CW00766371

For Grenville.

Pilot Cutters Under Sail

All the best.

Tom Cunliffe

P
P

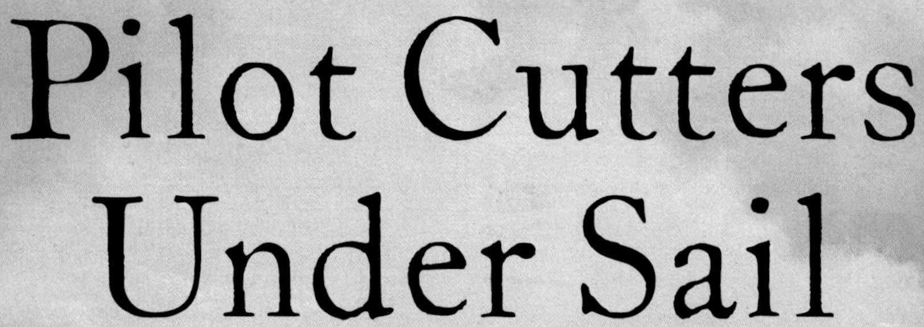

Pilot Cutters Under Sail

Pilots and Pilotage in Britain and Northern Europe

TOM CUNLIFFE

Seaforth
PUBLISHING
In association with the Royal Yacht Squadron

For Bernard and Michèle Cadoret

The publishers acknowledge the generous support of Ian Laing

Copyright © Tom Cunliffe 2013

First published in Great Britain in 2013 by
Seaforth Publishing,
Pen & Sword Books Ltd,
47 Church Street,
Barnsley S70 2AS

www.seaforthpublishing.com

British Library Cataloguing in Publication Data
A catalogue record for this book is available from the British Library

ISBN 978 1 84832 154 0

All rights reserved. No part of this publication may be reproduced or transmitted in any form or by any means, electronic or mechanical, including photocopying, recording, or any information storage and retrieval system, without prior permission in writing of both the copyright owner and the above publisher.

The right of Author to be identified as the author of this work has been asserted by him in accordance with the Copyright, Designs and Patents Act 1988.

Drawings in Chapter 13 *Pilot Cutter Seamanship* by Martyn Mackrill
Typeset and designed by Roger Daniels
Printed and bound in China through Printworks International Ltd

Competition in the early days

In this dramatic work by Admiral Richard Brydges Beechey entitled 'First Come, First Served' and painted in 1883, three pilot cutters are racing hell-for-leather to board an Indiaman which has hove to in heavy weather to await the winner. The scene is somewhat stylised, but it encapsulates the spirit of this book.
(© National Maritime Museum, Greenwich, UK)

Contents

Preface

In the late 1990s I was engaged by the French journal *Le Chasse-Marée* to produce a work on sailing pilots and their vessels. The book rapidly spiralled in scope and in 2001 two definitive volumes were published. These covered schooners in Europe and North America, as well as such diverse sideshows as the mighty pilot brigs of the Hooghly in Imperial India and the open-boat hobblers of Dublin Bay. A third volume was planned which would include the famous cutters of northern Europe but, as a result of restructuring in the publishing house, it was never written. Wishing in my heart to see this important material on the bookshelves, not only for myself and all those seafaring people who love a pilot cutter, but also for Bernard and Michèle Cadoret, without whose initiative and tireless creative work inside and outside the magazine office the project would never have begun, I sought another publisher. Over a decade later, backed by my shipmate Ian Laing of the Royal Yacht Squadron, I made contact with Julian Mannering of Seaforth Publishing who had been involved as a co-publisher with the original books. He proved an enthusiastic supporter and so, at last, *Pilot Cutters Under Sail* sees the light of a new dawn.

Whilst the book is based on solid research by myself, my wife Ros and others, the flavour derives from the years I have spent at sea in pilot cutters. As far back as the mid 1970s, Ros and I sailed from England to Brazil aboard a 13-ton Colin Archer called *Saari*, said to have been built for a pilot in the Gulf of Bothnia in 1920. Homeward bound we took the long route via the Caribbean, the US and the Grand Banks of Newfoundland. The extreme weather we experienced in the late-season North Atlantic convinced us that, for serious seafaring, these boats had few equals.

Saari's engine rarely functioned so we sailed largely without auxiliary power, learning the hard way how to handle a gaff cutter in fair weather and foul, in tight confines and hove to out on the broad ocean. *Saari* was followed in the 1980s by the 35-ton 1911 Barry pilot cutter, *Hirta*. Unrestored and unsullied by yachtsmen who imagined they knew better than the pilots, *Hirta* was a glory. Complete with original mast, boom and cockpit, she came to us so untouched that she was still without electric navigation lights. Like *Saari* before her, she spread a big mainsail of flax canvas. With her, we sailed to Greenland, America, Scandinavia and Soviet Russia. She made many memorable passages, including the long beat to Newfoundland from Iceland, a four-day run to the West Solent from Norway and

Hirta

Bristol Channel pilot cutter *Hirta* in mid Atlantic, 1983.
(Martyn Mackrill)

a traverse from North Carolina to the West Indies during which she weathered Hurricane Klaus, hove to in shocking seas on the edge of the Gulf Stream. As if this did not distinguish her enough, she also relished being short-tacked up the narrow, mooring-studded Beaulieu River sailed by a man, a woman and a teenage girl. She was an extraordinary sailing boat with the best manners I have ever experienced.

Following *Hirta* was a tough call, but the brand-new, wood-epoxy *Westernman* did us proud. Designed by Nigel Irens and built to our commission in North America, this 20-tonner, whose lines were inspired by the pilots of the Bristol Channel, ranted home across the North Atlantic in a highly respectable time, then carried on the good work by sailing to Arctic Norway, the heat of North Africa, and many a port in between. In all, we owned and cruised these cutters for over thirty years. Those decades formed us as individuals. Pilot cutters have a proud and charismatic history. They stir the souls of all who sail them, and attract the respect of people of the sea who have yet to do so. For me, this book represents something of a personal pilgrimage. Being given the opportunity to write it has been a privilege.

Tom Cunliffe, 2013

INTRODUCTION

Pilots, Cutters and Administration

Pilot boats have always been found wherever ships seek a safe haven. Europe has been no exception and many were the ports whose cutters did grand work. Readers from Scotland and Finland, to name but two countries, may scan the chapter list of this book in vain for coverage of their cutters, but space and time cannot permit a totally comprehensive account. The doors had to close somewhere, so the ports and sea areas included were chosen on the basis of importance and the availability of material.

The pilot cutters which operated around northern Europe under sail until the time of World War I possessed a magic equalled by few other working craft. Built with performance in mind by and for men who knew what a boat was supposed to look like, they had to match speed with seaworthiness in all weathers. The position was clear. If they failed to board their pilot, they made no money, so any that ran for home as soon as it came on to blow saw their owners rapidly 'going on the parish'. While some of the more prosaic pilot vessels

Trinity House on Tower Hill

The headquarters of the Corporation of Trinity House were new at the time of the Napoleonic Wars, following the move from Deptford to Trinity Square on London's Tower Hill. The foundation stone was laid by no less a worthy than William Pitt, who was Master of the Corporation. The building was badly damaged during the Second World War and today's headquarters were rebuilt behind the original 1796 façade, which somehow survived the attentions of the Luftwaffe. *(© National Maritime Museum, Greenwich, UK)*

were owned by corporations or cruised under other non-competitive circumstances, most vied one with another for the best jobs, and all had an overwhelming advantage over fishing and cargo vessels: in addition to a small crew, their only payload was one man or, at most, a few colleagues. So modest a burden meant that, like yachts, they would always sail to the same waterline. This gave builders a free hand to create the best possible forms, unhindered by the demand to perform adequately, whether drawing five feet of water or eight.

It has often been said that a boat which looks right on a mooring will be fine at sea, and few sailors would argue with the proposition. In the case of pilot boats, however, it rather puts the cart before the horse. Pilots were usually hard-bitten businessmen as well as thorough-going seamen. Their prime motivation was to serve their calling and earn a good living, so the way a boat functioned was a lot higher up their list of priorities than whether she was admired for a smart sheer-line. With a few notable exceptions, no yacht designer with an artist's flair laid pen on paper to create a sailing pilot cutter. They were built in the vernacular by men who left school early, if they went at all, and served long apprenticeships. The fact that many of the boats achieved an enduring loveliness says more than words ever could about a race of men who, without the benefits of formal education, were taught by time and experience to work successfully with nature.

Even in today's world of almost total electronic navigational knowledge, captains of ships coming into a strange port from seawards feel the need of someone with local knowledge to pilot them in. In the days before reliable, updated charts and position-fixing assisted by accurate chronometers, the requirement was fundamental. For centuries, pilotage was a casual service offered by anyone out in a boat who knew his way around his local waters. Fishermen were the classic operators. Seeing a ship approaching, they would offer their services, perhaps presenting a letter of approval from some previously satisfied customer, and strike a deal if they were accepted. No licensing framework existed, but in due course, as trade increased, local and national authorities realised that examining and licensing pilots made a lot of sense. It wasn't a big leap from there to dedicated pilots operating in purpose-built craft.

Inshore pilots and longshoremen doubling up to make an extra shilling or two generally worked from open boats, many of which developed from simple fishing craft into fast, multi-purpose craft such as the Deal galley punt or the great beach yawls of East Anglia. One day a man might be driving hell-for-leather to board a ship, the following night the same character, wearing a different hat altogether, could well be using the pilot boat to race seawards to salvage a wreck before his competitors could get a line onboard, saving life while he made a profit.

Hot competition in the Bristol Channel

Three Bristol Channel pilot cutters head seawards, some time after 1911. The middle boat with the white boot top is *Kindly Light*, the legendary cutter of Lewis Alexander, said to be the fastest pilot boat on the Channel at that time. Unlike the others, she is seen here unreefed and carrying a topsail. She is heeling accordingly, but no doubt is about to show the others her shapely stern. The boat survives to the present day and, after a long, lively history, is fully restored.
(Author's collection)

While many of these interesting and exciting craft never gave up right until the end, it was the far-ranging, dedicated pilot cutters that sailed into popular legend. *Jolie Brise* and *Marie-Fernand* of Havre, *Kindly Light, Mischief* and *Marguerite* from the Bristol Channel, and the outrageously lovely cutters from Norway out of the yard of Colin Archer – even today, these are as famous as any racing yacht. All were either privately owned or run by small co-operative units, competing with their fellows for the best jobs. They were obliged to move easily in the lightest breath of air on the long summer days when high pressure dominates and no gradient wind stirs the Atlantic, yet, like

Masefield's clipper ships, 'their tests were tempests and the sea that drowns.' No prisoners were taken, and there was no room for muddled thinking. In common with all working boats, 'seeking' pilot cutters were as honest as an archangel. Many sailed like witches and were surprisingly easy on the eye. 'Station boats' operated by corporations and amalgamated pilot services were very different. Prioritising ease of motion, dryness and safety, none are believed to have survived, few photographs were taken of them and there is a dearth of fine art representation. Only a handful of specialists can remember their names. Given time, and there has now been a century or so, the sea has a way of sorting such matters out.

Life below decks generally improved as the nineteenth century went on, but this was not always the case. Station vessels were often respectably appointed, but many self-employed pilots saw no reason to rough it more than was inevitable either. All decked boats were heated, typically by a permanently lighted solid-fuel galley stove burning coal or wood. Bunks were well boxed in for security, and most boats of any size featured a saloon of some sort where a pilot or his men could relax out of the weather. The exception, before Archer and

A seeking pilot cutter at sea

Much of this book is about specific cutters from many areas and ports. Here, the artist Martyn Mackrill has captured the spirit of them all in his depiction of a generic cutter cracking on far out at sea.
(Courtesy Martyn Mackrill)

A 'progressive list' of Dover or Dungeness pilots from the 1890s

When 'seeking' was finally done away with for London pilots operating from Dover, Dungeness and Deal, a system was put in place known as a 'progression', which allowed for pilots to work in rotation as far as possible. Pilots on this station had individual pennants which they hoisted after boarding a ship, indicating not only that a pilot was aboard, but who the pilot was. The lists themselves were beautiful documents. This one is delightfully archaic. Its primitive upper decoration depicts a scene from a century earlier, showing a Deal lugger flying a pilot flag approaching a warship, or possibly an East Indiaman, fifty miles down-Channel off Beachy Head. The ship is firing a gun to attract the pilot's attention. *(Dover Museum)*

Taking a pilot

An unknown brig takes her pilot in the late eighteenth century. Inbound to an unspecified port with her fore-topmast housed, probably as a leftover from some recent heavy weather, she is shortening down to lose way in the following wind. Her spanker-sheet has been let fly for brailing up and her main topsail yard is lowered. The hands are aloft and stowing almost before the sail is clewed up. Meanwhile, the pilot cutter has secured a painter and what looks like a negotiation is under way between a pilot in jaunty headgear and the brig's quarterdeck. The pilot boat herself is of no recognisable type. Indeed, while the brig is beautifully painted with useful detail, the small craft seems only roughly delineated. Never mind, the rapport between the two vessels is what this image is all about.
(Peabody Museum, Salem)

others transformed their lives, were the Scandinavians. One can only envisage the lot of the solo Norwegian apprentice, left on board after boarding his pilot, hove to out in the endless winter night, huddling over a makeshift open fireplace with no headroom, and nothing to sleep on but a palliasse stuffed with seaweed.

In addition to speed, seaworthiness and beauty, another requirement of the pilot cutter was a minimal number of crew. Once the pilot or pilots had boarded, a 50-ton cutter would be brought home by as few as two men. Bristol Channel boats of 35 tons were regularly sailed home single-handed, sometimes by a lad in his teens. These cutters had no winches and in order to ghost in light airs they were obliged to carry huge sails that were extraordinarily heavy by today's standards, yet the crew had to sail her into a tight harbour every week, bringing up quietly and without mayhem. The men, of course, were very good at their job, but they could only do it given a well-balanced hull form and a fully developed rig with no bad habits.

Of such stuff were the pilot cutters of northern Europe.

Administration of pilotage

It is impossible to understand pilot cutters or the men who sailed them without at least a nodding acquaintance with the rules and authorities which bound them increasingly tightly as the decades rolled by. In the special conditions of Norway, these were often as concerned with the safety of the pilots as they were with maintaining a reliable service. In Britain and France, things were more formalised. As the chapters of this book march forward, much of this interesting tale will unfold from port to port. French pilots tended to come under the control of local authorities. In Britain, the situation was less obvious and it is impossible to follow the story of UK pilot governance without knowing something of the activities of Trinity House.

It says much about the development of home-waters trade in the Middle Ages that the merchants and shipowners of the Hanseatic League were well ahead of their British counterparts when it came to safeguarding shipping. In London, these men of substance did their business at the Steelyard, a narrow passage now lying beneath Cannon Street Station. They were known as 'Osterlings' and left the British a legacy in the form of the latter part of their nickname. The word 'sterling' entered the English language to describe reliable silver currency, where it remains to this day, with the 'pound sterling' ironically putting up a manful fight against the marauding hordes of Euroland.

Among the home waters of the Osterlings were the German rivers Weser and Elbe, where they had already set up withies, beacons and navigation buoys to mark the ever shifting sands and channels. No evidence has come to light suggesting that they took it upon themselves to do the same in the equally challenging waters of the outer Thames, but it seems likely that their initiative shamed the new corporation of Trinity House, founded in 1514 by Royal Charter of Henry VIII to secure the safety of shipping and the well-being of seafarers. The corporation operated for many years under the grand title of 'The Master, Wardens, and Assistants of the Guild, Fraternity, or Brotherhood of the most glorious and undivided Trinity, and of St Clement in the Parish of Deptford-Stroond in the County of Kent'. The first Master in overall charge happened to be the captain of Henry's famously ill-fated *Mary Rose*, one Thomas Spert.

Captain Spert and his comrades must have been influenced by the men from the Steelyard, because Trinity House was soon following similar guidelines regarding its responsibilities. Like the Hanseatic League, the corporation founded its regulations and recommendations on the Laws of Oléron which went back to the times of the Crusades and had been drafted in the French Biscayan island of the same name. Most maritime law has its foundations sunk deep into these rules, which originated around AD500 with the great Roman lawmaker, the Emperor Justinian. He, in his turn, referred to regulations framed in the trading hotspot of Rhodes an astounding 1,400 years earlier. Most of 'Oléron' is concerned with responsibility for lost cargoes and other commercial considerations, but pilotage receives its due share of regulation. The brethren of Trinity House modified the rules to the needs of northern waters and it is interesting to note that from early times they required masters to employ pilots for English ports such as Boston, King's Lynn, Great Yarmouth and London.

Some of the rules laid down at Oléron would deter any but the most self-confident of mariners from putting themselves forward as pilots. The levels of retribution promised for poor performance must have concentrated many an unfortunate pilot's mind as an unkind wind shift set him firmly on a lee shore in a ship whose performance to windward resembled nothing so much as a haystack.

> The judgement is that they ought to suffer a most rigorous and unpleasant death; for there ought to be very high gibbets erected for them in the very same place, or as nigh as conveniently may be, where they so guided and brought the said ship or vessel to ruin as aforesaid, and thereon these accursed pilots are with ignominy and most shamefully to end their days; which gibbets are to be made substantially strong, to the intent that they may abide and remain to succeeding ages, as a visible caution to other ships that shall afterwards sail thereby.

Lest the reader may find this incredible and cast it aside as an anomaly, summary justice was also required by a law from Barcelona in 1494: 'if a pilot bring a ship into a haven and she is cast ashore by his lack of skill, the crew shall lead him to the hatchway and there strike off his head.' This last jewel of data was given to the author by Pilot David Barnicoat of Falmouth, Cornwall, who was quick to point out that, after 1667, pilots who fell short of the ideal were at least given a fair hearing. This, he suspects, was because of thinning ranks in the service.

At this time, the term 'lodeman', or 'lodesman', was generally applied to an inshore pilot. It seems reasonable to assume that the term derives from the Hanseatic 'loot', or lead. The word 'lead', 'lode' or a number of other derivatives appears again and again in connection with piloting in many languages, and from here, it is but a short step to the English 'pilot', since the word 'peil' has its roots in the sounding of depth, perhaps originally with a long stick. Hence, 'peil loot', or 'pilot'.

From snippets discovered by Trinity House, it is clear that pilots were operating between Britain and the Low Countries before the brotherhood was incorporated. From 1514 to 1808, despite the nature of King Henry's charter which, by implication, must surely have included pilotage and seamarks at least in the approaches to Britain's capital and main port, Trinity House had been mainly concerned with London and the inner River Thames. However, no responsible body could long ignore the ships lost in great numbers in the shoals of the wide estuary. Of these, the rich East Indiamen, both inward and outward bound, prompted the review of a situation which could not be allowed to continue unregulated. Many of the Elder Brethren had close connections with the management of the 'Honourable John Company', as the East India Company was known. Hit in their own wallets by disasters to these commercially important vessels, they shook themselves out of the general lethargy that had done nothing for the reputation of Trinity House in the early eighteenth century. The process took time but, as it gathered momentum, it went beyond providing beacons, buoys and lighthouses.

The origins of the word 'pilot'

In the centuries before our own very recent era of certain position, the lead was critical when approaching harbours, especially in reduced visibility. In ancient times, when the word for the 'sea guide' was being coined, the terms 'peil' and 'lood', 'lode' and 'los' were all in use for the sounding weight. It seems likely that a combination has led to the English 'pilot'.
(Author's collection)

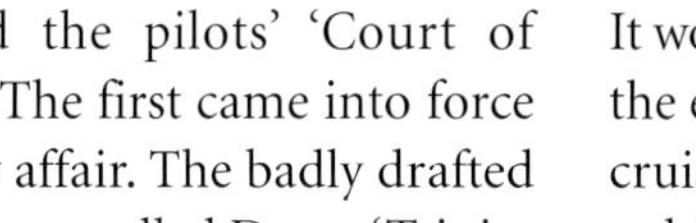

A succession of Acts was passed relating to Trinity House in London and the pilots' 'Court of Lodesmanage' in Dover. The first came into force in 1717 and was a shoddy affair. The badly drafted bill granted powers to the so-called Dover 'Trinity House', establishing the requirement for all ships navigating between Dover, Deal or the Isle of Thanet (the Margate area east of North Foreland) and any places in the rivers Thames and Medway to employ Cinque Ports pilots. A parliamentary inquiry into pilotage in 1732 was followed by an Act which confirmed these provisions. It also defined the jurisdictions of the several Trinity Houses by then in existence, but the first statute imposing compulsory pilotage nationally did not receive the Royal Assent until 1808.

A Cinque Ports pilot

The Cinque Ports pilot William Marsh, painted in 1875, in his best rig. He is posed formally with his spyglass in front of Dover Castle, wearing the watch and chain which would certainly have accompanied him on even the most frantic boarding of a ship. Pilot Marsh was involved in three shipwrecks during his apprenticeship. Originally from Deal, he moved to Dover with his family around 1859. Twenty years later he drowned when the pilot cutter *Edinburgh* was run down by a mail steamer off Dungeness. *(Dover Museum)*

The 1808 Pilotage Act handed Trinity House the responsibility for controlling pilotage in all coastal areas of England and Wales not governed by any existing authority. As well as the so-called Cinque Ports pilots of the Kentish shores, this meant that Bristol, Liverpool, the Humber and the Tyne maintained their independence from London, although the last two fell under the Trinity Houses of Kingston upon Hull and Newcastle upon Tyne respectively. Elsewhere, Trinity House passed on this new local authority to sub-commissioners of pilotage appointed from among local worthies in the same manner as magistrates. The commissioners did not employ the pilots as such, they merely oversaw their administration and activities. The pilots remained self-employed and hung onto their ancient independence, either individually or in groups. However, their licences now came from the over-arching authority of Trinity House. Not everyone liked this arrangement, but earlier heavy-handed attempts by the corporation to bring discipline to the London pilots from the North Sea and the English Channel had been far from happy, so for many it represented a marked improvement.

Pilots' liabilities

It would be shirking a vital issue not to discuss here the extent to which a pilot who had boarded via a cruising cutter was liable for damage to or loss of a ship under his pilotage.

The essential proposition has generally been that the master remains in command at all times, while the pilot is there to advise him. This was all very well, except where a ship's master was obliged to take a pilot he might neither want nor need, because of the requirement for compulsory pilotage. Among any other items, the Merchant Shipping Act of 1854 permitted Trinity House pilots to post a hefty bond of £100, plus the pilotage rates of the job in question, as the totality of their individual liability in the case of 'proved fault or inadequacy' in the conduct of a vessel. The Act also raised the recurring question of compulsory pilotage, whereby a ship-owner could absolve himself of liability for collision, damage to a berth, etc, by claiming that his vessel was under the 'command' of a licensed and compulsory pilot. In law, this was the so-called 'Defence of Compulsory Pilotage'.

The defence flew in the face of long-established tradition typified by the controversial case of the China clipper *Spindrift* in 1869. *Spindrift* was lost inside the London pilotage district outward bound for Shanghai with a valuable mixed cargo. The evidence, when examined with a seaman's eye, cannot be reconciled – the pilot being accused of drunkenness while protesting that a main witness to his condition, the steward, was also 'three sheets to the wind'. In the end, the Elder Brethren of Trinity House suspended the pilot for six months, creating the potential precedent that,

> in well conducted ships the masters regard the presence of a duly licensed pilot in compulsory pilotage waters as freeing them from every obligation to attend to the safety of the vessel, but are of the opinion that while the master sees that his officers and crew duly attend to the pilot's orders, he himself is bound to keep a vigilant eye on the navigation of the vessel, and when exceptional circumstances exist not only to urge upon the pilot to use every precaution, but to insist on such being taken …

It was pointed out that this view represented

custom rather than law, but it left captains in no doubt as to how much sympathy they would receive if they relied unreasonably on the compulsory pilotage defence.

This essentially unsatisfactory situation dragged on until the notion of a pilot being in effective command in pilotage waters was reinforced by the Merchant Shipping Act of 1894. In 1895 Lord Esher stated that:

> This doctrine of compulsory pilotage is an enacted doctrine no doubt. It was not enacted for the protection only of ships; it was enacted for the protection of ports; of commercial ports in particular because if a vessel is wrecked and lost and sunk near to the entrance, or within the entrance to a commercial port, she is not only lost herself, but she is a great danger and obstruction to the port and other vessels, and would interfere with the commercial business of the port.

Thus, the Defence of Compulsory Pilotage made the pilot responsible for any damage ensuing from the ship's movements under his direction. A good deal of injustice was caused, and the resulting remedy adjudicated by the courts was frequently unsatisfactory because a pilot, having been judged liable, typically had nothing like the means at his disposal to make full compensation. Under a non-compulsory system it was argued that the pilot was the servant of the shipowner for the term of his hire, giving 'advice' to the master, allowing the shipowner to insure against any act of his temporary employee.

This situation, unsatisfactory to the pilots,

Steam and sail in the Dover Strait

The superb image sums up the changes brought to sailing pilotage by the arrival of steam merchant vessels. The handsome, clipper-stemmed *Pinta* was built in Port Glasgow in 1898 for Robert MacAndrew & Co of London which had been trading with Spain, primarily in the importation of fruit, since the late 1830s. Not only could a steamer proceed into the eye of any reasonable wind, her tracks to her chosen harbour were relatively predictable and it was this assurance which sounded the knell of the seeking cutter. As this ship steams away to windward down-Channel from Dover, the backdrop is a menagerie of sailing vessels. From the humble coasting schooners to the majestic gypsy of the Horn at the extreme left, cracking on to catch her tide and her London tug, all were joined by the thread of uncertainty which had fed the hunger of the cruising pilot for centuries. The ketch-rigged pilot boat seen here is a 'station boat', built for comfort, not for speed. She is a classic example of the Trinity House ketches which replaced the older cutters in a number of areas, including Dover.

(The British Mercantile Collection)

pertained for some time and was further confused by anomalies caused by Local Acts which appeared to override general legislation until the abolition of the Defence of Compulsory Pilotage, in the years leading up to World War I, echoed the Antwerp Convention of 1910. This made a pilot the temporary servant of the shipowner as in the non-compulsory ports. It gave him the 'conduct' of a vessel – ie, the control of the navigation and manoeuvring of the vessel – assisted fully by the master and his crew, to whom the pilot tendered his professional opinion. Thus, the vessel proceeded under her master's orders and the advice of the pilot. This laid the balance of responsibility, both morally and legally, firmly on the master as the shipowner's representative, and the last of the sailing pilots doubtless slept more easily behind their high leeboards.

The coming of steam

Planning an ocean voyage or even a coastal passage under sail is very different from the same operation under power or steam. In the old *Ocean Passages for the World*, published by the British Hydrographic Office, three routes were generally given between distant ports. The first was the 'full-powered steamer route', such as might be chosen by ocean liners and other well-endowed ships that could steam into strong winds if they had to. Unless compromised by shoals or the likelihood of sea ice, this track followed the Great Circle route, or shortest distance between two points on a sphere. The second option was the 'low-powered steamer route'. This added distance by avoiding areas where strong adverse winds were likely to be encountered, for the simple reason that such vessels were seriously compromised by them. The 'sailing ship route' could well stray so far from the Great Circle as to be barely recognisable. This track was not merely trying to avoid too much unpleasantness, it actually had to go looking for fair winds, because the average merchant square-rigger would make little ground in anything else.

In a sense, these three route systems sum up the reasons why cruising pilotage under sail died out by the time of World War I. In the far-off days of pure sail, a Bristol Channel pilot, for example, might board a paying ship anywhere across the wide approaches to his domain. A ship inbound from Spain could have been fighting northeasterly winds and found herself far out in the Atlantic before tacking and hoping to lay her course straight in. Her position would be, at best, calculated to within a few miles, but if the sky were overcast, it might easily be fifty miles adrift from reality. To imagine that she would steer for some pilot station, knowing a cutter would be there waiting for her, is fantasy. She might never make such a rendezvous. The reality of passage-making under sail meant that the needs of shipping were in many ways better served by a multitude of cutters and pilots, well spread out, each motivated to find ships at all costs by the harsh economics of his trade.

This situation began to change with the advent of effective steamers in the mid nineteenth century, but it was a further fifty years before ships were arriving and leaving on something approaching a modern-style schedule. The author can testify from his own experience that, even in the 1970s, a typical coaster could make little or no headway into a full gale. Back in 1900, many a full-sized ship was similarly compromised. Thus, while pilot stations were useful, there was still room for cruising men seeking windjammers and steamers driven from the most direct route. The cream of such pilots would sail away from their home ports, often seeking far out to sea a ship which they knew to be due, and hoping to board her before she arrived in more densely served water closer to home. As late as 1911 in the Bristol Channel, and in 1913 at Le Havre, powerful new first-class cutters were still being launched for private owners. Such boats were fully developed and were among the finest sailing craft ever built, but as steam continued to improve and the wind-driven merchant fleet was increasingly eclipsed, the writing was on the wall.

By now it was obvious that the future lay in amalgamated pilot services, boarding at clearly defined stations from vessels supplied by the local pilotage authority, or Trinity House in certain areas of the UK. In the beginning, many such craft operated under sail, but they soon acquired auxiliary power. From there, it was a short step to steam or motor and so, by the time the great armies began marching, the final flowering of the cruising pilot cutter was over.

CHAPTER 1

The Channel Pilots

When a sailing ship came into the English Channel, her captain's first priority, if bound for an English port or further afield through the Dover Straits, was generally to take on a Channel pilot. If she were bound for Le Havre or one of the other major French ports, a seeking Le Havre cutter would supply the captain's needs. In today's world of certainty about a ship's position, electronic charts and the motor ship's ability to steam in whatever direction seizes her navigator's fancy, it may seem superfluous to pay a pilot in waters that start out over a hundred miles wide. This was not the case in times past.

Channel tides can run at over 3kts in areas where neither coastline is visible, even in clear weather. A sailing ship beating her way in or out would sometimes find herself in tight quarters at the end of a tack, yet still be outside the pilotage area of any particular port. Even if she were not, it was perfectly possible that she would have missed the local pilot

Illustrated London News

In 1885 the popular *London Illustrated News* published this beautiful double-page spread of piloting activities. It is a spectacular achievement, showing at centre a cutter hove to in what might pass for the lee of an early steamship, launching her punt in a shocking sea so that the pilot can be rowed or sculled across. On the left, the pilot is burning his night-flare; at bottom right, the punt is away, and at top right, the pilot is boarding a windjammer in very much better conditions than the rest of the montage suggests. *(Author's collection)*

cutter and hence have no pilot when she desperately needed one. Finding his ship embayed on a strange coast in thick weather, a master would have given a month's wages for the services of a competent expert who could recognise a misty glimpse of coast at a glance, or deduce his position from the depth and nature of the bottom as brought up by the armed leadline. Even today large ships, whose draught becomes a serious factor for safe navigation as the sea shoals towards Dover, take on Channel pilots as far west as Brixham, Devon.

In the case of British pilots who boarded in the Western Approaches, the term 'Channel' generally referred to all the channels between the islands of Britain as well as those separating them from the continent. Thus, a Channel pilot would be just at home taking a ship up to Greenock in Scotland as he would to the 'Downs' anchorage off east Kent, where ships bound to and from London waited for fair winds, or the approaches to Le Havre and Dunkirk. Even the Elbe in faraway Germany fell into his area of expertise. A Channel pilot boarding further up the English Channel itself, perhaps off Plymouth or certainly the Isle of Wight, was usually just what the term implied – a guide up the English Channel to the desired port pilot station. Once his ship arrived in the offing, the average Channel pilot would be content to hand over to the local man. Indeed, in later years he was obliged to do so by regulations. For London, this handover theoretically took place at Dungeness where a licensed Trinity House pilot would come aboard, but things didn't always work out as the Elder Brethren of that redoubtable authority would have liked.

An outward-bound Channel pilot stranded far from home would be delighted to take a ship down to his local waters once more, thus securing a fee as well as a free ride. By unwritten but universal agreement, any ship he had brought up was his to take to sea, but this might entail a long wait and was by no means always adhered to. Before the railways, however, the land-based travel alternatives were unattractive in the extreme, and even in the days of steam they remained a poor economic substitute for a ship.

Channel pilots were experienced deep-sea sailors who had returned to home waters to take up a career in pilotage. Before the Merchant Shipping Act of 1872, there were no licences for their work. The only qualification for the job was that a man was able to do it and could convince a ship's master that this was the case. A favourite device was to carry certificates or letters from satisfied masters and agents, but sometimes it was enough merely to step aboard from a pilot cutter and look convincing.

Some Channel men actually held an official licence for London as well as one or more for the many outports. As such, they were qualified to pilot a ship up to her berth. Outside of the Bristol

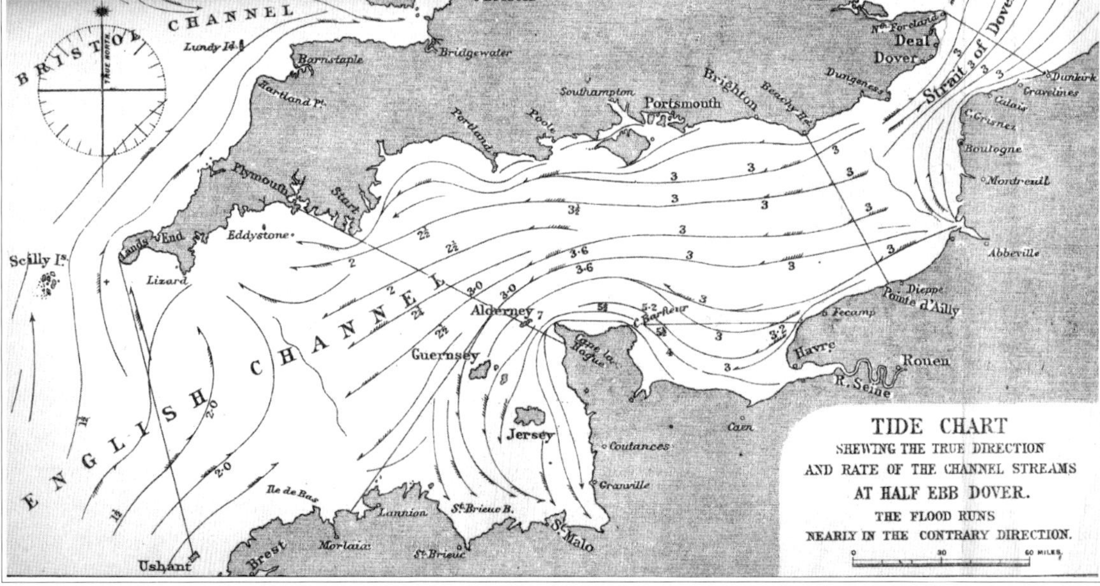

Chart of the English Channel

This late nineteenth-century chart of the English Channel shows not only the topography, but also the highly significant tides that the Channel pilots knew so well. Even today, circumnavigating yachtsmen from relatively tideless waters baulk at entering the Channel because of the streams encountered here. Looking closely, we see 3kts in the Dover Strait, over 5kts north of Cherbourg and a spectacular seven in the Race of Alderney.
(From the Admiralty Tidal Stream Atlas, *published 1899)*

Channel with its specific systems, many Channel cutters would be owned by a group of pilots offering a 'one-stop shop' service into the local port as well as the farther-ranging Channel pilotage up to London and beyond. After the 1807 Merchant Shipping Act which granted Trinity House jurisdiction over most of the Channel ports, the position of a Channel pilot was made clear; he could retain the part of the overall pilotage fee which concerned work outside the designated port limits to which his ship was bound. If a licensed port pilot took over for entry and berthing, he kept the rest. If no licensed port pilot presented himself, the Channel pilot could, like any other unlicensed pilot, keep the whole fee, so long as the master was willing.

In 1872 a new Act of Parliament made provisions under which Trinity House availed themselves of the right to grant deep-sea licences to Channel pilots. Ever willing to extend their jurisdiction, the Elder Brethren of the corporation now began to examine candidates of proven sobriety, good conduct, five or more years' sea service in addition to pilotage experience, and who were 'sound in wind and limb'. The licences they issued provided their holders with kudos and an implied seniority in the event of a clash with another pilot. Being licensed also made it easier for a pilot to convince a captain that he was the man for the job, but Channel pilotage remained non-compulsory and the work was still open to unlicensed pilots as well as Trinity House men.

As was the case in other services when licences were first issued, there was hard feeling from established pilots who had been passed over, and a tendency from those who had been selected and had succeeded under examination – often by good fortune rather than any superior ability – to kick away the ladder by which they had climbed. This tension is illustrated by an article from the *Shipping Gazette* of 20 January 1880. It concerns itself with the loss of the Italian ship *Erato*.

The *Erato* boarded an uncertificated Channel pilot at Falmouth who was to take her to the Clyde. All went well as far as southeastern Ireland, but here the pilot ran her ashore on the Barrels near the Tuskar Rock. The article is eloquent in its defence of the ship's master who took on the pilot in good faith, believing him to be competent on the strength of his professed recommendations. It goes on to state that the Court of Inquiry found the man 'unqualified and ignorant of the navigation' of the Irish Sea. Its conclusion was that while there may have been some unqualified pilots who were competent, there were certainly many who were not and that, were the Channels to be a compulsory pilotage area, all pilots would require certification and the problem would cease.

That this recommendation and its miraculous predicted outcome was held in low esteem by the majority of pilots is clear from a closing remark that, 'while [they] are not required to hold licences – although they may do so, if they think it proper to prove their competency to the satisfaction of the Trinity House or other authorities – few of the men avail themselves of this privilege.'

Boarding

A lovely drawing by Arthur Briscoe of the pivotal point of a pilot's work, the actual moment of boarding. The man in the punt is fending her off with an oar as soon as his pilot has his feet firmly on the Jacob's ladder. He now returns to the cutter and does not see his boss again until they meet up at some prearranged point at sea when the pilot brings another ship out, or in harbour when the cutter has chased this ship home. *(Private collection)*

Bound up-Channel, a ship would, if she were fortunate, find her Channel pilot waiting west of the Isles of Scilly. If she failed to board a man here, her next landfall was likely to be the Lizard Point where a Falmouth cutter was generally cruising, often in company with one or two Le Havre boats ready to service anyone bound their way. Once east of the Lizard, a northbound ship could be lucky off Rame Head with a Plymouth-based cutter or, finally, the Isle of Wight. If she had still failed to take on a pilot by the time she passed the Nab Tower southeast of the Wight, she was probably on her own until she fell in with the Trinity House pilots off Dungeness, unless she first met up with a casual lugger from Deal cruising down-Channel in search of business.

CHAPTER 2

The Far West – The Isles of Scilly

STANDING ON THE Isles of Scilly on a summer's day, it is hard to believe that one is on the outskirts of the English Channel. Were it not for the Cornish-style buildings, the colours of the shallow waters and sandy beaches could readily be taken for those of the tropics. The seas around the islands are a whirl of fast-running tides and straggling rocks, many of which will always remain unmarked. In the days of sail, and of steam prior to modern navigation systems, the toll they took of shipping was heavy and consistent, ranging from unknown trading schooners to the Royal Naval battle fleet under Admiral Sir Cloudesley Shovell, which famously ran ashore one nasty night in 1707.

There are a number of reasons for this, apart from the obvious one that the islands and their associated reefs lie athwart one of the main shipping routes of the world, at the confluence of the English, the Bristol and St George's Channel leading northwards into the Irish Sea.

Early days

Until very recently, of course, all deep-sea navigation relied upon the captain obtaining a view of the heavens from which to fix his position. Any sailor who remembers those days can testify that the facts of life in the Western Approaches are such that this is by no means always available. Ships which had had no confirmation of their position for days thus had two choices: either go with the

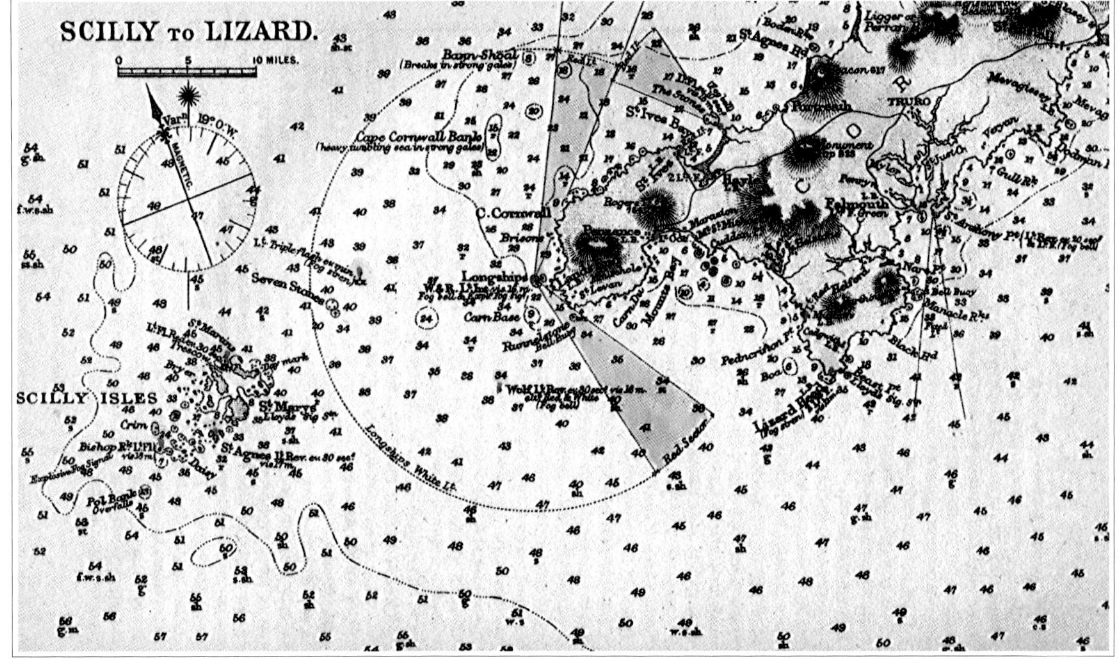

Cornwall and the Isles of Scilly

The Isles of Scilly lie approximately twenty-five sea miles from Land's End. In the days of sail, they had enough trade in their own right to warrant a pilotage service, but it was as Channel pilots that the men of the islands excelled. Their dangerous, rock-bound fastness was strategically placed for boarding ships inbound to Great Britain or Northern Europe from the Atlantic, and hence from the whole world. Many a ship's master was mightily relieved to be hailed by the Scillonian pilot cutter as he ran in, heart in mouth, perhaps having had no sight of the heavens for a fix for several days. *(From* The Pilot's Handbook of the English Channel, *1898)*

unpopular but safe option of heaving to until the sky cleared, or trust their dead reckoning and run in before the prevailing westerly weather. With crews who might have been at sea for months, it took a leader of strong moral fibre not to go for the soft choice and run in, hoping against hope to find a pilot. At night or in fog, things would be bad enough in themselves, but three further factors must be added to understand why even carefully estimated positions might well prove far removed from reality.

The first of these is the Rennell Current, whose existence was not fully established until 1793. This sets northwest across the entrance to the English Channel and can reach aggregate speeds of almost 1kt, even when the tide has been allowed for. A ship approaching from the Atlantic without having obtained a fix for some days could therefore find herself many miles north of her dead reckoning position. There are instances of ships whose navigators imagined they were passing south of the islands only surviving stranding because they were so far off track to the north that when day dawned they found themselves proceeding up the Bristol Channel rather than the sea high-road to London.

The effects of the Rennell Current were aggravated before about 1750 by the inconvenient fact that the charted position of the islands (and the Lizard – the next landfall point) was anything from five to fifteen miles north of their actual location. Yet another nuisance to navigation at this period was that compass variation, changing steadily as it always has and always will, shifted from east to west. Within a few years, this rendered an uncorrected chart (the usual state of affairs in those days) potentially dangerous and undoubtedly added to the wreck toll on the islands.

The Isles of Scilly were home to a substantial community and as such generated a coasting trade of their own, but they also attracted ships because they were the base of operations for a large group of Channel pilots. Many ships anchored in St Mary's Roads to await orders, or sailed close by, specifically in the hope of finding a pilot to take them up to Dungeness, the Downs or London. Many pilots from Scilly were capable of piloting into Havre, Liverpool, Glasgow, Antwerp, or any other important Northern European port, and so were in high demand. Pilot James Hicks of the cutter *Atlantic* piloted the crack China clipper *Thermopylae* to London on one of her famous races to be first with the season's tea crop. By the beginning of the nineteenth century, the pilot service was the mainstay of the monetary system of the islands.

Throughout the eighteenth century, appointment and control of the Scilly pilots was exercised from within the community by the so-called 'Court of Twelve', a committee of gentlemen who, to all intents and purposes, were the law in the islands. In those days, there were no pilots' licences of any

The stranding of Sir Cloudesley Shovell

In 1707, Admiral Sir Cloudesley Shovell was in command of the Grand Fleet of the Royal Navy when it ran ashore on the Isles of Scilly in darkness. Ships from small schooners to significant merchantmen piled up here every year, but the loss of many of Sir Cloudesley's warships made clear the need for pilots if anyone had ever doubted it. This plaque at St Clement's Church near Deal in Kent stands in memory of Admiral Sir John Narborough's two sons. The Admiral, a distinguished sailor, had married Elizabeth Hill, daughter of a Commissioner of the Navy. After his death, Elizabeth married Sir Cloudesley who thus became stepfather to the boys, both of whom perished with him in this disaster.
(Private collection)

A gig shipping flowers from the out-islands

As the advent of steam reduced shipwreck in the islands and competition from wealthy ports further east curtailed and finally tolled the bell on Channel piloting for the local gigs and cutters, the pilots and their men looked to alternative employment. Many found new careers in the burgeoning cut-flower business which remains a staple to this day. This load of flowers coming to St Mary's boxed up for shipping to the mainland shows the remarkable carrying capacity of a gig.
(Gibsons of Scilly)

sort for the Channel, so anyone capable of the work could take it on. The income from pilotage fees, wreck salvage and smuggling provided all that was needed to eke out the basic local economy of farming and kelp harvesting.

While pilot communities the world over have always been generous in saving life at sea, the Scillonians, like the men of Deal and the Norfolk beaches, were unusually prolific in this respect. The nature of their ironbound home ensured a constant stream of shipwrecks, while the fast and seaworthy six-oared gigs that were a local speciality allowed them to work out to the farthest rocks in most weathers. Using gigs or pilot cutters, the people of Scilly could, after saving what life they were able, remove cargoes from derelicts and either auction them officially, taking a salvor's share, or pass the goods unofficially into local trade. Both methods had a real effect on the prosperity of the people, but this was not the only way Scillonians benefited financially by supplying a service to those in need.

Smuggling was a long-standing business that worked at two levels. A big-time undercover trade existed between the islands and Brittany, generally carried on by gigs under oar and, if conditions allowed, sail as well. A gig was typically around 30ft overall, with a beam as little as 4ft 9in, yet, so long as they kept under way, they were as famous for their sea-keeping as for their electrifying turn of speed. The 1820 Cornish gig *Dove* was timed over a measured mile in 1928, rowed by a crew from Newquay, at 6 minutes and 15 seconds, which adds up to just a shade under 10kts! By rowing in shifts with a couple of extra crewmen to 'spell' the first team, an easily driven gig could comfortably maintain 4kts or more for long distances. This made the hundred-odd-mile passages to France achievable, with high-value goods such as spirits and tobacco being regularly landed for sale locally and in Cornwall. Pilot James Nance, for whom smuggling was definitely a 'second-string' occupation, boasted openly that he had rowed to France no less than twenty-five times. These activities were of increasing primary concern to the Revenue men stationed in the islands. In addition, the officers of the crown also took an interest in a widespread but far more innocent contraband activity carried on by the pilots.

From way back, hard currency had been sparse in Scilly, with an ancient system of barter existing in its place.

Inflation mattered not a jot when a pig was known to be worth ten bags of grain, or a bottle of rum a dozen loaves. Luxuries from outside the islands were highly prized and came in only as trade goods from Penzance, spoils from wrecks, or via pilots from ships in exchange for fresh produce. Supplies, needed urgently by homeward bounders, were bartered by pilots in exchange for the usual 'non-perishable comforts' carried on deep water. The proceeds were theoretically liable for excise duty, but by unspoken agreement this was never paid. For many generations, the preventive officers accepted that this business was a necessary part of the island economy and an official blind eye was turned, until things began to change in the nineteenth century, when the arrival of Victorian bureaucracy threatened this happy, simple state of life.

Until the late seventeenth century, the Isles of Scilly had little in the way of official aids to navigation. The islands had been active during the civil wars and shipping continued to increase in their aftermath. Vessels were now being driven ashore in such profusion that the major shipowners of Europe petitioned for a lighthouse and were given one, a fine tower stoutly built on rising ground in the centre of St Agnes and fired up in 1680.

St Agnes light was visible from the outer fringes of the reefs in the south and west, including the still-unlit Bishop Rock. It had such a beneficial effect on shipping that the governor of the islands complained he would now lose considerable income from the diminution of the numbers of wrecks in his bailiwick! So irate was this official that he demanded all ships anchoring in Scilly to forfeit their best bower anchors by way of rent.

While the governor ranted, however, the islanders saw things rather differently, recognising that this new safety aid would encourage ships to come looking for pilots. They were proved right, and piloting was consolidated as the major local occupation.

Wrecks off the Isles of Scilly

On 27 July 1879, the British iron barque *River Lune* of Liverpool stranded in fog on St Agnes Rocks, about a mile southwest of St Agnes, after a faulty chronometer put her off course. She had been on passage from L'Orient to Ardrossan in ballast and sank in ten minutes. The crew were taken off. A few hours later, the sailing barque *Maipu* was wrecked on Maiden Bower near Bryher in the same fog. Again, the crew were saved. The men of the islands performed sterling work in situations like these, saving life and, where appropriate, making a tidy profit on salvage into the bargain. *(Gibsons of Scilly)*

The men, particularly those who ultimately became Channel pilots, would typically go away in ships as youngsters, returning with a useful tally of sea-time to add to a natural ability which must have been stamped in the very DNA of these people whose kitchen thresholds stood almost literally in salt water.

In the early days, it was grab-as-grab-can for pilot work, sometimes with two men boarding a ship over opposite sides and arguing for the job. This led to serious undercutting of reasonable fees, but the pilots soon organised themselves to stop the practice. The result, with competition very much still to the fore, was the development of faster boats, with racing for paying ships an everyday occurrence.

Open gigs continued to be used by pilots to the very end, especially for local work. Some, like the *Shah* built in 1873, were so extreme in form that many declared them unseaworthy, yet losses were remarkably few in the flat-out competition that went on day and night to be first to board a pilot. Of the originals surviving today, *Bonnet* and *Slippen* were built in 1830 by William Peters of St Mawes for St Martin's pilots. *Golden Eagle* was also built by Peters in 1870 for pilots of Bryher. She was paid for by money received for saving the crew of the *Award*. The name was chosen because the handout came as new American gold dollars with the eagle on the back. Notwithstanding the sheer charisma of the gigs, a breed of all-weather, decked pilot cutter was also being developed which ultimately carried out the larger share of boarding Channel pilots in deep water. To the end, however, gig and cutter remained associated and many groups of pilots owned one or more of each, making the appropriate choice on the day.

In 1724 a law was passed stating that any money earned by piloting was to be taxed locally at 1s in the pound. The revenues thus raised were put towards a distress fund for pilots' widows and others brought low by the harsh service, in which death was a frequent caller. The fund seems to have been administered by the Court of Twelve, who were officially liable to provide for widows and orphans and who also supplied some housing for the most needy cases.

As the eighteenth century progressed, dues from the still-growing numbers of ships could not keep pace with the rising cost of living, and pilots knew hard times. The situation was exacerbated by new families and lone young men immigrating from Cornwall in search of work, many of whom turned to piloting from the 'off islands', as the smaller isles around St Mary's are known. These outsiders undercut the established pilotage dues and side-stepped the long-standing agreement that if a pilot brought a ship in, she was his to take out once more. In the end a deal was struck on this latter dispute, but the damage was done just the same, because the influx of humanity had left the islands effectively overpopulated. Some of the newcomers, though often discredited as pilots, were taken on as crew in the cutters, others turned to the easy contraband trade under cover of a nominal interest in pilotage.

Unfortunately for the islands in general, as the end of the eighteenth century approached, the Excise set up a preventive force of officers who patrolled in gigs, while powerful Revenue cutters ranged offshore. So potent were these services that mainstream smuggling was reduced to a trickle, and those who had made it their main occupation were brought to the direst poverty. Even for a pilot who was transporting a small amount of barter goods, 'a pound of sugar would expose the crew to seizure and the men to imprisonment'.

Rescue and salvage work grew with the numbers of ships piloted. The following sample incidents, taken at random as the years passed, are typical.

In 1825, the *James* of North Shields, laden with timber, had strained herself and was making more water than her crew could cope with. The pilots boarded her with extra men and brought her to safety by a short route through the rocks.

In 1830, a brave pilot, William Jenkins, was drowned in a do-or-die attempt to save the *John and Anne* bound up to London from Cadiz with a cargo of wine. The ship failed to weather the entrance to New Grimsby Sound between Tresco and Bryher. Jenkins boarded her and tried to work her off, but to no avail. She was wrecked with all hands including Jenkins, who left yet another widow and orphans for the islands to support.

In 1842, the Bryher cutter *Antelope* beat out to the Bishop Rock to save the crew of the steamer *Brigand* which had struck and was sinking fast.

Ships, even steamers, in trouble were sometimes towed in by pilots. This is a difficult feat in a sailing boat where the critical balance of the helm is easily upset by the tow-rope to the point of uncontrollability, yet two cutters managed to bring in the *Victor Jules* of Nantes, abandoned near the Seven Stones and laden with a valuable cargo of flour.

And so the piloting and rescuing continued, but always under the shadow of Customs activity. Alf Jenkins reports that, in 1824, when Lt Goldsmith of HM Revenue Cutter *Nimble* was himself prosecuted for a boyish prank construed by the locals as vandalism, there was much mirth and not a little celebration. This enthusiastic young officer had tired for a while of harassing his betters and had led his crew up a cliff near Porth Curnow on the mainland, heaving the well-known, much-loved and highly precarious Logan Rock seamark into the ocean. Feelings along the coast ran so high at this outrage that the authorities had no choice but to set up a court of inquiry, at which the Revenue man was found guilty. His sentence was to return the rock to its proper position and to pay the costs of so doing. He succeeded, but lost four years, seniority in the service for his pains.

All this still lay in the future, however, and through the dying years of the eighteenth century the pilots did what they could to help those families suffering from the efforts of the Customs men. Soon enough, however, they were to have troubles of their own.

Trinity House comes to Scilly

Responding to urging from the nautical authorities at Trinity House in London, the Parliament of 1807 passed an act bringing the Isles of Scilly within the compulsory pilotage area of the Trinity House Outports. The law came into effect on 1 October 1808 and after an interim period of two years during which the Court of Twelve continued to handle licences in the time-honoured way, Trinity House took over. Licences were now issued by sub-commissioners under their overall control and it is remarkable to note that the only Trinity House Pilotage Certificate ever issued to cover the whole of the British Isles was awarded to the Scillonian pilot, Captain Ashford.

The work of Channel pilotage remained outside Trinity House jurisdiction, but so far as island pilotage was concerned, the first demand of the Trinity from the old order was a list of pilots. This was duly supplied by Samuel Lemon, principal officer of the Customs in St Mary's. Mr Lemon was clearly alarmed at the prospect of the pilots being regulated by some distant administration, because in his returning letter, he went on to

> beg leave also to observe that the pilots here are extremely poor, and are ill able to pay anything considerable for their licences. I hope the pilots will be well rewarded for the great risk they are exposed to at this port in the winter season, since in my knowledge of these islands, a large number of men have lost their lives in endeavouring to board ships in gales of wind.

It is touching to hear the Customs chief speaking so caringly about men whom he well knew were not above a little modest contraband activity. The letter remains as evidence of the 'live and let live' relationship that must have existed at that time between the local Excise and the genuine pilots.

As for the pilots themselves, they are reported as being initially pleased to come under Trinity House, anticipating that their long hard times might in some way be alleviated. It was not to be.

Mr Lemon's report had named twenty-three pilots on St Mary's, eighteen on Tresco, seven on Bryher, fourteen on St Agnes and a further fourteen on St

Wreck of the Penzance ferry

On Monday, 22 July 1872, *The Times* newspaper reported the wreck of the passenger ferry *Earl of Arran*, stranded on the Isles of Scilly five days earlier as follows:

'The Cargo and baggage from the *Earl of Arran*, steamer, official number 26,933, from Penzance to the Scilly Islands, which was run ashore on the island on Nornour yesterday, after striking on St Martin's, have all been saved in good condition, with the exception of five small packages of cargo, which were saturated with water.'

A somewhat more colourful account advises that the ship struck St Martin's Neck and beached on Nornour after a pilot boat crew member – not a pilot – named Stephen Woodcock travelling as a fare-paying passenger, persuaded the skipper to divert from his usual track 'to give the passengers a better view'. This image gives as clear a picture as one could find of the islanders turning to for rescue and salvage work. The fact that the ninety-two passengers and crew of a ship bound from Penzance towards the islands (still the main ferry route today) must have included many of their friends and relations would have made little difference to their efforts.
(Gibsons of Scilly)

Martin's. The first act of the Elder Brethren of Trinity House was to announce that this was far too many, that less than a dozen licences would be granted to St Mary's, and that not a single ticket would in future be held by any off-islander. The result was immediate and riotous, forcing Trinity House to issue a compromise number of thirty-seven licences, several of which went to off-island men.

Thus commenced a situation which bled like an open wound until the end of competitive pilotage from Scilly. The tough truth seems to be that the Elder Brethren had no understanding of the ways of Scilly and had no wish to gain any. In disputes over the years they would hide again and again behind the claim that their only interests were for the good of shipping, which the pilots must serve in order to enjoy the fruits of a steady income. The reality was very different in these far-flung islands, where a spurned pilot of many years standing reduced to humiliation and poverty was hardly likely to give of his best.

The arrangement in the cutters had always been a communal one. The boats were owned by the pilots and some of their crews, with a share often taken by a shipping agent whose interests would be promoted by 'his' pilots. Scillonian cutters were originally comparatively small at 35–40ft but grew from 40 to 58ft in the first half of the nineteenth century. Leaving harbour to seek ships, the usual crew consisted of one or two seamen who could well be apprentice pilots, and eight actual pilots, of whom four might be for Scilly only and four for the Channel. Earnings were pooled and expenses shared equally. All this changed with the new bureaucracy.

The only pilots licensed to bring ships into the islands were the Trinity House men, but no cutter was supplied by the Elder Brethren. These favoured pilots could not have managed without the others even if they had been so inclined, so they were forced to mess in more or less as they had before. They could have claimed that they took precedence when a ship was to be boarded, but one can imagine the scenes that would have occurred on the deck of a hard-pressed cutter had such a claim been pursued. The only real advantages conferred by licences were a pension which, as we shall see, was sometimes not paid, and compensations for a pilot's widow were he killed in action. There were all too many of these, and pay-offs were pathetically small.

One method employed by the Trinity to try to reduce the number of pilots was to keep down the number of cutters by insisting that the boats themselves be licensed. This led to some reportedly fine vessels being refused the right to work.

In 1868, the new 59ft *Atlantic*, built by Mumford and Glyas of St Mary's at a hefty cost of £800 to replace a predecessor that had been wrecked after blowing ashore, was refused and had to be sold to a Milford Haven pilot. Another cutter put on the beach by official policy was the famous *AZ* of Bryher. All her crew were pensioner pilots except for James Jenkins, a licensed man who was distinguished by having been twice selected to pilot the Royal Yacht. The cutter was therefore for the time being temporarily short of pilots and working, officially at least, for Jenkins alone. The Trinity put a stop to this by the simple expedient of turning the *AZ* down and forcing Jenkins to take service in the cutter *Rapid* owned by a rival consortium. This was heavily against Jenkins's will but he was left with no option, eventually righting the situation by 'buying in' to the *Rapid*. This must have cost his own fortunes dear, because his share in *AZ* vaporised when the boat was broken up on the beach at Bryher.

No relief from poverty was thus occasioned by the intervention of Trinity House. Indeed, things grew even worse for a while when the pilots' unofficial bartering with ships was finally stopped. Not only had the pilots offered this service, wives and unemployed men had also always been ready to put to sea in the boats with poultry, fish and eggs to provide for a ship that had slipped through the pilot screen. By 1818, the preventive men had curtailed even this perk. Meanwhile, some of the licensed pilots were beginning to throw their weight around with their unlicensed colleagues, now officially referred to as hovellers.

It is never easy to ascertain the truth where official reports consistently contradict local anecdote. In the case of Scilly, an unexpected window on reality is opened by Augustus Smith, landlord of the islands from 1834 to 1872, who lived on Tresco. Augustus Smith has been described as the 'autocratic reforming creator of a stable Scilly'. Amongst his other legacies to the islands, he made education compulsory almost thirty years before it became so in England, by charging a penny for every child who attended school and two for every child who did not! Smith became increasingly outraged at what he perceived as the iniquity of Trinity House and finally took up the cudgel on behalf of the pilots.

One of Augustus Smith's actions was to report the *AZ* affair to his friend St Aubin, MP for West Cornwall. St Aubin put the matter before the House of Commons, but to no avail. Smith wrote that, 'if this sort of interference is to be exercised over the pilotage services by the Elder Brethren, very few will soon be found to follow that rough profession'. In the end, Smith left Pilot Jenkins the princely sum of £300 in his will, 'for his great distress caused by Trinity House refusing to renew licences'.

Smith was also incensed about the state of the unlicensed pilots, many of whom had been carrying on the work perfectly well for decades. When the Trinity House pilots tried to stop them working, Smith threatened dire retribution and eventually evicted some of the licensed pilots from their homes for interfering with his own more open-handed policy.

A further act of Trinity House roundly condemned by Smith was the levying of 6d in the pound on each and every activity undertaken by the pilots, whether official or not. There was little complaint about the levy while on licensed work, since Trinity House were in theory obliged to pay

Augustus Smith, Lord Proprietor of Scilly

Augustus Smith, seen here with a group of pilots, pilots' men and longshoremen, was landlord of the Isles of Scilly from 1834 to 1872. He acquired the lease from the Duchy of Cornwall for £20,000. Although a true philanthropist when it came to the pilots and their families, not all his actions seem to have been so well accepted. In 1855, for example, he expelled the ten inhabitants of Samson to turn the island into a deer park, but the plan backfired when the deer escaped in protest at the habitat.

Despite this and other unpopular measures, he represented the islanders strongly against Trinity House's more high-handed activities, recompensing one badly wronged pilot handsomely out of his own pocket. Smith also built a new quay at Hugh Town on St Mary's and opened schools on the well-inhabited islands. There was no coercion to attend, but fees were a penny (£0.004) if you showed up and tuppence if you did not. Augustus Smith lived at Tresco Abbey where he founded the now-famous gardens and encouraged the cut-flower industry. The estate was inherited by his nephew Thomas Algernon Smith-Dorrien-Smith, whose descendants still hold the lease.
(Gibsons of Scilly)

Scillonian pilot cutters

In this remarkable photograph from 1886, the pilot cutters *Atlantic* and *Presto* stand on beaching legs at low water. According to Scillonian pilot expert Luke Powell, they are laid up before being sold to Milford Haven pilots. The picture is full of interest, from the characters on the foreshore to the details of the boats themselves. Even granted that these people may not be tall, the draught of the cutters is huge, especially at the stem, where it plunges vertically to a prodigious depth. Unlike many similar vessels in the same service elsewhere, they rig powerful bobstays to keep the bowsprit down against the pull of their jibs, a vital feature if a cutter is to work successfully to windward. The hull on the left reveals a generous beam and a slack-bilged midships section of the style favoured in the West and known to generate less wetted surface than a wine-glass shaped yacht-like form. This confers the safety and comfort of heavy displacement without compromising light-weather speed. The massive mooring chains are said to have been salvaged from wrecked ships, and the arrangements on the starboard side of both bows for bringing these aboard must have been extremely strong, otherwise the monstrous links would have eaten the boats alive in anything of an onshore wind. Both boats have their shrouds fully rattled down, a sophistication unnecessary for the day-to-day sailing of a cutter. An easy route aloft, however, makes looking out over long distances a simple matter. These were boats that had made their living seeking ships well out in the Atlantic. *(Luke Powell)*

pensions out of the funds so raised. In due course, however, they began demanding it from income won from unlicensed activities, even including salvage. Smith pointed out that according to section 349 of the 1854 Merchant Shipping Act, 'any qualified pilot acting beyond the limits for which he is qualified by his licence shall be considered an unqualified pilot'. Smith drew the inference that no unqualified or unlicensed pilot could be made to pay a poundage on his earnings and that since Scillonian pilots were now expressly forbidden from seeking to board ships voyaging outside their licence area, it was unreasonable to demand poundage on earnings thus won.

All of this was expressed to the Board of Trade in a letter which pointed out that Smith had found it a waste of time to approach the Elder Brethren and was therefore constrained to seek the Board's intervention. In the same letter, Smith raised for the first time the sad case of Pilot Abram Stevens.

Stevens was turning sixty-six when he was suspended from his work by the Elder Brethren in circumstances that were at best inconsistent with judgements made on pilots from further up-Channel and at worst, notorious. The pilot's petition to Augustus Smith ran along the following lines:

> I was employed from boyhood in pilot boats and was licensed as branch pilot about 32 years ago. Not long afterwards, I was piloting an Italian vessel which struck Bartholomew's Ledge in St Mary's Sound and was wrecked near the Woolpack. I was suspended for two weeks. The accident occurred because the foreigner did not understand what I said. It was no fault of mine. The sub-commissioners agreed. That was 25 years ago.
>
> Nothing else ran amiss until 5 years ago when I was piloting an American brig. I was working through Broad Sound into St Mary's roadstead with the wind strong to the east. I thought to put her about when nearing the rocks called the Southern Wells, but the wind suddenly broke off and I had to sail her full. This caused her to run too far to pay off to go to leeward of the outer ledges, which she struck. The vessel came off immediately but made so much water that I had to run her ashore on Samson. Later, she was towed to St Mary's where her cargo of barley was discharged and the vessel repaired. My licence was again taken off me.
>
> Perhaps I went closer than I should, but I hadn't allowed for the wind dropping off. I have always been sober and never tasted liquor from the time I had my licence. I regularly paid 6d in the pound on all my earnings. I have often piloted ships to Havre, the Downs and London. I must have been to the Downs 30/40 times. I have been well known to many captains and received certificates of good conduct from them, although some of these are now lost.
>
> I looked to have had a pension of about £12 beginning just about the time my licence was taken away from me. I have nothing now to depend on for my support, but the share here in the pilot boat. I have piloted many vessels up Channel since losing my licence because you need no licence for that work, and whether you have one or not makes no difference with captains of vessels who are satisfied that you understand your employment.
>
> Last October I was rigging the new pilot boat *Atlantic*. While hoisting the [top]mast the cleat gave way and it fell on my back, laying me up for ten weeks. On my first day back, the foresail took me suddenly and knocked me down as dead as a hammer. Since then I have been laid up. As your petitioner, I therefore humbly pray that my case may have your merciful consideration and that through your assistance I may obtain some small pension in return for the sums I have paid through so many years to the Pilots' Fund.

The Secretary to Trinity House replied to the Board of Trade that Stevens was dismissed from the pilotage service for having on two occasions shown 'ignorance of his duties as a pilot' and 'want of knowledge of the locality' to wreck vessels in daytime in fine weather. The Receiver of Wrecks had advised that Stevens alone was to blame and that he saw no realistic excuse for the loss of the Italian ship. The secretary also pointed out that Stevens had only contributed £17 6s 9d over twenty-four years. This sum was forfeited with his licence. The secretary finished by writing that the withdrawal of Stevens' licence was 'an act of justice' and that failure to revoke it would have been 'an act of injustice to the shipping interest'.

Augustus Smith responded, still via the Board of Trade, that the Elder Brethren ought to see from

Stevens' statement that the first accident was owing neither to ignorance of duties nor want of knowledge. Smith had assured himself by further inquiries with people on board at the time that this was the case. He contradicts the secretary over the results of the first incident, stating that Stevens' licence had indeed been suspended but was immediately restored on inquiry and he had been exonerated from all blame. The Elder Brethren had ample opportunity to reopen this inquiry but did not do so and, as a result, they could only now complain about the second incident where the brig was temporarily stranded but not lost. Stevens, he repeated, had been harshly dealt with and now looked to the parish for support.

Smith stated clearly that the Elder Brethren had added up Stevens' contributions to the fund incorrectly, having failed to add the £1 1s which he had paid annually for his licence. This brought the total he paid as a pilot to £25 4s. Smith could not really believe that Stevens' poundage was so low and suggests that the sub-commissioners were remiss in supervision of payments. If it actually was the full sum, and Stevens had invested it in a Post Office savings account rather than paying it to the Trinity, he would have had £9 a year 'instead of being cast adrift in his old age'. Trinity House responded that Smith's letter merely repeated his previous communication and so required no further answer except that Stevens had been deprived of his licence for three months over the first incident – the full measure of term of punishment. They insisted that he was never exonerated from blame and that 'Mr Smith's ideas of justice most strangely differ from those usually entertained if he supposes any useful end could be attained by reviewing a question settled after 20 years and reopening it when those people are no longer available'.

Smith now wrote to the Board of Trade that the treatment of Mr Stevens by Trinity House was especially hard after the recent infamous loss of the famous clipper *Spindrift* further up-Channel in which the eminently culpable pilot, Martin, was only suspended for six months. The justification for this had been that Pilot Martin had twenty-three years' service. Smith notes that Stevens had twenty-four. He then reiterated his opinion that Stevens had not been guilty of causing any accident for which he could be justly blamed before having his licence confiscated over the recent temporary stranding of the American vessel.

The final letter in this interesting round of correspondence was a one-liner to Augustus Smith: 'The Board of Trade can no longer be a medium for correspondence between you and Trinity House.' One can imagine the impotent fury with which this decent and responsible landlord must have received the final shot from the bureaucrats' dusty locker.

Scillonian pilot cutters and the men who sailed in them

Set against this background of turmoil, it is hard to imagine the pilots maintaining their morale, but they managed to do so and to carry on the good work. Nearly all the local pilot cutters were built on St Mary's. The first purpose-built boat was launched in 1793, and by 1838, four yards were in full swing building cutters. As at many stations, the boats grew in length with time, beginning at 36–40ft on deck. By the mid nineteenth century, lengths were rising to 50ft or so, and in the 1870s four cutters of 60ft or more were at sea. Interestingly, two of these started life out at this large size, the heftiest being the 63ft *Gem* 2 of 1875. The other two had submitted to what in those days was the common practice of lengthening. *Presto* became the largest cutter in the Isles of Scilly after being lengthened in 1866 to 63ft – dimensions which the historian Sara Stirling advises may well refer to length between perpendiculars (more or less the waterline length for a plumb-stemmed cutter). If so, this could well give rise to a length on deck approaching 70ft, a view to which some of the spar dimensions mentioned below would certainly add weight. At the same time as she was lengthened, *Presto*'s beam was increased to 16ft, making her one of the biggest cutters on the Channel at that time, measuring up to her heavy Plymouth and Falmouth contemporaries.

Despite the efforts of Trinity House to keep boat numbers down, in 1848 when there were only thirty or so licensed pilots in the islands, at least twenty-eight cutters were fully manned with pilots both licensed and unlicensed, all working flat out.

The *Queen* ashore on St Martin's

The *Queen* was finally beached in 1889 and by the time of this photograph the sea had already begun to take its toll. Shortly after this photograph was taken she was broken up for fence posts. Piecing together the shape of these cutters is helped by the clear evidence here of the fact that the sternpost is as vertical as the stem. The downside of this is to increase drag from wetted area; the upside is that the rudder is carried as far aft as may be and attacks the water at the most advantageous angle. Most working gaff cutters tend to carry weather helm on some points of sailing. With some, it is a major vice. This feature would help minimise it in these big, tiller-steered creations.

The full-width mainsheet horse is in plain view, as is the cargo hatch for trade goods abaft the mast, a feature unique to Scillonian pilot cutters.
(Gibsons of Scilly)

The end of a pilot cutter

Photographic evidence for the pilot cutters of the Isles of Scilly is as sparse as images of the gigs are many. This rare shot of the cutter *Argus* paid off for the last time tells us about deep, ocean-worthy bulwarks, the lack of any cockpit, channels to increase the width of the shroud base and to provide a stout point of attachment for beaching legs, slightly swept deck planking and a cut-out in the starboard bulwarks forward to accommodate massive mooring chains. The shot also reveals a subtly sculpted bow with a hollow entry below the water blending into a carefully contrived reserve of buoyancy above, adding up to what seems a good solution to the dilemma of all straight-stemmers, to combine dryness and the power to lift to a sea with the ability to cut through a wave.
(Gibsons of Scilly)

When a cutter put to sea with her eight pilots, it was usual, if weather permitted, to cruise some distance westward from the islands, sometimes eighty or a hundred miles into the Atlantic. When all the pilots had been boarded, the crew, often no more than a lad on his own, would sail the boat home. On one occasion, the *Presto* was coming in single-handed. It being high water, the lad ran her right up to her beach mooring but could not pick it up in time to take off the last of her way. The mighty cutter kept right on going and ran her bowsprit in through the door of Duff's – now the famous Atlantic Hotel, still a favourite bar for locals. The drinkers turned out and shipped the cutter's beaching legs just in time to catch the last of the high tide.

Unlike the gigs, which seem to have achieved something near perfection at an early date and were never thereafter altered, the cutters changed constantly in form and rig. Most were decked cutters, but at least one was converted for a while to schooner rig, unsuccessfully it seems. Another tried her luck as a yawl, also without notable success. The Scillonian pilot cutter was of typical West Country form, with an exceptionally deep, straight stem stood up on the keel with no intervening curved forefoot. She was of traditional plank-on-frame construction, with her timbers well salted. She was fitted out with accommodation for nine men, complete with cooking and bunk facilities.

Planking was 2½in with a 3in garboard, fastened with iron and wooden trenails. Despite the obvious expense, the cutters' bottoms are reported by Alf Jenkins to have been coppered. Ballast was all carried inside and was normally of pig iron.

A typical cutter carried an immense running bowsprit of similar diameter to the mast, from which could be set a large jib and jib topsail. Her shrouds and forestay were heavy, and sail-carrying was her stock in trade, though once on station she might jog along under trysail, under which she could apparently sail herself forever. Alf Jenkins also notes that mainsails were, until the late 1800s, loose-footed on a long boom – ie, attached at tack and clew only. Substantial reductions in sail area could be achieved by removing the lower portion of the sail which took the form of a 'bonnet' laced along the foot of the sail.

In winter, some boats seem to have favoured their mainsails without the bonnet, while others 'changed down' to a small winter mainsail set from a shorter gaff and often known as a trysail. They also bent on smaller, stronger headsails. A staff for the pilot flag replaced the topmast of the summer days.

The sort of rig carried by the more ambitious pilots is evidenced by Alf Jenkins in his book where the *Atlantic*, given at 59ft on deck, carried a mast 61ft from deck to truck and a main boom 48ft long. This is huge when one considers that the 1913 55ft Le Havre pilot cutter *Jolie Brise*, rigged for pure speed by the master builder Paumelle, still carries a mere 38ft boom on a deck length of only 4ft less than the *Atlantic*. If one takes these dimensions as gospel, then the Isles of Scilly cutter has either fallen into anecdotal legend and 'grown in the night', or her crew were a world-class bunch of hard drivers. A more likely explanation is that, like the *Presto* described above, the *Atlantic*'s length was not in fact 59ft 'on deck', but 'between perpendiculars'. This archaic form of measurement does not include a boat's overhanging counter stern. If we add 8ft for this, the *Atlantic* becomes 67ft long and her rig suddenly looks more or less what one would expect, though such a boom must have surely taken some handling on a wild night west of the Bishop. Incidentally, the *Atlantic* and her attendant gigs were kept on the beach in front of the famous pub which today bears her name and where the *Presto* brought up in the bar.

There is no record of how well the boats sailed, save the usual claims of phenomenal performance, but with so great a lateral resistance from the extraordinarily deep forefoot, it is easy to imagine they would be slow in stays and might well be grateful for a backed staysail to help them through the wind when tacking.

Boarding was generally accomplished by means of a clinker-built stem punt. At around 16ft, this was substantially larger than those used in the neighbouring Bristol Channel. The pilot and the four-oared punt's crew were trailed astern on a long painter while the cutter sailed as close as she dared to the ship. At the crucial moment the punt was sheered off and under ideal circumstances would scramble alongside the ship without having to row. The cutter then took station to leeward so that the punt's crew could work back to her easily. The cutters were rigged with a gate in the bulwarks for launching the punt. This was achieved by manpower, using the roll of the cutter to facilitate heaving the boat in or out.

Many cutters carried a cage of pigeons for sending messages home. This enabled them to pass on information concerning ship movements as well as orders for fresh produce to flesh out the pilotage fees. Perhaps some of the more adventurous men bound far away up-Channel also sent sweet messages to young ladies, but we shall never know.

One surprising way of expanding the cutter's income was to collect mails from Australian wool ships, China clippers and other far-ranging vessels. Such ships would demand a premium for carrying mails, based upon their regular passage times. If held up by calms or a northeaster, it would pay them to maintain their good record by handing the mails to the pilot cutter for posting in Cornwall, together with a fee of up to £60. Further boosts to the funds were generated by the fact that, unlike most purpose-built pilot cutters, the boats from the Isles of Scilly featured a modest cargo hold with a hatch abaft the mast. The hold could carry supplies to sell to ships inbound from long voyages. Many of these would be pressing on for distant ports and would be glad of fresh fruit, meat and even essential dry goods, whether or not they were boarding a Scillonian Channel pilot. When piloting was thin, the cutters took advantage of the early spring which blesses their islands far out in the Gulf Stream by running new potatoes to Wales and Southampton. From there, the railways sped them to London and so the pilots of Scilly made their contribution to the finest dinner tables in the land.

One cannot leave the subject of victualling without making reference to an unusual account of a Scillonian Channel pilot. In 1851, the schooner yacht *America* was coming onto soundings on her historic voyage to Cowes, where she was to defeat the assembled might of the Royal Yacht Squadron and establish the *America*'s Cup, which was to remain in Yankee hands until the 1980s. A pilot was engaged and the mate of the *America* was bemused by the whole scene. Here is what he had to say:

> This channel beats everything and all conception that I had of its extent and magnitude. The pilot boats beggar all description, they are about 40ft long, sloop-rigged or cutter as they call them. Most of them carry only one or two pilots and these as dirty as chimney sweeps. The pilot steps aft and is introduced to the Captain. They make a bargain as to the amount. He next asked, 'Have you a bottle of spirits aboard for the boat?' I will give you the words that passed between our Captain (himself a New York pilot) and the pilot. In answer to the first question the Captain said 'No!' 'Have you any pork?' The Captain told the steward to get some of each kind and give it to the boats. 'Could you spare some tea and coffee? We have been out on this trip three weeks last Tuesday.' Here the Captain filled away and the boat had to leave. The pilot told me that he spoke and boarded every vessel he met and asked the same questions. He told me that he supplied a ship last Wednesday with 200lbs of beef and port, besides other things for which they received £3 sterling. They are without any exception the damnedest beggars I ever fell in with.

Towards the end of the nineteenth century, many merchant sailing ships were growing too large to navigate conveniently into St Mary's Roads and steamers were coming into general service. Both these factors tended to hurry shipping past the islands and on towards Falmouth to collect their orders and pilots. As a result, the now-diminishing numbers of pilot cutters from Scilly experienced a growing problem with rival cutters from Falmouth vying for the same Channel trade. Ship numbers were falling as tonnages grew and tracks had become more predictable. Pilot work was thinning out and competition for what remained was increasing. Sometimes two or three Falmouth cutters beating down west looking for work would join forces to out-manoeuvre a Scillonian boat, leaving her sadly short of trade. A typical example took place on 8 April 1884, when the cutter *Agnes* was at sea with Scilly bearing East, fifteen miles. From Alf Jenkins's excellent book, *Gigs and Cutters of the Isles of Scilly,* the following poignant log entry is lifted,

> Boarded brig *Sommeville,* Scilly for orders.
> Spoke several ships bound east.
> Falmouth cutter No 1 close alongside.
> Scilly East 15 miles
> No 2 close to Scilly with her flag up.
> Have two other cutters in sight, no chance to speak to a ship before them as they enclose you in the middle of them all.

One advantage a local cutter could always bring to bear, in light weather at least, was to tow a gig and send her pilots in that speedy craft from an apparently hopeless leeward position. In harder going, gigs were even said to have been carried on the decks of some of the larger cutters. There would be no answer from Falmouth to these lithe, six-oared boats stretching away, leaping to windward through the tumbling seas, but fate in the guise of world economics was on the move and even this bold expedient was not enough.

The last cutter working from Scilly was the *Agnes,* operating from the island of that name with the pilots serving a rota system. In her last years she was nicknamed the 'Roster', because all the pilots had to take their turn. Her service ended in 1894 when she was converted to ketch rig in Plymouth for use as an island collier. A number of cutters had finished their time in this way, carrying island potatoes up to South Wales and returning laden with coal for home. This trip gave every chance of a reach, at least outward bound, and times were recorded both ways that would not disgrace a modern racing yacht. The *Agnes* was broken up for fence posts on Tresco on 7 November 1902.

There were still pilots in Scilly, and for many years to come the seas were scanned in search of a homeward bounder, with the remarkable gigs and their crews – as thrilling to watch then as they still are today – ever standing by to put their man aboard. In truth, however, it was all over. In the words of J G Uren, the postmaster of Penzance in 1907, 'No longer does the white-winged barque or a full-rigged ship with royals set and courses hauled well aft appear in the offing, and, to the delight of the islanders, hoist her number and ask for a Channel Pilot to take her to port.'

CHAPTER 3

The Falmouth Pilots and their Cutters

As it evolved in most ports, piloting in Falmouth began on a casual basis but was regularised in 1808 when the harbour became a Trinity House outport subject to compulsory pilotage. The waters within its jurisdiction stretched eastwards from Black Head just north of the Lizard to Dodman point ('The Dodman', or 'Deadman') half-way to Fowey. The first Falmouth licence was issued to Henry Vincent of St Mawes, which lies on the east side of the harbour opposite Falmouth itself. The two communities were in great rivalry for the piloting of ships. Both maintained cutters and competition between them ran high.

Pilots' licences were issued under Trinity House by local sub-commissioners who were also responsible for discipline. On the whole, the pilots were a law-abiding crowd but one or two notable lapses added colour to the scene, in addition to the usual complaints about the occasional man being on duty the worse for drink.

One pilot was temporarily suspended for laying out the harbourmaster with a shrewdly placed fist. We are not told the cause of the altercation, but while many port officials have done a fine job down the years, more than one misunderstood sailor has fallen foul of them or their representatives around the seven seas, so it seems likely that the pilot's peers at least would have supported his enterprise.

Another incident resulting in disciplinary action began with a joke which backfired, and one can only hope that the reaction of the sub-commissioners was not too severe. One balmy afternoon with not much going on, an apprentice lad had a bit of fun penning a message which he corked up in an old rum bottle and tossed into the sea. So far as we know, the Falmouth pilots were not a notoriously bawdy crew, so the lad was probably joking when he wrote, 'Lovely day, pilots all drunk.' Unfortunately for the apprentice, the bottle drifted ashore and was returned to the authorities who, it is reported, read its tidings with mixed feelings.

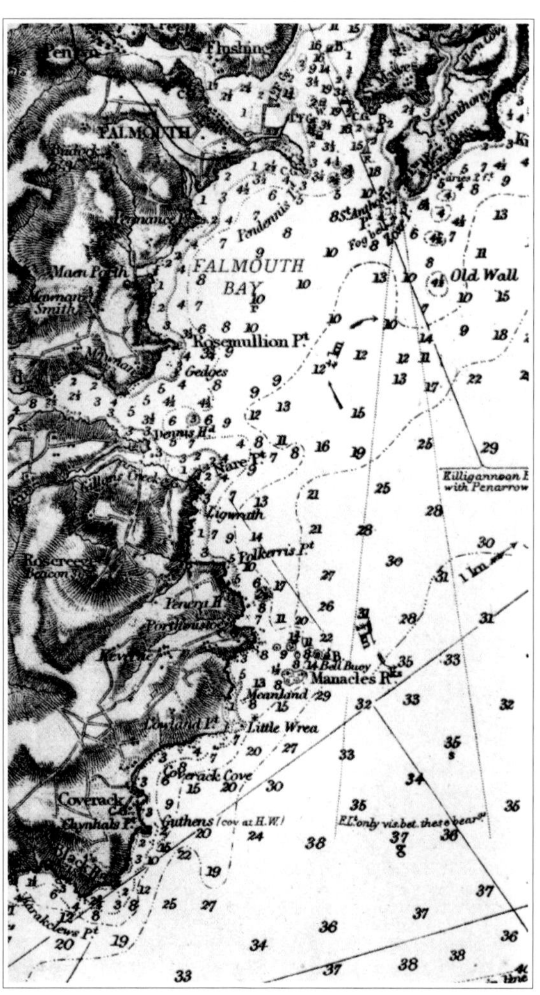

Falmouth Harbour

This period chart with depths in fathoms shows Falmouth Harbour (upper central). The inlet on its east side, north of St Anthony Point, is St Mawes where one group of pilots had their base, and from where they had a clear view of the Manacles and incoming ships. On the west side, inside the walled dock, lies Falmouth, better sheltered from prevailing westerlies. Between the two sit Carrick Roads, easy to enter under sail with a leading wind, and with water enough for all but the deepest sailing ships to lie waiting for orders. Outside, Falmouth Bay offers shelter for larger vessels anchoring in winds from southwest through to northeast.
(From The Pilot's Handbook of the English Channel, *1898)*

In 1809 nine first-class pilots and sixteen second-class men were working from Falmouth and St Mawes. By 1873 there were sixty-five pilots in all. Between 1830 and 1875, a total of no fewer than thirty-eight cutters operated from the two sides of the harbour, to say nothing of pilots working from the inevitable Cornish gigs. These men were wild, independent characters, many of whom seemed from another age altogether. One such man, Bob Dash, claimed that the longest trip he ever made from St Mawes was on the pilot gig. He had only once visited Falmouth, and that was to consult a lawyer. He never went on a train, but he signed on as crew on a gig to go out seeking a Norwegian ship due to berth in Falmouth. The ship was finally boarded in a fresh breeze near the Eddystone Rocks off Plymouth. Bob Dash boarded her with the pilot hoping for a quick trip home, because he knew full well the gig-men would put in somewhere halfway back along the coast to refresh themselves with a few pints of the right stuff. His ruse failed miserably when the wind died completely. The gig pulled home the same evening with all hands in merry mood. Dash and his boss, the pilot, arrived three days later.

Boats were often owned by families in which the pilot tradition ran strongly. The Vincents, the Lowrys, and the Andrews were typical. The pilots themselves were originally the proprietors and it was not unusual for a whole crew to be related either by blood or marriage. Many of the women took a share also. Hesther Chard claimed 56/64 of the *Victoria* worth a nominal £328 2s 6d, of which her husband was the managing owner; Kate Pope owned 16/64 of the famous *Arrow*, and Philippa Bellman was up for 4/64 of the *Antelope*.

As shipping thinned out towards the end of the nineteenth century, competition between pilot cutters stiffened steadily. Falmouth boats had always carried Channel as well as Falmouth pilots, many of the men being ready for either work. Now, the boats began ranging out beyond Scilly where they vied with and ultimately eclipsed the local craft in their zeal to put their men aboard eastbound ships.

The sad fact was that there were now too many pilots and too many cutters. Competition had become counter-productive. To cut their losses, therefore, the thirty-three pilots of Falmouth and the thirty from St Mawes joined forces in 1887, forming the Falmouth and District Pilot Boat Association (FDPBA). Their first chairman was Samuel Collins. The twelve cutters then working were bought by the association at a total cost of £4,525.

In the early years of the association, carrying orders to sailing ships bound for northern European ports was a major additional occupation. At this time, ships would often sail not knowing their ultimate destination. A classic example would be a barque bound in round the Horn from Chile loaded with nitrate. The cargo might be bought and sold several times while she was on passage and it was only on arrival at Queenstown (Cork), Falmouth, or perhaps Cowes – the main ports where ships went 'for orders' – that she would report in and be told her final destination. All three stations had immediate access to wide, well-sheltered anchorages suitable for sailing ships.

First, the agent of an expected ship would arrive

Pilots and their pay

On 22 May 1897, the *Falmouth Packet* newspaper published the following article:

Public sympathy will be on the side of the local pilots in their efforts to secure a revised tariff. At a meeting of the Harbour Board this week, Mr Thomas Webber, retired merchant, of 'Woodville', Falmouth, gave publicity to the matter, and lucidly explained the grievance of those who follow the dangerous and responsible calling of navigating the vessels comprising our mercantile fleet through dangerous passages of water. The very basis of the tariff stands in need of alteration. Instead of being paid according to the tonnage of vessels, the pilots charge according to the number of feet a vessel draws.

Comment is hardly necessary, except to mention that with increased tonnage invariably comes increased responsibility.

But the pilots have what they regard as a still bigger grievance. To pilot a vessel drawing eight feet from outside the Manacles to within Pendennis point, the charge is thirty shillings, whilst there is a reduction of ten shillings on this amount if the pilotage only extends from inside the Manacles to Pendennis. Captains take every advantage of this, and the fact that stormy weather often prevents pilots from boarding vessels outside the Manacles, the men suffer man losses year in year out, through no fault of their own.

What they want is the same pilotage inside and outside the bay, and as there is little fear of the port suffering as a consequence, it seems very likely that this important change will be made.

at the Custom House and bind himself that if orders were delivered to his ship, he would pay her light dues. Next, the orders were presented in a sealed envelope to the pilotage secretary. The envelope bore an undertaking to pay both the inward and outward pilotage. When the ship came in, this document was duly presented to the captain and the appropriate arrangements made, often to the benefit of any Channel pilots who were on hand to take the ship onwards. In 1884, 1,945 vessels sailed into Falmouth, anchoring in Carrick Roads for orders. This represented over a million tons of shipping.

Under the amalgamated arrangements of the FDPBA, a fresh cutter left Falmouth every evening to take up station off the port. The following day, the next one came out and the first sailed down to the Lizard to relieve her own predecessor, which now worked west to the Scillies to seek ships and harass the locals. Thus, right up to the end, each cutter had a fair chance to board her Channel pilots in the old-fashioned way.

Complaints inevitably came in about the new system as against that of the old, free-ranging pilots, but these were handsomely rebuked by the *Falmouth Packet*, the local newspaper which wrote, 'It is a fine thing for landlubbers and interested tradesmen to be snugly anchored in "blanket bay" on dark and stormy nights. It would be better for the finest part of their nature to be disciplined by having a winter's experience with our brethren in their perilous duty.'

The Falmouth pilots had always indulged themselves in the local passion for serious racing, a tradition continued today by the working oyster dredgers that still thrash it out once or twice a week in fair weather and foul. The pilots raced annually at the town regatta and their participation was popular with the townsfolk. There was invariably a full turnout and contests were hard won.

In 1864, the creatively named *Gorilla* from Penzance came up from Mount's Bay to try her luck against the local hotshots. For her pains, she had her bobstay and main earring cut through and was given verbal abuse whenever she came within earshot of her competitors. According to John Leather, the *Arrow* won this unsporting contest and was played in by the town band with 'See the Conquering Hero Comes'. The wooden spoon was serenaded by another favourite of the time, 'Cheer up Sambo, don't let your spirits go down'.

As professionals, it was beneath the pilots' pride to race for a stake of less than the £40 offered to them as prize money and this, sadly, proved their undoing.

In 1878, the race officer was the pompous Major Read of the Royal Cornwall Yacht Club. This gentleman, who clearly understood how things should be run in a proper outfit, decided that 'the £40 prize money would be better spent on races for bona fide Corinthian yachtsmen', and churlishly withdrew it. The fact that in those days many of his 'Corinthian' cronies probably watched their yachts race from the club bar while their paid crews worked out in the rain must have escaped him.

Falmouth pilot cutters before the 1887 amalgamation

A rare, very old image showing two Falmouth pilot cutters, fully rigged as seeking vessels with main booms and sizeable mainsails. The cutter with the punt gate in her bulwarks showing aft of the vessel in the foreground is the *Vie*, No 3. She has a distinctly 'yachty' sheer but, despite the racy stow of her mainsail, she lacks a tall yacht topmast. The short pole is typical of pilot cutters of her day. The *Nautilus*, No 11, in the background with her main and topsail hoisted is a classic. Both these handsome, powerful cutters date from the 1820s. This picture will come as a relief to many a sailor who has puzzled over how the Falmouth pilots can have been serious about sailing their boats with the boomless cut-down mains photographed so famously in later years when the days of competition were long past. *(Luke Powell)*

As shipping under sail declined into the early twentieth century, the Falmouth pilots became fewer and fewer until by 1922 only one cutter was left working, along with a new motor launch. The cutter was the *Arthur Rogers*. In her latter days the *Rogers* was refitted with two 13/15hp Kelvin engines and a cut-down ketch rig. She was moored off the Town Quay and worked forty-eight-hour shifts. Jimmy Morrison of Falmouth recalled that, in a northerly wind, her station was below Pendennis Castle at the harbour mouth. In easterlies she was to be found anchored by Mallennon. In southwesterlies she lay behind Porthlellow, handy to The Manacles rocks, a mile south of Nave Point. Thus, she was near the harbour at all times, ever ready for service. Mr Morrison also remembers going aboard

8
7

Vincent at her work

This colourful artist's impression by Kenneth Grant shows the *Vincent* working into position to board an inbound sailing ship in a heavy sea. The pilot and the punt's crew are going to have a lively time of things in the very near future and much will depend on how effectively the ship heaves to and gives them a lee. *Vincent* was a St Mawes-based cutter named for the Vincent family who had been pilots locally for generations. *(Courtesy Kenneth Grant)*

Alphabetical List of Falmouth Pilot Cutters Under Sail from 1820

Vessel	Sail/Motor	Built	Length (ft)
Alarm	Sail	1847	44.3
Alarm	Sail	1857	61.2
Alliance	Sail	1841	43.7
Andrew	Sail	1857	56.0
Ann	Sail	Unknown	Unknown
Antelope	Sail	1870	62.5
Arrow	Sail	1862	66.8
Condor	Sail	1874	57.8
Constantine	Sail	Unknown	Unknown
Dan	Sail	1850	46.0
Dash	Sail	Unknown	Unknown
Experiment	Sail	Unknown	Unknown
Fal	Sail	Unknown	Unknown
Gem	Sail	1845	48.1
Harriet	Sail	1844	46.2
Harriet	Sail	1852	54.7
Lively Sail	Sail	c1820	Unknown
N Jenkin	Sail	1847	44.2
Nautilus	Sail	c1820	Unknown
Pearl	Sail	c1820	Unknown
Providence	Sail	1841	43.6
Providence	Sail	c1820	Unknown
R Green	Sail	1866	58.0
Scilly	Sail	1847	56.3
Solace	Sail	c1825	Unknown
Spy	Sail	1837	54.2
Telegraph	Sail	1857	63.3
Union	Sail	Unknown	Unknown
Victoria	Sail	1837	44.4
Victoria	Sail	1852	52.8
Vie	Sail	c1825	Unknown
Vincent	Sail	1820	Unknown
Vincent	Sail	1852	68.0
Wasp	Sail	1848	51.1
Water Nymph	Sail	1844	56.0

Pilotage rates

As far back as the Napoleonic Wars pilotage dues were laid down succinctly by the authorities in Falmouth.
(From Instructions to Masters of Ships: A Digest of the Provisions, Penalties etc of the Pilots Act, *Trinity House 1809)*

TABLE OF THE RATES OF PILOTAGE,

For piloting Ships within the Falmouth District.

FROM	TO	8 feet & under	8 to 10	11	12	13	14	15	16	17	18	19	20	21	22
		s.	s.	s.	s.	s.	s.	s.	s.	s.	s.	s.	s.	s.	s.
Sea, and vice versa	Carrick Road, Falmouth, and St. Mawe's Harbours, and St. Just Pool	24	30	35	42	46	50	55	60	67	75	84	94	105	120
Ditto....ditto	Helford Harbour	21	24	27	30	34	38	42	47	52	60				
Carrick Roads, and vice versa	Falmouth and St. Mawe's Harbours, and St. Just Pool	*One Shilling and Sixpence per Foot of the Draught of Water.*													

Masters of Vessels taking a Pilot at Sea, are to pay,

	£.	s.	d.
For putting a Pilot on board without a Line drawn from the Manacles to the Dodman	2	2	0
Ditto from the Entrance of Helford Harbour to the Gull Rock	1	1	0
Ditto a Mile without the Shag Rock, or Pendennis Point	0	10	6
Ditto off the Lizard, or in the Parallel of the Lizard, or meeting a Vessel there, and running before her, not being able to put a Pilot on board, provided the Master of the Vessel consents to receive a Pilot at that distance	3	3	0

N. B. No Allowance for a Pilot going on board a Ship in the Harbour to take her out, except in extremely bad Weather, or when Ships are on shore, or making Signals of Distress, in which Cases a reasonable Compensation is to be made.

41

Richard Green on station

Richard Green, No 10, fore-reaching under backed staysail with jib and trysail both drawing. The rig is in cut-down, post-amalgamation (1887) form. A cutter of the same name and number was reported as having dragged her anchors in a gale on 2 September 1887, to be driven ashore in Helford River after putting in for shelter with four pilots and three apprentices on board. Forty to fifty fathoms of chain were let out on one anchor and the full length of the hawser on the other, but to no avail. The cutter struck on the rocks just under Mawnan Church. The crew saved themselves in the punt, but lost all their effects. According to *The West Briton* newspaper, the *Green* became a total wreck. However, no record has been found by this author of a replacement and the extreme sheer of the boat seen here is archaic in form, so one wonders if she was in fact salvaged and refitted, or whether this image was taken just weeks before she was lost. She has no peak halyard purchase and, in contrast to the *Harriet*, the halyard is clearly dead-ended aloft.
(© National Maritime Museum, Greenwich, UK)

Falmouth pilot cutter *Harriet*

Harriet, No 1, is seen here fore-reaching on station in post-amalgamation days with her staysail sheeted to windward, her jib drawing and a small, boomless mainsail. In this trim, she could be left to her own devices to work slowly upwind with no need for a helmsman. Her galley stovepipe is a feature one might expect. Perhaps of more significance is the boom-jaw collar on the mast, a left-over from her glory days as a free-ranging cutter when she carried a full mainsail and pilots hungry to be well upwind of the next cutter. The peak halyard purchase is in clear view immediately above and to leeward of the gaff, and the mainsheet block is on the leeward side of the stern. Cross-checking with the shot of *Richard Green* seems to confirm that this block moved across the boat somehow when she tacked, a potentially hazardous practice unless it was rigged to a horse and was thus self-tacking. There is a suggestion of a mainsheet horse in the photo but it is by no means clear and conclusive.
(© National Maritime Museum, Greenwich, UK)

the *Arthur Rogers* and has a vivid memory of her hull being so 'sharp' that she had little more than 5ft headroom.

The brave old cutter was finally pensioned off when she lost her counter on being driven ashore into the back of Marks and Spencer's new shop. Even then she was not finished. She was sold to a man who refitted her, then sailed her to the South Seas where she carried copra with, as legend has it, an all-woman crew. She ended her days on a reef, having dragged her anchor with nobody on board.

Falmouth pilot cutters

Falmouth cutters came from the town itself and also from St Mawes across the harbour. Traditionally, St Mawes cutters were built at Porthmellon, hard by Mevagissey, while Falmouth boats often came from Flushing and the yard run latterly by the Trethowan family. A classic example was the *Arrow*, built by Trethowans in 1862 for £810 6s 10d.

Falmouth pilot cutters were similar in size and form to the larger of the Scillonian boats, typically running out at 60ft or more on deck with a sweet counter stern, a plumb stem and a long, easy run. They evolved little after the first three decades of the nineteenth century, although they did grow somewhat 'sharper' as time passed. The boats were classic gaff cutters setting a mainsail, a topsail in fair summer weather, a jib tacked down to a long bowsprit and a staysail. The only anomaly is that after 1887, all available evidence suggests that they sailed without a main boom. Neither is any sail-carrying topmast to be seen. Instead, the boats seem to have rigged a 'chock pole' from the topmast irons for flying flags.

Lack of a boom would have compromised performance considerably, especially off the wind. It is convenient to speculate, as some authorities have done, that the boats were thus rigged to make them safer. This conclusion is drawn on the mistaken basis that a gybe with a boomed sail is likely to cause mayhem. Nothing could be further from the truth as anyone who has gybed a Bristol Channel pilot cutter will advise. In any case, the boom of any working 60ft gaff cutter with a decent suit of sails will be well above head height at the helming position. Furthermore, tacking a loose-footed main in a hard breeze is a potentially hazardous undertaking with heavy sheet blocks flailing around to brain the unwary.

However, there is no denying the evidence of a series of fine photographs dating from well after the amalgamation that form the main pictorial support for these boats. Like many other large cutters of their time, including racing yachts on passage from one regatta to the next, they are shown setting a down-sized gaff sail which looks for all the world like a winter rig. Perhaps it was, but no illustrations from after the amalgamation show a boom rigged, so it is certainly arguable that after this date the boom was not, in fact, used at all. The trysail shown is comparatively generous and could perhaps have served in place of a full summer mainsail on boats which were not competing with one another and whose cruising area was now curtailed to a line joining the Lizard and the Dodman – both headlands being a mere 10 miles or so from Falmouth Harbour. The big trysail would have been cheaper than a full-on mainsail; no topping lift gear would be required; hoisting would have been easier too, but sailing the boat would certainly not have been. A boom-jaw collar is clearly seen in a photograph of the cutter *Harriet* (No 1), and a spar which could possibly be a boom is seen in the scuppers in a photograph on deck from the same series, so while the evidence for permanently rigging the trysail is strong, the jury is still hovering in the doorway.

Another interesting observation about the Falmouth pilot cutter winter mainsail is that it was extremely short-luffed, its area being apparently made up by means of a 'bonnet' laced neatly to the foot. There was therefore no messy roll of canvas at the foot with the sail shortened, as is invariably otherwise the case with a loose-footed sail reefed in a hurry at sea. The bonnet would simply have been unlaced. From careful study of the photographs of these unusual sails, one can conclude that either the bonnet was rigged with at least one set of reef points, or a choice of bonnets was carried to give scope for fine-tuning. The mainsheet has been said by some sources to have been hooked to a specially strengthened stanchion on the lee side that was armour plated with a square hole for the shackle pin. However, an athwartships horse arrangement seems more likely.

A photograph of the Falmouth cutter *Vincent* taken in 1924 also shows this small, boomless mainsail. By that time, the boats were generally motorised, so it seems likely that the sailing rig was maintained for auxiliary and emergency purposes. Using the winter rig for this would have been a logical step.

Staysails were self-tending, sheeted from a horse forward of the mast, and jib-sheet leads were outboard of the bulwarks where they should be, indicating a full understanding of how to drive a cutter to windward. We should expect nothing else.

As in Scilly and the Bristol Channel, boarding was by way of a clinker-built punt. These are reported to have been 15ft long and manhandled through a bulwark gate to port with the cutter hove to on starboard tack. So large a punt would have been excellent at sea once launched. Recovery would certainly have been done to leeward. By making use of the reduced freeboard and anticipating a roll, a substantial boat can be dragged aboard a pilot cutter with surprisingly little difficulty. In light weather when the cutter was not heeled, the men

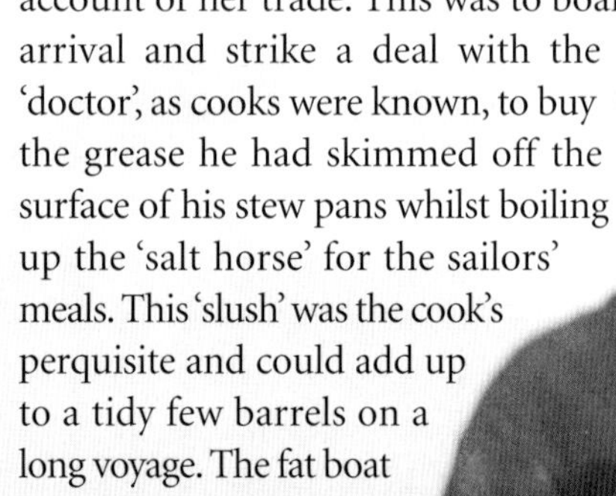

The *Vincent*, No 8, on deck

This priceless image of the deck of a late Falmouth cutter shows no cockpit, a strongly-built companionway, the punt in its chocks to port and surprisingly deep, safe bulwarks. The mainsheet purchase is a mere 4 : 1. It is rove to advantage, but even so, heaving it in must have called for some stern effort in a blow. The dark horizontal line behind the helmsman could well be a mainsheet horse. The heavy spar chocked off in the starboard scuppers is perplexing. It would be satisfying to suggest that it is the main boom, waiting for its moment of glory when summer comes around and the men shrug off the winter trysail, but in light of all the available photographic evidence of post-amalgamation boats, this seems unlikely. It is too big to boom out the staysail downwind and lacks fittings in general. Perhaps it served to pole out the main clew on a run. If it did, a spar of this weight would have needed a topping lift and a simple jaw-style gooseneck. Sadly, if these existed, they are out of shot, so perhaps we shall never know. *(© National Maritime Museum, Greenwich, UK)*

would generally have left the punt in the water and towed her.

Falmouth quay punts and others engaged in casual pilotage

Like many busy harbours during the age of sail, Falmouth developed a whole range of service industries whose transport requirements were supplied by 'bumboats'. These handy, capacious craft were known locally as 'quay punts'. Typically 28ft long with a straight keel and plumb stem, a transom stern, a large open cockpit and a foredeck sheltering a cuddy, as their name suggests, they put to sea from the quays of Falmouth and Flushing. A score or more were regularly to be seen plying their various trades, operated by family groups such as the Morrisons, the Wests and the Tonkins.

The services offered by Falmouth quay punts were typical of the British bumboat. Personnel were certainly ferried, and this would undoubtedly include pilots, at least on a casual 'taking-off' basis. While the punts were not official pilot cutters, it made sense from time to time for a pilot to avail himself of a passing punt in order to leave a ship which had missed the cutter that would ideally have taken him off. Pilots stuck on foreign-bound ships from other ports might also signal for a punt to come alongside as the ship passed by so as to regain the land before it was too late.

In addition to humanity in many forms, the punts also traded in fresh produce, water, newspapers, chandlery, and anything else a ship could possibly require. One unique punt was always known as 'the fat boat', not because of her plump lines but on account of her trade. This was to board each new arrival and strike a deal with the 'doctor', as cooks were known, to buy the grease he had skimmed off the surface of his stew pans whilst boiling up the 'salt horse' for the sailors' meals. This 'slush' was the cook's perquisite and could add up to a tidy few barrels on a long voyage. The fat boat

is the only quay punt recorded as having sunk at sea while working. One commentator remarked that, 'one minute she was sailing along, the next, I turned round and she had vanished.' Whatever happened to her, the ballast keel dragged her down far harder than the buoyant barrels of fat could hold her up.

More sophisticated business was also pursued by the quay punts, such as carrying tailors to seaward of the Lizard to meet incoming ocean wanderers short of a respectable rig in which to step ashore. This was a lively occupation in Falmouth, as it was in Cork, because of the numbers of ships arriving for orders, and the town was famous for tailors, having a considerable Jewish population, many of whom had traditionally specialised in this work. A seaport tailor could turn out a smart suit overnight on the basis of a deposit collected off the Lizard. The sprightly punt would often have delivered the order long before the ship was anchored. By the time the captain or his mates were ready to head for the agent's office or the flesh-pots, the tailor would be alongside with a made-to-measure go-ashore outfit.

Some tailors owned their own quay punts, but 'Henry Rusden, outfitter' was sole proprietor of the *Sally*, a powerful 64ft cutter more like a pilot boat than a bumboat, built locally in 1861. The *Sally* came to an unfortunate end eleven years

Falmouth pilot cutter *Arrow*

Arrow, No 6, built in 1862, was big vessel of 53 tones and 66.8ft overall. (*© National Maritime Museum, Greenwich, London*)

Falmouth pilot cutter *Vincent*

This fine shot of the *Vincent*, No 8, was probably taken around 1914, by which time the Falmouth pilots had been amalgamated for many years. The deep, straight stem is to some extent mitigated by a small amount of round at the bottom of the forefoot. Even so, it must have often asked for a backed headsail to help her tack, especially with the cut-down boomless mainsail being employed at this period. She is beached for maintenance and the channels for the main shrouds are in use as prop-points for the beaching legs, a feature already noted on similar craft in the Isles of Scilly. The pulling boat in the righthand foreground is the cutter's punt with her number up, mirroring the parent vessel. *(© National Maritime Museum, Greenwich, UK)*

later when the *Royal Cornwall Gazette* reported her as run down off Black Head (just inside the Lizard) by a Falmouth pilot cutter. Both cutters were soliciting a barque inbound from the East Indies. The outfitters were sailing under the lee of the barque at around 3am one December night. They were trying to strike a deal with the officer of the watch, when Pilot Cutter No 8 swept round the ship's stern heading for the same favoured position for negotiations. Neither cutter was carrying lights, preferring to rely on the moonlight, but they failed to see one another and the pilots rammed the tailors fair and square. The *Sally* filled rapidly and sank after what is described as 'three lurches'. Three of her crew jumped into the punt as she went down, rowed ashore to Coverack and walked home. The fourth made a leap for it and just managed to grab the pilot cutter as his own vessel sank beneath his feet. The only human damage in this incident was a broken finger among the tailors. The pilot cutter lost her bowsprit but the *Sally*, valued at around £700, was a total loss and uninsured to boot.

Falmouth quay punts – construction and rig

The quay punts were locally built by R S Burt, W E Thomas, and various other yards. They carried their chain plates either inboard or carefully faired into the rubbing strake to prevent damage when coming alongside shipping in a seaway. They were yawl-rigged with a small mizzen, often of the 'leg-of-mutton' or Bermudan form, to assist manoeuvring under sail in tight quarters. This rag of canvas also allowed the boats to lie head to wind when waiting for ships off the Lizard, or anchored in one of the bays down west. Rather than step the mizzen off the centre-line to permit a full sweep for the tiller as did some West Country yawls, many quay punts featured an iron tiller with a deep 'crank' to enable it to clear the mizzenmast.

Quay punts had a very short mainmast so that by simply lowering the peak of the mainsail they could work in alongside square-riggers without fouling their gear on the lower yards. This rather odd-looking arrangement did not compromise the luff length of the sail. The only real downside was that the peak halyards ended up pulling from an awkward angle which imposed high compression loads on the gaff, although there is no record of this causing problems.

Quay punts followed the usual Falmouth practice of carrying the forestay on a stump bowsprit of iron rigged by an inner bobstay. This has the benefit of moving the centre of effort of the rig forward and encouraging a lighter helm. In winter, a staysail set from this was the only headsail carried, but in summer a long bowsprit was sent out.

As the twentieth century dawned, yachtsmen began to take an interest in these fast-sailing craft and builders developed the traditional form to suit their needs. Within twenty years, the old straight keel had been refined by the addition of some rocker, as well as considerable drag down to a deep heel. This made them more lively and responsive on the helm.

The boats were always deep draughted and were among the few true working craft to carry outside ballast. The *I C U* (pronounced 'I See You') was a large example built in 1890 by Burt for 'Dinah' Morrison. She was 32ft overall, 6ft 6in draught with 11ft of beam. Her ballast keel was iron and weighed 3 tons 7cwt. When racing, she loaded a further 1½ tons inside. Under her crack helmsman William Morrison she became 'the boat to beat' in local regattas.

The most famous quay punt of them all is now undoubtedly the 28ft *Curlew*, built fifteen years after the *I C U* by Burt for the Jose family and described as having 'walked away from everything in the port'. Owned for many years by Tim and Pauline Carr, she has cruised the world's oceans and been honoured for her pioneer sailing in the Antarctic. Still without an engine, *Curlew* cleaned up at the Falmouth regattas during a rare visit home in the early 1990s, maintaining her original reputation after nearly a century. She can now be seen at the National Maritime Museum Cornwall in Falmouth where her distinguished life began.

Classic casual pilot work – an eyewitness account

The extract below is lifted from *The Yachting Monthly*, 1921, and written by Percy Woodcock, a yachtsman on a winter holiday in Falmouth with his shipmate, Sam. Woodcock had struck a deal with the skipper of a quay punt to take them for a jaunt across to the Helford River. The weather had been atrocious and the article about the trip they finally managed to make is filled with interest. The observations about the vessels sheltering from the tempest recount a very different time to ours, and the relationship between the 'humble boatman' and the gents seems prehistoric, but what shines through is the supreme seamanship of Bill, the boatman, especially in close quarters with a ship big enough to smash his boat to matchwood and not even notice.

> The wind was still strong, especially in the rain squalls which drove up at intervals, but once aboard the *Petrel*, Bill's able 28ft quay punt, we were soon under way. With treble reefed mainsail, double reefed staysail and small jib-headed mizzen, we ran rapidly out through the fleet of anchored boats and past the docks. Anchored on Falmouth Bank was a Norwegian barquentine rolling her rails under as the westerly wind held her broadside to the heavy southerly swell; and as we passed under her lee a most objectionable smell made itself very obvious. Sam and I stared at each other interrogatively.
>
> 'Guano,' said Bill with a grin. 'She's from round the Horn and got her orders for Liverpool yesterday, but she'll have to hang on till the weather moderates. Hullo, sir,' he broke off. 'Here's a lame duck. I heard she passed the Lizard.'
>
> Just entering the harbour in tow of a tug was a big full-rigged ship. Her fore-topmast lay a tangled mass of wreckage over the starboard side, and her main topgallant mast had also gone, only a splintered stump remaining. A string of flags fluttered from the tiny monkey gaff on the still-intact mizzen, her 'number' topped by the blue, white and red of France. Following her in was a small tramp steamer.
>
> 'She'll be the boat that picked her up,' said Bill. 'She'll be a nice little hobble, sure enough. If I had half what that steamboat's captain'll get for his salvage share, I wouldn't turn out at two o'clock in the morning to go seeking for another six months.'
>
> 'There's quite a fleet,' I said as we opened up Falmouth Bay, which was dotted with steamers. With two or three exceptions they were all in ballast, being bound 'around the land' [Land's End] to load coal in South Wales. I counted fourteen of them from a lordly five thousand tonner to a diminutive coaster with her snub nose cocked aloft by the weight of her engines aft. Unable to face the gale with the dreaded north coast of Cornwall as a lee shore they lay at anchor waiting for the weather to moderate.
>
> Passing Pendennis Point we laid a course for the Helford River. Dodging about in the Bay was another quay punt, whose skipper, on seeing us appear, let draw his staysail and started to sail down ahead of us.
>
> 'He doesn't know we're pleasuring,' explained Bill; 'he's afraid we may get below him and do him out of a job.'
>
> 'What sort of a job?' asked Sam.
>
> 'Oh! if a vessel should come along and want a boat, sir; or he might knock a hobble out of one of the steamers – take a telegram ashore for the cap'n or something like that. There you are, sir,' he added, pointing to windward, 'We're going to get it.'

An ominous black cloud was rising over the land, and with the rain came the wind. The *Petrel* lay over till her lee rail disappeared in the swirl that rushed past, and the tops of the waves whipped off by the wind, mingled with the rain in stinging spray, making it almost impossible to see to windward. Bill seized the tricing line and hauled the mainsail tack well up. For several minutes he nursed her along through the flying spume while the squall howled and the rain turned to hail and pelted us pitilessly. In the midst of it all we passed the quay punt that had been ahead of us. She lay hove to under staysail and mizzen, plunging in the short steep seas. We watched her as we swept past to windward and soon she was lost in the smother astern.

A Falmouth quay punt in working trim

Bumboat, tailor's boat, butcher's boat and without doubt occasional unofficial pilot transport, the quay punt was the Jack of all trades of Falmouth harbour. This joyous little image by the artist Ian Heard shows all sorts of detail of these eminently useful craft. Note the iron bumkin on the stemhead to extend the fore-triangle without the need for a vulnerable bowsprit, the long-boomed 'leg-of-mutton' sail set from a mizzenmast stepped on the transom, and the tiller which will certainly have a crank to allow it to clear the spar. Also of note is the very short mainmast which allowed the boat to come alongside a sailing ship without fouling her lower yards. *(Courtesy Ian Heard)*

Presently, the rain grew less violent and the wind gradually eased so that Bill was able to sail her once more on her course. We emerged again into sunshine that seemed to dance joyously on the foam-crested waves, while to seaward the squall receded in a blueish grey pall, out of which, one by one, the fleet of anchored steamers slowly hove into sight. Sam pointed to a steamer nearly a mile to leeward of us, from whose bridge a couple of flags were being hauled up.

'She's signalling, isn't she? I wonder what she wants.'

'Shall we run down and see ?' I suggested.

'Well, sir, if you don't mind, sir,' said Bill doubtfully. 'But what about Helford?'

'Helford can wait,' said Sam. 'It'll be more interesting to "knock a hobble" out of the steamer, so carry on if you feel like it.'

So Bill put up his helm, and we soon approached the three thousand ton, rusty-sided, stump-masted, long-funnelled steamer, flying light in ballast. Her skipper hailed us.

'I want to go ashore for provisions, boatman. How much there and back?'

'How long will you be ashore, sir?'

'Not more than a couple of hours.'

'Shall we say a pound, sir?'

'Very good! Come alongside,' and the skipper disappeared into the deckhouse. Presently a long rope ladder came squirming down as Bill unearthed some huge fenders and fixed them in position along our port side. Then, waiting until the steamer sheered so as to give us a lee – with her high sides and small grip of the water she was steadily 'sailing' at the end of the anchor chain – we dropped the staysail and, sweeping round, ranged up alongside. A line was tossed down. As Bill made it fast the burly figure of the captain straddled the rail and climbed rapidly down the ladder. Under Bill's direction I sheered the *Petrel* in as he reached our level and, leaning out to catch our shrouds, he swung himself aboard. By this time the pilot was half way down and he too soon stepped aboard us. Before the steamer had reached the end of her sheer Bill had cast off the line, run up the staysail, and got us under way again.

We picked up our moorings just as another tremendous squall burst on us and the mainsail was lowered to the accompaniment of a wild slamming. After it was over Bill rowed ashore with pilot and captain, leaving Sam and I to eat our lunch. Scarcely had we finished when Bill again appeared.

'There's water in alongside the quay now, sir,' he said. 'We'll go in for the provisions if you don't mind.'

Making the dinghy fast to the moorings, he climbed aboard and we sailed the *Petrel* in under the lee of the quay, rounded her up and nosed into the middle of half a dozen quay punts. Presently a butcher's assistant appeared trundling two huge baskets of meat and vegetables on a trolley. They were handed down and lashed in a corner of the well. 'The captain'll be along in a minute,' said the butcher's man with a grin. 'He's just gone to have a farewell refresher.'

Ten minutes later the two appeared. With her line cast off the *Petrel* slowly dropped back clear of the ruck, where her mainsail was hoisted and the staysail run up. Once more we headed for the outer harbour. As we reached Pendennis and again opened up the Bay, the pilot asked if we had a spyglass aboard and gazed long at a tiny patch of sail under the land beyond Helford.

'I believe that's my boat,' he said at last, handing back the glasses. 'I don't know what they're hanging about there for. I thought they'd have jigged her down around the land last night.'

I stared at him in mute astonishment. A night that had shaken the bed on which I lay and which kept large steamers in shelter was scarcely the night in which to expect a thirty-ton cutter to 'jig away' round Land's End, but the pilot seemed to take it as a matter of course. I could only thank my stars that life had not called on me to assist at jigs of that sort.

'We shall have to be quick this time,' said Bill as we rounded to in the lee alongside the steamer.

'Hurry up, boys, and let me have a rope,' called Bill to the heads high above as their captain and pilot swarmed up to join them. Presently one was thrown down, and Bill dexterously made fast one of the baskets which was hauled up and disappeared inboard. The second basket followed suit.

'Hurry, boys, hurry!' cried Bill anxiously. The steamer had reached the end of her sheer and was rapidly coming head to wind.

'Stand by the staysail halyards, sir.' Bill stood impatiently, glancing aloft at the rail, then, 'Hoist away, sir, hoist away. We can't wait no longer.'

But we had already waited too long. The steamer, past head to wind, gave us no further shelter, the full force of the wind filled the sail and pressed us against her weather side while waves swept down on us. Then followed a mad minute of veritable nightmare as the waves heaped themselves into irregular, unbalanced pyramids that came aboard on both sides and set the *Petrel* plunging and rolling in a wild abandon.

'Down staysail, sir,' shouted Bill to Sam as he let the mainsail down with a run. At his order I cast off the mizzen sheet and unshipped the boom; then we pushed and scrabbled at the rusty plates, trying to force the *Petrel* back and so drop clear astern without being pounded to pieces. Now I realised the utility of *Petrel*'s enormous rope fenders as she reeled and shuddered against waves which flung themselves at her as though determined on her destruction. What the end would have been I can only guess, had not the pilot seen our plight. He threw us a rope and shouted to Bill, who took a turn with it round a thwart. Then, helped by some of the crew, he commenced to drag us astern while we, half dazed and wholly bewildered by the deluges that fell upon us, continued to fend off as best we could. At last, with a deep breath of thankfulness, I saw the rudder and the scored edge of the mighty propeller slowly pass ahead as we drifted into the comparative peace of open water, miraculously uninjured.

'Well! that was a close call, that was,' said Bill, as we once more headed for home. 'If my missus could have seen us then, she'd have had a fit. Sure enough she would,' he added cheerfully.

A quay punt in trouble

Every boarding sailor's nightmare was for the ship to swing so that her side became a lee shore. This has happened here. The boat is smashing against the ship's steel plating and the men's only hope is somehow to wrestle her around the stern without being torn to pieces by the rudder or the propeller blades.
(Yachting Monthly)

Tricing the mainsail

Already reefed well down, this quay punt is further reducing canvas on a temporary basis by heaving the tack of her loosefooted mainsail up the mast. The process, known as 'tricing' and executed with a simple up-and-down line from the gaff jaws, is not available to boats whose mainsails are laced to the boom. It offers a rapid and large reduction in sail with very little compromise in performance as the whole length of the leech is not affected. A spin-off benefit of tricing is that it hugely improves the helmsman's vision forward. The depth of hold of the quay punt is clearly visible here, with two hands hiding under the weather coaming to keep dry while the helmsman muscles it out through the squall.
(Yachting Monthly)

CHAPTER 4

Plymouth

With its network of tidal rivers and sheltered waterways fronting onto the western English Channel, Plymouth has been a centre for maritime trade and other activities since before historians first set quill to parchment.

It seems probable that Celtic seamen were trading from Plymouth to Brittany by the eighth century BC, while goods found locally imply that merchandise was appearing from the Mediterranean by the early Iron Age. In Roman times, continental sailings thinned out, giving way to a bustling coastal trade. According to Crispin Gill in his book, *Plymouth River*, the first ship actually recorded in the eastern arm of Plymouth's two main waterways carried a cargo of slate from Plympton to Southampton in 1178. Soon after this date, Plympton ceased to have any real importance as a port owing to silting caused, some say, by the growing practice of 'tin streaming' upriver on Dartmoor. The river, from its sea reach called the Cattewater, up to Plympton and beyond, is known as the Plym. As its waters became impassable, more and more vessels chose to carry on their business nearer the sea at Plym Mouth. Plymouth appears in the Pipe Rolls of 1211, and by 1368 a town seal existed under the name of 'Sutton-super-Plym Mouth'. Sutton Harbour is still busy today, incorporating the famous Barbican.

Anyone navigating the waters of Plymouth in the late twentieth century would naturally assume that the western streams of the river Tamar, including the Hamoaze, would be of equal significance to the Cattewater and Sutton Harbour. Historically, however, this has not always been the case. Most of the docks encompassed by the western area are, or have been, part of the great naval dockyard of Devonport, whose importance only began to rise in the nineteenth century.

The military significance of Plymouth city itself probably dates back to the days following King John's loss of Normandy in 1204. After this sorry affair, England's main French territories were in the Bay of Biscay. Partly because of Plymouth's situation, which is well down-Channel without being as remote from London as Falmouth, local seamen made regular voyages to Bordeaux and the neighbouring provinces. This gave them specialised knowledge and rendered them and their growing port of particular interest in subsequent international misunderstandings.

The role of Plymouth and its sons, Drake, Hawkins and the rest, in the catastrophic effort by King Philip of Spain to rid the world of the English Protestant menace in 1588 has passed into legend, and further strategic references are made to the port as the centuries roll on towards modern times.

Despite efforts by the Navy to discourage merchant shipping, the commercial wharves steadily expanded and trade flourished. In 1812, work commenced on the low, 'island' breakwater which still renders the entrance approachable in all weathers, at least to those familiar with the waters, and later in the century, with the arrival of the railways, new services were created at Millbay. An advertisement for Plymouth Docks placed in the *Shipping World Year Book* in 1897 by the Great Western Railway boasts of floating basins, an outer harbour, a graving dock 464ft long, capacious sheds and warehouses, rail connections throughout the land, tugs and tenders for passenger liners, and many other temptations for the shipowner.

The Plymouth pilot cutter *Leader*

Said to be one of the fastest boats of the seeking era, the first-class cutter *Leader*, No 3, was designed in the closing years of the nineteenth century by H Grigg (reported elsewhere as H V Prigg) for the Glinn family, pilots of Turnchapel. Few details of the vessel survive, but the artist has given us what seems a proper image of how she must have been in her heyday. With her mast set well aft, West-Country fashion, and her long topmast and bowsprit, she would have been a powerful performer on a reach with her overlapping 'tow' foresail set. The generic resemblance to a Devon trawler is inescapable. The *Leader* was sold as a houseboat in 1926 and survived at the top of the Cattewater until finally being broken up in the 1980s.
(Crispin Gill)

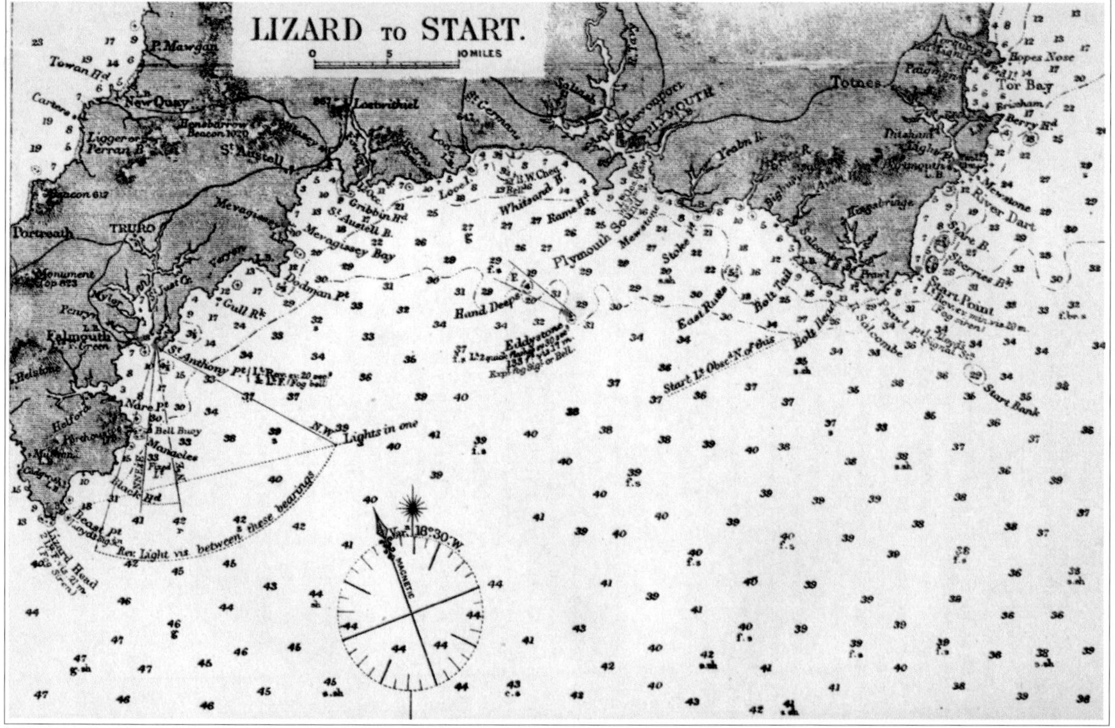

The Lizard to the Start

Despite Trinity House's insistence that one cutter remain on duty in Plymouth Sound, the second half of the nineteenth century saw the flowering of the big, seeking cutters operating from Cawsand in the Sound and Turnchapel within the rivers of Plymouth. Although they might on occasion go further, their main area of operation was between Start Point in the east and the Lizard in the west. Save for the Eddystone, the Manacles and one or two other notable dangers, the area is relatively free of hazard. Navigators will be interested to note how the compass variation has decreased by over 15° since this beautiful chart was published more than a century ago.
(From The Pilot's Handbook of the English Channel, *1898)*

Pilotage at Plymouth

Plymouth was traditionally served by pilots from either Cawsand or Turnchapel, with the classic Cornish village of Cawsand better placed for rapid response to inbound shipping. Standing on sharply rising ground beside its neighbour, Kingsand, its lower buildings were virtually lapped by the tide over a small beach shelving hard down to an open anchorage on the west side of Plymouth Sound. Sailing craft could work readily in and out of this roadstead, and from time immemorial its situation had made it the favoured place from which unofficial pilots could sortie. Cawsand's problem was, and still is, that it is wide open to easterly weather. Gales from the southeast on the lead-up to a warm front are not uncommon, especially in winter months, and it needs little imagination to conjure up the scene with a storm blowing in. Huge seas literally broke over houses while fishing boats and pilot cutters were tossed like wild horses, snatching in rage at their moorings. Anxious seamen strode up and down watching for hours, fearing lest a weak link in their chains should part. Many vessels were lost on the rocky foreshore over the years, yet still the people persevered.

The settlement of Turnchapel tumbles down an equally steep hill, but is sited well up the Cattewater on its south side. It is fully sheltered from all weathers, but to run a pilot service from there involved working a sizeable sailing cutter out of the river, beating into the prevailing westerly winds, then through the deep-water channel with its awkward dog-leg turns off Mount Batten shoals into the more open area behind the offshore breakwater.

Neither site was ideal, and fierce rivalry developed between pilot groups from the two villages where small, related co-operatives ran both their operations like proprietorial family businesses. Sons were regularly apprenticed to their fathers so that the special skills were passed on in the most direct way possible.

Before the mid nineteenth century, time-served pilots from Cawsand boarded from their own fishing craft which were often of the highly capable 'Plymouth hooker' type. These sweet-lined, semi-open fishing boats sailed with a pilot and crewman. When business was slack they would head out for the fishing grounds to top up their income with hook, net and pot, but if the chance offered, the pilot would board a ship and leave his mates to bring home the boat. In 1808 the Pilotage Act specified that a pilot boat should have her sides painted black with the upper strake white and should carry at the masthead a vane or flag of large dimensions consisting of two horizontal stripes, white over red. It seems unlikely that these men in the far west would comply with much that Parliament wanted to lay on them, but they did at least always fly their pilot flags.

In the reign of George III, pilotage was formalised by the Outports Pilotage Act, following which a list of recognised Plymouth pilots under Trinity House of Deptford was published in the 1809 *Instructions to Masters of Ships*. These pilots were licensed for the coast from Looe in the west to Start Point in the east, and these same limits remained throughout the days of sail and oar. Pilotage rates were also now set, with ships of over 14ft draught paying 5s (25p) per foot, and 4s below that limit. Pilots boarding offshore were rewarded accordingly, with a 3-guinea (£3.15) fee for 3 leagues off, 4 guineas for 6 leagues and 6 guineas if the ship were 10 leagues out to sea. By 1827, Trinity House was insisting that all ships entering Plymouth must take a pilot, even those registered there. This notorious piece of bureaucracy created a furious controversy locally, but the regulation stood.

One pilot found in the early Trinity House records is Andrew Glinn, licensed in 1812. The Glinn family became a major influence among the Turnchapel pilots, but Andrew, the forefather of the clan, worked from Cawsand. In the early years of the nineteenth century, the respectable business of smuggling, or 'free trading' as the Cornish preferred to call it, was in decline. The wickedly fast eight-oared pulling boats used for lightning trips to Brittany to load up on brandy and other luxury goods had been outlawed by the Revenue men, and excise regulations were generally being more resolutely enforced.

The employment vacuum left by this tightening up of law enforcement was to some extent filled by increasing pilotage possibilities. For Andrew Glinn, however, smuggling seems to have been his destiny, on one side of the fence or the other. He was only a youth when his uncle, a boatman for the Revenue, was shot by smugglers. He himself was drummed out of the pilot service after a career spanning thirty-five years when he failed to out-run the preventive officers while engaged on a little private business. His descendants settled at Turnchapel and became a thorn in the side of the Cawsand pilots for several generations. The 1891 census mentions four Glinns living in Turnchapel working as pilots, out of a total of twelve in all.

In addition to being taken by the Revenue Men, it seems another hazard to honest pilot work was a readiness to accept a drink when offered at the right price. The *West Briton* of 24 February 1837 reports as follows:

> **Melancholy Accident**
> On Sunday se'nnight, John Spriddle, Thomas Andrews, Francis Spriddle, and Pascoe Spriddle, put to sea, from Cawsand, in the pilot boat *Elizabeth*, and after sailing some distance southward, they fell in with an Indiaman, from the Commander of which they received a mail for delivery at the Plymouth Post-office. They were also given two bottles of spirit, of which it appears, they drank freely on their way back to Plymouth, when, after delivering the letters, they again drank together until they became intoxicated. In this state three of the party determined to return to Cawsand, Pascoe Spriddle, remaining behind. They reached Cawsand in safety, but finding their punt was gone adrift, went in search of it, when, in attempting to put about the craft missed stays, and was driven upon the rocks. Two of the unfortunate men then attempted to swim to shore, contrary to the wishes of the third. The other man, after some time finding himself alone, made a similar attempt, and, with much difficulty, effected his purpose, and reached the beach. From some cause, probably from stupefaction, this man, John Spriddle, instead of giving the alarm, or making inquiry as to the fate of his companions, retired to bed. In the morning, the vessel, valued at about £100, was seen upon the rocks a complete wreck, and the two unfortunate men, Thomas Andrews and Francis Spriddle, were missing. Their bodies were subsequently picked up, and an inquest held before A B Bone, Esq, Coroner; and the jury, after a patient inquiry, returned a verdict of found dead, but would not take upon themselves to say from what cause they came to their end, as from the extraordinary conduct of the man John Spriddle, they could not put faith in his testimony.

By 1850, larger boats were favoured by both communities, although the Glinns of Turnchapel kept a hooker, the *Dorothy of England*, as a reserve for their first-class cutter, the *Leader*. Competition amongst pilot families was now no longer confined to rivalries between Cawsand and Turnchapel. The three main families within Turnchapel itself also often found themselves racing for the same ship. The Glinns in the *Leader* would be pitted against Staddons and Skiltons in the *Drift*. As it had long been among the ruling families of Europe and was soon to come with the gangsters of Chicago, the pilots decided that a marriage to enjoin the blood of the warring families would be mutually beneficial. In 1902, therefore, James Glinn, great-grandson of Andrew Glinn the smuggler, married Ida Staddon, whose father had already united his own family by marrying a Skilton daughter. The two cutters belonging to the Glinns and the Staddon/Skiltons dressed overall in the Cattewater that day, but nobody now remembers whether or not the union was a diplomatic success. As Crispin Gill has remarked, though, 'old habits die hard!'

The number of vessels using Plymouth continued to increase through the 1850s but, from around 1860, owing largely to increasing tonnage of individual ships, the count began to decline. This led to even keener competition. Trinity House had ruled that one cutter must always be on duty in the Sound and, as in most other stations, this job was strictly circulated. The remaining cutters were free to range far and wide to be first with a pilot ready to board incoming ships. Typically, they would be found scouring the Channel as far afield as the Lizard or the Start, flying their white-over-red flag in daylight, or showing a blue flare every fifteen minutes after dark, always hungry for the hurly-burly of an impromptu race with a rival for a ship both fancied.

Retired seamen known as 'lumpers' were stationed at Penlee Point to spot incoming 'mail boats', as steamers were known. Flag signals ensured rapid communication with the pilots, but they were not the only beneficiaries of these old sailors' vigilance. Sailing-ship crews arriving off the Lizard after voyages of extreme length were often at the end of their endurance. Fresh food had not been seen for months; even staples might be in short supply, while sweet water was regularly at a premium.

In response to this need, Plymouth chandlers ran an 'at-sea' replenishment service for ships bound on up-Channel. The pilots were delighted to offer a few comforts on their own account in the way of joints of beef, potatoes, fish or fresh eggs, discreetly exchanged for tea, spirits or other dutiable goods.

With these varied possibilities for profit from a steadily diminishing clientele, pilots had to employ more than sheer speed to get the better of one another. Tony Carne, a local historian descended from a Cawsand pilot, advises that stealth and misinformation were also high on the shopping list. Running on black nights without lights was a well-known ruse, but in the latter days such ancient smuggling skills as muffling the oars of the boarding punt were resorted to in order to 'steal a march' on the others. Late-evening plotting in the bar of the Pilot Boat Inn above the beach grew so heated that on one occasion the chimney caught fire and the pilots had to clamber onto the roof to extinguish it with buckets of water. Sadly, this popular institution was closed down by the authorities after a series of nasty midnight falls from the precipitous steps leading from the 'outside' gentlemen's urinal directly to the rocks below.

The general diminution of available trade as the nineteenth century wound to its conclusion, coupled with a series of tragic accidents and the loss of the Cawsand cutter *Mystery*, led the Turnchapel and Cawsand pilots to amalgamate in the early 1900s. After this time, the remaining cutters no longer engaged in competitive seeking, but worked a roster on three agreed stations. Parliamentary reports on pilotage reveal that at least in terms of remuneration, Plymouth pilots were better off as a result of this change of circumstances. In 1888 with competition in full swing, a select committee was advised that the average net earnings for a typical pilot were £85 per annum. By 1910, a similar statement tells of an amalgamated pilot making £125 from the pooled funds, which was £13 per annum better than neighbouring Falmouth was achieving.

The 1910 report also offers a neat insight into the realities of piloting in those days. The pilots brought before the committee complained that 'boatmen' and other unlicensed characters were boarding ships which rightfully belonged under the compulsory pilotage provisions to the official Trinity House men from the cutters. Often, a boatman would hop onto a ship with the captain's full compliance and go up to the bridge to take the wheel. If an official pilot should board later, the boatman would insist he was merely there to 'make up the numbers' for docking as the ship was short-handed. If no pilot offered his services, the boatman's speculative boarding had paid off. He would scoop the pool and take a pilotage fee.

A few such gambles won were well worth the time lost to a boatman through those that failed. Ships' masters would often be perfectly satisfied with their services, as many of these unlicensed men were well up to the job, and would no doubt settle for less than the official fee. If the ship could give the pilot cutter the slip, everyone but the Trinity House pilots was happy, especially if the ship were registered in Plymouth and did not really need a pilot at all.

This information from the select committee report ties up with anecdotal evidence of these practices from Cawsand, where one of Mr Carne's elderly relatives recalled climbing aboard a ship that had slid past the cutter in the fog. He piloted her into harbour and was amazed to discover the size of his fee. Thereafter, he had more respect for the pilots – if not for their professional skill, at least for their ability to strike a good deal.

Mud pilots in Plymouth

Once inside the harbour, if a ship or barge required to proceed any distance up one of the rivers she was handed over to one of seven 'mud pilots'. This unprepossessing title gave away nothing of the potential earnings from the job. Mud pilots bore no certificates, but were appointed by a local committee comprising the Collector of Custom, the Cattewater Harbourmaster and the Sutton Pool Harbourmaster. Often, these officers were hired from outside the local area, so the candidates knew far more about the waters and the mechanics of the task than did their inquisitors.

Rather than turn down a job because he already

An archaic pilot yawl off the Eddystone Light

This undated lithograph is entitled, 'Lord Harborough's lugger under small sails and a pilot yawl near the Eddystone Light House off Plymouth'. We see two shapely vessels, the closer one presumably a yacht, but no detail of any sort is given. Nothing has been turned up by this volume's researchers concerning pilot yawls like the one shown here, but it seems unlikely that the artist invented the scene from imagination. The yawl was either therefore a common form of pilot boat – perhaps a racy forerunner of the yawl-rigged Plymouth hooker – which had vanished before people started writing down what they were sailing, or she was a one-off. The latter is not unlikely in this area. The only clues we have concern the date. The lighthouse is unambiguously the one modelled 'on the shape of an oak tree' by John Smeaton and built of granite blocks secured by dovetail joints and marble dowels. Construction started in 1756 at Millbay and the light was lit in 1759. The 59ft tower remained in use until 1877 and was rebuilt on Plymouth Hoe as a memorial which still stands. This pins the date to before then, but after 1808 Plymouth pilots were obliged to fly the standard red-over-white pilot flag, while this craft is clearly doing no such thing. The feel of the painting is very eighteenth century, so all in all it seems probable that this pilot yawl is a very early type that was eclipsed in due course by the ubiquitous, cheap and handy Plymouth hooker which preceded the big, charismatic cutters.
(© National Maritime Museum, Greenwich, UK)

had a vessel in charge, it was not unknown for one of these hard-bitten professionals to run a client's ship onto the mud where she would have to wait for him, safe but stuck, until he had shifted a second customer about to float off from a similar 'berth' further downstream. He would then return on the last hour or two of the flood to finish his original task. Two wage packets and occasionally even three could thus be extracted from a single tide by a man clever and able enough to keep all the balls in the air at once.

Piloting for the Admiralty

'It is the duty of the Masters of HM Ships to pilot them into and out of Plymouth Sound'. So say the *Plymouth Port Orders* of 1858. Civilian pilots were never used for warships, 'except in the case of a Master of a Ship declaring himself incompetent to perform the duty, when in the absence of the Queen's Harbour Master a Pilot may be engaged: but every such case is to be reported to Their Lordships, who will consider the propriety of charging the expense of such pilotage against the pay of the Master.'

The orders go on to clarify the important issue of how old-fashioned British class distinction was to be maintained. Trinity House pilots were to be messed in the wardroom, but any other pilots, if fed at all, were to be seated according to the whim of the commanding officer, who was 'to exercise his discretion as to the Table at which the Pilot should take his seat'.

We shall never know whether the Trinity House men of Cawsand were comfortable in the rarefied air of the wardroom to which, by this directive, they were entitled. Perhaps they would have preferred the banter of the lower deck. Regardless of changing dining arrangements, however, the general order has remained in force at naval ports in Britain down to present times, with 'QHM' or his representative piloting men-of-war where necessary, and regular pilots being used only as a last resort.

Success and disaster

Because the Plymouth pilots spent much of their time cruising in the port approaches, they were frequently involved in emergencies and were often the nearest available help in a crisis. By virtue of their proximity to the land, which is always the dangerous part of any voyage, and the inherently hazardous nature of the boarding operation, their own lives were not without self-imposed risks. Incidents involving pilot cutters and their crews were therefore often to the fore in the newspapers of the nineteenth century.

Pilots never knew what extra roles might land upon them in the course of their duty. In 1860, a pilot boarded the 906-ton SS *Havering* of London and was immediately asked to witness the reading of ship's articles to a mutinous crew. On arrival in the Sound, the pilot cutter brought the captain ashore to get a warrant for the crew's arrest; the master's luck was out, however, because when he returned to his ship he found that during his absence she had dragged her anchors and stranded on Batten Reef. Sadly, we are not told what became of the mutineers.

The Cattewater pilots met with tragedy in 1872 when three of them lost their lives on duty. It was 8pm on 13 February, and cutter No 5 *Surprise* was three miles off Penlee Point with the 3,000-ton West India mail steamer *Nile* signalling for a pilot. When cutter and liner were less than a hundred yards apart, the pilots lowered their boat and senior pilot Edward Glinn (50) and his son Edward (24) set out to row the duty pilot, George Phillips, across to the ship. Tragically, the *Nile* misjudged her stopping distance, her bowsprit ripped through the cutter's mainsail and forced her over with her hull against the liner's bows. The boat was crushed between the vessels, and all three pilots were drowned. The last that was heard from them was a cry of 'My God' from the younger Glinn as the boat disappeared.

As if this were not enough, the *Nile*'s stem damaged the cutter's stern and she began making water. It soon became clear that without extra manpower she would sink, so Edmund Driver, the cutter's skipper, shouted for assistance. After some delay caused by the *Nile*'s boats being double-lashed, one was launched and the second officer went aboard with five seamen to man the pumps. The *Surprise* managed to keep afloat and make way until the tug *Volunteer* took her in tow and beached her up the Cattewater. Edward Glinn senior and George Phillips both left widows with large families to mourn their passing.

Many years earlier, the Cawsand pilot Richard Eddey found himself in unusual circumstances in the terrible gale of 23 November 1824. A 110-ton ketch, the *Coromandel*, was bound from Portugal to the Downs with a cargo of cork when she was overwhelmed by heavy seas in a southwest gale off the Eddystone. She actually capsized, and the watch on deck were swept away and drowned. The inverted ship, with her captain and three others miraculously alive, airlocked inside the coalhouse, drifted rapidly inshore and six hours later was swept onto the uncompleted Plymouth breakwater. The ship began to break up as the tide receded, but the determined survivors managed to scramble onto the rubble.

Pilot Eddey was sheltering behind the breakwater and saw what was happening. At great risk to himself, he and his skiff's crew of six brought the befuddled mariners off safely. Eddey received the silver medal of the Royal National Institution for the Preservation of Life from Shipwreck for this rescue.

Tragedy in the latter part of the nineteenth century was not confined to Turnchapel. By 1880, only two cutters were working from Cawsand, including the *Mystery*. On midsummer's day 1881, *Mystery* was on turn for inshore station in the Sound, anchored in light winds and fog. Suddenly, a mail boat, the Direct Demerara liner *Blenheim*, steamed out of the murk, flying a 'G' flag requesting a pilot. Clearly, the cruising cutters had missed her in the fog, so five of the *Mystery*'s crew manned their punt in high spirits and put Pilot Sam Hancock aboard. On their way back to the cutter, they were rolled over by an unexpected wave while crossing Draystone Reef. Two men were drowned on the spot, while a third was struck by a heavy line thrown down from the *Blenheim* and lost to view. The sole survivor was a lad who couldn't swim and so had clung to the upturned boat. After the incident, Trinity House offered him a full pilot's licence, but he preferred to return to the fishing. His morale never really recovered and he ended up selling teas to tourists on the beach. One of those lost was James Eddey, whose wife, Ann, was standing at the window of their home with her three-month-old baby. She witnessed the whole affair and saw her husband drowned, leaving her with seven children.

The folly of attempting to enter Plymouth without either a pilot or a boatman was demonstrated in December 1890, when the 3,550-ton P&O liner *Nepal* was approaching in fog, homeward bound from Calcutta. For one reason or another, Captain Brady did not pick up a pilot and having overshot the western entrance to the anchorage, rashly decided to use the eastern passage. Within moments the mate was shouting, 'Breakers ahead!' and *Nepal* grounded heavily on the Shagstone. Her forefoot was torn away and she pivoted on the rock with her stern swinging toward the land.

Nepal's distress rockets were seen by the duty pilot cutter which went in immediately and took off those passengers due to disembark. Shortly afterwards, the Queen's Harbour Master went out in an Admiralty tug and found 5ft of water in the forward hold. Without delay, the remainder of her passengers, mail and baggage were lightered off by the GWR paddle tenders *Sir Francis Drake* and *Sir Walter Raleigh*. In the morning, the ship's condition had considerably worsened and she became a total loss.

Plymouth can look an innocuous entry to a small-craft sailor on a summer's afternoon, but the *Nepal* incident serves to underline the vital work carried out in all weathers by the pilots. Had their services been taken up, the *Nepal* would certainly never have come to grief. That her entire complement was saved without loss is largely due to their prompt action, selflessly working their cutter alongside in pitching, dangerous seas and hurrying to the rescue.

A Plymouth hooker on the foreshore at Cawsand, *c*1905

Dried out on legs on what looks like a Sunday afternoon, this hooker is enjoying a low-tide rest on the beach at Cawsand with Fort Picklecombe and the entrance to Plymouth via the 'Bridge' passage clearly visible between the masts. Villagers have strolled down to the shore, with two ladies in their chapel best, a brisk little lad collecting what appears to be driftwood, and a smart young fellow in casual pose against the punt. On board are a number of characters, once again mainly dressed to the nines, while under the quarter stands a solitary working seaman, clad in the time-honoured fisherman's smock and sou'wester. Hookers, while not generally purpose-built pilot vessels, were often used as such. They had reasonable all-round performance under sail, were surpassingly handsome craft with their counter sterns, and could stand a press of weather. The high-value 'PH' number and lack of the official white sheer strake of the pilot cutter suggests that this boat's work was primarily fishing, but Cawsand was a pilot port and it is more than likely that, at some stage in her career, she served her turn with the pilots.
(Tony Carne)

The Plymouth pilot cutters

By 1850 or so, large, classic gaff cutters, purpose-built for the pilots, were coming into service in Plymouth. This left the previously favoured hookers or other smaller vessels on the beach, except for occasional back-up duties. The new cutters were crewed by five pilots and two 'strappers', fishermen or apprentices who would bring home the vessel after all the pilots had boarded.

The biggest of the Cawsand boats was said to be the *Alarm*, built in Plymouth in 1859. She was 64ft

Cawsand Beach on a flooding tide

Modern yachtsmen complain frequently about how good anchorages are becoming choked with moorings. A glance at this shot from the early years of the last century confirms that this is no new issue. The number of moored small craft in Cawsand Bay southwards towards Penlee Point is startling. In the foreground, a Plymouth hooker with the classic West-Country yawl rig is just floating off on the flood. The skipper has the haul-out line in hand, but the starboard beaching leg seems still to be in evidence in the shadows beneath the channel for the main shrouds. If, as seems likely, this photograph was taken around 1905, the Cawsand and Turnchapel pilots had already amalgamated. This means that the gaff cutter under short sail in the distance looking suspiciously like a pilot boat is probably the *Alarm*, which stayed in backup service with a paraffin auxiliary engine into the 1920s. *(Francis Frith collection)*

on deck, 14ft beam with almost 10ft draught and was owned by the Parford family. This makes her far and away larger than a first-class Bristol Channel pilot cutter which ran out at 50ft or so, but on a par with the heftier cutters of Falmouth or the Isles of Scilly. Later Turnchapel boats were even greater in size, culminating in the *Allow Me*, at 67ft between perpendiculars – probably around 73ft overall. *Allow Me* was designed by H Grigg, who, according to some records, also drew up the fastest cutter of them all, the *Leader*. The researcher's lot is rarely simple, however, and conflicting evidence has this designer's name as H V Prigg. The same source, John Leather, announces that the largest cutter was the *Verbena* built by Jackman in Brixham which once ran the forty-five or so miles from the Lizard to Rame Head in 4 hours and 10 minutes. An average of over 10kts for any cutter is a remarkable effort.

The boats were strongly built and required the same sort of competitive edge of speed typical of pilot cutters of their period. Few photographs or accurate paintings exist of these craft, but a sheer plan and sail plan of the *Ferret* is reproduced here from Tony Carne's work, bearing an uncanny likeness to a fast Plymouth trawler of the same period. So far as one can tell, the cutter-rigged trawler smack *Erycina* looked very like this vessel, and she was acknowledged to be one of the most notable performers among the working fleets of the English Channel.

Plymouth pilot cutters were tiller steered, carried a short counter, and a straight, slightly raked stem. The rig was long and of a low aspect ratio with the usual astonishing variety of jibs for the skipper to choose from. Lest this plethora of headsails might be considered a fancy of the architect of the sail plan, there are photographs in existence of Bristol Channel boats wearing jibs of all these sizes, including the tiniest. The only anomaly in the rig shown is the fact that the cutter is rigged with running backstays to the lower mast. This was unusual in West Country working craft of this size. Topmast preventer backstays to counteract a jib topsail might be used occasionally, but main runners were rare indeed. Nobody doubts their usefulness, but the nuisance value of handling them deterred most fishermen and pilots. Perhaps they were tolerated in Plymouth because there were generally more men aboard than in some other services.

In the fairest of weather, the Plymouth pilot cutter would come alongside a ship to be boarded, but more normally the task was accomplished by means of a boarding punt. This was launched when needed, then rowed across from the cutter by the strappers after being towed into the ship's lee. If the sea were particularly heavy, the cutter would signal the ship to follow her behind the breakwater, after which the pilot was always able to board. It would be a mistake to assume that seas to leeward of the barrier were totally subdued. The degree of shelter can be more a matter of comparison than of complete respite; in onshore storms, serious breaking waves can still be encountered.

The last of the sailing cutters

The *Mystery*, so called because according to rumour nobody knew how the money had been raised to build her, was driven ashore from her moorings in a blizzard on the night of 9 March 1891. Those boats that could do so clawed off to seek shelter elsewhere, but nine out of the ten craft that remained off Cawsand were sunk. The *Mystery* fetched up on rocks next to the beach where her bottom was smashed clean out of her. Her owner, Pilot John 'Bunker' Hooper, a man who had lost two fingers in an accident, raised fresh funds and the smaller

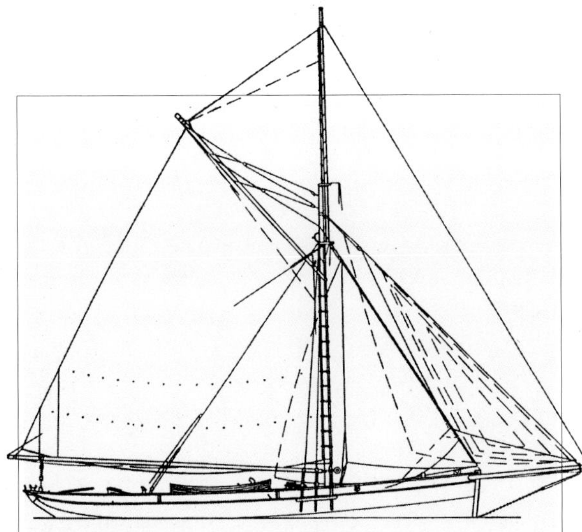

The *Ferrett*

The *Ferret*, a noted flyer in her day, is a fine example of the big, seeking pilot cutters operating from Plymouth before the amalgamation in the early 1900s. The low freeboard and big rig imply a deep-draughted craft with reasonable windward ability for her type and period. The low-aspect-ratio mainsail is typical of a late nineteenth century gaff cutter, whether working or yachting, although the jackyard topsail favoured by yachtsmen is notably and sensibly absent. The 'tow foresail', or reaching staysail, depicted in the painting of *Leader* on page 49 is shown in pecked line, as are the multiplicity of jibs. Five are indicated, including one large overlapping sail for light weather. By far the most useful would be the working sail sketched with a solid line. It sheeted naturally to the single lead on the bulwarks forward of the shrouds. Many of the other sails would pose sheeting issues that would have had makeshift or semi-permanent solutions. It seems unlikely that all of these jibs would actually be taken on board at one time, for reasons of space and simply that unused canvas sails literally rot in the bag if stowed wet. A suitable selection for the season is more likely, with the tiny 'spitfire' serving to hold the cutter's head down when sailing in conditions too extreme to hazard the bowsprit with a more powerful sail. Plenty of photographic evidence for using these diminutive sails at this period is available from the Bristol Channel (see Chapter 10). *(Author's collection)*

but closer-winded *Ferret* was bought from Turnchapel as a replacement. *Ferret* would be the last cutter to operate from Cawsand. After the amalgamation, she was sold to a Norwegian, but she never arrived in Norway, being lost in a winter storm in the North Sea on passage to her new home.

According to the excellent manuscript of Martin Langley and Edwina Small, *The Plymouth Pilots*, to which considerable reference has been made for this work, the remaining cutters worked from the Cattewater until after the Great War. Seeking and competition were done away with, and the cutters now patrolled three stations in turn. The last sailing boat in service was the *Alarm*. Fitted with a paraffin engine, she was used as a standby vessel into the early 1920s.

Another survivor, the *Drift*, boarded pilot John Pascho onto the first German prize brought into Plymouth in World War I. The pilot's grandson, also John Pascho, recalled being taken aboard, but his main memory was that she was infested with more cockroaches than he could ever have imagined possible. *Drift* was sold to France and became a Breton onion boat, while the *Leader*, the third cutter to outlast the war, was sold by the Glinns as a houseboat in 1926. She survived well into the 1980s, still in Hooe Lake at the top of the Cattewater, until she finally submitted to the chainsaw as being beyond economical repair.

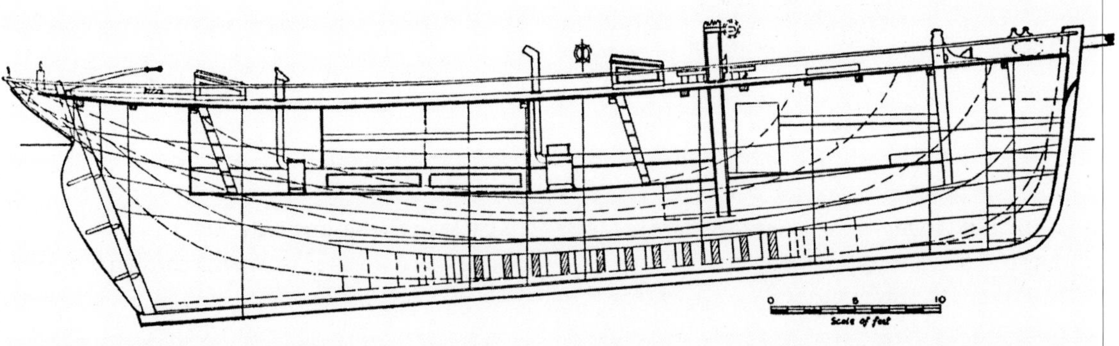

Accommodation aboard a Plymouth cutter

This side-view of the general arrangement of a Plymouth pilot boat is described at source as a 'Cawsand hooker'. The hookers captured photographically at Cawsand are far smaller than this 55-footer, suggesting beyond reasonable doubt that this is a full-scale pilot cutter. Aft is the saloon with direct access to the helm and its own stove just forward of the companionway. Depending on whether the bunks were two-tiered, up to eight pilots could be accommodated here. Further forward is a second companionway leading to the crew quarters and galley with its own range. The fo'c'sle may have contained crew berths or be used for sail and general stowage but, as in the Bristol Channel, little would have been placed forward of the bitts in order to keep the ends of this heavy vessel as light as feasible. The long run aft, dragging down all the way to a very deep heel, would maintain balance under sail, although the straight forefoot with minimal curve from the stem into the keel would make demands of the helmsman when tacking. It would, however, guarantee a quiet ride when hove to on station. This is a boat where performance and comfort have successfully combined to create supreme fitness for purpose. *(Author's collection)*

CHAPTER 5

Isle of Wight Pilots

After passing Plymouth, a ship bound up-Channel had to round the Bolt Head/Start Point complex of land, then keep a good offing from the potential horrors of the Race of Portland before coming up with her next chance of a Channel pilot, usually off the Isle of Wight. The sound separating the island from the mainland is known as the Solent. It shelters the major ports of Southampton and Portsmouth as well as Cowes and various other secondary harbours, so a good number of ships would be bound here and no further. In 1809, Trinity House records show several columns filled with pilots licensed in Portsmouth and Southampton, which ran their own services under sub-commissioners of the Trinity.

Not all ships bound up-Channel would pass south of the Wight. A serious volume of shipping was posted to Cowes for orders, while many more simply worked into the wonderfully sheltered and accessible Solent to anchor and escape bad weather. All this shipping was serviced by a thriving Isle of Wight, or Cowes pilotage service, licensed in its own right under Trinity House sub-commissioners.

Some Cowes pilots were Channel pilots; others, as in most places, were not, but despite this, they had traditionally sailed down-Channel in their powerful cutters seeking ships. The following jolly account from the *Caledonian Mercury* of a boarding in 1825 describes a Cowes pilot cutter taking off passengers southeast of Portland Bill.

> Sept.12.— This afternoon, about four o'clock, the Mary of Cowes, Isle of Wight, pilot boat No 6, Mitchell, master, came alongside, a little to the south-east of Portland Bill, and conveyed my two fellow passengers and myself to Weymouth, in Dorsetshire, where, with heartfelt joy and gratitude, after an absence of exactly two years and nine months, I once more stepped on my beloved native land.

It may seem odd today that a pilot for Cowes would go the hundred miles down to the Start in search of a ship, knowing that most of the vessels bound east past that headland would not need his services, but it should be remembered that some of the pilots on the cutter would be 'Channel' and could go on up to Dungeness or beyond. When a Cowes-bound ship came alongside the cutter, a local pilot could board and the master's troubles were much alleviated, because, although unlicensed for the Channel, the pilot would undoubtedly have an excellent idea of the waters leading up to his home patch. A master might not be obliged to pay for this part of the trip, but many would, on the 'fair dues' basis.

When a Parliamentary committee member asked a Cowes pilot giving evidence in 1888 as to whether a ship could be misled into thinking a cutter off the Start might carry pilots for Dartmouth or Portland, the pilot responded simply, 'But they could not be misled. If a man did not want a Cowes Pilot, he would not take one.'

When a pilot cutter came alongside a ship in those days before radio communication, the loudspeaking trumpet was brought out and the duty pilot called, 'What ship and where bound?' He might add, 'And what is your cargo?' The response removed any possible ambiguity. If the pilot boat carried the man a ship was looking for, he would go aboard, present his licence if he had one, and the deal would be struck. If the cutter did not have the right pilots aboard, she sheered off and continued seeking.

At the beginning of the nineteenth century, a large number of pilot cutters were registered at Cowes, though many operated from Yarmouth, at the island's western extremity, immediately inside the Needles Channel. Many pilots lived here, and from its safe harbour they were ideally placed either to cruise locally to seaward of the Needles, or to press on a little further down-Channel. Evidence for this activity is supplied by a newspaper report from Monday, 26 November 1865. The article refers to the death of Pilot Charles Dyer and his man, William Brimson, of the Cowes pilot cutter *Spider*. Apparently they and another hand had been ashore in Portland 'on business' the previous Saturday night. Returning to their moored vessel in a gale, they were on the point of boarding when a terrible squall capsized their dinghy. The third man scrambled aboard, but the pilot and Brimson were lost. Portland is still known as a dangerous place to get ashore in a gale because, although it is sheltered from westerly seas, the wind can blow very hard in the funnel between the peninsula known as the Isle of Portland and the Nothe of neighbouring Weymouth.

Once a year, all the Cowes-registered pilot boats were obliged to muster in town for the annual review and regatta. First, the pilots were given a supper at the Custom House near the present site of the Cowes Corinthian Yacht Club, with first-, second- and third-class pilots sitting in their own divisions. The following morning, the cutters were inspected before sailing in numerical order to a start line for a race around the buoys. This contest has been said to be the forerunner of the great Cowes yacht races and it was ultimately taken over by the 'Yacht Club', soon to become the Royal Yacht Squadron with its base at the Castle.

In those early days, pilots were sought after by gentlemen to become masters of their yachts. This tradition certainly continued into the 1860s when Samuel Caws, who began piloting in 1858 but was not licensed until 1864, is known to have spent two or three of his thirty-plus years at sea as a yacht skipper. Samuel Caws was a member of a family prolific in producing pilots. The Portsea Census of 1881 lists four of that name from two generations among the crew of the pilot cutter *Hornet of Cowes*.

The Western Approaches to the Solent are beautiful in fine weather, but are extremely

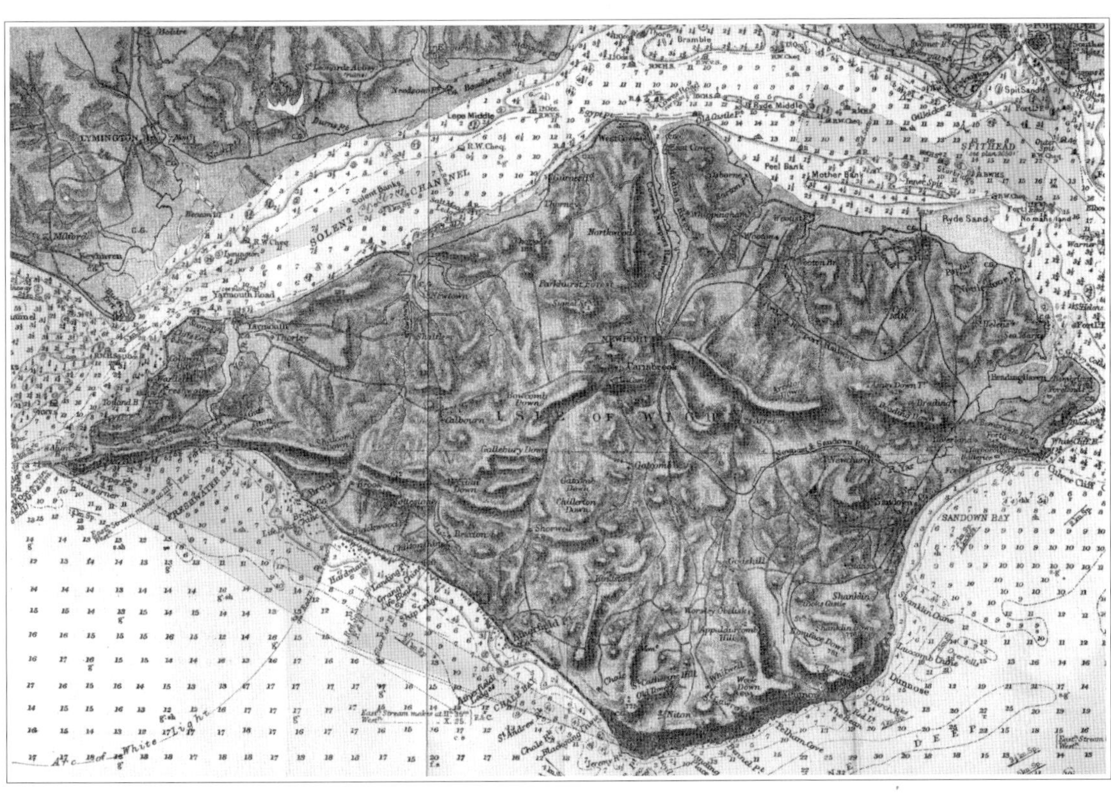

The Isle of Wight

Halfway along the English Channel coast, 'The Island' sits from one to two miles seaward of the mainland, enclosing the sound universally known as the Solent. Tides run swiftly here, but the water is generally sheltered, giving safe access to such ports as Southampton, Portsmouth and Cowes.
(From The Pilot's Handbook of the English Channel, *1898)*

An Indiaman drops her Channel pilot off the Isle of Wight

No direct information is given with this E W Cooke engraving, but it remains the only image that, to the author's knowledge, shows a seeking pilot cutter off the Isle of Wight. The English shoreline lies to starboard of the Indiaman *Thames* so she is outward bound. The profile of the headland is not conclusive, but the concentration of shipping indicates the proximity of some important port. The East Solent with Portsmouth, Cowes and Southampton seems most likely. The brig in the background under topsails looks like a gun brig that could well be cruising out of Portsmouth. The headland is probably therefore Dunnose, and it is more than likely that the ship has just dropped her Channel pilot off the Eastern approaches to the Isle of Wight. The 'C' on the pilot cutter's sail almost certainly indicates 'Cowes', although her blue-over-white flag tells us nothing directly, but it is known that many plots carried their own flags at this time, and that half-coloured bunting at the masthead was often used as a pilot-boat signal. What is certain is that the wind is east or northeast, which would mean a swift passage out towards Ushant and then down the Atlantic. The Wight could well have been the pilot's last chance to disembark before Calcutta.
(© National Maritime Museum, Greenwich, UK)

dangerous in foul. Lives are still lost there every year. The main channel leading into the shelter of the Isle of Wight runs between precipitous cliffs and a shingle bank. It is far too narrow to allow a big square-rigger to beat to windward. Tidal streams run up to 4½ kts and with a southwest gale blowing against a spring ebb seas can be prodigious. There is a quieter North Channel on the mainland side of the Shingles, but this passes perilously close to a lee shore. Running in with a strong wind behind him, the last thing a master would want would be to have to heave to for a pilot with the tide setting him down onto these dangers, so the earlier he could board one, the better he must have liked it.

Edgar March recalls hearing from Captain A G Cole that, in the early years of the nineteenth century, the cutter *Pallas* was moored at Yarmouth under the ownership of Pilot John Long. Long was always ready for work and on Christmas Day 1820 he put to sea before dawn when nobody else cared to chance their arm. A southwest gale had been blowing for days. To beat down to the Needles he must have taken the ebb tide since making ground to windward against the flood is not a proposition, so the sea state off the 'Bridge' shoal at the entrance to the Channel would have been diabolical. At first light, the cutter discerned a ship running up-Channel straight towards the Shingles. The shoal was breaking heavily. The pilot thrashed up to her and called for her to heave to with her head to the southward. This she did, but lost her mainmast in the process. The ship was held off the shoals by the swingeing ebb tide and Long managed to clamber aboard through the wreckage. Getting it cleared away, he set a course for the Needles. The ship proved to be an East Indiaman crowded with passengers and carrying a cargo of great value. The captain had not managed a sight for twelve days and had imagined himself to be off Falmouth.

Long anchored the ship in Cowes Roads and collected a handsome salvage payment for his Christmas present. Pilot Long finally slipped his cable at the age of eighty-two in 1842.

Not all Isle of Wight pilots were without fault in the mid nineteenth century, a proposition borne out graphically by the finish of the first transatlantic yacht race. On 11 December 1866, the 200-ton schooners *Fleetwing*, *Vesta* and *Henrietta* lined up off Sandy Hook, New York, to race to the Isle of Wight across the winter North Atlantic. All three were crewed entirely by professionals. The only owner on board was James Gordon Bennett, Jnr, son of the newspaper tycoon. The race was born out of a drunken argument in a New York club over the relative merits of centreboard and deep-keeled yachts. The two young playboys who owned the shoal-draughted *Vesta* and the powerful, heavy-displacement *Fleetwing* each bet $30,000 that his yacht would beat the other across the Atlantic. Sitting quietly in the corner was Bennett, who asked humbly if the other two might include his $30,000 in the stake if he were to enter his *Henrietta*.

After an appalling crossing during which one yacht lost six of her complement to a single wave which swept the cockpit, all three incredibly arrived off Portland Bill within a tide of one another. The race was by no means over.

Vesta began signalling for a pilot at 1600 on Christmas Day, but her luck had run out. The light was fading, the pilot launched his punt too soon in the heavy sea, and was soon lost to sight in the gathering gloom. *Vesta* gave up waiting and stood on once more, firing off blue rockets, but no other pilot showed up until nearly 2100. On boarding, this burly fellow was immediately asked the inevitable question as to whether or not *Vesta* was the first. The bad news was that *Henrietta*, Bennett's schooner, was already through the Needles.

Vesta was now only about eight miles from the light, but the pilot somehow blundered and set course for St Catherine's Point instead, twelve miles or so to the east. By the time he realised his error the tide was flooding, leaving the huge yacht to beat against it all the way back to the Needles. While *Vesta* was flogging her dead horse in this way, *Fleetwing* foamed past the Needles at midnight going like a train, to anchor in Cowes Roads at 0130 on Boxing Day.

Lest any well-informed reader should find such an error incredible – as did the author when first acquainted with the facts – the shameful truth is confirmed by a letter from the pilot himself. It reads as follows:

> The great yacht race having caused so much excitement in the country, and the character of each yacht being at stake, I beg to say that I boarded the *Vesta* at 8.50 pm, ten miles WSW from the Needles, as I supposed, but owing to the misty weather I mistook the St Catherine light for the Needles light, and thereby caused the *Vesta* to be last in, instead of the second, as I could have been at the Needles at 9.50pm the 25th, instead of 12.40am the 26th.
>
> Signed
> Edward Webb, Pilot Cutter No 35

Somewhat earlier, another pilot who seems to have lived a far from blameless life lost his cutter when she was confiscated by the Revenue men. This was Pilot John Steward of Ryde, whose *Palmerin* was built at Seaton in Devon in 1816. She was 41ft long and 21½ tons, with a beam of 11ft 2in. After being re-measured in November 1824, her rig was altered to 'smack', but twelve years later she was re-registered in Cowes, Isle of Wight and purchased by the pilot. Within twelve months, his nefarious activities had been discovered, the *Palmerin* was seized while smuggling by the Revenue cutter *Stag*, and broken up for her trouble.

Perhaps because of the complexity of Solent waters and the number of ports within them, the jurisdiction of pilotage in this area was often confused and frequently the subject of controversy. At one stage in the nineteenth century there were over fifty Cowes pilots, but owing to a shift in the responsibilities of the sub-commissioners to the Portsmouth office and the running down of the Cowes office, this number was alleged by a marine insurance expert (an 'Average Commissioner') to have fallen to two over the period of twenty years leading up to a Parliamentary Select Committee report in 1888.

The Average Commissioner insisted that the loss of the Swedish barque, *Magellan*, on the Shingles in 1883 was a direct result of this reorganisation.

The vessel was bound towards Cowes for orders. She had tried unsuccessfully to find a pilot off the Lizard, the Start, then Portland, and had no better luck off the Needles themselves. The master decided to enter without a pilot, got into difficulties, and hired a retired pilot who was unlicensed by virtue of his superannuation. The ship was lost because the elderly pilot made a fatal error which, the Average Commissioner averred, was the ultimate fault of Trinity House for running down the Cowes Pilot sub-commissioners. The argument seems plausible until one reads the evidence of the next witness, a Trinity House pilot.

Pilot Samuel Caws, the ex-yacht skipper, was quick to state that there were any number of Isle of Wight pilots, but that they did not happen to be resident in Cowes. He went on to point out that if the master of the *Magellan* had hove to outside the Needles as a number of vessels had done that same night, he would have been served with a pilot the following morning, as were the others (for a fuller analysis of this situation, see below). Caws then grabbed the opportunity to voice a number of complaints about the way the local pilotage was administered. Ships coming down-Channel in charge of a Dungeness or Channel pilot were permitted to penetrate the East Solent all the way to St Helen's Road off Bembridge without taking on a Wight pilot. If no Wight pilot offered, the man from the east could pilot the ship to wherever she was bound in Wight waters. This last provision was modified by the rule that from St Helen's inwards any fees such a pilot charged could only be levied at half the rate a licensed pilot would receive.

The Isle of Wight pilots' area ended at the Owers shoals off Selsey Bill east of Chichester, and a further source of irritation to them was the hovellers who operated from that low, shingly headland. These were beach fishermen equipped with a variety of boats. The men were unlicensed, but performed useful work helping out ships that came foul of the complex and dangerous shoals off the Bill. No doubt they were also ready for salvage opportunities, but it was as unlicensed pilots that they were a thorn in the sides of Caws and his colleagues.

Some of the Selsey fishermen had a form of local licence to pilot ships that found themselves inside the Owers, a highly technical business for which local knowledge would have been as vital in those days as it still is today. Until the recent arrival of the GPS waypoint, many a yacht has run down towards the 'inside passage' and the narrow, tide-swept Looe Channel in misty weather, with the skipper's heart in his mouth as he searches the water ahead for the two tiny channel buoys. The potential maelstrom between this precarious passage and the Outer Owers buoys remains the private domain of the Selsey fishermen.

The Isle of Wight pilots were infuriated by the hard-bitten beach operators skulking around outside the Owers when fishing was poor, and picking up a ship or two that should rightly not have been theirs. Such unlicensed men would often bring their charges in to St Helens or further when their semi-official area of operation was supposed to stop at the west end of the Owers.

And so the confusion and pilot piracy continued. The provisions for 'who went where' dated back to the Outports Act of 1807, and the Isle of Wight pilots had been complaining about them ever since. Caws made the most of his chance to hammer home his grievances before Parliament, but received little in the way of immediate benefit.

Trinity House cutters under sail at the Wight

The main change that had come about between the time of the Caws complaints to Parliament in the 1880s, and the 'good old days' of the cruising cutters owned by the likes of John Long sixty years earlier, was that Trinity House now supplied the pilot vessels and stationed them as they saw fit. By the late 1890s, the practice of seeking was to all effects abolished. By 1907 the policy of fixed cruising stations was well established, but two years later the Isle of Wight pilots faced the same dilemma as their colleagues in the North Channels to London. Their boats were worn out. They could not afford to replace them themselves and nobody else saw fit to make funds available. Trinity House again used the Pilot Fund for the London District to buy out the Isle of Wight cutters, retaining a few and selling the remainder to the highest bidders.

The Trinity House Isle of Wight pilot craft were generally to be found outside the Needles and off the Owers, the better to catch ships bound into the Solent from west or east. Most pilots were content

An early Trinity House ketch

This fascinating image, taken from the boat deck of what is probably a liner, shows a Trinity House 'station' pilot cutter. The unmistakable fort in the Eastern Solent provides a backdrop. The 'wing' collar of the officer suggests strongly that the shot was taken before the First World War, while the pilot boat herself is very much in sailing rather than motoring trim. She is using a main boom, her staysail is set from the forestay to her stemhead and her jib is a serious sail. Interestingly, when compared with later shots of these boats, she appears to have a full-length fidded topmast capable of setting a useful topsail. Given this, she carries more than enough canvas to be a proper sailing boat. She almost certainly had an engine also, but at this early stage, it was treated as an auxiliary, rather than the full-powered version seen so clearly in later photographs. This image has sometimes been said to depict *Titanic* on her fateful voyage and, indeed, the great liner did indeed call at Southampton, but she arrived at midnight and left in daylight. This image shows an inbound vessel with Bembridge and the East Solent in the background.
(© National Maritime Museum, Greenwich, UK)

The Trinity House 'cutter' *Totland*

From around 1907, until the modern era, Trinity House supplied motor-sailing ketches for the Isle of Wight pilots. While illustrations of early Wight pilot cutters are sparse or non-existent, we are fortunate in that Beken, the great yacht photographer, shot some clear pictures of these latter-day station boats. *Totland* is shown here under a main trysail. The boom which is clearly visible must have been largely redundant by this time, as any attempt to square off before the wind would be frustrated by the davits.
(Beken of Cowes)

with this arrangement. The real essence of the dissatisfaction felt by a few was that incomes now tended to even out, and there was no longer the opportunity for an energetic pilot to seek ships farther afield on the gamble of boosting his earnings.

The new system worked well for the ever-increasing proportion of steamers, ploughing their straight furrows to their destination. For most ships, the net result was that a master knew where he would find the pilots, and the pilots could be confident of meeting most of the ships that needed them. It caused problems for the sailing ships, however, of which the loss of the *Magellan* was typical. As the Average Commissioner pointed out, the cutter was not on station on the night the ship arrived. A steamer could have maintained her position while waiting for a pilot by 'leaning on the tide' at slow revolutions. This was harder for a windjammer to achieve and so the master decided to 'go it alone'.

There is some truth in the Average Commissioner's contention that the wreck was directly caused by the reorganisation of the pilots and the keeping of a station (or not, as the case may be), but the truth was that they and their authorities were now aligning themselves more and more to meet the needs of the new steamers. This explains the Trinity House pilot's opinion that the *Magellan* should have waited. As time went by, the number of sailing ships requiring pilots dwindled away so that the 'cutter on station' system caused even fewer problems.

Among the Trinity House sailing 'cutters' were the ketches *Selsey* (No 2) and *Totland* (No 3). These were timber-built motor-sailing craft in the order of 70ft on deck. They carried a modest rig which was nonetheless capable of driving them to windward when required. Unlike the Dungeness cutters, they had no topmast, the mainmast being a 'pole' spar. Otherwise they were classically rigged with all the appurtenances of a classy gaff ketch – bowsprit with tricing bobstay, jib set from a traveller, mizzen boom overhanging the stern, etc. No lines and lamentably few images survive, but so far as one can tell, the hull form of these Wight Trinity House cutters was not unlike that of a sailing trawler. This would give them a notably easy motion on station as well as a useful turn of speed when needed. Their sheer was subtle and not exaggerated and they had elegant elliptical counters. They carried their number painted in white on the knee-high bulwarks in way of the main shrouds. The boarding punt was in davits amidships, and the *Selsey* boasted a whaleback shelter for the helmsman. The man steering the *Totland* had to be content with a canvas dodger lashed to the mizzen shrouds. In due course these craft were added to and perhaps superseded by larger vessels of an even more cut-down rig. These bore the legend 'Pilots' on the hull and their number on the mainsail in the form of 'IW No 1'.

A Trinity House Isle of Wight pilot cutter and the RMS *Berengaria* 1921

This delightful postcard shows a classic Isle of Wight scene of the period. The ketch-rigged pilot cutter is almost certainly the Trinity House boat *Selsey* on, or near, her station by the Nab Tower. Dunnose Head is in the background and the boarding punt is pulling manfully towards the liner at the extreme right as the inbound ship takes off way in the southwest wind. Originally the German liner *Imperator*, built in Hamburg for Ballin and launched 1912, the *Berengaria* was transferred to the British after the First World War as a reparation for the *Lusitania*. She became the new flagship of the Cunard Line until the advent of the two great 'Queens' later in the century. *(Author's collection)*

A steamer bound up-Channel towards Dover and London might well lay a course to the southward of the Owers station. She would certainly be many miles off as she passed the Needles. Her requirements were then met at Dungeness, where the Trinity House cutters waited on station. As in days of old, a sailing ship must have been grateful for any pilot she could catch as she approached the ever-narrowing waters up to the capital, or onwards into the North Sea.

Hovellers of the Solent

The fact that Cowes Roads and the East Solent provided such a heavily used anchorage meant not only that many sailing ships called here for orders, it also made the area an ideal place for dropping off or picking up a Channel pilot. If no pilot cutter were on hand, which would often be the case, trans-shipment could always be achieved by making use

A Trinity House ketch towards the end of sail

The rig on this boat is cut well down and the engine is clearly giving adequate power for most circumstances. Compared with the earlier photograph of the *Totland*, the staysail is now set inboard, rather than from a stemhead forestay, and no bowsprit of any sort is in evidence. She is proceeding powerfully almost dead into the wind, so no sail has been hoisted. The punt is in tow ready for action.
(Beken of Cowes)

of the numerous hovellers that any major anchorage bred in the days of sail. These craft carried anything that could be sold at a profit, from newspapers to spirits and tobacco. The longshoremen who manned them were among the most inventive characters in the working world of those days. There was little a Solent waterman was unable to turn his hand to aboard ship, and if he could not himself fix a problem that had baffled a vessel's company, then it was sure that he 'knew a man who could'. Inveterate 'wheeler-dealers', they could wield a saw and chisel as well as an oar, their mothers were probably bakers of renown, their fathers fishermen and vegetable merchants, and their great-aunts midwives. It might be discreet not to enquire about their sisters.

In Cowes Roads, the local watermen plied the fleets in their skiffs for any trade they could pick up, while in the East Solent and Spithead, wherries came out from Portsmouth with the same ends in view. Portsmouth wherries came in two classes: the so-called 'class II wherry' was a shapely, double-ended rowing boat, clinker-built and smartly painted, generally crewed by two or three. These were used both in harbours and out on the Solent in moderate conditions. In their latter days they ran trippers around the great warships at anchor.

When the going was hard, the alternative 'first-class wherry' was almost never incapacitated by virtue of a gale of wind. These double-ended half-deckers were from 27–30ft long, 9ft or so beam, and up to 4ft draught at the sternpost. They were built largely of oak and were copper-fastened. They set two spritsails with a staysail from a tiny ketch rig and were ballasted with up to 4 tons of movable stones that could be shifted to the weather side while beating in a hard breeze. Wherries had a fine run and entry, and are said to have sailed surprisingly well. Interestingly, it seems they were steered with a yoke and lines instead of the more powerful conventional tiller, so they must have been very well-balanced under sail. Many made expeditions to the Channel Islands, cooking under way on a tiny stove set up in the forward cuddy. The results of these trips would not have pleased Her Majesty's Customs and Excise, had they known about them.

First-class wherries could be seen in any weather taking passengers and pilots on and off from anchored merchantmen. They also traded in fruit, vegetables, and any other fresh produce a ship could be induced to purchase at a premium rate. Even Portsmouth men-of-war often preferred to adopt a wherry to transport their officers rather than lower their own less seaworthy boats when a strong wind against a spring tide whipped the Solent waters into steep, awkward seas. Many a pilot would have been glad to catch the services of one of these craft, and the tough, ever-ready hovellers who manned them.

The Selsey beachmen

There is no harbour at Selsey and the local hovellers' craft included a type of small, deep-draughted, half-decked cutter kept moored off the beach, as well as a clinker-built, beach-launched galley. The galley was a large, powerful pulling boat, long and narrow, and crewed by up to twenty-two oarsmen. The cutters were unusual in that they might be either carvel or clinker-built, but the shape of both was similar. They had sharp bows, a low, wide transom stern and a simple gaff cutter rig with no topmast that was similar to the working rig of the famous Itchen Ferry punts of Southampton.

In 1903, seventeen cutters were recorded at Selsey. They spent most of their year riding to moorings off the beach enjoying only minimal protection from the offlying shoals associated with the Owers. When not engaged in 'hovelling' as their crews called pilot work, their official calling was lobster fishing. Although not fully licensed pilot craft, they carried their name on the transom together with their hailing port and also the name of the principal pilot who might be connected with them.

Selsey cutters were not notably pretty, but they were evolved for the specific requirements of working in the Owers shoals. With their rounded forefoot they must have been handy under sail, while their long boom and bowsprit suggest plenty of dash and elan from their owners.

The cutters' moorings were reached from the shingly shore by using a smaller punt that also served as a seine net boat.

A Selsey galley (above)

Selsey Bill forms the extreme eastern end of the influence of the Solent and the Isle of Wight. Together with the off-lying Owers shoals, it stands in the path of anything approaching from along the shoreline from the direction of Dover. Its beachmen were not slow to take advantage of their geographical situation and, with their unlicensed operations, were a constant thorn in the side of the official Trinity House men in the station cutters. Seen here is a sixteen-oared galley, certainly used for pilotage amongst other even less legal pursuits. Pulling to windward in moderate weather, such a boat could put anything afloat below the horizon until the arrival of reliable engine power. *(© National Maritime Museum, Greenwich, UK)*

The Selsey cutter *White Wings*

Cutters like this one worked the perilous area around the Owers shoals from the beach at Selsey, officially as lobster boats, but unofficially as pilots. *White Wings* is laid up ashore with her rudder dismounted for beaching. She shows a small cutaway in her stern post indicating some degree of auxiliary power, which is no surprise, but she still carries her full sailing rig with its long boom and bobstayed bowsprit. Note also the 'plumb' sternpost, the wide, heavy transom and the rounded forefoot which ensured confident tacking in awkward shoal waters. *(© National Maritime Museum, Greenwich, UK)*

CHAPTER 6

The Last Lap to London – The South Channel

A SHIP BOUND UP-CHANNEL towards London must pass around the eastern end of Kent, either west of – 'inside' – or east of – 'outside' – the Goodwin Sands. Inside the sands lies the ancient anchorage known as the Downs and the town of Deal which, in the days of sail, had a large complement of luggers and pilots, licensed and unlicensed. After the Downs comes the turn to port off the North Foreland, then the passage west through the sand banks of the Thames Estuary to the great river itself. Here, at Gravesend, the river or 'mud' pilot is shipped and any pilot who has brought the ship thus far is taken off.

As far as the South Foreland immediately east of Dover, the Channel is comparatively free of dangers, always excepting the long, narrow shoals of the Varne and the Colbart lying far offshore. Thereafter the horrors come thick and fast. In an ideal world, the topography would have been arranged so that there were no hazards to safe navigation until a ship had passed north of Deal, because the waters in the lee of Kent are generally calm except in easterly weather. A ship could then have turned the corner and taken a pilot from the Deal beach in comfort and safety. Because of the Goodwin Sands and various other shoals, however, this sea area is by no means as simple as it might appear on a landsman's road map. The alternative was to board a pilot somewhere down-Channel.

Although Channel pilots were available at

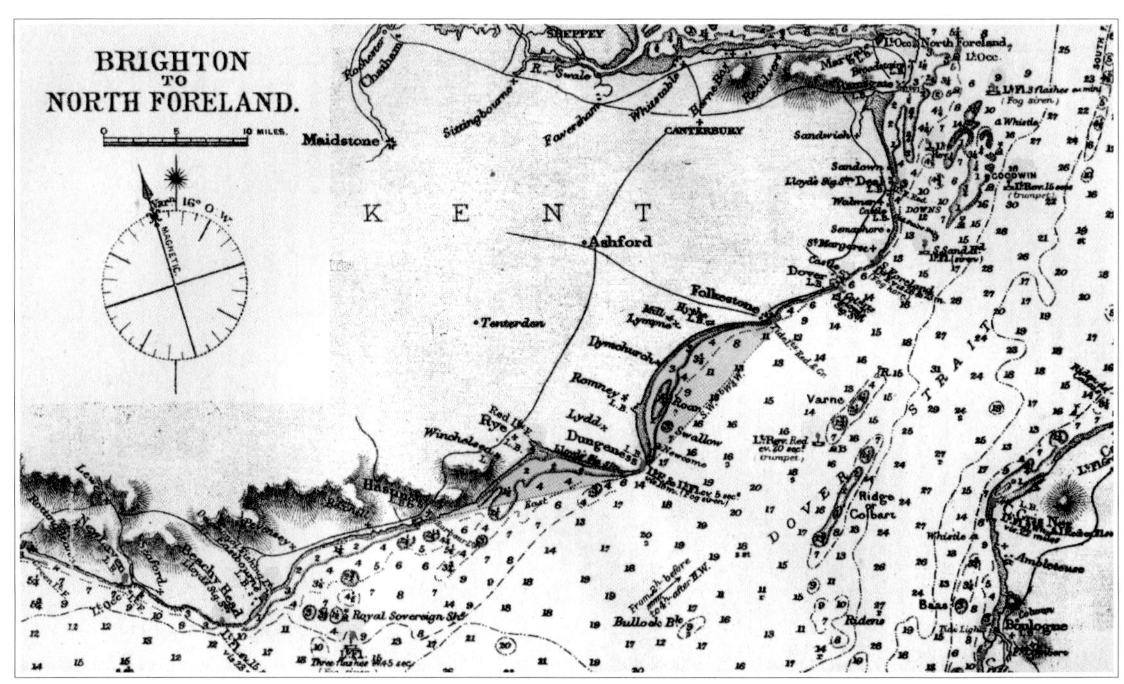

Brighton to the North Foreland

This chart from the late sailing era shows the salient points for London's 'South Channel': Dungeness, offering a small amount of shelter from westerly weather; Dover within its harbour walls; the Downs anchorage lying north of the South Foreland between the Goodwin Sands and the eastern shore of Kent and, finally, on the northeast corner of Kent, the North Foreland, beyond which lies the Thames estuary itself. *(From* The Pilot's Handbook of the English Channel, *1898)*

numerous locations from far-cruising cutters as far west as Scilly and beyond, they were often either missed by sailing ships or ignored by steamers. The hope was to save money by shipping a pilot only at the point where pilotage became either a pressing necessity or compulsory. The last viable open-water rendezvous was the low promontory of Dungeness twenty miles west of Dover.

Now rendered unmissable from seaward by a huge power station which appears to rise out of the sea itself, Dungeness in the days of sail was a low, featureless headland identifiable from a distance only by a lighthouse standing starkly beside the stump of its predecessor. As a final 'pre-Downs' pilot station, the advantages of this dismal, shingly promontory as against Dover itself were many: its tongue of land protrudes so far into the Channel that a ship can pass close to it without a major detour; the water is deep on its seaward face comparatively close inshore; from early times it has had a lighthouse; it is close enough to Dover or Folkestone to be readily serviced with fresh pilots and cutters, and if a cutter were not in the offing, a ship might well signal for and secure a pilot who would board directly from the shore by means of a small boat. It is for these reasons that 'from Dungeness inwards' became the official boarding point for London after the Pilots Act of 1807 made pilotage compulsory. From then on, unless exempt from the regulations, a ship's master must either take a licensed pilot or come up with a good reason for not having done so. Certain classes of vessel were not required to use a pilot by virtue of the master or mate having been examined for a port which he frequently visited. This exemption still exists for Channel ferries and others. At differing periods in history, any or all of the following might also be exempt:

> Ships in the UK coasting trade, ships of not more than 60 tons burden, ships trading to Boulogne or to any place in Europe north of Boulogne, ships from Guernsey, Jersey, Alderney, Sark or Man, who are wholly laden with stone, being produce of those islands, ships navigating within the limits of the port to which they belong, ships passing through the limits of pilotage between two places situated

Dover

The Dover foreshore looking westwards beyond Shakespeare Cliff towards Folkestone; and beyond there lies Dungeness. Adjacent to the shore is the pilots' lookout, while a punt is being being launched and various longshoremen await their chance for profit out on the water. *(Dover Museum)*

> outside such limits, not being bound to any place within the limits, and not anchoring therein.

Penalties for infringing the compulsory pilotage rule were stiff and in the nineteenth century might typically involve a double fee plus a further payment. Fines of up to £20 were levied for failure to fly a 'pilot required' flag when entering compulsory pilotage waters. Originally, the signal was a union flag at the fore-masthead or in the fore-rigging, but as years went by this developed a white border and became known as the 'pilot jack'. By night, a blue flare would be shown. After 1897, the new International Code of Signals prevailed and the blue and yellow vertically striped 'G' flag took over. Once the pilot had boarded, this was replaced by the red and white striped 'pilot on board' flag, below which, on this station in particular, every pilot flew his personal recognition signal. This allowed the authorities to see who was doing the job as well as keeping them advised as to manning requirements out on the cutter.

The administration and licensing of pilots on the English side of the Dover Straits and on up to Gravesend really began on 26 February 1526 when Sir Edward Guldeford, Lord Warden of the Cinque Ports and president of the then brand-new pilots' Court of Lodemanage, enrolled fourteen Dover 'lodesmen', together with one from Deal and another from Margate.

Under their own Trinity House set-up at Dover, the Court continued to manage the licensed pilots through good times and bad in succeeding years, and there were certainly plenty of bad ones. Being empowered to fine and imprison mariners without the accused having any right to see the regulations, or to defend himself for having broken them, probably led to arrogance on the part of the officials. By 1616 there was more than a hint that officers of the Court were personally pocketing the fines they levied. Bickering and backbiting continued to be a way of life for two centuries until finally the Duke of Wellington took over as Lord Warden.

The Duke did things with a touch more class than his predecessors. Not only did he take a genuinely keen interest in bringing equity and fairness to the proper business of the Court of Lodemanage, he also restored full ceremony to its meetings. Wellington is said to have processed to St James's Church dressed in a blue coat with a red collar, followed by the pilots, immaculate in brass-buttoned jackets set off by primrose waistcoats. Meetings were held behind the altar.

The last Court of Lodemanage was held on 21 October 1851. Shortly afterwards the Duke passed away, the local Trinity was dissolved, and the Trinity House of London took over all responsibility for Dover pilotage.

Between the 1807 Act, which first brought the London Trinity House onto the scene, and the Act of Parliament of 1853 which secured their final ascendancy over the Cinque Ports, pilots could be licensed by either body. The pilots qualified to bring ships up to the Thames were traditionally divided into two equal groups between Deal and Dover, with a further backup group in Ramsgate to take care of ships that, perhaps because of fog, had failed to find a pilot at Dungeness and had no better luck even in the Downs, where Deal remained a pilot station. In the nineteenth century eight pilots were often stationed at Ramsgate, and a further, absolute 'backstop' group could be found around the North Foreland in the Margate area. This was known in the service as 'on the Island' because it was part of the ancient Isle of Thanet. By the early years of the twentieth century, the islanders had disappeared and there were rarely more than three men to be found at Ramsgate.

One might imagine that a ship approaching the corner without a Dungeness pilot would be compromised, but this part of the passage often presented no particular problem because many masters would have already taken a Channel pilot much lower down to the west. While these men were generally unlicensed, particularly for Dover Strait and beyond, most had a practical knowledge of the waters equal to that of many London pilots.

The scene at Dungeness in the heyday of sailing pilotage was a busy one. In addition to the London pilots, 'Dundee-rigged' ketches, schooners and cutters cruised there in all weathers from France, Holland and Belgium, seeking ships bound for Calais, Dunkirk and Flushing. Dungeness was also the official easterly limit of seeking for Le Havre pilot boats, so these handsomely proportioned

Deal beach, September 1840

A sketch by Henry Moses depicts two luggers and a galley punt standing ready for launching. In the offing is the Downs anchorage where a lugger is carrying on her business with the anchored ships. *(Deal Museum)*

Deal beach – boatmen gather round a capstan

In this view of Deal beach by Henry Moses, a fast, slippery galley punt waits to be launched. Used for smuggling as much as assisting ships and pilot work, they were dragged up the beach like the bigger luggers by capstan. Once the haul-in warp was secure, their crews and any beach loafers they could rope in would tramp round while rollers were thrown under the keels. *(Deal Museum)*

Launching a lugger off Deal beach in a gale

Many of the boatmen of Deal were unlicensed pilots. They were among the most accomplished small-boat seamen the world has seen, working their heavy boats off a stony beach in all weathers short of an onshore storm. Here, in a sketch by Henry Moses, the wind is southerly and blowing great guns, but they are getting off to serve the anchored shipping which seems in urgent need of help. In this case they are more likely to be carrying out extra ground tackle than serving their pilots. *(Deal Museum)*

cutters were often in evidence with their elegant sails marked with their number and the anchor of the pilot service. Despite all this activity, a London-bound ship still slipped through quite frequently. She would then be obliged to board a pilot in the Downs if she could find one, and there was nothing the authorities could do about the fact that she had run twenty-five miles through compulsory pilotage waters without a pilot. Indeed, in heavy weather it often proved impossible to board a pilot in the big seas running off the Ness. A supremely seaworthy Deal lugger manned by some of the finest boat handlers in the Channel might manage a transfer if she were at hand. If not, the ship had no choice but to seek the shelter of the Downs and hope for a pilot there.

The fact that pilots were officially stationed at Deal speaks for itself, but it is interesting to note that as late as 1901, ships were complaining that they had tried to board a pilot at Dungeness but that none had offered. The Elder Brethren of Trinity House were, by this time, always on the lookout for ships that were using 'no pilot offered' as an excuse for having actually evaded the cutter to save money. On 22 September 1902 the secretary to the Elder Brethren wrote to the sub-commissioners at Dover that the master of the steamer *Mazagar* was to be penalised for just this offence on the 14th of the same month. Speedy justice indeed!

After 1808, the Cinque Ports authorities were obliged to have eighteen pilots at sea at all times. So far as it is possible to tell, pilots in those days seem to have been responsible for getting themselves aboard ships. Some may have been rowed out from the beach, but for most it proved best to arrange some sort of cruising cutter. The Deal lugger was a classic example, where a number of licensed men shared the expense of cruising down-Channel seeking ships. Not all Deal boats carried licensed pilots, however, and in the eighteenth century and earlier, a ship's master was often more than pleased to accept a man without the official papers so long as he knew the waters comprehensively.

More formal cutters were certainly operated

Dover pilot boat

This 1831 lithograph by John Atkinson depicts a galley punt being used for pilotage in the Dover Strait. In strong westerly weather, the crew are scrambling their boat to seaward with a half-hoisted fore lug. The rag of canvas will blow them out beyond the breakers, giving steerage to keep the boat head up so as not to be upset by the awkward sea regularly encountered off Dover. It will be fully hoisted as soon as the extreme seas die down. *(© National Maritime Museum, Greenwich, UK)*

from Dover, with Dungeness as the most likely cruising area. No significant details survive of these, but they were undoubtedly the forerunners of the Trinity House cutters of the second half of the nineteenth century.

As soon as Trinity House established their rule, they moved ten pilots from Deal to Dover. This was highly criticised for the sensible reason that boarding at Dungeness was so often not accomplished and there was a need for more men at Deal. The Elder Brethren, however, like many official bodies of their time, seem not to have been admirers of the Deal boatmen and hastened to do what they could to reduce their power.

One such boatman-pilot was William Alexander Marsh who was born in Deal early in the nineteenth century. In due course he became a sailor and married Mary, a straw-bonnet maker. After being wrecked three times during his apprenticeship and losing a brother, drowned, Marsh was made a Cinque Port pilot. He lived with his wife at number 89 Beach Street, Deal. By 1861, however, a census

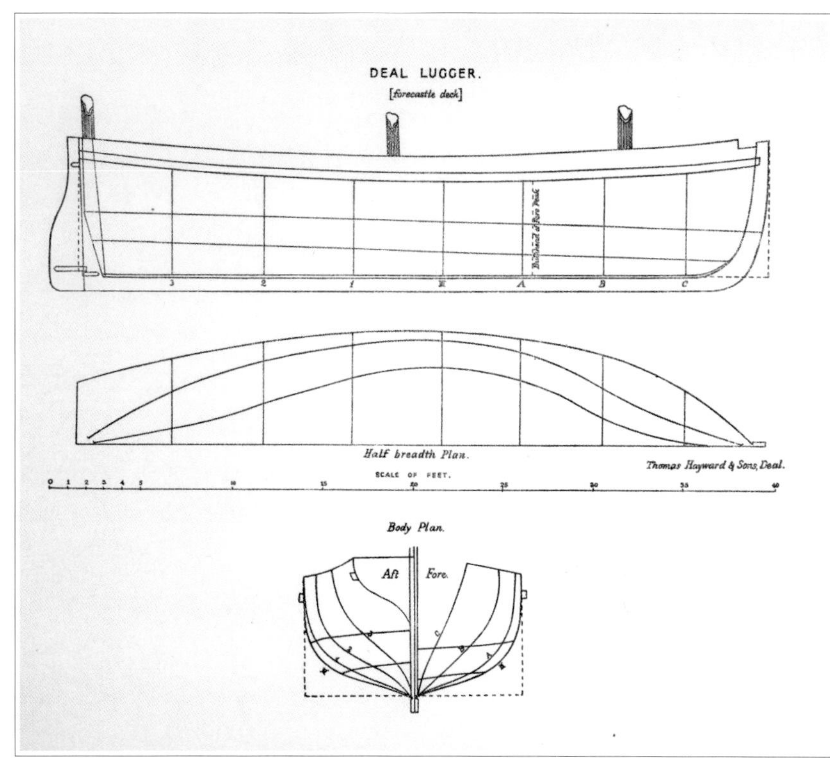

Lines of a Deal lugger, 1848

It is immediately obvious from inspecting these lines that a Deal lugger was a heavy-duty sea boat. Decked over in the forepart, she could stand a great press of weather in the hands of her highly skilled crews. Launching such a massive vessel from a stony beach on what was sometimes a lee shore was an everyday job that required phenomenal teamwork. *(Author's collection)*

Deal pilots' list

A remarkably beautiful plaque indicating the various Deal pilots and their colours. This one is noteworthy because of the name, 'Willm Stanton'. Stanton was born in 1803 and on the strength of his father's excellent smuggling income was sent to a good private school. After a period in deep-sea ships, he bought a share in 'a set of boats', which included a lugger. He was not, however, a fully licensed pilot because, for a Deal boatman without money or noble influence, securing a Trinity House or Cinque Ports licence was a major challenge.

Finally, after Stanton and others lobbied Parliament, a select committee was appointed and the Duke of Wellington, who was Lord Warden of the Cinque Ports, declared the situation intolerable. After being turned down twice, Stanton asked for an audience with His Grace. The Iron Duke gave him dinner at Dover Castle and in 1834 Stanton finally gained a Cinque Ports pilot's licence. He retired in 1867 with a pension of £50 per annum, minus £6 tax. *(Deal Museum)* lists him as being resident in Dover. It seems likely that the Marshes moved as a result of the unpopular Trinity House policy of keeping extra pilots at Dover. Evidence of the children's birth dates indicates that the family moved in about 1859.

Marsh was drowned in September 1879 when the cutter *Edinburgh* was run down by a mail steamer at night off Dungeness. The catastrophe left fifteen dead and sixty-five fatherless children. A collection in town raised £772 for them, a large sum in those days, though none too big when divided among so many. For the remainder of her life, Marsh's widow received a pension of £2 10s per quarter. The pilots themselves set up a relief fund for the orphans, who were paid 18s annually until their sixteenth birthdays.

Having arranged the imbalance in manpower to the detriment of Deal, the Elder Brethren now decided to assist matters by supplying cutters for the Dungeness pilots, paid for by a levy on their earnings. This must surely have been a help, though how popular the arrangement was is hard to say. Certainly, not all pilots complied without a struggle. As late as 1902, Pilot Thomas Blaxland was dismissed for falsifying his earnings, presumably with a view to paying less than his share to the Trinity.

Unlicensed pilots were totally illegal within the London pilotage area by the time Trinity House took over, yet they continued to operate. Penalties were severe, with fines of £50 being not unusual. A curt letter from the Trinity to Dover in April 1901 complains of four cutters at Dungeness offering unlicensed pilots to shipping. The very next month, the Brethren are reprimanding Pilot Jago for neglecting to board a vessel that asked, and for permitting an unqualified pilot to take her. He is further cautioned for undermining discipline on the cutter by attempting to intimidate the mate and for subsequently being abusive to the clerk to the sub-commissioners, one A West, Esq. Pilot Jago was given a week's suspension and required to apologise to Mr West. One suspects he got off lightly.

Not all pilots boarded their charges from cutters. From time to time, a request was made to send a pilot to a foreign port to bring a ship in. This would usually happen when, for some reason, the vessel would not wish to risk any delay in waiting for a pilot. In September 1901, the secretary was ordered to supply a 'competent pilot' to bring the Royal Yacht, *Victoria and Albert*, from Flushing. Earlier in the same year, the German Kaiser's men had also contacted the secretary with a request to provide a pilot for His Majesty's Ship, *Princess Wilhelm*, from Nieuwe Diep in Holland to the Thames.

The pilot vessel *Maisie Graham*

Maisie Graham, known as *Kindly Light* during her time as a pilot schooner in the Dover Strait, was a purpose-built German pilot vessel constructed in 1879. Operating as a freelance pilot schooner from 1879, her performance was so disappointing that she failed to make a living and was sold to Scarborough Sea Scouts who successfully sailed her for 14,000 safe and stately miles. *(Scarborough Maritime Heritage Centre)*

The Trinity House cutters at Dungeness

The Trinity House pilot cutters of the Dungeness station were large wooden ketches with berthing arrangements for up to twelve pilots. Few details of their construction are now available, other than that they were heavily built working craft of the smack genus. The 69-ton *Vigilant*, the last sailing vessel to work for the pilots, was built as a cutter at Wivenhoe in 1879 and later converted to ketch rig. The ill-fated *Edinburgh* was also built at Wivenhoe at a cost of £1,425. She came into commission in 1869 and appears to have replaced the *Queen*. In 1877, the pilots acquired an additional ketch, the *Granville*.

These ketches were rigged with a main topmast and, unusually for a working pilot vessel, running backstays on the lower mast. They had high bulwarks, a straight, trawler-type stem, and a square counter stern. Their number was painted on the bulwarks forward and was also stitched into the mainsail, together with the word 'London'.

Edgar J March has remarked that their sail plans were enormous and, on the strength of original sail-makers' bills, this does seem to have been the case. Surviving photographs of the boats in the ketch-rig mode show a more modest set-up.

Another 'cutter' in the Dover Straits pilotage business was the *Kindly Light*, a schooner built at Bremen for the Weser Pilot service in 1879. She is said to have operated on a 'freelance' basis, but sadly she was so slow she could not get out of her own way and was a failure. Sold to Scarborough Sea Scouts, she was renamed *Maisie Graham* and successfully logged fourteen thousand steady miles in their ownership.

The Dungeness cutters were serviced and operated from Dover and there were always three available at any one time. In 1871, the western station was five miles west of the Ness, the middle was between Romney and Folkestone, while the eastern cutter was kept in reserve waiting for the western boat to heave in sight bound home to pick up more pilots.

Pilots felt that awaiting a ship while standing by on the cutter was the worst part of their life and that once on board a ship, when their actual work began, their difficulties were largely over. However, as in most pilotage areas, transferring to a ship from the Dungeness cutters was also fraught with peril. The usual method was to be rowed across in a small boat and clamber up a pilot-ladder. 'Boating', as it was called, carried with it the ever-present danger of capsize, either close under the cutter, or when coming alongside a much larger vessel. A specific hazard was that of being forced under the lee quarter of a hove-to ship as she made leeway, with the punt coming up on the weather side as matchwood.

In most such incidents the crew managed to scramble up ropes lowered from the deck, but when the cutter herself was run down, loss of life almost inevitably followed. One such incident occurred on 24 May 1862, as *The Deal & Walmer Telegram* reported:

> The *Princess* (No 3) Pilot Cutter left the Downs for her station at 7.30 on Wednesday evening last with a crew of 8 persons, consisting of the master, mate, cook, steward, four seamen and 14 Deal Pilots. Shortly after midnight, a strong wind with rain prevailed, and as they were in the act of reefing the sails, or had done so, they saw a ship approaching them. The cutter burnt the usual flare-ups, and the mast-head light was also clearly visible. The ship, however, failed to notice these signals, when the order was given to shift the cutter's helm and get her before the wind; but before this order could be carried out into execution, it became evident to those on deck that the ship must strike them. The master then gave the alarm to the pilots below, who had all turned in, and implored them to prepare for the catastrophe which afterwards befell them; but before anyone could reach the deck, the ship struck the cutter violently on the port bow, hooking some part of her on the fluke of the ship's bower anchor, which dragged the cutter through the water with velocity, carrying away masts, bow-sprit, in fact everything above deck. At the moment of the collision tremendous efforts were made by the pilots to spring on board the ship. Many succeeded in gaining the deck of the ship. Mr JOHN PEMBROKE had succeeded in laying hold of some part of the ship, but before he could haul himself up a heavy sea struck the cutter and jammed him between that and the side of the ship, by which he was, no doubt, instantly killed. Mr PEMBROKE was much esteemed in the town generally, where he had been known since his birth, his father having formerly held the position of Storekeeper at Her Majesty's Naval Yard at Deal. We are informed that the mate is also lost, and we believe belonging to Dover. The ship proved to be the *Stirlingshire*, from Trinidad, West Indies, she was afterwards took charge of by one of the pilots, Mr JOHN POTTS.

Worse was to come. The *Queen* (No 4) piled up on Dymchurch Wall, four miles from Hythe on 30 November 1867. Her crew claimed that the weather was thick and the boat had missed stays, but the enquiry found a 'want of judgement in hugging the shore too closely'. The truth is probably a mixture of both conclusions, with the boat creeping inshore to cheat a foul tide, then running out of water at the end of a tack faster than anticipated. The loss to the commissioners was estimated at £2,000.

In February 1875, the *Louisa* was sunk by the ss *Humbolt* of Stettin which claimed not to have seen her. Three men were lost and those saved were lucky to be able to scramble from the sinking cutter's rigging to safety aboard the ship. And then, in 1879, came the *Edinburgh*, lost with ten pilots and five crewmen, all drowned.

The powerful luggers of Deal were by no means averse to seeking ships for their Channel pilots as far west as the Isle of Wight and it was inevitable that with them, too, losses resulted from time to time. The 18-ton pilot lugger *Pride of the Sea* was wrecked there off Shanklin on 30 October 1887. The previous night the wind had blown at hurricane force and had veered sharply into the northwest. Nothing is known about how the stranding came to pass, because the lugger went down with all hands. John Moss (53), William Moss (48), Charles Moss (36), Charles Selth (51) and Henry Kircaldie (34) were all lost. The *Pride of the Sea* had left home twenty days earlier and it is a commentary on the rapidly diminishing returns of such enterprises that she had picked up but one solitary ship in all that time. She had sailed far down-Channel and boarded one of her pilots, Thomas Adams, off St Alban's Head thirty miles west of the island. Adams piloted this ship to Dunkirk before returning home to his family, unaware that the lugger had gone and that all his shipmates were drowned. Back in Deal it was assumed that he had still been among them, and he appeared to his family 'as one from the dead.'

A number of newspaper accounts survive of this disaster. The most sympathetic is from *The Ventnor Gazette and Isle of Wight Mercury*:

> Shortly after six o'clock, as daylight crept over the scene, a glance southwards showed a wreck of some kind beating in over the rocks of the Yellow Ledge, the most prominent point between this place and Luccombe. The vessel proved to be a Deal lugger or pilot boat, and bore the name painted on the stern *Pride of the Sea*, Deal, John Moss. She was on her beam ends with masts and other spars snapped off short, and the rocks over which she was driving were crushing in her under side. No sign of the crew was visible, and an empty punt too plainly indicated that they must have perished. As soon as the tide permitted the vessel was boarded, when numerous articles of wearing apparel in bags, in bundles, and loose, were found, showing that her crew had left in haste. These Deal luggers are well known all round this coast, also their crews, which usually consist of six men, who frequently put in here for provisions. They are consequently familiar to the watermen and others, and when at about eleven o'clock the body of a middle-aged man, fully

The Dover cutter

In this painting by Pat Donovan the ketch-rigged Dover pilot cutter *Vigilant*, heads up to board a barque. The ship is taking off way prior to heaving to. The fore royal halyards have been let go, the outer jib has been hauled down and she will shortly round up to back her main yards which are already braced round. *Vigilant* was the last sailing pilot vessel out of Dover. *(Pat Donovan, RSMA)*

MONTROSE

> attired in sailor's costume from sea boots to oilskins, was discovered on the shore between Shanklin and Sandown, it was quickly recognised as that of the captain of the wrecked vessel. Hundreds of persons visited the wreck when the tide receded in the afternoon. She was then high and dry on the rocks immediately under the lofty cliffs just inside the point. Wreckage strewed the shore around, and it was a pathetic sight to look upon the different articles of dress – sailors' stockings, shirts, jackets, woollen caps, shoes, etc – whose owners were in all probability lying at the bottom of the sea near by.

Life on the Dungeness cutters

> It having come to my notice that the decks of the cutters are frequently left during the night, with only one man instead of two, and that man frequently asleep, and thereby risking the lives of all aboard. This is such a disgrace to all concerned, that I shall feel obliged to any pilot reporting to me so serious a breach of discipline.
>
> I therefore give notice that the parties so complained of will be immediately dismissed the pilot service.
>
> Signed,
> John Cow, Superintendent Pilot Officer,
> Dover, 11 July 1878

At that time, Mr Cow administered the affairs of four ketches on the Dungeness station. Each carried a master, mate and four or five hands, paid on a monthly basis with a share in the pilotage money also. The order from him about sleeping on watch sets the scene on the tight regime demanded by 'shore control' over the men at sea. Things were not always operated as the authorities might have wished, however, and the pilots and their crews kept the human element afloat until the Dungeness service was finally discontinued after World War II.

The scene in the approaches to the Downs in the days of sail must have been busy in the extreme. Not only were there large numbers of ships on passage to and from London with the Dover pilots out looking for them, there were also numerous pilot boats from the continent seeking ships on passage towards their own patch of salt water. Cutters from Holland were particularly common. Le Havre boats came this far, and so did many others.

In 1877, the Elder Brethren became so concerned about their own vessels not being recognised after dark that they issued an order for the London pilot cutters to show not only the all-round white light and a flare every so often that had been accepted up until this time; they now wanted two flares in rapid succession every fifteen minutes.

On the question of lights, students of the International Regulations for the Prevention of Collision at Sea will be interested to read that a Notice to Mariners of November 1891 requested that pilot vessels show the white over red all-round lights that they still show today. Trinity House circularised their skippers demanding that this Notice be observed. In the same year they also took the trouble to order that riding lights at anchor were not to be hoisted more than 20ft above the hull. This sensible provision ensured that an approaching ship would receive a useful perspective on the pilot boat's position, a factor forgotten by modern yacht builders who insist on siting a permanently available riding light at the masthead.

The turnover of pilots on the Dungeness cutters was fairly rapid, so the long periods of one another's company that used to be the lot of the seeking pilot were generally a thing of the past. Also, a system was now in place known as a 'progression', whereby senior pilots from the list were awarded jobs that turned up in the hours of daylight. Their juniors generally got the night work.

The progression lists are beautiful documents which show the pilots' individual pennants. These were hoisted after boarding a ship, so that all who were privy to the system could see at a glance not only that a pilot was aboard, but who that pilot was.

The cutters kept the sea in fair weather and foul, and when one ran for Dover Harbour in a hurricane-force storm, the Elder Brethren were affronted and wanted a full explanation. This attitude probably would not have impressed Pilot Parish, who was washed along the deck of *Vigilant* and fetched up jammed beneath the windlass. The only way of extricating him was by levering him out with handspikes. He was fortunate to sustain no more damage than broken ribs.

Opportunities for pilots to practise their traditional sideline as petty smugglers were few on the new, controlled cutters, but some still managed a

***Vigilant*, No 4, the last sailing cutter in the Dover Strait**

The 69-ton *Vigilant*, the last sailing vessel to work for the pilots, was built as a cutter at Wivenhoe in 1879 and later converted to ketch rig. Seen here weighing anchor in Dover Harbour with a handsome steam yacht and a Channel ferry in the background, she is carrying a full complement of pilots dressed in their Sunday best. The crane for her mast lights is visible at the doublings of the mainmast. Unusually for a working craft, the rig is supported by a running backstay set up with a powerful 8 : 1 Burton purchase. There is no sign of an auxiliary engine running and she looks every inch a sailing boat.
(© National Maritime Museum, Greenwich, UK)

little activity. This seems to have been mainly in the way of small dealing with whoever had the key to a ship's bonded locker, and on 28 January 1892, Pilot Gillman was caught by the Customs with 8oz of tobacco and one tenth of a gallon of what they describe as 'perfumed spirit'. Whether this last was Dutch gin or scent for a lady-friend is now obscure, but the Elder Brethren took an uncharacteristically lenient view of the proceedings. The pilot was fined three times the duty payable, presumably by the Revenue men, and his offence was 'recorded' by the secretary to the Trinity.

In 1879 an order was issued expressly forbidding the 'shameful practice' of the men in the boarding punts asking ships' crews for grog and other comforts, on pain of instant dismissal. Three years later, an Elder Brother may well have boarded a cutter for a snoop around without being announced, because an order came down on 6 December that trysails were not to be stored in boats on deck. Boats, he said, must always be clean and ready for hoisting in an emergency. This is a hard demand, particularly in winter, because every sailor knows that dragging wet sails below is the sure route to damp, condensation, mildew and misery. Small boats stowed right way up on deck invariably become repositories for items nobody wants below, and if there really had been an emergency, one can be sure that the pilots would lose no time in throwing the trysail out of the boat in as few seconds as it took to hook on the tackle blocks.

Another order coming down to the cutters from on high was a reminder that second-class pilots should stick to ships for which they were qualified, which were those of 14ft draught and under. This division reflected the ancient arrangement at Deal between 'lower and upper book' pilots.

Apart from unlicensed piloting and, in later days, the boarding of both licensed and unlicensed pilots from the shore, the thing that really upset the big names of Trinity House was when a pilot cutter was discovered taking a tack close to the beach. This was a periodic practice allowing the pilots a quick run ashore to buy the latest newspapers and generally stretch their legs, but the gesture of freedom so incensed their bosses that all excuses were set aside as 'frivolous', and the direst penalties promised for any repeat performances. Such activity, it was pointed out, meant that the cutter had to be off station for at least two hours. It is not for us to judge.

The end of the sailing cutters for the South Channel

Perusal of Dover pilot records for 1891 shows an increasing interest in the value and condition of the ketches. No 3, *Princess*, was first valued at £180, then sold to a Mr Groom. The *Granville* fetched £350 from Thomas Adie and Sons, who offered to purchase 'the ketches' in the plural. On 11 October, a letter authorised the yard to make good the kentledge (iron ballast) found missing from an inventory to be 'replaced from one of the other ketches'.

All this activity took place alongside the commissioning of the first two steam cutters for Dungeness, the *Pioneer* and the *Guide*. These two fine vessels were to replace the sailing boats forever, but the last of them, the *Vigilant*, remained in service as a tender to the steamers and also a reserve operational pilot cutter. For years, she supplied the Dungeness steam cutters with pilots and sometimes provisions, flying her flag when on passage and always authorised to board a pilot should any ship need one from her.

It is clear that a positive decision was taken in 1892 to keep the *Vigilant* on, because she was re-caulked following a minor collision the previous autumn. Quotes were then taken for a new suit of sails, with the words 'London' and the pilot number sewn on the main. Sharp and Enright quoted £50 6s 2d, plus 28s 6d for a pair of shrouds. Simpsons undercut them by £10 and got the job. It is salutary to note that, in 2012, Sharp and Enright are still in healthy business as first-class traditional chandlers opposite the Wellington Dock in Dover. The fate of their rivals is unclear.

The steam cutters flourished and in due course the *Vigilant* was lost when she struck a mine during World War I, but still the commissioners kept up their tireless work for their pilots' comfort. In the year of the new steamers' launching, they authorised a payment of £2 5s for repairing the lavatory in the pilot house, and at Christmas they approved a £1 10s tip for the man who filled the steamers' water tanks and boilers. This payment was to be given annually in future. Perhaps it is only to be expected that since the ships had not been in service a full year, the gift for 1901 was reduced pro rata to 15s.

Christmas aboard the Dover pilot boat

Christmas dinner served aboard the early steamer off Dover. We may only speculate about the ghost in the background on the left. Is he real, or did he move so fast the lens could not keep up? *(© National Maritime Museum, Greenwich, UK)*

Below decks on an early steam cutter

Pilots doing what pilots do all over the world - playing cards as they wait for a ship to board. Accommodations are surprisingly spartan despite the remarkable innovation of electric lighting and what appear to be chintz bunk-curtains, but they will be warm, and probably considerably drier than the old sailing boats. *(© National Maritime Museum, Greenwich, UK)*

Steam arrives in Dover

Pilot Boat No 1, one of the two steam cutters, the *Pioneer* and the *Guide*, that took over from the Trinity House ketches around 1891. These handsome craft worked alternate watches off Dungeness, where ships could now be certain of acquiring a pilot. This is the *Pioneer*, manned by a crew of thirteen in all, with accommodation for twenty-four pilots.
(Dover Museum)

A second-generation steam pilot cutter

The Dover cutter from between the world wars, photographed from the western Admiralty Pier as she steams out past the Prince of Wales Pier, shows a more sophisticated vessel than the earlier auxiliary cutters. Sail is still bent on, however, and beautifully stowed. The hull itself bears a marked resemblance to the striking sailing ketches that preceded her.
(Dover Museum)

A Dover pilots' progression list

The Dover pilots' progression lists are not only handsome documents, they indicate the individual pilots' pennants that were hoisted by any ship they were piloting, thus making clear who was doing the job. According to tradition, older pilots generally bagged the day jobs, while less popular night work fell to the youngsters. *(Dover Museum)*

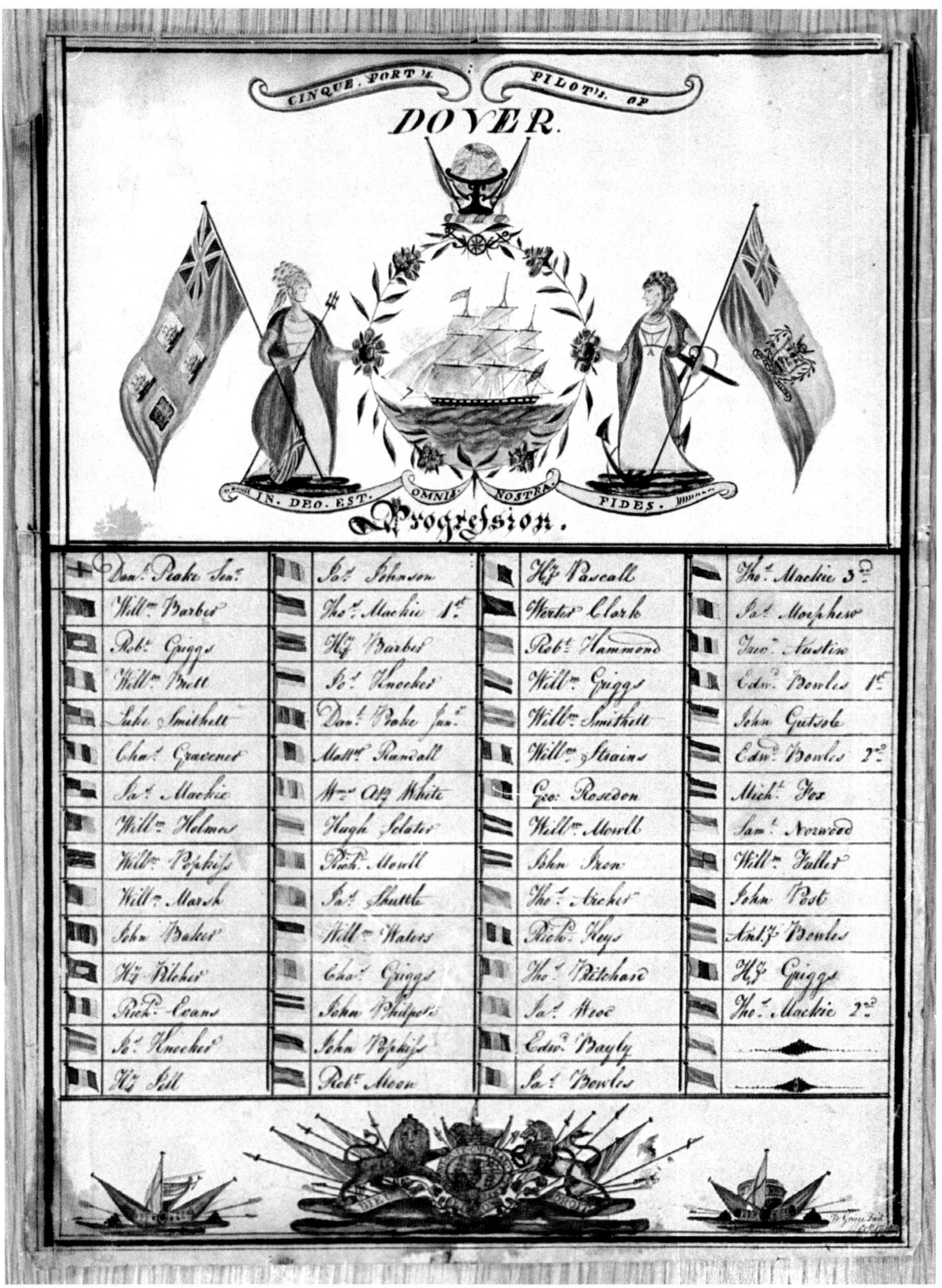

CINQUE PORT'S : PILOT'S OF

DOVER.

IN. DEO. EST. OMNIS NOSTRA FIDES.

Progression.

Danl. Peake Senr.	Jas. Johnson	Hy. Pascall	Thos. Mackie 3rd
Willm. Barber	Thos. Mackie 1st	Webster Clark	Jas. Morphew
Robt. Griggs	Hy. Barber	Robt. Hammond	Jno. Austin
Willm. Bell	Jos. Knocker	Willm. Griggs	Edwd. Bowles 1st
Luke Smithett	Danl. Peake Junr.	Willm. Smithett	John Gutsole
Chas. Gravener	Matthw. Randall	Willm. Strains	Edwd. Bowles 2nd
Jas. Mackie	Wm. Atty White	Geo: Rosedon	Michl. Fox
Willm. Holmes	Hugh Sclater	Willm. Mowll	Saml. Norwood
Willm. Popkiss	Richd. Mowll	John Iron	Willm. Fuller
Willm. Marsh	Jas. Shuttle	Thos. Archer	John Post
John Baker	Willm. Waters	Richd. Keys	Anty. Bowles
Hy. Pilcher	Chas. Griggs	Thos. Pritchard	Hy. Griggs
Richd. Evans	John Philpott	Jas. Wood	Thos. Mackie 2nd
Jo. Knocker	John Popkiss	Edwd. Bayly	
Hy. Sell	Robt. Moon	Jas. Bowles	

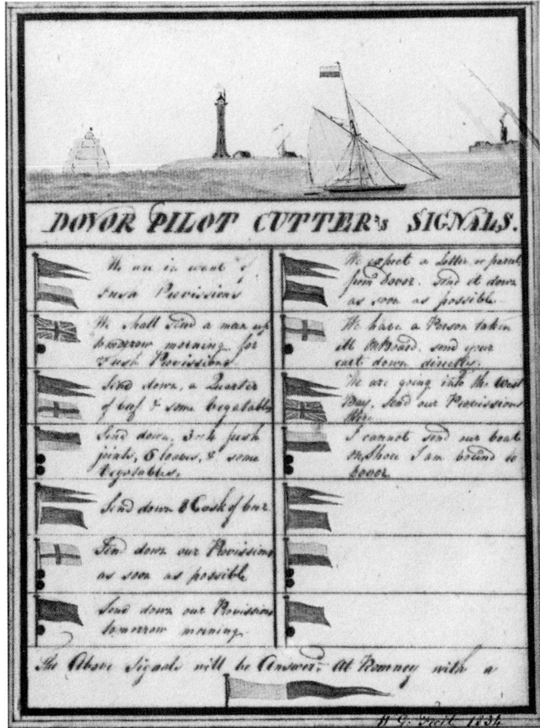

Dover pilot cutter signals

A glorious piece of folk art from 1834, showing private signals arranged between the pilots for such banal items as 'Send down a cask of beer', and 'Send down a quarter of beef and some vegetables'. The image at the top shows a ship bound up-Channel, stunsails set on both sides, and a very fine pilot cutter sporting a big rig cruising with her mainsail tack triced up. The cutter is in the lee of what is clearly Dungeness, indicating that at this stage, unless the artist was using a large degree of licence, true cutters were working this stretch of coast.
(Charles Miller)

The arrival of the steam cutters marked not only the end of official cruising pilotage under sail, it also tolled the funeral bell for the hovellers of Deal who had done so well over the years by carrying pilots themselves. In January 1907 the spare cutter was stationed off Dover to take off pilots from outward-bound vessels. This almost ruined the Deal men who had been landing these 'down' pilots for centuries. The boatmen and hovellers now petitioned the King, who reacted in favour of the common man. Perhaps he recognised the usefulness of these great seamen and saw their potential for the nation in time of war, or maybe he just felt sorry for them. Whatever the reason, Trinity House was obliged to withdraw the spare vessel and allow the hovellers to carry on their ancient craft.

Finally, when enemy activity during the First World War made the Dungeness cruising station too dangerous to operate, all shipping was ordered into the Downs for examination. The transfer of pilots was now carried out by the duty cutters working within the anchorage, squeezing the boatmen out. When peace came, the 'down' pilots almost invariably disembarked off Dungeness once again, to be landed by the cruising cutter. By the end of the 1920s, the Downs had fallen silent to shipping, the pilots had left, and the last of the hovellers had disappeared.

An early Dover pilots' list

A beautifully decorated list of Dover pilots, this one from 1824. The artwork at the top shows, yet again, a true cutter. She has an archaic lug topsail and is answering the call of a signal gun fired by the man-of-war hove to with her main topsail aback.
(Dover Museum)

CHAPTER 7

Local Pilots in the English Channel

In the days of sail, most of the many English Channel harbours of any significance were served by pilots, either officially or unofficially. Information on these ports is hard to come by on the English side and largely anecdotal. Le Havre and Dunkirk with its ketches and schooners are very much the exceptions in France, but elsewhere, data have proved even more difficult to obtain.

Pilots generally worked from vernacular craft which, like the quay punts of Falmouth, had usually been designed and built for some other purpose. Typical among them are the Channel Islands and Poole, which find a home in this volume for no better reason than that their pilots' lives were not without incident and that at least some information has been unearthed.

Channel Islands piloting

If ever a region needed pilots to bring ships in safely, it must surely be the Channel Islands. These dots of land (Jersey is the largest, measuring barely ten miles across) lie amongst some of the most

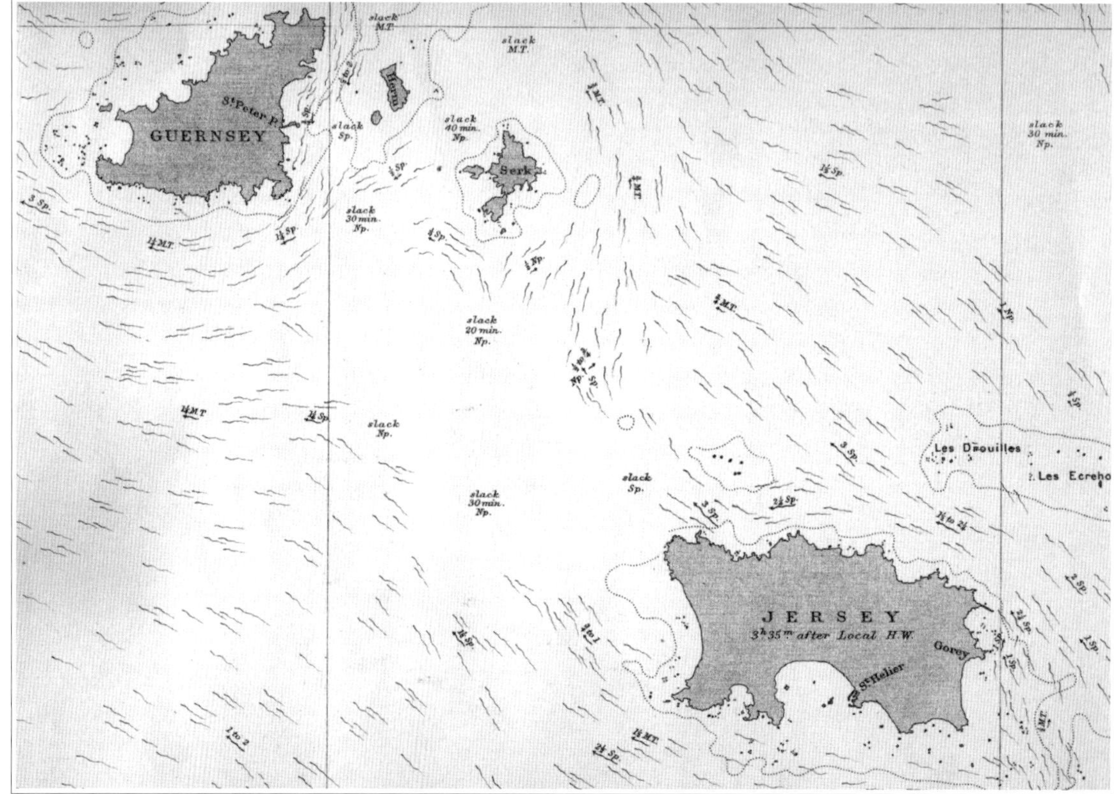

Guernsey and Jersey

The two largest Channel Islands are sited in the tide-swept waters of the bight running between the Cotentin Peninsula and North Brittany. Tide is king here, and even today when yachts have reliable diesel engines, no small boat puts to sea without consulting the stream atlas. *(From* Tidal Streams Channel Islands, *Admiralty publication 1903)*

St Peter Port waterfront and a pilot boat

The small craft in this image of St Peter Port waterfront are fine examples of the sort of generic craft favoured by local pilots. The one on the left with a 'P' on the bow is almost certainly a pilot's boat. Her sister to the right could be taken for a fishing craft, except for the gentleman in a boater and the rather smartly turned out tender, both of which suggest that she may have been bought by a yachtsman.
(The Priaulx Library)

St Sampson's, Guernsey, around 1890

Two sailing coasters are dried out in this harbour that lies a few miles north of St Peter Port in the Little Russell Channel, east of Guernsey. Outside the pier, three general-purpose small craft are moored. Any could act as one of the pilot boats that are known to have operated from ports other than the main harbour.
(The Priaulx Library)

extensive and dangerous areas of rocks in the world. The tides are also prodigious, with a rise of up to 38ft and streams which can run at 7kts and more. Indeed, the sea's rise and fall governs the very size of some of the land masses. The Plateau des Minquiers, south of Jersey, consists of a few isolated outcrops of barely inhabitable rock at high water. At low tide, a wasteland the size of the English city of Birmingham is uncovered.

The islands became a part of Britain when William of Normandy incorporated his homeland into the extensive conquests in the larger island to the north for which he is famous. Very much a geographical part of his old domain, they nestle close in to the French coast, sixty miles and more from the British mainland. While as a result of this historical anomaly they have become politically and linguistically British, the Norman French influence on their culture is unmistakable. This is particularly noticeable in the locally built working craft, which look far more French than they do English.

In recent years, Jersey, Guernsey and Alderney have become international tax havens with their main industry that of banking and finance. It was not always thus. The islands are 'washed by the sea', and the proximity to Gulf Stream water ensures that their mini-climate is friendlier than that of continental France or Britain during the cold winter months. As recently as twenty years ago this natural benefit was used for fruit and flower growing, with 'Guernsey Toms' (tomatoes) a well-known export. Stone and other commodities were also transported to England in some quantity. Like most island communities, the Channel Islands have had to rely on imports for many of the necessities of life, coal being a notable case in point. As a result of this trading, shipping has moved in and out of the islands for centuries. Much of it has required pilotage.

The earliest references to pilots in the Channel Islands date back to the Middle Ages, but they are vague. There is no doubt that even by the eighteenth century, the charts for the area were still generally inadequate for safe navigation. British naval vessels at least always preferred to ship a local pilot rather than rely on dubious published material.

Early in January 1783 a convoy of transports is on record as having arrived at St Peter Port, Guernsey, with troops from Portsmouth. Here, the commodore's nerve must have failed, or maybe he had been well advised. In any event, he procured the services of an old man for pilot and sailed on to Jersey.

Guernsey

Until World War II, piloting in Guernsey remained more or less as it had been from much earlier times. By 1878 pilotage was compulsory for all steamers of over 50 tons arriving from foreign ports, and we know that while it was, surprisingly, not compulsory to take a pilot for departure, many captains made the wise decision to do so. It is interesting to note that the rate for taking a sizeable collier to sea from St Peter Port was around 17s, while for bringing in a ship of over 200 tons, the rate was £1 10s. There was a St Peter Port pilot operating from the harbour itself but, in addition, a number of pilots worked from outlying anchorages and harbours.

Pilots were licensed for different parts of the coast, and most of them were also fishermen. Typically, when a ship requiring a pilot was due from mainland Britain, a fisherman with a pilot's licence who fancied his chances would set sail to the north towards the Casquets rocks or the Race of Alderney. Sometimes, two or more pilots would put out, and an impromptu contest would ensue. For a man working primarily as a fisherman, the rates of pilotage would have represented an attractive bonus to a modest income.

If the fishing were poor, or shipping heavy, the men would sometimes put to sea seeking a ship to bring in. Although this was not the normal way of things, a man could at least cruise on the fishing grounds awaiting his chance, so that even if he missed the ship, his trip might not be a dead loss.

A wooden watchtower was erected on the old St Peter Port careening dock, where pilots could get an early view of ships coming round from the south of the island, or across from Jersey and St Malo. Such a structure must have been of scant use for vessels approaching from the north down the Little Russell Channel, unless they had already shipped a 'coast pilot' further out. These vessels would have required a pilot on board long before one could have been sent to them after being spotted from the harbour. Bound south, they would be roaring along on a fair tide, while a pilot coming out to meet them would have had to struggle against the powerful south-going stream, so it seems logical that Little Russell pilots would have stationed themselves at the north end of the island.

That this was often the case is confirmed by the reminiscences of a gentleman still living in Guernsey in the 1990s, who sailed with a pilot before World War II. His home in the early 1930s was near Bordeaux harbour in northern Guernsey, and he went to sea from time to time aboard a small fishing boat owned by a pilot. He was not the pilot's official mate, but the great man was pleased enough to take the lad along, particularly on days when his indentured apprentice failed to turn up.

The pilot's boat was a typical Guernsey-built fishing boat. Such vessels had changed but little in the preceding century, except that by the 1930s many had been fitted with auxiliary or primary power units. This one had not. She was more or less open, around 21ft long with 4ft 6in draught. Like the rest of her kind, she was carvel planked on sawn frames with caulked seams. As can be seen from the illustrations, such boats carried something of a French look about the stem, while the stern also

The careening dock – St Peter Port, Guernsey

This remarkable early photograph of the coaster *Channel Queen* shows not only the south side of St Peter Port harbour, but also takes in the unique pilots' watchtower on the left. The tide is not high, which is perhaps why the pilots are not using their facility, but the huge range between high and low water make the Channel Islands a favourite for drying out and scrubbing a vessel's bottom to this day. *(The Priaulx Library)*

displayed more than a touch of the steep rake of their continental cousins. The run is sweet and long, set off by powerful shoulders and a steep drag aft to the rudder post.

These boats came in various sizes, from a little over 17ft up to 23ft or so; 17-footers were popular because of a law which exempted craft under 18ft from harbour dues.

Fishermen who wanted a larger vessel were well advised to buy 'foreign', and many did well with second-hand Cornish mackerel drifters, or 'drivers', renowned throughout the Channel for speed and weatherliness. Pilots were ready to use either local or bought-in craft.

In earlier times, Guernsey boats favoured the sprit rig for their usually three-masted sail plans. By the twentieth century, however, gaff rig prevailed on the main- and foremasts, some boats setting full jackyard topsails with a club yard on the clew as well as the long, canted luff yard. The old spritsail sheeted to an outrigger remained on the mizzen only.

The gentleman mentioned above recalls that, 'The mizzen was set all the time, and we only bothered to attend the sheet if we were racing or in a real hurry.' A big jib was set from a very long bowsprit and some boats, but by no means all, hoisted staysails as well. An unusual feature of open Guernsey-built boats was that their pumps discharged into a hollow thwart, opening via a port to let the water out. Sheets for the foresail and jib led aft via the knee above the centre thwart, and the halyards were often belayed to half-pins beneath the thwarts using a slippery hitch. This system permits instant lowering of the powerful lugsails in a heavy squall and was favoured by other open boats in Britain, such as the Yorkshire coble and the heavily canvassed Deal galley punts.

Such craft were unstable without their ballast. One day, the boy from Bordeaux harbour and a friend were cleaning out the bilge of a sailing boat they had dried out on the tide. The ballast took the form of round, smooth stones of about 40lbs weight known as 'killicks'. The English slang for 'anchor' used to be 'killick', a term which stems right back to Viking times, when stones enhanced with wooden stocks were used as anchors. On the day in question, all the ballast had been lifted out of the boat for scrubbing, because the stones and the bilge were coated in fish slime. As the tide began to return, the ballast had not yet been replaced and one young man remarked to the other that there was no hurry, because the water was still way short of floating the boat. They reckoned without the extra buoyancy that came with an unballasted hull, however, and she floated far earlier than they expected. To their consternation, as she lifted she made no attempt to float upright, but simply lay down gracefully and filled with water.

The Bordeaux pilot was 'a hard man', always ready to clip a boy's ear if he were slow about his duties. Whether popular or not, however, he is recalled as a fine sailor, always insisting on the boat being given plenty of air. 'Let her go!' he would cry in frustration as his youthful helmsman pinched her too tight to the wind.

A typical piloting trip for him was to catch the north-going stream up the fifteen or so miles to the Casquets Rocks. There, he would come alongside a ship and climb aboard as best he could, usually via a rope Jacob's ladder lowered from the deck. His lad would have to bring the boat home. Unlike their more aristocratic colleagues out in the Channel, Guernsey pilots at this time showed no interest in dressing up for the job. They went aboard their ships wearing the same 'Guernsey' jumper they wore for fishing and digging their gardens but, lest anybody should imagine they were lackaday about their work, or that a mere fifteen-mile sail down-tide was easy, the nature of the Casquets should be borne in mind. Anybody who has sailed a small vessel anywhere near the Casquets, Alderney, or more particularly, the Ortac Channel, knows that this stretch of sea with its uneven bottom, land looming to leeward and a tide-race that is sometimes hard to credit, is one of the worst wave engines of the eastern Atlantic shore. Seas here are notoriously heavy in all but the finest weather. No joke at all for the little boy left in charge of an open boat while his hard-case boss clambered off to the comparative comfort of a collier and a profitable ride home.

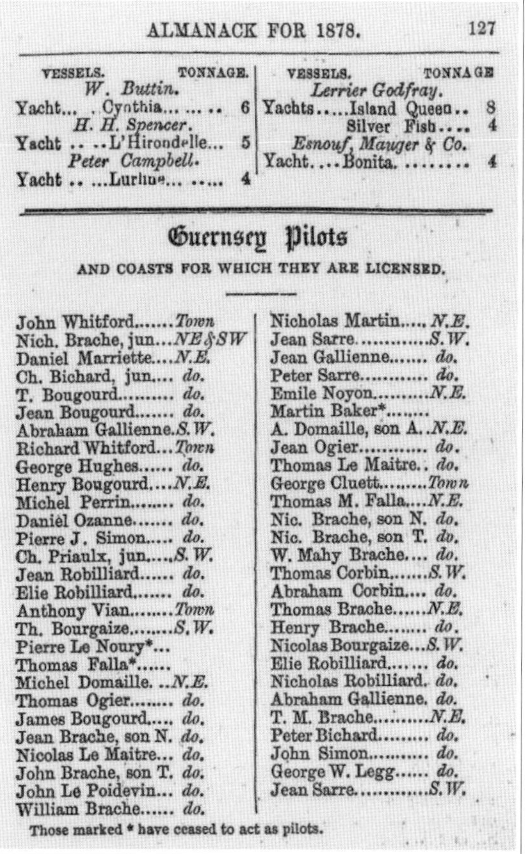
ALMANACK FOR 1878. 127

VESSELS.	TONNAGE.	VESSELS.	TONNAGE
W. Buttin.		*Lerrier Godfray.*	
Yacht... . Cynthia...	6	Yachts.....Island Queen..	8
H. H. Spencer.		Silver Fish....	4
Yacht .. ..L'Hirondelle...	5	*Esnouf, Mauger & Co.*	
Peter Campbell.		Yacht....Bonita.	4
Yacht .. ...Lurline...	4		

Guernsey Pilots

AND COASTS FOR WHICH THEY ARE LICENSED.

John Whitford.......*Town*	Nicholas Martin.... *N.E.*
Nich. Brache, jun...*NE&SW*	Jean Sarre............*S.W.*
Daniel Marriette....*N.E.*	Jean Gallienne....... *do.*
Ch. Bichard, jun.... *do.*	Peter Sarre........... *do.*
T. Bougourd.......... *do.*	Emile Noyon..........*N.E.*
Jean Bougourd....... *do.*	Martin Baker*........
Abraham Gallienne.*S.W.*	A. Domaille, son A..*N.E.*
Richard Whitford...*Town*	Jean Ogier........... *do.*
George Hughes...... *do.*	Thomas Le Maitre.. *do.*
Henry Bougourd....*N.E.*	George Cluett.........*Town*
Michel Perrin........ *do.*	Thomas M. Falla....*N.E.*
Daniel Ozanne....... *do.*	Nic. Brache, son N. *do.*
Pierre J. Simon..... *do.*	Nic. Brache, son T. *do.*
Ch. Priaulx, jun.....*S.W.*	W. Mahy Brache.... *do.*
Jean Robilliard...... *do.*	Thomas Corbin.......*S.W.*
Elie Robilliard....... *do.*	Abraham Corbin.... *do.*
Anthony Vian........*Town*	Thomas Brache......*N.E.*
Th. Bourgaize........*S.W.*	Henry Brache........ *do.*
Pierre Le Noury*...	Nicolas Bourgaize...*S.W.*
Thomas Falla*......	Elie Robilliard....... *do.*
Michel Domaille. ..*N.E.*	Nicholas Robilliard. *do.*
Thomas Ogier........ *do.*	Abraham Gallienne. *do.*
James Bougourd..... *do.*	T. M. Brache..........*N.E.*
Jean Brache, son N. *do.*	Peter Bichard......... *do.*
Nicolas Le Maitre... *do.*	John Simon........... *do.*
John Brache, son T. *do.*	George W. Legg...... *do.*
John Le Poidevin... *do.*	Jean Sarre............*S.W.*
William Brache...... *do.*	

Those marked * have ceased to act as pilots.

Guernsey pilots' list, 1878

This list of pilots leaves no doubt about the French ancestry of many Channel Islanders. A few English names are creeping in, but the old families are in the majority.
(Mackenzie & Co's Almanac, *1878, The Priaulx Library)*

Secondary activities of Guernsey pilots

Like many pilots, the men of Guernsey became involved in the saving of life and the salvage of goods from time to time. According to the records of Mr Sarre, the great-grandson of a Guernsey pilot, the dismasted brig *United Kingdom* was found by pilots drifting abandoned in 1854. They boarded her and managed to beach her, but tragically, a boat was overturned and two of their number drowned.

A notable incident involving Mr Sarre's forebear is described in the Guernsey newspaper, *The Star*, in February 1904. The 750-ton Blue Cross liner ss *Roman* owned by Elders of Newcastle upon Tyne had run into difficulties down off Ushant, shipping a large amount of water in a severe gale. The influx damaged her cargo and doused the fires in the stokehold. Two of the crew died from inhaling ammonia fumes from the cargo and another was washed overboard as the ship drifted helpless for a day and a night. On the morning of 15 February, Pilot Pierre Sarre was looking seaward with his telescope from his home behind Les Hanois rocks, when he spotted the *Roman*. He sent a telephonic message to St Peter Port and the ss *Assistance* was sent to the rescue. She was unable to find the casualty and returned to base. A further sortie that evening also proved fruitless, but Pilot Sarre would not be talked down. He knew what he had seen and so he travelled to St Peter Port and boarded the *Assistance*, taking her to sea the following morning. The *Roman* was discovered and towed into safety in a violent gale with blinding snow.

Mr Sarre reports that in 1861 the Rocquaine pilots from the west coast of Guernsey were engaged for ninety vessels, of which Pierre Sarre piloted forty and his brother Jean several others. Most were proceeding to Guernsey or Jersey, but some were bound for French ports in the Bay of St Malo. The same two pilots guided the tug and its barges which carried the stone, water, oil, and workmen from St Peter Port for building the Hanois Lighthouse. The authorities had long resisted the construction of this light, but the pilots had continued to demand it. Finally it was built and not a day too soon. The idea of navigating the southwest corner of Guernsey with its notoriously rough seas without its reassuring flash is not attractive, even today.

Vigilo, a Guernsey boat

Vigilo is a classic example of a Guernsey boat of the type used for inshore fishing or pilot work. She was built by de Garis in 1890 at St Peter's and fished until 1970. In the mid 1990s she was restored by Major Eddie Parks.

Like many of her type, *Vigilo* was originally constructed at £1 per foot to a length of 17ft 6in. This kept her inside the 18ft lower limit of harbour dues. Her beam is around 6ft 6in and her draught

Pilot cutter *Mary*

This rather fanciful lithograph from 1850 depicts the Guernsey pilot cutter *Mary* (N Brache, master) rescuing survivors from the wreck of the cutter *Experiment* on the morning of Sunday, 17 March. The name Brache features nine times in the list of Guernsey pilots from 1878 on page 89, suggesting that the N Brache in this image is, if not their father, then another member of a typical pilot dynasty. A further point of interest is that by the time of any written history of Guernsey pilotage, the boats used were general workboats. Cutters were confined to Jersey. Here, we have a cutter working out of Guernsey. *(The Priaulx Library)*

The Casquets Rocks

A Guernsey pilot boat negotiates the vicious tide-rips of the Ortac Channel between the Casquets Rocks with their remote lighthouse and the isle of Alderney. Pilots would sail up to this area on the north-going stream to meet southbound shipping. *(Author's collection)*

is 2ft 6in. She carries about a ton of ballast.

Vigilo had a motor installed later in her life and at this time her freeboard was raised by one plank. Evidence of this was clear during the restoration. The practice was typical when converting the old sailing boats to power, because the sailing freeboard was very low. As soon as the weight of an engine was added, the boats became uncomfortably wet and tended to 'squat' by the stern under power. Motor craft to the traditional form were built with higher topsides and a vertical transom. The original sailing models thus required modification. A filling piece was inserted abaft the raked sternpost to permit space to install a propeller forward of the now vertical rudder. The extra board in the topsides increased the bow overhang, raising the overall length to 18ft, but by then the cheap deal for 17-footers had fallen by the wayside, so nobody much cared.

Considerable pains have been taken in restoring *Vigilo*'s rig, complete with main topmast and lug-yard topsail. Major Parks has rigged the main and foresails with brails for ease of handling and notes that *Vigilo* is so directionally stable that it is necessary to sail the boat through a tack, easing away fore and jib sheets and hardening up the main to help the little boat to fly through the wind. The fore and mainsheet blocks originally attached to the sail with a long, heavy iron hook, which could be simply moved up a cringle for reefing. This arrangement proved dangerous with inexperienced cadets in the fore part of the boat, so Major Parks replaced it with a bullseye set-up which works just as well.

The pump was an unusual feature on these tiny craft. As noted above, it was normally formed by an oblong box emptying into a hollow thwart and thence outboard. *Vigilo*'s has been replaced with a novel innovation. After World War II, the occupying German forces had left the island rather untidy. Spent anti-aircraft shell cases and the like littered the waterfronts, so a local plumber had the bright idea of converting some of this useful junk into pumps. Nearly half a century later, the brass tube of an ack-ack shell proved a perfect fit for *Vigilo*, so Major Parks installed it during his refit; a historic reminder of a period which long precedes the birth of most of those who now sail her, but which for her was merely a halfway house in a working life which still stretches ahead.

Working craft of Guernsey

These jaunty, mainly schooner-rigged semi-open boats are typical of the craft that were favoured by Guernsey pilots. Similar boats can be seen today at any French traditional regatta. They owe far more to their Norman and Breton neighbours than to any British working craft of this era. *(Author's collection)*

Jersey

The pilot service in Jersey was rather more formal than that of neighbouring Guernsey. According to the local historian John Jean, the island was a hive of shipping activity in the nineteenth century, with 1,600 men employed as sea captains. Many of these had old French names, including Renouf and Larbalestier, an anglicised form of the Norman *l'arbalestier*, a crossbowman. In 1852, twenty-eight pilots served the west coast of the island, while a further eight were stationed on the east side overlooking the difficult and dangerous approaches from the French coast.

By the year 1900 there were around ten full-time pilots, sharing a pair of elderly 40ft cutters of a very French hull form, the *Rival* and the grandly named *Yacht*. Thanks to the memoir of Captain F B Renouf, we know that in 1902, when he was taken on as apprentice aboard the *Rival*, his shipmates were Pilots Thomas Roberts, the captain, Phil Roberts, Frank and George Renouf, and Mr Jack Allix. Aboard the *Yacht*, the captain was yet another member of the Renouf clan. His messmates were Pilots Edward and Jack Larbalestier, George Roberts, and Ernest Keeping. From this, it is immediately obvious that in Jersey, just as in Guernsey, Falmouth, the Bristol Channel and faraway New York, piloting ran in seafaring families.

The Jersey cutters worked a 'three days on watch, three days off' arrangement at this time. Pilots generally boarded in the vicinity of La Corbière point, with its powerful light and off-lying shoals. The boats anchored up off Bouilly Port (called 'Beauport' by Captain Renouf) in St Brelade's Bay, where they would lie safely if not always comfortably in all but southerly or southeast winds. A yachtsman of today who wishes to anchor in St Brelade's Bay must keep his wits about him to avoid various unmarked rocks, but for the pilots of a hundred years ago, entering and leaving was literally all in a day's work.

Life was tough during the winter, because the cutters remained on duty, watch on and watch off, just as they did in summer. In hard weather from the southwest or even the west, however, the winter swells and gales could render St Brelade's Bay completely untenable. At such times, the duty cutter would slink off to the lee of Noirmont Point, the western sentinel of the larger and more sheltered St Aubin's Bay. At neap tides, they could lie behind Belcroute beyond St Aubin's Fort, but the extreme low waters of spring tides rendered even this unapproachable, leaving the boats 'rolling their masts out' in the wide bay itself. Once again, the approaches to this dubious haven are strewn with rocks and shoals.

In heavy weather, it was impossible for pilots to board ships at sea from the cutters, so their customers had to work into St Aubin's Bay to take on the pilot for St Helier. No doubt they were pleased to see the pilot coming over the rail, because although a stranger who had safely negotiated the numerous deadly hazards in the offing without assistance was entitled to a high level of self-satisfaction, any captain would be glad of all the help he could find for the last lap.

In fair conditions during the summer months, life on the cutters was said by Mr Renouf to be idyllic. The boats would cruise out to the west of the island, hooking mackerel down in St Ouen's Bay, and north up to Grosnez Point. If all the pilots had boarded before the three-day 'tour' was up, the cutter would run for St Helier with a large pilot flag

St Helier in the days of sail

A brig lies alongside the quay of the drying English Harbour, shot from the high ground at Fort Regent at a place known locally then as Pilot View. Elizabeth Castle, with its associated pier, supplies shelter from the west as it still does today. *(Société Jersiaise)*

hoisted, indicating that her sister was to sortie with a fresh complement. This was a popular state of affairs for the boy bringing home the empty cutter, but it was hated by the apprentice on the other boat, and by some of the pilots as well. There was no help for it, however. The service had to be maintained no matter what private domestic arrangements went by the board in the process.

On one occasion, the young Renouf was anxious to be home to see a girlfriend he was missing badly after two winter nights at sea. He was keeping lookout from the companionway and decided to fool the pilots into going home, so he took out his mouth organ and blew the bottom note quietly. It sounded just like the siren of a distant ship to the pilots below. He did it again, waited a decent interval, then blew once more. The pilots now got under weigh, but when they had opened the red isophase blaze of Corbière light, no steamer could they see. After a brief effort to discover one, they ran for

Jersey pilot cutter No 1

By the end of the nineteenth century, the Jersey pilots were operating from two cutters. One would take around five pilots aboard and go out seeking ships, while the other remained in port. When the active cutter came in, either at the end of her turn or because she had boarded all her pilots, the second cutter went to sea, and so on. This one is the *Yacht*. *(Société Jersiaise)*

The second Jersey pilot cutter

This photograph of *Rival*, No 2, is full of useful detail not recorded elsewhere. The cutter is of the old-fashioned 'cod's head and mackerel tail' hull form still favoured in France at this time. It also appears that the Jersey pilots had followed suit with their colleagues in Falmouth and done away with their main booms. These, of course, are far smaller vessels and the boomless mainsail would cause no more problems than it does on such successful boomless cutters as the Thames Estuary bawley fishing craft. The boat has a handsome open counter and weatherboards permanently rigged to protect the helmsman. She is really quite small to be spending three days on station with so many men aboard. The pilots must have been good friends, or at least have learned to rub along together in search of their common goal.
(Société Jersiaise)

Jersey pilots

Another view of *Rival* with her conspicuous weatherboards. A small crane appears to be set well up above the hounds of the mast on the starboard side. From this would be swung the pilots' lights after dark. Also in view is the stock of the traditional bower anchor stowed across the capping rail forward of the mast. This was common practice in working craft, to keep the weight of their heavy anchors well inboard and reduce any tendency to pitch. These boats spent a lot of time anchored, and a large fisherman-style hook would be the preferred tackle. Deploying the anchor from this position was simply a matter of slacking away a few fathoms of chain and heaving it over the side.
(Société Jersiaise)

A mystery cutter in St Helier

Described in the archive as a typical Jersey-built cutter (named *Welcome*) in St Helier Harbour, this vessel does not give the appearance of a pilot cutter. With her staysail of a different cloth than the rest of her canvas and no running backstays, she is probably not a yacht either. She has a roller-reefing mainsail like a Bristol Channel pilot cutter, but she has a taller and lighter rig. Like the much humbler Jersey pilot cutters, she has had weatherboards fixed above the capping rails.
(Société Jersiaise)

home, it being not worth going back to anchor for the night. It seems the lad understood that his superiors were as tired as he was of bouncing around at anchor on a filthy evening, looking at the lights of snug cottages so close to windward.

From time to time, a pilot would choose to disembark from a ship he had taken to sea and return promptly to St Helier rather than being taken off by the cruising cutter. Very often the transfer took place right outside the breakwater. This practice was particularly popular at times such as Christmas when a man would prefer to be home with his family, even at financial loss, than slopping about on the rough, cold Channel. These transfers were typically handled by the 'yawls', heavy 16-footers that were clinker-built by Allix of Havre-des-Pas. These seaworthy little boats were rigged with a lugsail and centreboard and were turned out by the yard in 1900 at £1 per foot of length.

Apprenticeships

A typical Jersey pilot's apprenticeship at the turn of the nineteenth century began, sometimes as young as sixteen, with a couple of years in the cutters, after which the lad was obliged to do six months' sea-time in a square rigger. For both these services he would receive £2 per month. A trip much favoured for sea-time was to ship out in a Collas-owned vessel bound for Newfoundland, thence to Rio de Janeiro or Santos with salt cod, and so back to Jersey in the springtime. Sometimes these ships were temporarily beset in the ice off Cape Race. On one occasion, the youthful crew played football on the floes while local hunters clubbed seals to death alongside their pitch.

After a further year working the cutters, a young man could be examined for his full pilot's licence.

The examination for a Jersey pilot in the days of sail was a colourful affair. First, the candidate submitted to an oral test in the harbourmaster's office where that official and another old sea captain questioned him over a large-scale chart. The following day was set aside for a practical inquisition. The would-be pilot was then taken to sea aboard the *Duke of Normandy* and obliged to demonstrate comprehensive knowledge of the various channels as well as the shore marks which delineated them. The test was carried out at high water so that many significant rocks were submerged. The party then anchored in St Catherine's Bay for a slap-up lunch served aboard at the candidate's expense. Since the pilotage committee consisted of twelve hungry men whom the poor fellow was anxious to impress, this could prove an expensive binge, with fine food and wines in quantity.

It is hard to imagine a candidate enjoying this feast, knowing that his fate was already decided, for it was not until the committee had eaten their fill that the outcome was announced. Captain Renouf advises that when a successful result was revealed, the newly appointed pilot's health was drunk in his

The Jersey pilot cutter *Yacht* in later life

In 1907, the *Yacht* was owned by ten pilots, and remained in pilot ownership until 1928. Four years later, she passed into the hands of none other than the writer Hilaire Belloc, who renamed her *Jersey*, keeping her until after hostilities in 1946. She finally disappeared from view with her final entry in Lloyds Register in 1954, once again named *Yacht*.
(Private collection)

***Jersey* hoists her topsail**

The pilot cutter *Yacht*, under Mr Belloc's ownership as the *Jersey*, heaves to with jib and staysail aback in order to hoist her topsail. Note that as a yacht she is sensibly carrying a main boom.
(Private collection)

own champagne. We are not told what doom awaited those wretches whose navigation was not up to the mark, or whose lunches failed to reach the required standard.

The pilot cutter, *Yacht*

The second Jersey pilot cutter during the last days of pilotage under sail was the *Yacht*, locally built at St Martin in 1846. More is known of her than might otherwise have been the case because of her latter-day association with the famous Anglo-French writer and commentator, Hilaire Belloc.

In 1862, the *Yacht* was sold to a pilots' consortium consisting of Messrs Renouf, Sampson, Larbalestier and Keeping, each carrying sixteen shares. Her service continued through the ownership of a number of pilots until 1928, when she was finally sold to a fisherman. It is hard not to conclude that this man, one Frank Lawrence, was something of an entrepreneur, because he got rid of the *Yacht* the very same day (13 July) to a Mr John White Reynolds. A man from Hayling Island on the south coast of England bought her in 1930. In 1932, she passed into the redoubtable ownership of Hilaire Belloc.

By this time, Mr Belloc was well on in years, but he ran his 'new' yacht, which he renamed the *Jersey*, in the same robust traditions he had worked up in his previous maritime experience. From all accounts, it seems Mr Belloc was not a skilled seaman in the accepted sense of the word, but he managed to keep the old pilot cutter off the rocks nonetheless. According to Dermod McCarthy's delightful book *Sailing with Mr Belloc*, the boat was 'parish rigged' in the extreme, with antiquated blocks and creaking gear. She always leaked and creature comforts were, quite simply, zero, but Mr Belloc cared nothing for such fripperies.

The *Jersey* had no sea toilet, the calls of nature being served by a useful bucket, partly screened in the forward accommodation. Once completed, the fruits of the daily duty could be hauled up the fo'c'sle hatch and discharged in a healthy and direct manner into the sea. Washing facilities were non-existent until a guest bought the ship a large enamel bowl, which for a brief period took up home on the saloon table. The guest in question was engaged in writing a book about the sumptuous baths of ancient Rome and found the arrangements on board too much of a climb-down. Mr Belloc and his crew were delighted to discover that the book was to be entitled *No Bath Yet.*

Hilaire Belloc's system of navigation consisted of setting up a small table on the aft deck, folding a chart onto it and holding it down with a couple

Pilot No 1 on her home mooring

Looking across St Helier's Old Harbour to a crane beside the Great Western Railway building on the North Quay, with pilot cutter No 1 at her moorings. Why she has been painted white is unclear. Note the beaching legs under her main shroud channels, indicating that she is not about to put to sea and will dry out on the next tide.
(Société Jersiaise)

of enamel mugs of the red wine which he bought in bulk from a favourite vineyard to bottle at home and lay down. He would glance around him and draw surprisingly sensible conclusions using little more than a well-developed, but carefully disguised, store of common sense. His ship did boast a compass, but he spurned such modern excesses as the trailing log to measure distance run.

Hilaire Belloc sold the *Jersey* in 1946, when even he had to admit to being too elderly to enjoy her anymore. By then she had achieved her first century. Eight years later, she disappeared from Lloyd's Register of Yachts and has not been heard of again.

Perhaps we should leave the Channel Islands with the musical voice of Hilaire Belloc, still with its hint of French accent into his old age, especially in the question of his 'r's. One night in Poole harbour, he and his crew had been ashore celebrating their deliverance from the deep in a nasty incident off St Alban's Head earlier in the day. Dermod MacCarthy describes the scene:

> Exhausted, we turned into our bunks and dealt with the drips from the deck above by draping an oilskin or lying to one side of the wet patch. Mr Belloc lay down on his large rubber mattress with many groans and sighs. He took off his coat but nothing else, not even his boots, and covered himself rather clumsily with a blanket. His sighs became high-pitched gasping sounds, interspersed with 'my children, my children!' Others may have fallen asleep quickly but I could not. The noises of an anchored ship become very loud when there is no sleep and no talking or work to do. Things clanked and knocked and the rigging howled. In the small hours Mr Belloc's high-pitched sighs began again, very unhappy, suffering sounds. In an instant Peter was by his berth and asking 'What is it, Papa!' 'I can't sleep, my dear, I'm cold.' 'Yes, yes Papa, I'll see to it.' Peter covered him with a lot more blankets and tucked them warmly round him like a child, Mr Belloc saying all the time, 'Thank you, thank you. Thank you, darling boy.'

Poole Harbour

Poole Harbour, which provided shelter for Hilaire Belloc's tortured night, and to countless seamen since before the time of the Romans, lies half a tide's sail west of the Solent. It is an unusual natural haven, extensive in area but shallow in depth, with a thriving port in its upper reaches. A deep-water channel leading around a wide sweep up to the quay was the main route to town until recently. In the days of sail, a secondary, shallower channel known as 'The Diver' (since dredged as the main channel) offered a more direct route. Because of some mid-English Channel anomaly, the rise of tide here is surprisingly modest, but the enormous body of water inside the narrow entrance generates powerful currents, particularly on the ebb. Once outside, a long buoyed fairway stretches southward towards Handfast Point and Swanage, bounded on one side by the shore and on the other by the extremely shoal Hook Sand. At the seaward end of this channel lies a bar which can be crossed safely by ships at high water but is subject to dangerous seas in south-easterly gales, to which it is wide open.

Although off the 'main road' to London and with Channel pilots notably absent, Poole was of considerable local importance in the days of sail. The town had major interests in Newfoundland and northern Europe which, together with a rich coasting business, created a serious demand for pilotage. Before the Outports Act in 1803, this was met largely by casual operators competing off the bar in good weather, while hanging around inside the harbour hoping for a better break in foul. Immediately within the entrance is a safe anchorage where the local pilots were wont to lie in their cutters, waiting for a fair tide, a stronger wind, or whatever other help they needed to negotiate the challenging narrows.

Poole pilot cutters

In the second half of the nineteenth century, there appear to have been two cutters in Poole. They were of different designs and though few details remain, we can safely assume them to have been of the local fishing type, which is usually half-decked.

The *Content* was given as a square-sterned pilot cutter, 40ft on deck, 10ft 6in beam, with a depth of hold of 7ft 6in. The actual draught was later stated to be 5ft, which is more than enough in these shoal waters. Her displacement was something over 17 tons. The boat was owned in 1870 by Pilots John Brown, James Stone and Thomas Wills, but by 1872,

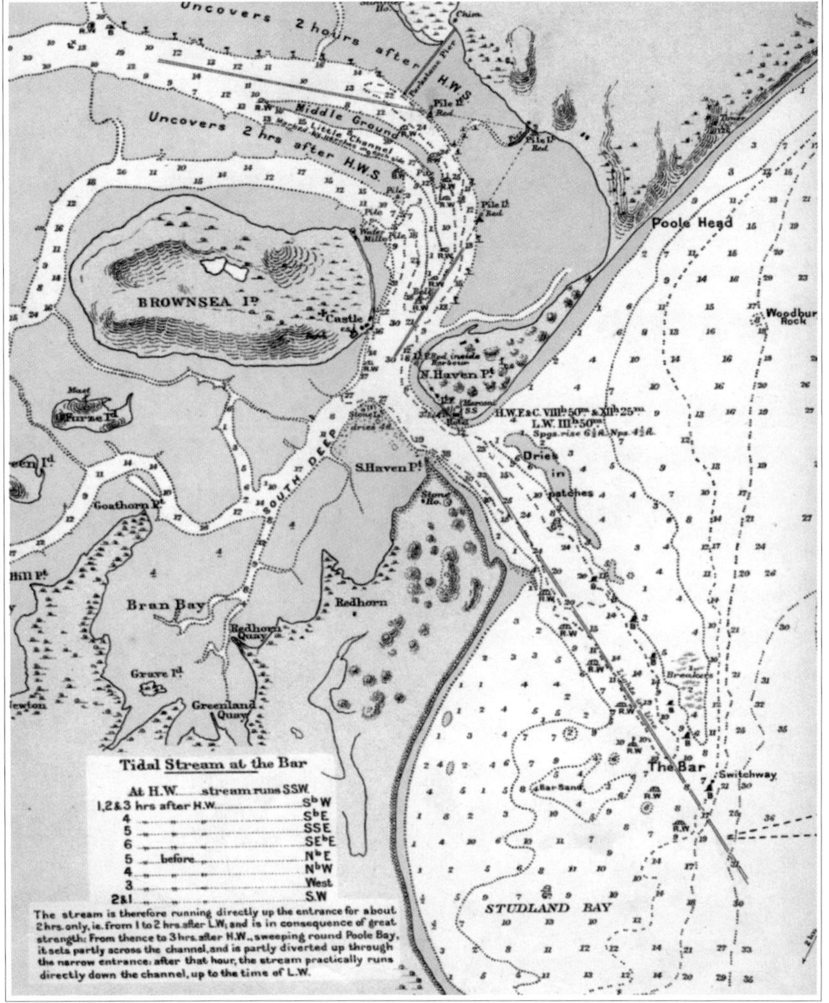

Poole Harbour and approaches

Poole is one of the largest natural harbours in Europe, but because of its extensive shoals, drying flats and strong tides it has never quite rivalled Southampton and Portsmouth for the biggest ships. Nevertheless, it has always been a port of considerable significance. Note the long entrance channel running south-southeast inside the Hook Sand. This fairway and the bar at its seaward end can be a death-trap in an onshore gale when a spring ebb is ripping out of the entrance.
(Royal Cruising Club Chart, 1908)

Brown's share had been passed to a Thomas Tilstead. After a further fourteen years, Tilstead had either sold up, retired or died, because he ceases to appear on the register. Stone and Wills were still partners however.

After a few more changes in ownership, the *Content* was sold to Guernsey in 1899. Her sister ship, *Ela*, first appears on the books in 1863 and was still on Lloyd's Register in 1937. By then she was described as ex-*Pilot* and had a Parsons engine. She was slightly larger that the *Content* and had a 'round stern'.

With information about the sort of cutter used by Poole pilots so sparse, the author was pleased to discover a letter written by the famous amateur yacht designer, Dr T Harrison Butler to the editor of *The Yachting and Boating Monthly* in the annual for the winter of 1909/10. It concerned the search for a good hull form for a small cruising yacht:

Sir

The correspondence upon this interesting subject has now reached a practical stage; at last yachtsmen are giving the lines of boats which appear to fulfil the conditions of seaworthiness, speed, comfort, and handiness.

I therefore venture to send you the lines of a little ship which I have designed, taking the sketch lines of a Poole pilot-boat by Ashton & Kilner, which you published in May, 1908, as a basis. When I came to lay off this boat to scale I found that the run was rather lean, so I filled it out a little, and even now the curve of sectional areas is not too full aft.

The stem has been drawn out to admit of the 'ideal rig' and the sternpost raked more than in the pilot-boat. Freeboard has been added to.

With these slight alterations the design is substantially that of the Poole boat you published …

T Harrison Butler

Further research and the kind assistance of the staff of *Yachting Monthly* produced the 1908 magazine with the article to which Dr Harrison Butler referred. It describes a yachting interlude at Poole in that year and while it is full of interest, it remains somewhat tantalising on the subject of pilot cutters. It describes in some detail the excellent fishing craft designed and built locally by Ashton and Kilner, and it features a lively drawing of a 'pilot boat at work' in heavy weather. It also carries the lines plan mentioned by Harrison Butler, which is clearly labelled as 'The Poole Boat'. Since this looks remarkably like the one in the pilot-boat drawing, and we know that fishing craft were used by pilots, it seems most likely that Harrison Butler drew the right conclusion. If so, we can safely construe that this, indeed, is the best likeness we shall now find of the elusive Poole pilot cutter.

Poole pilots suffered a number of problems in their days under sail, most of them caused by the exposure of the bar to the southeast. A letter was sent to Trinity House in 1847 complaining that the pilots did not always keep 'watch' at the entrance to the harbour, and it certainly appears that they were understaffed, particularly after the railways opened up the steamer trade with the Channel Islands in 1848. At that time, the sub-commissioners wrote to Trinity House and asked for one extra pilot, which hardly seems enough. One morning in 1860, most

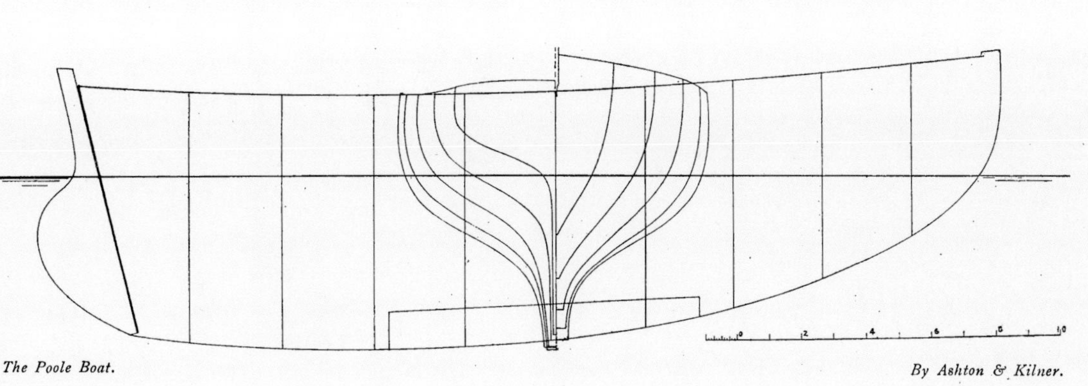

Lines of a Poole pilot boat, c1908

This is the lines plan referred to by Dr Harrison Butler in his letter to the *Yachting and Boating Monthly* of 1909/10. The plan comes from the builders, Ashton and Kilner. It marries up well with the sketch below, showing a transom stern and a potentially weatherly hull for one of such relatively shoal draught with more keel rocker than would normally be found on a working craft. The hollow run begins a long way forward, indicating that speed and sharp handling took precedence over comfort and load carrying. *(Yachting Monthly)*

of them were engaged in taking ships to sea just as a vessel called the *Vivid* arrived signalling for a pilot. The wind was rising from the east and the bar was nasty. The ship waited until she could bide no longer, then ran for shelter in Portland. Whether she found safety there is not clear, but her owners complained to Trinity House about the pilots at Poole.

William King wrote back to Trinity House on behalf of his brother pilots and pointed out the circumstances. He also advised the Elder Brethren that the *Vivid* was noted among them for being tricky to handle and that the solitary small steam tug was engaged elsewhere. The ship was drawing 14ft, which was also the depth on the bar and, in Pilot King's opinion, to have essayed the shallows would have been to court disaster. In his own words, she would have been 'a lost ship'. The final result of this exchange is not on hand, but it seems unlikely that the matter went any further. It is reproduced here to indicate the difficulties pilots often had to face from unreasonable ships' masters and subsequently irate owners.

At this time, Poole pilots had been used to trouble with owners complaining about their watch-keeping for many years. In 1847, a group of owners had written to Trinity House, stating that as a result of the pilots' failure to do their duty, their property was being jeopardised. Anyone who has entered Poole Harbour in hard southeasterly weather understands full well that a pilot cutter simply would not be able to maintain station near the bar. Nor is any shelter to be had in Studland Bay, another obvious place to lie, or further out in Swanage Bay. On this occasion, the merchants and owners were lobbying the Trinity for an extra pilot, a protégé of theirs named William Hixon, to be established as a branch pilot at Swanage. The Bay of Swanage lies close to the main shipping lanes rounding Anvil Point, so it was a possible jumping-off point for Channel pilots, but as a base for Poole pilots, in 40ft sailing boats or smaller, it would hold no advantages over Studland Bay. One hopes for the sake of Pilot Hixon, if he were ever appointed, that he was granted more than his share of westerly weather!

Poole grew steadily with the new century and is now an important port for continental ferries. The old Diver Channel has been dredged, the pilots bustle in and out aboard their motor cutters, and all trace of the sailing boats operated by Pilots Brown, Stone, Wills and their colleagues has disappeared. It is a well-organised scene in which it is hard to imagine the goings-on a mere century ago, when one pilot was so disgusted with a sub-commissioner that he shot him dead.

A Poole pilot cutter working seawards

Information on Poole pilot cutters is scarce, so this drawing from the pages of *The Yachting and Boating Monthly* in the winter of 1909/10 is of prime importance. The boat is beating southwards down the Swash Channel lying between the Hook Sand and the training wall that keeps the channel self-dredged. The fairway lies outside the harbour proper and the stacks seen here are the famous 'Old Harry' rocks. The boat is nowhere near as big as the West-Country pilot cutters of Falmouth and Plymouth, but she has enough weight to work the very rough waters sometimes encountered on Poole Bar when the powerful ebb tide runs in the face of a south-easterly gale. Her transom stern is confirmed by the lines plan above. *(Yachting Monthly)*

CHAPTER 8

Le Havre

IN SPITE OF BRITAIN's undisputable claims to being a great maritime nation, in the area of organised pilotage it does seem that, across the Channel, the French stole a march on their neighbours.

History of the pilotage service

As early as 1517, King François ordered the construction of 'Le Havre de Grâce' by the mouth of the River Seine, because the river-based ports of Honfleur and Harfleur were rapidly silting up. While he was at it, he instructed his architect Jérôme Bellamarto to fortify Le Havre. The most imposing tower was named *La Tour de François Ier*. There, the pilots kept watch, as they do to this day.

François' son, Henri II, carried on the good work and by 1551 was already laying down laws about what was, in effect, compulsory pilotage.

An early fishing/pilot boat

This engraving by Jean-Jérôme Beaugean in his 'Recueil de Petites Marines' of 1817 shows a typical work boat of Le Havre from the days before the great cutters. As her pilot number on the mainsail shows, this one is working officially, but the 18ft lugger could just as well have operated as a Seine Bay fishing boat, of which she is a classic example. (*Valetoux collection*)

> The ship's master, in order to avoid all danger to his crew and cargo, will in all places where it is necessary, take a pilot. If not, he will be punished each time by a fine of 50 'reals' of gold. The pilot will be paid on the merchandise of the shipper and he will be fed by the captain if his wage is not more than 6 Flanders pounds.

In 1556, a full set of rules was drawn up and formalised in *Le Guidon de la Mer*. A short while later came 'Pilot instructions' and *Le Petit Flambeau de la Mer*. This modestly named document was in reality a formidable work, laying down pilotage instructions for the whole coast of France and onwards to the Barbary Coast, down to Cabo Verde in West Africa. It was, in a sense, the ancestor of modern pilot books and sailing directions.

At this early stage, pilots were divided into three categories. The *pilotes hauturiers* were educated men who could navigate not only by coastwise bearings and transits, but were also at home with mathematics and astronomy. Ships' captains were often of noble ancestry or favourites of the King who, knowing nothing of the sea, needed specialist pilots to look after them. By the eighteenth century the captains had regained their status as navigators and these deep-sea pilots were no longer necessary. Their job was eliminated during the revolution. The *pilotes côtières* were recruited for their local knowledge. They worked within sight of land and were often fishermen who knew their job but lacked the status of an officer.

Specialists at bringing ships in and out of port were of the third category, the *lamaneurs*, whose name seems likely to derive from the usual sources of 'lootsman', etc. These manoeuvres could not take place under sail where really big ships were concerned, so the *lamaneurs* organised tow-boats and capstans ashore. As a modern-day Le Havre pilot noted, it was less romantic, but a lot more sure.

As aids to navigation improved, the work of the *pilotes cotières* and the *lamaneurs* came together, but in 1938 the two branches of the profession separated once more. Thereafter, the pilots manoeuvred the ships and the *lamaneurs* handled the ropes. Just as it is today, pilots never replaced a ship's captain. In practice, however, so long as the ships' officers had confidence in him, they were happy for him to give the orders.

In those far-off times, however, their situation was not protected and they were obliged to shoulder full responsibility. Any mistakes were heavily punished. A pilot was rewarded with three years' hard labour if he so much as grounded a ship – all too easily done in these tidal waters – while summary death sentences awaited those adjudged to have acted maliciously. Hangings were to be from a gibbet planted near the wreck, a technique of learning by example later championed by Voltaire, whose character noted that it was just as well to shoot the occasional admiral, *pour encourager les autres*. The practicalities of these executions were not always easy to arrange, especially when a ship stranded on one of the banks associated with the Seine which run well out to sea, but compromise was not encouraged and the legislation remained in force until 1913. Drunkenness was treated more leniently. Records show that any unfortunate *lamaneur* discovered to have taken a glass too many was fined 100 sols and banned from piloting for a month, although the draftsman framing the rules seems not to have been without a certain humanity. He notes that some pilots were well known to be braver after taking a drink or two.

By the time of Louis XIII in the first forty years of the seventeenth century, pilots appear to have abandoned their old ways and become distinctly pious. At this time, the brotherhood of Notre Dame was formed for the men who spent much of the year at the Newfoundland fishing grounds. It allowed Christian burials for those lost at sea. Many of the ships employed deep-sea pilots and in 1662 the archbishop of Rouen authorised the captains, masters and their pilots to process slowly through Le Havre, duly lined up behind the clergy. This ceremony, complete with all possible pomp, banners and sanctified by various masses, was organised on the quay at Epiphany. It was commemorated by a magnificent window, destroyed in 1944 along with a good deal else of Le Havre's history. All these men were highly religious, perhaps encouraged in their faith by the fact that few of them could swim.

This tendency to godliness was mirrored at sea. Whether he liked it or not, a boarding pilot was obliged to recite, 'Captain, after God, I take command of this ship, and with the help of Notre Dame and Ste Anne, I will bring you to a safe harbour …' No doubt many a deep-sea skipper running in with a hard westerly wind astern was more grateful for the reassuring presence of the pilot himself than for the promise of divine assistance.

Napoleon's administration liked to see things cut and dried. On 12 December 1806, a decree was signed at Potsdam in Germany, where Napoleon was running the show at the time, which tied down the organisation of the pilots, their licensing and examinations, their wages, their taxes and the rules of the service. Also laid out in this instrument were a formalised list of punishments which were less severe than of yore, a statement of the head pilot's duties and responsibilities, and a system for dealing with retiring pilots and bringing on their replacements. This must have been well-drafted

A pilot lugger of the 1840s

The luggers doing pilot service at Le Havre by the 1840s were substantially heavier than their earlier counterparts. The one seen in this engraving from Antoine Morel-Fatio (1810–1871) is a highly capable vessel. During the hundred years spanning the eighteenth century, the French developed uniquely fast luggers for warlike and smuggling purposes which led the British naval and revenue cutters many a merry dance. The technology was used for the phenomenal bisquine oyster luggers of West Normandy and doubtless it spilled over into the pilot boats also. However, a lugger was less handy than a cutter and had the general limitation of requiring more hands to sail to her full potential. Shortly after this picture was produced, cutters gained the ascendancy. (*From* Les Clippers Français)

'Souvenir du Havre'

The cutter in this early twentieth-century postcard is the *Marie-Madeleine* H25, built in 1890 by Le Marchand for Pilot Picard. The fact that she has been chosen for this postcard on sale to the general public is a strong indication of how the pilot boat had become symbolic of the relationship between the city and the sea. (*Valetoux collection*)

legislation because it stuck until 1928 when a different world finally recognised that it was out of date.

Napoleon didn't stop at whipping the pilots into line. He also poured money into developing Le Havre so that it would rival the great ports of neighbouring countries and make a serious profit for France. He made a good start. Soon, the industrial revolution, the railways, and steam at sea brought his dream into powerful reality. Meanwhile, the pilots were organising themselves in areas where it really mattered, and from 1812 they developed a pension scheme and an insurance for widows by tossing 5 centimes out of every franc they earned into their mutual savings account. Retirement age was set among themselves at sixty.

By 1850, the pilots of Le Havre had developed into as fine a body of seamen as existed, disciplined not only by the sea itself, but also by the regulations and hierarchy that were now accepted and firmly in place. At around this time Frédéric de Coninck, one of the biggest local merchants, wrote:

Nowhere are the pilots better organised than at Havre. They number 48 in total, with a further 12 cadets. In addition, 100 *lamaneurs* crew the pilot boats and the '*barques d'aide*' (hobbler's boats) which assist ships by retrieving and supplying anchors in the avant-port (outer harbour) or the roads. The service has 20 beautifully constructed and fitted-out boats, capable of keeping the sea in all weathers. A Chief Pilot chosen from among the senior pilots or captains is in charge of the details of the service, reporting to the Harbourmaster.

Since 1855, the limits of cruising for pilot cutters are the Meridian of the Casquets in the west, to that of Dungeness in the east. The pilots provide a watchman, or duty pilot, from sunrise to sunset on the François I Tower. Four *lamaneurs* are also on hand to assist him, should any ship want help. A fierce, but paternal, discipline is meted out by the

An early pilot cutter

This painting by Joseph Frédéric Roux (1805–1870), depicts the American ship *Solon*, built 1834, hailing her pilot off Le Havre on 29 May 1847. Note the lug topsail on this early cutter, and the mainsail triced up to take off way and to give the helmsman a better view ahead. (*Peabody Museum, Salem*)

Le Havre Regatta, 1841

Two races are in progress in this lively scene, one about to start, and the other finishing. The rowing craft are whale boats from the many whaleships which used the port at this time, and the luggers are pilot boats. They are running in past Cap de la Hève on the prevailing westerly wind setting every stitch they can find. Note the booming-out poles rigged on both sides, and the lugger in the foreground dropping her sails, presumably after being first home. (*Valetoux collection*)

harbourmaster on the pilots and *lamaneurs* and he only allows sober and honourable men. As a result, there is almost never any problem between captains and pilots. The sort of attempted violence by pilots on the ships' captains that is frequently encountered in England [*sic*] simply does not happen at Le Havre.

The price of piloting is proportionate to the distance and tonnage of the vessel. 13 cents in the Petite Rade, 26 cents up to 21 miles, 39 cents for more than 42 miles. The tonnage of vessels is only going to increase and that will be good for the pilots. However, the question of whether or not the pilotage tariff applied to very big ships isn't becoming exaggerated must soon be addressed in the interests of commerce.

Marie-Madeleine arrives home

Sailing into the Avant Port, *Marie Madeleine* is snugged down for a strong breeze with a reef in her main, the tack triced up a foot or so, and a small jib to balance her. It is interesting to note that her punt is chocked off upside down. This makes obvious sense for a vessel that is facing heavy weather, for a punt full of water is liable to damage, and so much weight on deck represents a compromise to stability. Yet Bristol Channel cutters, similar in so many ways, invariably carried theirs 'right way up' for ease of launch and recovery. In order to gain a two-fold purchase, her jib sheets are rove through full-sized blocks at the clew, rather than the more usual bullseyes.
(*Valetoux collection*)

Early in this quote, de Coninck mentions officially recognised hobblers performing much the same service with anchors and salvage as was carried out by the men of Deal in the Downs anchorage off Kent, as well as off Lowestoft and Great Yarmouth. All these roadsteads are vulnerable to winds from certain directions. The English ones are open to the east, Le Havre to the west. The offlying anchorages at Le Havre are clearly no place for a pure sailing vessel in a northwesterly gale, even today. Many must have been either driven ashore or obliged to cut and run, leaving their ground tackle behind. If they wanted to see their expensive anchors and cable again, their only choices on returning for it were to retrieve it themselves, or bargain with a hobbler who had already dredged it up.

In the Second Empire, the tower of François Ier was demolished and replaced by a modern semaphore which stood until 1904. The restrictive practice of 'choice pilotage' also began to rise at this time, as steamship lines with their predictable scheduling started to gain the ascendancy. By now, each pilot owned his own boat crewed by a skipper known as the *patron*, a *lamaneur* and a *mousse* (cabin boy or 'nipper'). The crew worked as a highly motivated team, so that the speed of the boat and her qualities of manoeuvring were used to the best advantage when boarding the boss onto the biggest, best-paying ships.

Changes in the port at the end of the nineteenth and beginning of the twentieth century were all good news for the pilots. In 1898, breakwaters were finally built to protect the port from the eternal Channel swells. A new semaphore was erected and, perhaps best of all, a berth for transatlantic liners and a big dry dock were dug. The benefits of these improvements and the development of such supreme examples of the pilot cutter as Paumelle's 1913 *Jolie Brise* enjoyed only the briefest day in the sun, however. The end of seeking pilotage under sail took place in Le Havre, as in so many places, at the time of World War I. After hoisting her pilot flag on 8 December, it was all over by the following August, and on 1 November she was commandeered by the Navy. All the cutters were called in as 1914 ran its terrible course and the pilots' expertise was pooled to assist convoys running between northern France and Southampton.

The pilots and their lives

Perhaps a suitable introduction to the Le Havre pilots themselves might be an extract from the diary of the Princess Langsdorff, returning from Brazil in 1843 with her husband who had been ambassador of the court of King Louis-Philippe. They had shipped aboard the frigate *Belle Poule*. An interesting footnote is that this same ship had carried Napoleon's remains back to France from St Helena in 1840. It would be satisfying to conclude that the dates have become muddled and that this account is of the closing stages of that historic voyage, but it cannot be. The hero's remains were actually landed in Cherbourg and only came on to Le Havre later in a steamer, thence upstream to Paris. The Prince Joinville was certainly aboard *Belle Poule* for the repatriation, but it was a different trip.

> We heard the gun. My husband Emile came to tell us that they were signalling for the pilot. All eyes were fixed on Ushant. After 5 minutes, a second shot was fired and we continued going. A further five minutes later, a small white sail appeared on the horizon and we heard, 'There's the pilot.'
>
> The Princess Joinville and I leaned as far out as possible to hear the conversation between *Belle Poule* and this little craft, but she was so far below us and the waves roared so much that the words were carried away on the wind and we could hardly hear them.
>
> 'Will you take command of this vessel?'
>
> 'Under God I will take it,' replied the pilot, pronouncing the words religiously. Then he climbed up. Shortly afterward we saw him on the poop beside the prince who stepped aside to allow him to take his place in the middle of the poop. I can't described the emotion and the respect I felt for this 'brave marin'. There was something so simple, so dignified, so lacking in pomposity about him, while there was something grand in his bearing and the tone of his voice.
>
> He had no spyglass, nor any instrument whatever, and he left his little ship which seemed so miserable and came on our bridge which was like a palace. He didn't appear either astonished or upset.
>
> I saw him take a ribbon from his pocket, attached to a small painting of the Virgin. When he was on the bridge, he said to the prince.
>
> 'Sir, we've been waiting for you for three days and nights. We only brought a bit of cheese to eat, my crew are famished. Would it be possible for you to give them something?'
>
> The order was quickly given. I saw the little boat which was dancing up and down still tied to the frigate by ropes, and seeing her I thought with dread, 'Three days and three nights.' Yes, all this time, these four men have been tossing around on the high seas.
>
> Somebody asked the pilot if he'd like something to eat and drink before taking up the command of the boat, but he said,'Later, when we've got the anchor down.'

The golden age of pilotage

As was the case for British pilots in the Bristol and English Channels, expanding trade, steamships, superior cutters, and organisations that allowed pilots to use their initiative led to a golden age of pilotage between the middle of the nineteenth century and the outbreak of World War I. Pilotage for all French ports had begun centuries earlier with fishermen keeping a weather eye open for the main chance. These were men who could not read a chart even had one been available, much less a compass, but they knew the coast by heart, both the sea marks and the depths. They also knew the underwater contours which they called 'the stairways of the Channel' and could use them to navigate in dense fog using a deep-sea leadline armed with tallow to bring up a sample of the bottom. What stuck to the tallow might confirm or discard a location where depth alone could confer an ambiguous result.

Coming home in fair weather

Marie-Madeleine, H25, sailing into the outer harbour in full dress. She is holding all her canvas until the last minute, suggesting that the pilot is anxious to be home. The halyard and crane for the night-lights can be clearly seen below the masthead, and the rope fendering used to protect both cutter and punt while launching the small boat makes an interesting feature rarely seen in contemporary photographs. *(Valetoux collection)*

Back in 1560, fishermen were acting as pilots, and vice versa. These were the working pilots of the port. At the same period, the King regained a number of dedicated pilots whose job was to look after the King's ships and no other. Even those who had achieved a certain standard of education were still considered seamen, frustrated that they did not have the status of officers. However the pilots gained in expertise and standing until, by the nineteenth century, the final flowering of the trade bloomed with glorious cutters and famous men.

By 1890, the port employed around forty

Summer in Le Havre

Pilot cutters alongside at the Quai des Casernes in the Bassin du Roi at Le Havre. This was the preferred berth because the basin, snug inside its tide gates, maintained a constant depth. The topmasts hoisted up to the fid, and sails drying in the sunshine, suggest that this is summer. H22 in the foreground is taking the opportunity to air her trysail that has probably been too long stowed away wet. The boats and their crews are taking it easy as they await their pilots' orders. *(Valetoux collection)*

permanent, qualified pilots and a dozen cadets who shared the work as follows:

The *Petit Métier* covered an area between Fécamp and Ouistreham.

The *Métier du Nord* went from Dunkirk to Dover.

The *Métier de l'Ouest*, also known as the *Grand Métier*, was limited only by a line from Land's End to Ushant, but in heavy weather a cutter would often *demanche* (literally 'de-Channel'), or go over the line by sixty miles or more. Some undoubtedly 'demanched' deliberately to seek ships, even though this was expressly forbidden. Some justification was offered by the established fact that at the end of a long passage, a captain making landfall in thick weather who had not seen the sky for a week or more to take a position fix, had no way of knowing where he was. Add a degree or three of compass error, a chronometer that could easily have gone unchecked for ninety days, the 50ft tides and 10kt streams in the Bay of St Malo, and we find a man who needs a pilot more than a flower needs rain.

This liberty to plough up and down the Channel, effectively without limits, was often queried, and

Painting of *Eole*

A quite primitive depiction by the artist Eugène Grandin of *Eole*, H22, setting out to cruise in fair weather. *Eole* was built by Le Marchand in 1888 for Pilots Boudin and Viel. She was decommissioned on 20 August 1914 and sold to Belgium in 1917. *(Valetoux collection)*

Home berth

The Quai des Casernes around 1900 with the celebrated Hotel Suisse on the right. In the foreground is the machinery for the tidal gates and a capstan for manoeuvring ships. In the background is a fine yacht which may well be a visitor from across the Channel with the hull shape of an earlier day. By this time the spoon bow of the King's G L Watson-designed *Britannia* had replaced the plumb-stemmed fashion of the mid nineteenth century. Who the urchins are will forever remain unclear, but they give this lovely picture a distinctly French edge.
(*Valetoux collection*)

the suggestion that pilots only looked for the big ships and ignored the little ones must often have had more than a grain of truth in it. From the shipowner's and the harbourmaster's point of view, a further downside to the free-cruising arrangement was an old, old story so familiar to London pilotage authorities. Despite the 'screen' of cruising cutters fanned out to the east, north and west, ships still managed somehow to arrive off Le Havre having slipped through the loose-woven web. In 1855, new limits were set between the Casquets and Portland in the west, and the meridian of Dungeness in the east. This was not a success, because it kept the cutters nearer the land and forced ships to steam into dangerous waters before boarding a pilot. Three high-profile shipwrecks, the *Stella,* the *Chatillon* and the *Jean-Goujon,* spurred shipowners and their insurers to demand a change. Once again the pilots were given leave to rove the Channel as far as they wanted.

A further example of ministerial meddling at this time laid regulations on the pilots to alternate every ten days between inshore and offshore work. This didn't work either, for the simple reason that it ignored the psychology of the seeking pilot. As Pierre-Henri Marin, whose forebears had been '*patrons*' of pilot cutters, put it, 'You don't ask birds of the ocean to stay on their nests for ages.' The rule was adjusted in 1897 when the pilots were divided into sixteen groups of three. On twenty consecutive days they could alternate between being at sea and keeping inshore. The head pilot always had two qualified men at his disposal. The other fourteen could go where they wanted.

Unlike many pilot stations throughout Europe and the rest of the world, where a pilot stranded on board a departing ship had to make the best of his lot, in Le Havre the results of this thankfully uncommon mishap were mitigated by regulation. When a ship left with a pilot on board, the captain had to make sure the pilot could disembark, and a boat followed the ship out for that reason. A pilot might also arrange to meet with his cutter, perhaps much further afield, but if all failed and he couldn't get off he was considered an officer at the disposal of the captain. Even if he ended up in New York, he was paid 150 francs a month for his trouble until he could be repatriated.

Between 1866 and 1896, records indicate that an average piloting rate over the course of six months was ninety-two ships. At four ships per week, that is a snappy work rate. The record-holder was Pilot Louis Guerrier, whose luck, fuelled by enterprise and sheer hard work, saw him boarding 139. To encourage competition, the Chamber of Commerce organised a financial incentive for the three pilots who assisted the most ships.

Mistakes were still made, of course, some of them serious, but by the 1800s, the immediate execution of pilots, aboard or close to the wrecks over which they had presided, had been replaced by more humane retribution. In 1855, for example, Pilot Charles Guerrier was banned for two months for running a British ship aground in the Petite Rade of Le Havre. Most of the punishments meted out to pilots, however, resulted from commercial decisions made in contravention of the regulations. The usual form was for a cutter to 'fail to see' a smaller ship because her eyes were averted in her search for a much bigger one. The penalty for this popular crime was a fine. Another common source of annoyance to the authorities was when a reckless pilot pushed his luck over the restricted times for entering harbour. At this period, a pilot had only about three hours' safe operating per tide. If he were caught trying to bring in a ship much beyond this limit, suspension awaited him.

Returning to port

Hirondelle, H28, returns to port with everything set. The mainsail is well triced up to improve visibility while the boat enters an area of heavy traffic. The 'girt' across the mainsail is caused by the topping lift which has been set up early to make for one job less when it all starts happening very shortly. *Hirondelle* was built by the brothers Paumelle in 1894 for Pilot Durécu. She was sold to La Rochelle in 1921 and passed to the Ile de Groix a year later. Her transom board has been preserved for the Le Havre pilots of today. (*Valetoux collection*)

On a brighter note, recognition of bravery in the form of medals outweighed the fines. The awards were not always for such obvious acts of courage as taking survivors off a sinking ship and, in 1895, Pilot Prosper Pileur of the *Charles-Héloïse* (No 17) noted what must have been a unique event. An early gas balloon had drifted out over the sea, to ditch a dozen miles off Cap de la Hève. Pilot Pileur was alone on board with his *mousse*, but the pair did not hesitate. Despite the real danger of explosion, they brought the cutter alongside the wreck and rescued two extremely wet aeronauts.

The money and the office

Remuneration for Le Havre pilots was good, but the winnings were not so generous as those enjoyed by successful men in the Bristol Channel, whose work and lives were comparable in many ways.

The *mousse* earned 25 francs a month, then 30 to 35 after six months. He was the only one who received a fixed salary; all the others were paid on a share basis.

After paying the lad, the cutter's gross revenue was divided into six shares. Four went to the pilot, which he generally divided into half for him and half for the cutter. The *patron* received one share; so did the *matelot* or *lamaneur*, which speaks well for the respect in which these able seamen were held. When, as sometimes happened, the *matelot* was replaced by a couple of young novices they were known as a *demi-lot* and each received half the pay of the *matelot*.

The cutter's total take depended entirely on how many ships she had managed to board, and how profitable they were. Pilotage fees were based on tonnage and the distance from home. Three tariffs were in place during the golden age. The first was for ships brought in from further than forty-two miles, the second from a limit of twenty-one miles, the third for vessels already in the roads. The bottom line varied from 0.19 francs per ton to 0.06.

Swallows of the Channel

A souvenir postcard commemorating *les hirondelles de la Manche* (swallows of the Channel). The nickname probably came about because of the black hulls with white bulwark strakes, the white sails and the way they seemed to dance upwind. Whatever the reason, the name stuck fast. *La Charité*, H31, seen here towing her punt, was built in 1903 by Paumelle for Pilot Mérieult. She was sold out of the service to become the yacht *Lucy* in 1911.
(Valetoux collection)

These dues were taken by a collector in the pilot office on the Grand Quai opposite the Hotel Continental. In addition to supplying all the administrative backup and general governance of pilotage, the office housed the chief pilot, supplied a mess with a basic bedroom for the duty pilot and, in the back, maintained a section specifically for the *lamaneurs.* Like the homes of some of the more advanced pilots in the Bristol Channel, the Le Havre pilot office boasted a telephone.

The life of a pilot: the *mousse*

From the moment the *mousse* signed on a cutter at the age of twelve, his day went something like this:

Out of the bunk at 0345 to light the stove, which was tricky in bad weather or with the wind from astern. Prepare coffee for the change of watch, then back to bed until 0600. Up again to clean the boat quietly so as not to wake any sleepers. Next, he cooked breakfast – a mess of eggs, spuds, or soup in winter. Mackerel in summer. Then, if not wanted on deck, wash up, polish the brass, prepare vegetables and make lunch. More washing up. In the afternoon he was on deck learning his job – the compass, chartwork, plotting a course and knots and splices.

An older pilot cutter goes seeking

Shortly before 1900 *Saint François*, H34, built in 1872 by Crandalle Brothers, sails out of Le Havre to commence a seeking cruise. So far as one can see, the hull has fairly bluff lines, which is to be expected of a cutter built at that time. Her sails are showing signs of age too, but the huge jib is of particular interest. Such sails are never seen in photographs of comparable Bristol Channel boats, perhaps because they are notoriously difficult to sheet close-hauled, often creating more drag than lift, but they appear to have been commonplace in Le Havre. The pilot is at the helm in his waistcoat and white shirt.
(Valetoux collection)

Coming home in a stiff breeze

Beating into the harbour under short canvas around 1890, *Charles-Héloïse,* H17, makes a fine sight. She has two reefs in her mainsail, the tack is triced up and she is setting a small jib which is just starting to luff as the *patron* shoves the helm down for a tack. The punt is seen inverted on deck, confirming that this was the preferred method of stowing the boat. H17 was built in 1884 at Cherbourg by the Bienvenu yard for Pilot Prosper Pileur. *(Valetoux collection)*

As if this wasn't more than enough, he was also in charge of the deep-sea lead which weighed 8kg. Sometimes, this had to be hove in depths of over 120m to find the deep trench north-northwest of Alderney and Guernsey, or off the Triagoz which were principal boarding points for the pilots on the French side of the central Channel. He was also obliged to learn the nature of the bottom from what the lead brought up in the blob of tallow in a recess in its lower face. Handling a leadline is a miserable business when it goes on for more than a few minutes. The lead gets heavier and heavier, the boat seems always to be going too fast to swing the lead far enough ahead to achieve a true sounding as she sails over it, while the water running off the line as it is coiled back aboard soaks the poor sailor, first to the elbow, then to the armpit and finally to the bottoms of his seaboots – no fun on a freezing night. The job certainly put muscles on the lads, especially around those deeps off the Casquets. The *mousse* would be interrogated on depths at the end of each day by the skipper or the pilot. If he was wrong he'd get a taste of a rope's end for his trouble or, if his luck was really out, he'd be awarded the graveyard watch from midnight to 0400.

Dinner had to be served up at exactly 1800. Then it was back to the dishes. By 2000 everything had to be squared away and shipshape, with the fire made ready to be lit in the morning.

Pilots' examinations

Despite this gruelling schedule, learning on the job had its advantages, and many a *mousse* eventually made the grade to become a pilot. In 1896 the minimum age for qualification was twenty-four,

Dried out with all hands present

Like all sailors, the crew of *La Joyeuse,* H14, are making sure their vessel performs as she should by keeping her bottom clean. Dried out for a scrub-off on the grid in Calais they are grabbing their chance between ships. Close inspection of the bulwarks forward reveals that the various items of headgear are all led aboard neatly via eyes set in exactly the right places. The anchor chain is ranged on deck on the side nearest to the wall to ensure the boat lists inwards as she takes the ground. *La Joyeuse* was built in 1873 for Pilot Auguste Guerrier from one of the great pilot dynasties of Le Havre. Also on board is Fernand Guerrier who has signed the card. *(Valetoux collection)*

with no upper age limit. Also required were six years' sea-time on merchant or naval ships, enrolment in the maritime district, and a pass in an exam which included both written and oral sections. After 1896, six months at sea on a commercial steam ship of more than 500 tons was required, plus six months on sailing ships over 300 tons.

The examiners were a local administrator, a ship's officer, two captains, and two pilots. The president was a naval officer to ensure that no favouritism was shown. The candidate had to know the details of the French coast from Cap Gris-Nez to Ushant perfectly. He also required a working knowledge of the whole Channel coast of England. In spite of all that, candidates still showed up who had never practised in Le Havre Roads, so they were also put through a further 'oral' based on what the candidates could actually see out of the window. A bright applicant could second-guess what these were likely to be and would then learn the replies by heart. Most potential pilots had started as a *mousse*, often on their family's boat, and they didn't have to cheat to get the examiners on-side, but a good result was still far from guaranteed. The written exam comprised maths and spelling, which many who had been at sea as *mousse* rather than attending school hadn't had the time or inclination to study.

Just as it was in many other countries, being a Le Havre pilot ran in families, and veritable dynasties such as Guerrier, Biard, Prentout and Bonzans keep cropping up in the records. Coming from a long line of pilots, having a physical aptitude, an unimpeachable knowledge of the coasts and a rock-solid grasp of the rules of navigation inclined the jury to leniency, even if the spelling left something to be desired, yet injustices were still done. One Jean Saliou's coastal know-how astonished the jury, but his academic prowess fell so short that he could scarcely write. His wife drafted his own pilotage notes under his dictation, but the couple's honest efforts were to no avail and he was failed. It was, notes M Marin, a shame that such a man was brushed aside, although further research has revealed that his grandfather and great uncle had suffered the same fate.

Once a successful candidate had received a letter signed by the Minister of the Marine, he could wear a small silver anchor in his buttonhole or on his watch chain. With his licence in his pocket, a likely young man who was qualified but lacked the funds

A model in frame

This magnificent model of a Le Havre pilot cutter was made at the end of the twentieth century. It is a generic form but looking at the thrilling lines, especially aft, it is impossible not to conclude that it was inspired by *Jolie Brise*. (*Valetoux collection*)

At the helm

Engaved by Bonquart for *Le Journal des voyages* No 406 of 11 September 1904, this image offers a good deal of interesting detail. The *patron*, Müller, is at the helm of *La Fauvette*, H6, in heavy weather, which he has described as a 'maritime cake-walk'. The mainsail is neatly furled on the boom, which is secured not only by the mainsheet, but also an extra line led down to leeward to hold it rigid. The sheet alone can never do this, as some degree of triangulation is required. The trysail is set loose-footed with its clew held by three-part sheet tackles, one either side. Surprisingly, bearing in mind the solid water coming aboard, the companionway is wide open. Less surprising is the fact that the *patron* is using a relieving line on the tiller. This was standard practice on all tiller-steered working craft and most yachts of any size.
(*Valetoux collection*)

as yet to buy his own boat, would sign on with an established pilot. It was a standing joke in the service that men with the best-looking daughters attracted the likeliest young pilots as their 'number two', while those with less well-favoured offspring sailed alone.

Pilots ashore

Most of the pilots lived near the port, south of the Rue de la Mailleraye in old Le Havre. They rented properties in the Rue du Perrey, Rue Augustin-Normand and the Quai des Etats-Unis, rarely buying, because success in business depended on having a fast, seaworthy cutter. The boat was everything, so, perhaps despite voluble protestations from some of the wives, that is where their money went.

A pilot was not allowed to take days off without written permission. If he did, he might well suffer eight days in prison or the withdrawal of his vital certificate. He was also obliged to survey the rivers, anchorages and port entrances on a daily basis when not at sea, reporting changes in depth, buoyage or channel variations. Duties also included salvaging unbuoyed anchors, which had to be declared to the authorities within twenty-four hours. In the moon's first quarter, the pilots joined forces with the choice pilot responsible for the ocean liners – the so-called 'transatlantic pilot' – to check the depths in the harbour.

All in all, a pilot's life was considerably restricted by his profession, but when he did take a lay day he made the most of it, strolling with his family along the Rue de Paris, or on the boulevard with a new woollen black hat, wearing a blue suit and yellow shoes, taking great care to show that this was his 'mufti' rig and not his uniform. Across his waistcoat, perhaps covering an ample stomach, would stretch his watch chain and hanging from this was always the silver anchor symbolising his profession. The chain fob would also have his gold watch, usually with his initials engraved on the case. In his pockets were silver cases for his matches and toothpicks.

It's usually an indication of good morale in a service when people are given nicknames. Le Havre pilots were no exception to this, and nicknames abounded. Pilot Roze was called *Le Dératisateur* because he chain-ate garlic. Rats apparently hate the smell, and his cutter was never troubled in this respect. Pilot Saliou was *L'Ouaro*, the gull, because of his rolling gait; Pilot Rolland, who never said a word unless it was absolutely necessary, was known as *Le Muet*. Pilot Berest was the *Roi des Huns* because of his habit of beginning every sentence with '*Hein, hein*'. Auguste Guerrier found himself with the nickname, *Père Canard* because he was always calling people, '*Mon canard*'. Another member of the Guerrier dynasty, Charles, was of so pleasant a disposition that everyone knew who you meant if you referred to *Le Marquis des Belles Croquette* on account of his beaming smile.

At sea on the cutters

Being a commercial vessel, a pilot's cutter either worked or lost money, so his days of promenading with his wife were few and far between. Back at sea, he was in charge again. He and his colleagues enjoyed a monopoly which left ships no choice but to call on their services or to recompense them if they chose not to do so. If a captain hired an unlicensed fisherman, for example, he would have to pay him off if a pilot turned up, leaving the chancer with a free ride home, but no pay for his trouble. In times very different from our own, where men were born to a hard life and expected to work long hours for little reward, achieving the status of a Le Havre pilot would seem to have been one of the local waterfront's happier occupations, yet still there was a general shortage of licensed men because the administration limited the number of licences for reasons of quality control. As the pilots no doubt observed, 'Less pilots, more trips.'

The cutters were tools of the trade for pilots who worked for themselves and were paid by the owners of ships they brought in. This 'every-man-for-himself' modus operandi led to an enormous sense of freedom and also to great rivalries which ensured that the boats were maintained like racing yachts. For those who opted to go west, being first at the Lizard was vital. A pilot choosing to seek ships coming down-Channel was best served by being in the vicinity of Dungeness before anyone else leaving Le Havre at the same time.

A boat's turn at sea could run for fifty days, whatever the weather. Once a pilot had boarded a ship he took her up to Le Havre then, if another were waiting for him, he would come down on her to meet his cutter at some predetermined position. Failing the certainty of an outbound ship, he might tell his crew to go to a port far down the pilot route, then he himself might take land transport after bringing in the ship, meeting his cutter as far away as Brest or Aber Wrac'h. Occasionally he would even ship out on a ferry and join his men in Falmouth. Just like a Bristol Channel pilot, he would find out from Lloyd's or a local paper when the most likely ships were due. Some had arrangements with shipping company clerks who might slip them the wink, and no doubt other sidelines were in full swing to keep one man ahead of another. As soon as he knew what was coming, a pilot would telegraph to his skipper and be on his way. Albert Guerrier, who was *mousse* on board his brother's cutter, remembers that he would cable 'dinghy to the station' if an expected ship was particularly urgent. 'We went directly to find Fernand straight off the train and as soon as he leapt over the rail we left for the Channel …'

Fine dining aboard

Whether preparing for one of these long voyages, or while the cutter was in harbour between one ship and another, the *mousse* did the shopping. He was also the cook, which wasn't so enjoyable a task in hard weather when he was sometimes to be found soldiering bravely on, getting no sympathy, with a sick bucket between his feet.

Meat would be laid on for three days only in summer, because it wouldn't keep for longer. There was roasted sirloin steak, boiled beef, and a stew. They always ate the boiled beef first and Joseph Vatinel, to whom we are indebted for the following recollections on gastronomy aboard, recalls that once he got it the wrong way round and boiled the beef that was meant for roasting. When he roasted the stewing beef it was tough and the pilot stormed into the butcher's shop in the Rue Faidherbe when they returned and tore him off a strip. The wretched *mousse* confessed his crime ten years later as a *lamaneur*, but nobody believed him. The butcher's name was still mud.

When the meat was all gone, the crews turned to eggs, salt fish and, when even these dubious delights were exhausted, they settled for ship's biscuit. The bread, although baked specially for pilots, soon

The wreck of the cutter *Fellow*

An illustration by Bonquart taken from the *Journal des Voyages et des Aventures de Terre et de Mer* 1904. It depicts the wreck of the pilot cutter *Fellow*, overwhelmed by an extraordinary storm. Three men were lost but the *mousse* and another youngster were saved. The detail of what remains of the cutter's foredeck is beautifully portrayed.
(Author's collection)

became hard and mouldy, so *le sac du pilote* was always welcome. This was a sort of 'goodie-bag' which some shipping companies traditionally gave to the cutter when the pilot boarded. It contained fresh bread, cheese, sometimes fruit, wine and a bottle of *goutte*. This was a spirit of the Calvados genre, made in backyard stills with a 50 per cent content of the magic ingredient. After a week or so on ship's biscuit and board-hard salt fish near the end of its tether, the *patron*, the *lamaneur*, and the long-suffering *mousse* may well have needed it. The bag prepared aboard the ships of the Chargeurs Réunis company was the favourite, with four loaves of bread, 3kg of green coffee, sardines, two bottles of wine, two bottles of tafia and an Old Amsterdam Dutch cheese in a round, as famous for its longevity as the same product is today aboard far-ranging yachts lacking refrigeration.

While the meat was still good, the big moment came at midday. In the evenings there was vegetable soup with *graisse de Cherbourg*, which is old-fashioned beef dripping, boiled with the vegetables to give them more body. The bought-in victuals were often augmented by 'a bit of fishing'. In those days, mackerel were more prolific in the Channel than they are today, and fresh fish was a good boost for morale. Anyone who has trolled for these lively shoals knows well that the waiting diner is invariably treated either to a feast or a famine. On a good day, far more would be caught than could be eaten by four hungry men, but, being French, nothing went to waste. Any fish not eaten fresh were pickled in brine, laid on the dinghy to dry, liberally peppered, and taken home to appreciative wives as a delicacy. Another mackerel recipe was to boil the fish in salt water with onions and parsley. The flesh

Fauvette

The classic pilot boat featured in the account by Bonquart which is so rich a resource into how life was lived on the Le Havre cutters. *(Painting oil on board by Dominique Perotin)*

fell off the bones and in summer the resulting soup was a favourite alternative to the ubiquitous vegetable broth. Aboard *Espérance* (No 37), a system had been devised for netting the more difficult herring. Lunch following a good catch was boiled herring and potatoes, cider or coffee.

Perhaps the final word on these inventive diners should be left with young Vatinel. He reports that, after victualling in Penzance following the boarding of their pilot, the crew treated themselves to a 'full English breakfast'. Inexplicably, the fragrant bacon and sizzling eggs failed to hit the spot with these sons of the sea, and in future they always referred to the meal derisively as 'brave steak'.

At sea aboard the *Fauvette*

The pilots didn't keep a log book, so day-to-day details of life on board would have been hard to find but for the work of a man called Bonquart, a painter and writer. Bonquart produced a series of articles for the *Journal des Voyages et des Aventures de Terre et de Mer*, published in 1904. He shipped out aboard the cutter *Fauvette* as a supernumerary shortly after a fifteen-year-old *mousse* and a young crewman had been rescued from the pilot boat *Fellow*, overwhelmed by a hurricane-force wind. The other three on board were lost, and Bonquart provides a dramatic representation of the rescue in his artwork. A sailor studying this will be much the wiser concerning the detail of the foredecks of these cutters in their working days.

As to his own trip, Bonquart's first-hand account supplies a rich source of atmosphere as well as hard fact. He and his shipmates sail from Le Havre on the morning tide with a perfect sailing breeze and a long swell from the west. He writes in the present

A unique rescue

This unusual painting commemorates the life-saving efforts of Pilot Prosper Pileur with his cutter *Charles-Héloïse*, H17, and her bold crew. Two aeronauts were saved in this idiosyncratically French operation. (*Valetoux collection*)

Lines and plans of *Henriette-Marie*

The *Henriette-Marie*, H2, was launched in 1847. She worked as a pilot cutter in Le Havre until 1890. H2's lines show an early form of classic pilot cutter. The waterlines indicate an uncompromising cod's head and mackerel tail design, while her convex midships section spells out notably heavy displacement. The deep forefoot would confer excellent sea-keeping characteristics, but would have the effect of making her relatively unhandy on the helm in a tight situation. Her near-vertical sternpost would offset this to some extent by placing the rudder as far aft as possible so as to maximise turning effort when compared with the more sporty, raked sternposts of later years. The stern itself is more of a lute stern than the genuine counter which appeared as development continued. The rig is, as one would expect, a simple gaff cutter, whose lug topsail exactly concurs with the one set by the pilots in the illustration (page 103) showing the arrival at Le Havre of the American ship *Solon* in the year of H2's launch. The letters on the mainsail in this image confirm the cutter as *Henriette-Marie* herself, perhaps picking up one of her first paying jobs. *(Author's collection)*

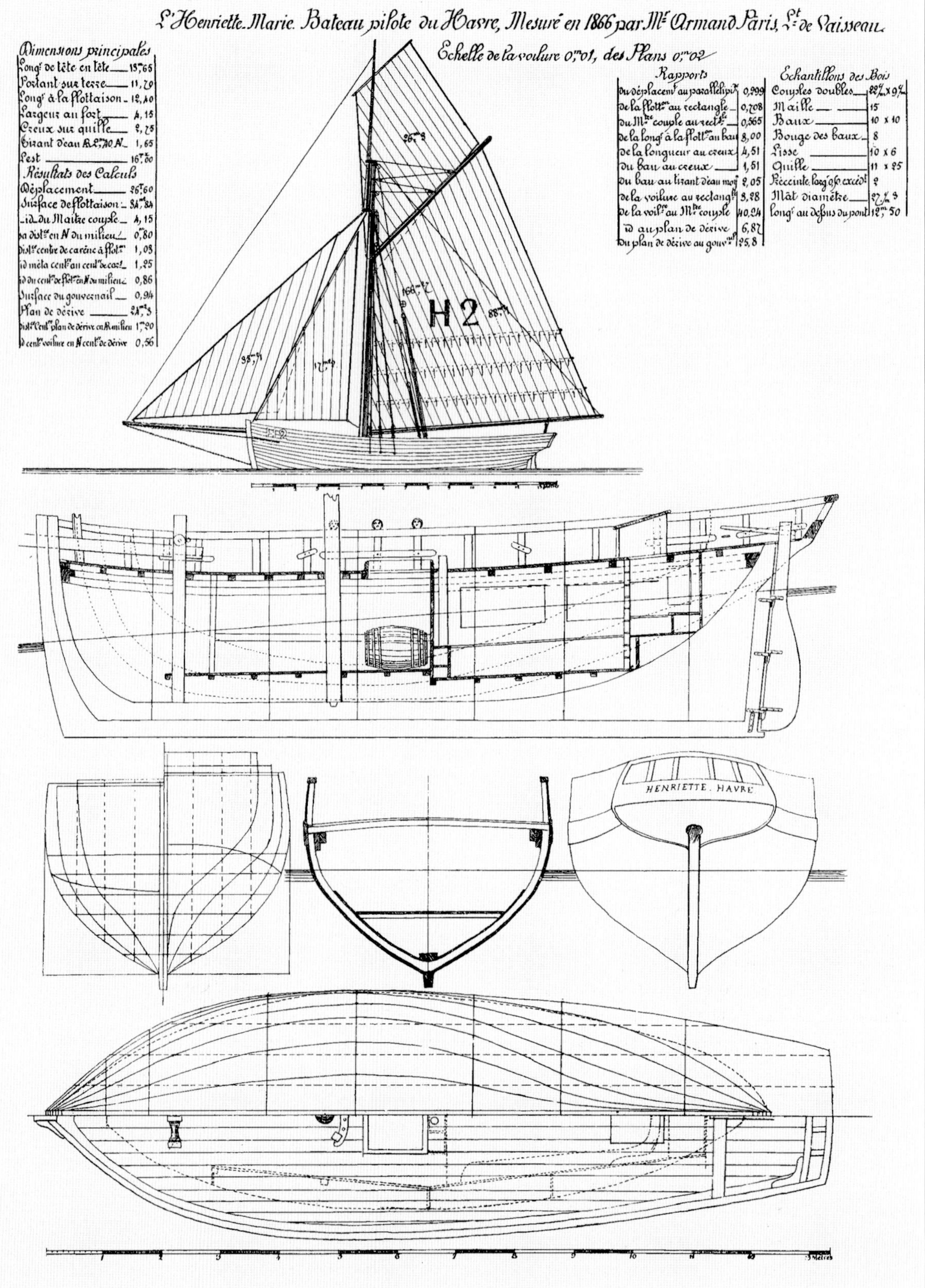

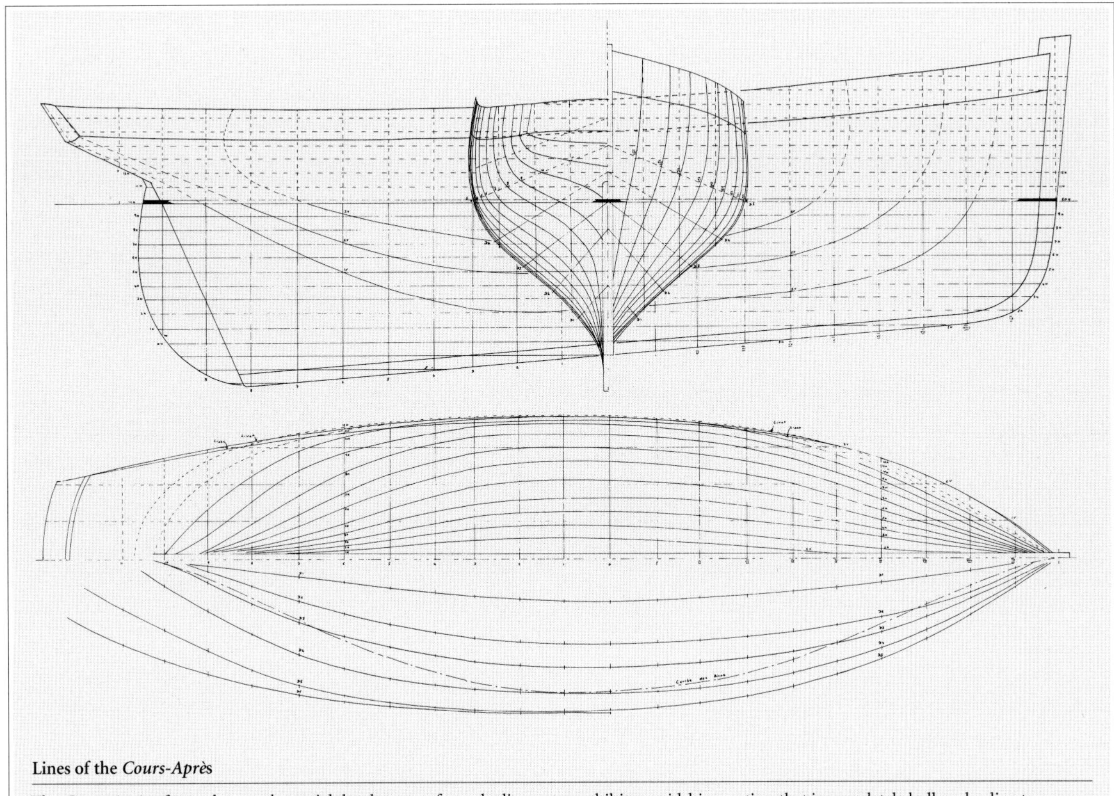

Lines of the *Cours-Après*

The *Cours-Après* of 1871 shows substantial development from the lines of H2, a quarter century earlier. Her stem is somewhat less severe and is also rounded into the keel, promising a more athletic performance close-in to a ship. Her sternpost has taken on the characteristic rake of French working craft of later years although this is by no means extreme. The biggest change, however, is seen in the body plan, which exhibits a midships section that is completely hollow, leading to a balanced set of lines which has left the older, bluff-bowed form behind. Her buttock lines have not yet reached the perfection seen in the ultimate developments of the twentieth century, but she is on the way to being a useful performer both close-hauled and off the wind. *(Author's collection)*

tense which confers a certain immediacy to his account. Although what follows is not a direct translation, we will emulate his example. There is much to be said for it.

The pilot is Dupernet, a strapping man with a kind face and blue eyes. In spite of his large family, he finds time to help the widows' and orphans' funds. The '*patron*' is a big fellow, Ferdinand Müller, who knows his job inside out and is capable of being a pilot in his own right. The pilot has every confidence in him. He's as solid and upright as the mast. Always in a good humour. He's always joking while the *lamaneur* Alexandre from St Vaast is quiet and silent. He has just qualified as a sailor; he's just married too, and although he sometimes breaks out into a broad smile, his thoughts seem far away. It is to be hoped that Mme Alexandre sees more of the smile than his shipmates.

The *mousse*, M Baptiste, is Alexandre's brother. He does the cooking, housekeeping and is a sailor too. He makes coffee, tea, brings out sails for changing, he's in charge of stores and he works all day and night – there's scarcely an hour goes by but someone shouts, 'M Baptiste, a coffee, pull up this sail, or it's the firing squad for you tonight …' And so he keeps watch with a deck broom as his watch-mate, but being threatened doesn't make him unhappy. He takes his job seriously.

The last person in the team, and by no means the least, is the boat. *Fauvette* is eight years old, solidly constructed by the greatest builder and designer of them all, Albert Paumelle. She is fast, like all Paumelle's boats, and sound in every way. The accommodation isn't luxurious, but it has every comfort a man really needs. The interior is divided into three. The forepeak contains sails, beautifully folded, the vegetable store, two barrels of water – 50 litres each – kept in reserve and changed at every opportunity. The main water tank is in the hold, which is the next compartment aft. It carries 500 litres drawn with a lift pump. Only the pilot washes and shaves every day. All cooking and cleaning of food is done in sea water. The stove is in the hold too, near the foot of the mast with a coal box to starboard and crockery stowed above it, along with the ship's supply of biscuits. These are kept for emergencies and changed every year, whether they need it or not! Under the sole of the hold lie three independent chain cables for the anchors.

The hold is separated from the saloon by a bulkhead and a door. The door is varnished, pitch-pine, the saloon deckhead is painted white and the whole compartment is lit by the only skylight in the vessel. There are four berths called cabanes, two on each side, closed off with curtains with chests and drawers underneath where the crew can stow their kit. Each man on board has his own bunk, but if an extra hand is shipped they have to hot-bunk it when the pilot is on board.

At the centre of the saloon, a drop-leaf table is bolted to the cabin sole. Either side are the chests where the crew can sit to relax or eat. In each corner there's a cupboard – two aft for the crew, the forward ones are for the pilot's clothes and bottles of conserve. More conserves, margarine, bottles of wine, cider and liqueurs; a foghorn, a compass, a telescope, a barometer and flag boxes are found in the saloon, and on some boats there's even a

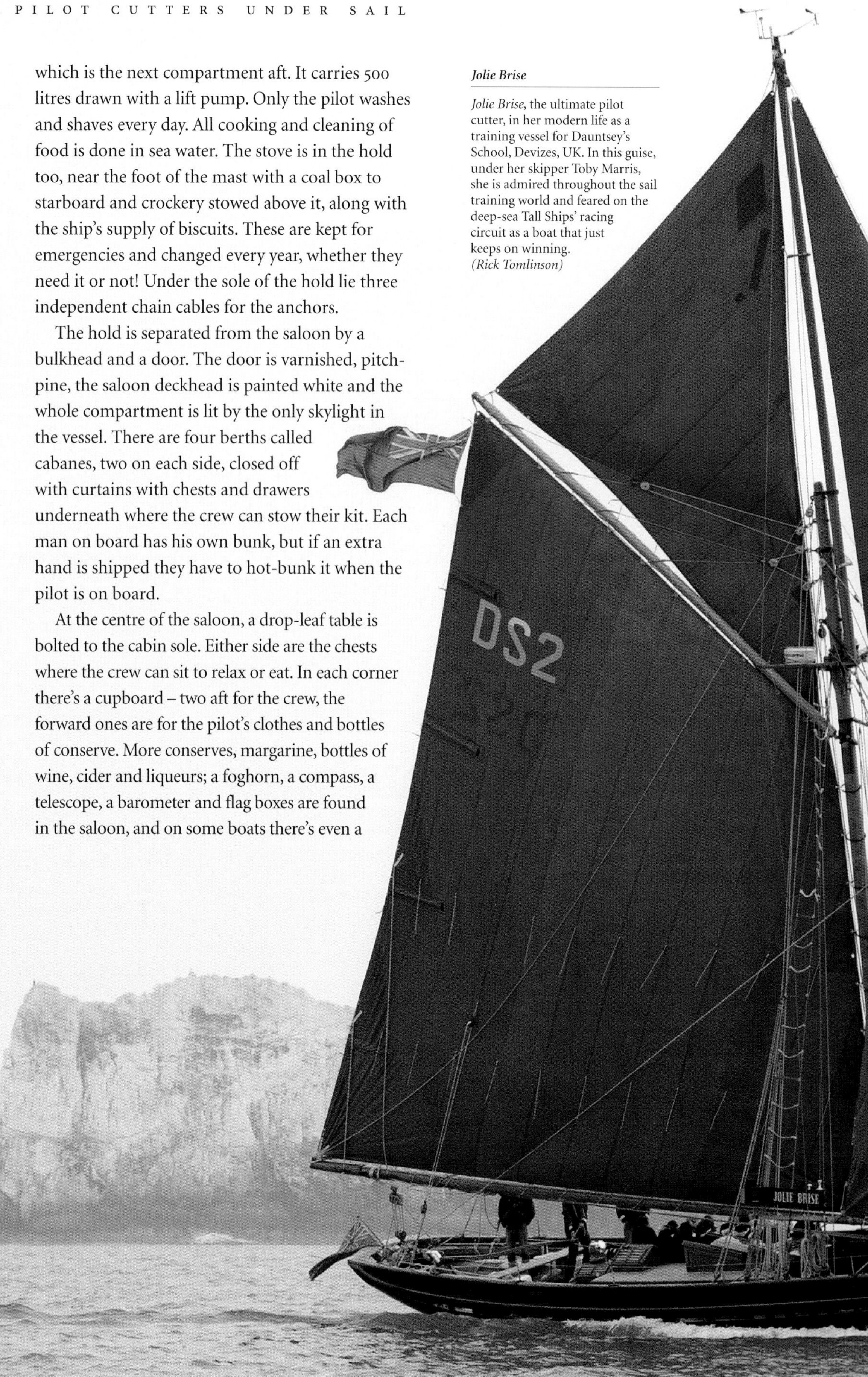

Jolie Brise

Jolie Brise, the ultimate pilot cutter, in her modern life as a training vessel for Dauntsey's School, Devizes, UK. In this guise, under her skipper Toby Marris, she is admired throughout the sail training world and feared on the deep-sea Tall Ships' racing circuit as a boat that just keeps on winning. *(Rick Tomlinson)*

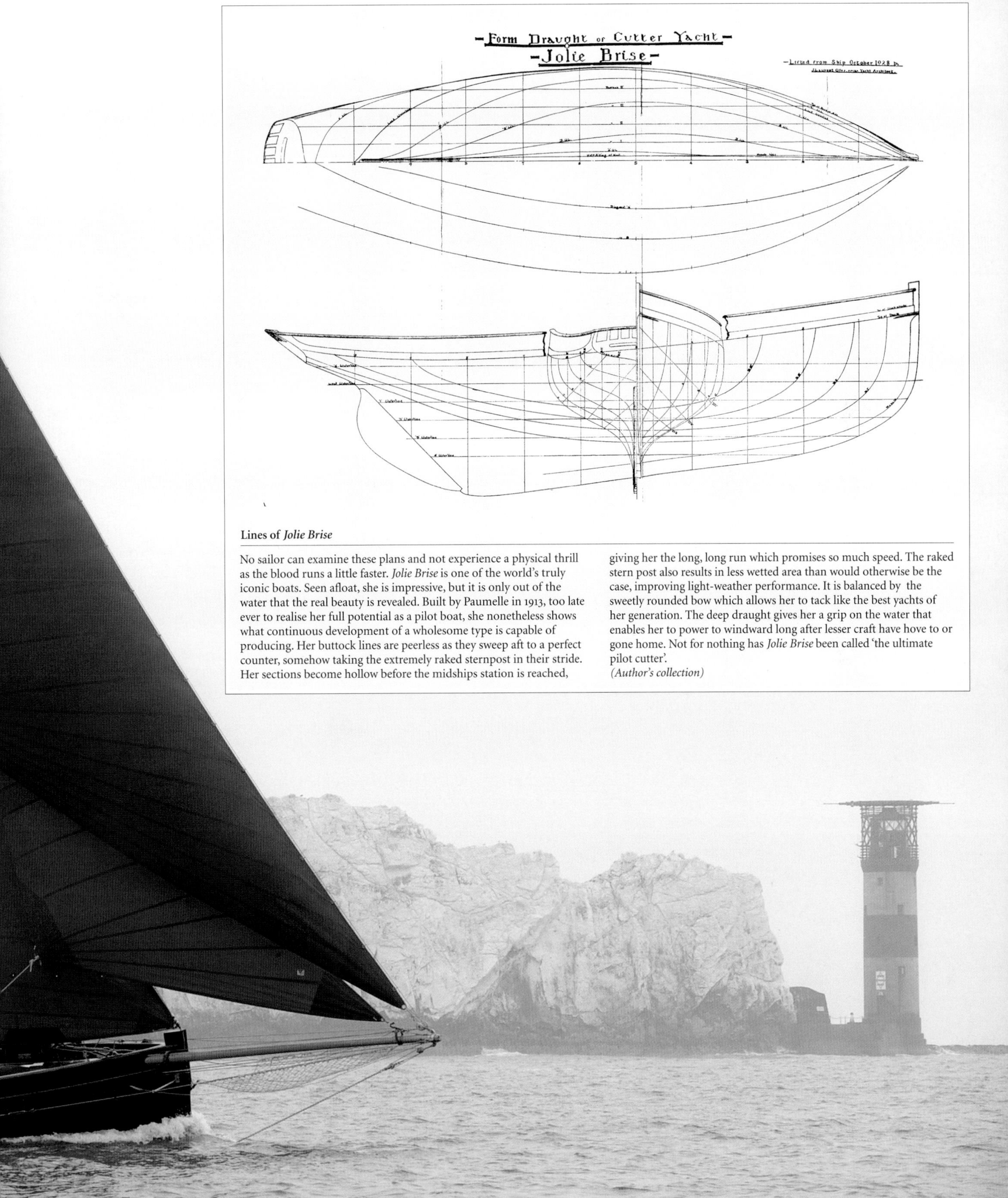

Lines of *Jolie Brise*

No sailor can examine these plans and not experience a physical thrill as the blood runs a little faster. *Jolie Brise* is one of the world's truly iconic boats. Seen afloat, she is impressive, but it is only out of the water that the real beauty is revealed. Built by Paumelle in 1913, too late ever to realise her full potential as a pilot boat, she nonetheless shows what continuous development of a wholesome type is capable of producing. Her buttock lines are peerless as they sweep aft to a perfect counter, somehow taking the extremely raked sternpost in their stride. Her sections become hollow before the midships station is reached, giving her the long, long run which promises so much speed. The raked stern post also results in less wetted area than would otherwise be the case, improving light-weather performance. It is balanced by the sweetly rounded bow which allows her to tack like the best yachts of her generation. The deep draught gives her a grip on the water that enables her to power to windward long after lesser craft have hove to or gone home. Not for nothing has *Jolie Brise* been called 'the ultimate pilot cutter'.
(Author's collection)

statue of Notre Dame. A powerful oil lamp swings above the table from the skylight. And that's it.

Down aft, in a cabin separated by a bulkhead and a curtain, a ladder gives access to the deck. Lockers for tools line the sides, and just abaft the ladder lies the trysail and its gear. All neat and tidy.

The bilge is largely full of ballast of iron or lead, much of it set in concrete. A well, or sump is left at the deepest part for the bilge pump suction.

Bonquart notes next that while the cutter left Le Havre in a nice breeze, this soon fell away and, coming on deck after lunch, there isn't a breath of air. They are drifting in the vicinity of Cap de la Hève, just far enough east to be able to see the powerful light on Cap d'Antifer to the northwards. The view of the bay is spectacular, but not what they want right now. Nothing much changes after dark. Bonquart smokes a pipe and yarns with Muller on the helmsman's seat. They go off watch at midnight and Alexandre takes over. At daybreak there still isn't any wind so they fish for mackerel with some success, while the pilot reads yesterday's newspapers. Finally, the following night, the wind comes up and we find *Fauvette* gliding silently over a calm sea. La Hève disappears and Barfleur light pops up ahead, followed by Cap Lévi close to Cherbourg. Next comes Cap de la Hague and in short order the Casquets Rocks light is sweeping the horizon, across the great tide race known locally as the Raz Blanchard and to the British as the Race of Alderney. There is still a big swell running and *Fauvette* makes the best of it that she can. In the cabin the names of the ships they are seeking and their tonnage are chalked up on a slate. It's the big ones they are after. The others can have the tiddlers which they must pretend not to see if they are signalling for pilot, because they are then obliged to board, whether they like it or not. The pilot and the *patron* fear there may well be three or four other boats waiting in the dark. Bonquart points out that the pilots will do all they can to be first to a ship, including running without lights, as they all try to get to the westward first.

As day breaks, out come the telescopes, scouring the horizon, but there isn't another pilot cutter in sight. Although they have the sea to themselves, they manage to miss two ships and are far from happy. They take it out on the *mousse* for not polishing the brass well enough and not trimming the lamps to perfection – well, why not, it has to be somebody's fault – but in three days' time there should be at least one big ship coming in past the Lizard (Cap Lizard) in the far west of England bound for Le Havre. All the pilots are well aware of when certain capital ships are likely to be due, and their probable route into the Channel, so they make for Plymouth to clear Customs and anchor in the Cattewater. The Customs come on board, the pilot talks to them with English described as being as good as that of Chamberlain himself, and the officials are liberally plied with rum and other benefits.

With the formalities complete, *Fauvette* sails for Falmouth. They run out of wind just by St Anthony's Point and the luckless Alexandre gets the tough task of towing them in past Black Rock in the dinghy. They moor in the harbour and take a well-earned watch below. In the morning, the hands go cockling off Trefusis Point while Pilot Dupernet appears to be giving them all a treat by preparing Sunday lunch, but it turns out that his underlying motive is to invite Captain White, an old chum who is skipper of a local tug, to join them. They smoke and talk, then go ashore with the intention of doing some shopping, but they discover everything is shut because it's the weekend. Somehow, they wheedle their way into the shops they need because, as Bonquart points out with glee, the back door is always open to the Havre pilots.

If trade had been slack, of if they had been waiting for the pilot to come back from a ship, the crew would have taken the opportunity now to dry the cutter out on the tide against the wall and scrub her bottom. This was done at least every couple of months to keep her on the cutting edge of performance. This time, there's no chance. Dupernet has struck a deal with his guest and, if the following day should dawn calm again, Captain White will tow them to Black Head, almost as far as the Lizard. It's as well he did because, yet again, there isn't a breath of air. The tugboat skipper fulfils the obligations incurred by his excellent lunch, the fishing is good as *Fauvette* trundles along over the long Atlantic swell, and the pilot gives the *mousse* another break by commandeering the stove. This time, it's curry. They are still panting from the spices when they sight the Lizard with its octagonal light tower and the semaphore station marking the start of the Channel proper.

All day steamers pass by. There isn't one for Le Havre, but the boys look on the bright side because there's not another pilot boat in sight. They are expecting the *Lorraine*, a liner from New York, and next morning Müller calls to the pilot, 'Frederic here she comes!'

All hands swarm up on deck to see the mighty masts come up over the horizon in the clear air, followed by two red funnels. Dupernet has a quick spruce up, then he leaps into the punt, saying, 'See you in Cherbourg.'

As the pilot boards the ship, she will hoist the 'G' flag to signal his presence to any other pilots who might offer their services. If the flag isn't shown, he may find himself liable to pay compensation to any rival who comes out of his way to board. While a deck apprentice is hoisting the flag, the captain will be advising the pilot about how much water the ship draws, as well as pointing out anything that might affect her ability to manoeuvre.

Down on the cutter, by the time the punt has been dragged back on board, the breeze has filled in as though it means business, so the men left on board *Fauvette* heave in a reef and square away towards Cherbourg at 8kts. This places them comfortably to windward of Le Havre, and the pilot rejoins them there by train after berthing the *Lorraine*. Without further ado they head out down-Channel in filthy weather, but they are well rewarded for their effort, because they board the big Chargeurs Réunis liner *Chargeur* off the Wolf Rock in a rough sea.

It is worth noting that while these pilot cutters were undoubtedly among the finest sea boats of their size ever built, there is little pleasure in being on passage in any 50-footer in a gale of wind. M Bonquart eloquently describes it as being tossed like a salad.

Boarding

Boarding is always the central issue in a pilot vessel. Le Havre boats were similar in size, form and work to their cousins in the Bristol Channel. Both used small open boats, or punts to make the sometimes-dangerous transfer. Often, these were sculled with a single oar. We are fortunate in that Pierre-Henri Marin has reported the memoir of Pilot Julien Capard which describes a typical boarding process in full:

1. The ship heaves to across the wind and sea, creating a lee.
2. The cutter runs downwind with her mainsail pinned well in to keep her speed down and to be ready for a subsequent gybe. As she passes under the bows of the ship, she launches her punt on her own lee quarter. The pilot and the crewman hop in.
3. The cutter continues to sail to leeward and the punt casts off, pulling over to the ship in the shelter of her lee.
4. While the punt is boarding the pilot, the cutter runs downwind and gybes, coming to the wind close-hauled and heading up slowly.
5. By now, the punt should be away from the ship and the pilot well up the ladder. The punt pulls downwind and passes under the cutter's stern, grabbing her taffrail on the lee side as she does so. If the punt is having a struggle to get back in time, the cutter can back her headsails and heave to.
6. The crewman scrambles aboard the cutter. Depending on how she is lying relative to the ship, the punt is either retrieved now or towed away into clear water for retrieval in safety.

All this sounds like routine work and so it was, but it doesn't do to forget that the manoeuvre required skill, strength and judgement of the highest order. These were no ordinary seamen.

The boats

It seems universal that pilots in the early days of their history used whatever local boats presented themselves, and Le Havre was no exception. Happily for them, the chaloupe-rigged fishing luggers of northern France had a charisma all their own. The boats from neighbouring Trouville were fast, strong, delightful to the eye, and the pilots used them or their equivalents until the mid nineteenth century. Early paintings reveal that some boats were sprouting gaff mainsails before this time, but one cannot ignore the fact that the great cutters of Le Havre began to distill out of the menagerie at about the same time as a parallel evolution took place in the Bristol Channel.

Marie-Fernand in frame during her restoration

Marie-Fernand, H23, was launched on 7 July 1894 for Pilot Eugène Prentout and was named after his two eldest children. She enjoyed a distinguished career which included some grand racing results until she was decommissioned like the rest of her sisters around 1914. Amongst other things, she then had a long and successful life in Scotland under the ownership of Archie Cameron and the name of *Leonora*. From him, and through the vision of Peter Gregson of Wooden Ships brokerage in Salcombe, England, she was ultimately sold to the Association Hirondelle de la Manche at Le Havre who restored her to full pilot trim and sail her to this day. A wonderful achievement. This photograph shows her in frame during the restoration, being planked from the garboards up. *(Valetoux collection)*

The *Henriette-Marie* (H2) was built in Cherbourg and appeared in 1847, entering the pilot service in 1849 and working until 1890. She has become famous after Admiral Pâris, an officer of the French navy, took off her lines in 1866 and published them in a large volume of vessels from around the world. She was a pure cutter with the big fore-triangle favoured for ease of handling by Bristol Channel boats and the later cutters from Norway. She also carried a fidded topmast and an old-fashioned lug topsail, but her hull shows her fishing-boat ancestry clearly. Her forefoot is angular which would have made her slow in stays; her sternpost is almost upright to assist in helm balance and make building easier, while her body plan shows a 'cod's head, mackerel tail' format with a slack, fishing-boat style bilge carrying the inevitably associated heavy displacement. Nonetheless, she is a true pilot cutter.

By 1871, the *Cours-Après*, H1, is already exhibiting noticeable signs of development. The body plan is becoming more wine-glass shaped and the entry is sharper. The forefoot, while still very severe, is rounded off, and the sternpost is distinctly raked. As the decades passed, the cutters became steadily larger and finer in line as the design trend set by *Cours-Après* developed through *Marie-Madeleine* and *Marie-Fernand* to find its ultimate expression in Paumelle's masterpiece, the 56ft *Jolie Brise* of 1913.

In these twilight years, pilot cutters in many areas were outstripping their forebears. It was happening in the Bristol Channel with craft such as *Frolic* and *Kindly Light*, but in *Jolie Brise*, Le Havre had the final word. It is hard to imagine any working gaff cutter standing against her in light weather or heavy. Powerfully built on grown frames interspersed with steamed timbers, this glorious vessel was never to fulfil her original destiny. She was launched too late to work as a seeking pilot, so history overtook her, yet she found even greater fame in an unexpected direction. After working seven months for the pilots on the close-inshore 'Petit Métier' anchorage in the early years of World War I, *Jolie Brise* was requisitioned by the French navy, then sold to a Concarneau tunny fisherman in 1917. She fished as best she could until 1923 when her fortunes came good in a big way. She was purchased by a British yachtsman, E G Martin, who had recently crossed the Channel in *Marie-Fernand* and realised the potential of Le Havre pilot cutters.

Marie-Fernand, H23

A depiction of *Marie-Fernand* during her working life. *(Valetoux collection)*

His plans for *Jolie Brise* outstripped the usual yachting round of inshore racing for those who wanted it and gentle cruising for any who didn't. Martin had vision. He recognised that the real test of a yacht was to pit her against her peers on the high seas in whatever weather came along. To this end, he inaugurated 'The Ocean Race', soon to be known as the Fastnet Race, from Cowes to Plymouth via the Fastnet Rock off southwest Ireland. This was exactly the sort of seafaring she was born for and she cleaned up the silverware against a small fleet of yachts. The Ocean Racing Club which was founded among the competitors soon became the world-famous Royal Ocean Racing Club with the Mayfair premises it still occupies, and *Jolie Brise* repeated her performance in a further two of these great events. She also won her class in a Bermuda Race during this period, after crossing the Atlantic to compete. Had it not been for some gear failure following her long haul westwards, she might well have won overall.

The story of this remarkable pilot cutter is not yet ended. After a long and happy sojourn in Portugal owned by Senhor Lobato, she was offered to the pilots in Le Havre and the French nation at large, but there was no interest. Instead, she came to Dauntsey's School in Wiltshire, England, in the late 1970s to be used for training their students. The author has had the privilege of skippering her to Spain and back from the English Channel and can personally testify to the fact that on one night watch off the Casquets where she was built to work, she ran forty miles through the water in four hours. During much of this spectacular dash, the mate, who had sustained a back injury on the outward passage, was seated in a kitchen chair which was not even lashed to the rail, so steadily did she reach. We were very young and it was too dark to see the topmast bending, but we overtook more than one struggling coaster that night as we swept by with all of history thrumming in our sails.

Today, *Jolie Brise* is a world-renowned sail training yacht, winner of Tall Ships races, competing 'trans-atlantic' under her captain of fifteen years, Toby Marris, a man of whom Paumelle and E G Martin would have approved wholeheartedly. Of all the pilot cutters of Le Havre, she and the carefully restored *Marie- Fernand,* twenty years her senior, are the only survivors still in commission. They carry the flag with justifiable pride.

CHAPTER 9

London – The North Channel

Ships bound for London from the North Sea had no choice but to enter the Thames via one of a number of passages through the sands of the estuary. These guts, deeps and passages were known collectively as 'the North Channel'. Administering pilotage here was more difficult than the relatively straightforward Strait of Dover/North Foreland route, so it was late in the day before it was brought under control.

Fifteen miles of shifting sands lurk just a mile or two off Lowestoft and Yarmouth on the easternmost bulge of the coast. To the north, Haisborough Sand lies seven miles off the Happisburgh light. Bank after long, narrow bank extend further seawards parallel to the shore along the run of the tide, with squeezed channels separating them. Shipping bound for London closed on the area from Scandinavia, North Holland, Germany, Russia and the Baltic, to say nothing of the regular fleets of Geordie and Whitby brigs carrying the capital's coal south from Newcastle. Shipwrecks on the outer banks and the beaches were numerous and few onshore gales came and went without leaving widows somewhere. A short stretch from Lowestoft past Southwold and on down to Orfordness is relatively clear of dangers. Then come the broken inshore shoals of Essex and the Thames River itself.

Before Trinity House began to take an interest in the North Channel, pilotage was conducted mainly by unlicensed local fishermen. Fishing tended to be seasonal, rising and falling with the movements of the shoals of herring and mackerel. In those pre-industrial days, the North Sea literally swam with fish, and men who were half-seaman, half-farmer flooded annually to the shore to grab their share of the enormous hauls. When the fish moved on and the landsmen returned to their farms, the boat-owners had to keep their vessels working, so lifesaving, the attendant business of salvage, and pilotage took over.

From Great Yarmouth southwards, rivers – many of them tidal – offer ports of varying quality which could shelter deep-water pilot cutters or fishing cutters seconded to the job. On the essentially uneasy shoreline further north, harbours are few or non-existent, so boats were inevitably launched off the beaches, which offered the best of a bad job for pilots to put out and meet incoming ships.

Although not strictly cutters, the enormous open beach boats of northern East Anglia did sterling service to London pilots. Their story has been told in full elsewhere by this author, but it remains colourful in the extreme, so to leave them out of this book would have seemed nothing short of churlish. It is therefore offered here in brief without apology.

East Anglian beach yawls

By the third decade of the nineteenth century, beach companies existed at Sheringham, Great Yarmouth, Lowestoft, and a number of small towns and villages. They had become an established part of the scene and although their day in the sun was brief, it was glorious.

Every beach company was an independent unit. They were entirely unsupervised, having divested themselves of any influence that might have been brought to bear on them in previous times by the Shipmen's Guild of Great Yarmouth or the Osterlings of the Hanseatic League. All along this shoreline, their simple huts were rendered splendid by trophies of salvage action. Famous figureheads, trailboards and other memorabilia festooned the wooden walls, while equally notable characters hung around smoking, spitting and yarning, waiting for yet another ship to pile up on the outer shoals, or for one of their pilots to need a boarding boat.

There were always watchtowers associated with the beachmen's headquarters. From these, a man with a telescope could hope to gain an inch or two over the opposition a short way up the strand, and competition was fierce.

The community of Southwold between Yarmouth and Orfordness was home to several beach companies. Southwold does have a harbour, but the beach was preferred for pilot and salvage work because the narrow entrance became heavily silted up. The beach lies at the foot of a cliff, which gave the companies an excellent vantage point for spotting business. The Long Island Cliff Company set themselves up at the end of East Street with the yawl *Jubilee* in 1810. Four years later, the 50ft boat was involved in a cutting-out expedition against the French. The log of the incident has been recorded, apparently from the hand of the skipper, W Woodard, who is infuriatingly understated in his description:

> Re-took a collier Brig with the *Jubilee* pilot boat, from a French luger. ben a Bout 3 miles to a head put 5 Frenchmen on Shore at Southwold it came on to blow at NE and i toke the brig to Harwich. W Woodard.

This spirited little action towards the end of the French wars must have delighted the men, striking a blow at the old enemy.

Another recorded incident involving the *Jubilee* in 1818 was a more typical piece of work. The ship *Eliza* had lost her ground tackle in a fierce southerly gale while lying in the Downs off the Kent shore on the south side of the Thames estuary. She had drifted across the Thames to be carried by wind and tide to a point off Dunwich Church a few miles south of the company's lookout. Here, she had been precariously brought up, presumably with a kedge. The *Jubilee* was launched and two pilots were put aboard. They brought the *Eliza* to Yarmouth Roads where the yawl, which had easily out-run her in the gale, was waiting with fresh anchors and cable. Things then went from bad to worse, with the gale increasing in fury. Several ships in the roads cut away their masts to lessen windage, and three sank at their anchors. The *Jubilee* stood by her prize and brought out yet more ground tackle which undoubtedly saved her. We are not told the amount of her salvage claim, but in 1830, her sister yawl, the *John Bull*, performed a similar service for the *Mary* of Guernsey and received £125.

The *Jubilee*'s days ended with the loss of one of her crew during a launch to a vessel signalling for a pilot during an onshore storm in the winter of 1844/5. She was thrown back onto the beach and smashed.

One generally associates disasters with heavy weather, but off this treacherous coast, anything could happen. One fine, moonlit night, the Caister yawl *Zephyr* was sailing out to a schooner stranded

The Old Company of Beachmen, Lowestoft

The beaches of Suffolk were studded with companies like this one, photographed around 1910. A more colourful and capable collection of old salts was rarely met, even in the 1800s during the rough-tough days of the great beach yawls. Their huts were decorated with trophies from ships they had salvaged and when it came to racing, no 'rock star' of today was ever more committed. When a rival beach company won the regatta with the *Georgiana*, these men of the Old Company commissioned no less an architect than G L Watson – designer of the King's cutter *Britannia* – to produce lines for the *Happy New Year* with which they intended to redress the balance. Although a successful salvager and pilot boat, the *Happy New Year* never did beat her rivals. *(Robert Malster)*

A brig heaves to for her pilot off the Suffolk shore

This lithograph, depicting a brig signalling for a pilot, was published *c*1850 and shows a beach yawl on the left probably making her way towards the brig to deliver a pilot. On the right is a fishing lugger. Stanford light vessel, with two masts each with a circular topmark, is in the distance, while in the far background can be spotted the two piers of Lowestoft harbour. *(Robert Malster)*

on the Barber Sand immediately offshore. The coxswain recalled the stump of a mast on a wreck he had salvaged eight years previously.

'Now, dear boys,' he said quietly, 'keep a lookout for that old stump.' Almost before he had finished speaking, the broken tooth of a spar took the yawl's bottom out of her. Some of the crew began heaving ballast over the side, but the realists sat on the disappearing gunwale and stripped to their underwear. One of these, John George, struck off as the boat went down underneath them saying, 'Fare ye well, boys, I'm off to the shore.'

On the way, he hailed a Yarmouth shrimper, *The Brothers*, which picked him up in amazement. He quickly told his saviours about his shipmates, and the shrimper made her best speed to the scene. 'There's fifteen of us in the water about here,' said George, but only six more were picked up. The remaining eight had gone away on the tide and were lost, leaving six widows and twenty-nine fatherless children. An incident such as this was worse than a tragedy, it was an economic calamity from which a small community like the Caister of those days would take years, perhaps decades, to recover.

Boarding pilots

According to the late historian, Edgar J March, when a ship was seen signalling for a pilot on a nasty night, there came a wild rush from all directions of folk completely focussed on getting the yawl into the water. Skids were shoved under the bows while many hands gathered along both sides, literally holding her up as the shores were knocked away. As the boat started down the beach, the crew tumbled aboard with bags of ballast, sails and gear. There was no stopping her now in her headlong slide into her native element with gravity and greased ways in charge. As she hit the water she was given an extra heave with a long spar called a sett. By that time the mizzen would be hoisted. It was followed on the instant by the mighty foresail and the yawl was away, accelerating with improbable speed. As she clawed off the breaking shoreline in pitch darkness, she was driven fearlessly through seemingly impossible breakers, sometimes shuddering as her keel touched an offlying shoal, sometimes with her foresheet eased to keep her on her feet as she leapt off a steep wave with seven men bailing for everyone's lives, and the whole wild thing dashing to windward, not pointing high, but hissing along through the broken water until finally she reached the deeps. Here, like a hound off the leash, she set her course and flew away towards the flares burning aboard her quarry, very probably with another yawl or two for company, all bound for the same job which only one would secure.

A somewhat different scene would have been presented on a pleasant summer's afternoon, and we are fortunate to have an eyewitness account of what went on in these conditions. Aldeburgh, just north of Orfordness, the low headland which could reasonably claim to be the beginnings of the Thames Estuary, is a logical place for pilots to be stationed, and so they were. Beachmen and pilots occupied many of the cottages in town and two beach companies were active here in the nineteenth century.

Aldeburgh was once a port with a true harbour, but North Sea movements and silting have shifted the mouth of its river ten miles south of Orfordness, to where the River Ore now debouches at the fearsome and virtually unchartable bar of Shingle Street. The beach was thus the only useful place for local men to carry on their work, and the Reverend J Ford, a local clergyman, wrote down his impressions of the launch proceedings and subsequent competition of a couple of pilot yawls.

Beachmen of Aldeburgh

This remarkable collection of sailors and longshoremen is from a painting in the Moot Hall Museum in Aldeburgh. These are the men who manned the great yawls. They are as follows:

Behind: James Ward ('Dony').

Second row from back: William Ward ('Drooks'), his brother; Jim Fisher; Catmore; Sam Filby (known for always wearing a blue jersey).

Third row from back: Robert Easter (nickname 'No-Thank-You'); Sam Ward (sexton and gardener); Charlie King (brickmaker and 'Professor' on festive occasions).

Fourth row from back: Charlie ('Sanko') Nicholls; George ('My Lord') Cable; William Cable (known for reasons obscure as 'Dick McCarthy'), his brother; John Scarlett.

Fifth row from back: Robert Thorpe (a man with a red hat who belonged to a trading coaster); Jack ('Twee') Beame, with a Dutch-style cap; Ned Burwood.

Sixth row from back: Charles Burwood; his cousin, Christopher ('Kit') Fisher; and Robert Wilson, from the Lloyd's Signal Station.

(Aldeburgh Museum)

> I will suppose that there are clusters of boatmen at their respective stations, with the pilots also, and that a strange vessel has just hoisted a signal or 'jack' at her foremast head, denoting that she wants a pilot. She is observed by both 'ends' of the beach. All is now hurry and confusion. There is a small breeze, so one of the medium-sized yawls is taken. The 'Up-towners' launch their boat, the 'Down-towners' theirs. Prior to starting, the pilots of each party draw lots and he who draws the longest goes with the boatmen.
>
> The start. They are pushed through the breakers; they cross the shoal. One started slightly before the other; she keeps the lead. Her sails fill with the breeze and gracefully she glides through the waters. All is excitement on the beach. The sailors use the telescope freely and freely exchange opinions of the probable results of the chase. The sailors' wives mingle on the beach and they also express their opinions on the merits of each yawl:
>
> 'The *Kate*'s ahead.'
>
> 'No, she's not.'
>
> 'Why don't they do so-and-so?'

'Who's off in the *Louisa*?'

Such, and a hundred more remarks, are bandied about until the contest is decided by one of the boats reaching the prize first and leaving her pilot on board to conduct it to her destination. ...

... These chases are generally very amusing, but occasionally they are carried so far as to become dangerous. I do not think this division of boatmen occasions any feelings of hatred on the part of either, it affords much amusement and interest and fosters perseverance. It occasionally causes a 'squabble', but even then drink is more culpable than division in originating it. The spirit of 'Up-town' and 'Down-town' exists in greater intensity among the small boys than the parties concerned, and many a hobby-de-hoy goes home with a disfigured face and a sorrowful heart because his pal said the 'Up-towners' always beat the 'Down-towners' and he, courageously contradicting him, got a punch in the head for his trouble.

Beach boats

The great yawls of the Norfolk and Suffolk coast seem to have evolved over a long period, but reached the height of their development at the end of the eighteenth century. They then remained more or less as they were until changing economic conditions, brought about largely by the advent of steam power, finally eclipsed them at the end of the nineteenth century. Their name was pronounced 'yoll', which might be a pointer to ancient origins dating from the Vikings who ruled this coast for hundreds of years.

Beach yawls were undoubtedly the most exciting working sailing craft ever developed in Britain. Impossibly large, open boats with a pointed stern, fine ends and narrow beam, they carried enormous lugsails whose area defied nature in that the frail shells that carried them ever stayed the right way up. To say a beach yawl was easily driven would be an understatement, and they were enormously fast when reaching in a strong breeze, their slender sections and shoal draught carrying them well beyond the usual limits imposed by wave-making on hull speed. A Yarmouth yawl was reliably recorded as making 16kts under ideal conditions.

Clearly, so shallow a hull was not a great performer to windward, but, like a racing multihull today, the yawls more than made up in 'knots per hour' what they gave away in pointing ability. They would certainly have sailed far faster and made

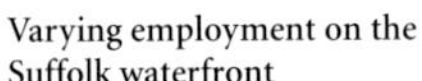

Varying employment on the Suffolk waterfront

After the Duke of Marlborough's wars came to an end in 1711, trade, including pilotage, took a dive. Shortly after 1765, however, holidaymaking began to come along as an accepted activity, with the beaches of East Anglia securing their share of the new business. This is a sketch of Aldeborough beach with its bathing machines in the early days. The cutter, which seems to be carrying a pilot flag, could well be one of the pilot cutters built for Southwold men in Aldeburgh. Aldeburgh itself was using beach yawls, as we know from the account of the Reverend Mr Ford on the previous page. *(Aldeburgh Museum)*

Suffolk pilot skiff

A nineteenth-century pilot skiff drawn up on the beach at Lowestoft. This brightly painted, high-performance boat is a pulling version of the larger sailing yawls for which the Suffolk and Norfolk beaches were justly famous.
(Mersea Museum, John Leather collection)

much less leeway steering a point or two free of the wind, while their ability to work off a lee shore in a gale was remarkable.

In light conditions, a yawl could also be rowed by her crew of up to twenty-five men. Leverage was supplied by coppered square holes in the wash strake which were shuttered over when sailing. Like the coble of Yorkshire and other open boats, the yawl, when sailed hard, seemed to sink her lee gunwale below the surface of the sea, yet by some mystic process tied up with her great speed, little water came in.

Ballast was beach shingle in bags and was pitched across from bilge to bilge as the yawl tacked to keep the weight to windward. Off the wind, the crew sat on the bottom boards to keep the centre of gravity as low as possible. The huge forelug was dropped and manhandled around to the lee side on each tack, and it was sometimes necessary to row the boat's head through the wind. The mizzen sheeted to an enormous outrigger was known all along these beaches as an 'outligger'.

Masts were stepped on the keelson and partnered at gunwale level by beams called 'dowsings' set at the top of the wash strake. This gave the maximum cantilever for support. Two conventional thwarts below this level further supported each mast; these were joined together by fore-and-aft members that served as tabernacles and helped guide the mast as it was raised and lowered.

The foresheet of a yawl was never made fast, but always held in the hand with a turn or three around a samson post on the main tabernacle. The man on this sheet was critical, not only to performance, but also to the survival of all hands. The sheet block was hooked to an eyebolt outside the lee gunwale and one was rigged on either side to facilitate setting everything up again after a tack. The mizzen sheet was also held on a turn and was often eased to prevent a broach when the boat was running hard in a quartering sea. The mizzenmast was stayed forward by a tackle from the masthead and secured to an eyebolt in the keelson known as a 'Tommy Hunter'. Oddly enough, this peculiar name was also in vogue in the West Country, but who Mr Hunter might have been is lost in time. Ernest R Cooper, whose excellent articles on beach boats have been referred to here, suggested that perhaps he might be a shipmate of Matthew Walker ...

As for scantlings, Cooper gives the data for *Bittern* on the following page. She was built by Beeching Brothers of Yarmouth in 1890.

The Suffolk beach yawl
Happy Return

Open yawls like this, between 50ft and 80ft long, were among the fastest working craft the world has ever seen. Twelve men would crew them on a day-to-day basis, but up to twenty-five came aboard on race days. Keeping such a vessel upright when driving hard was more of an athletic feat than a piece of humdrum seamanship. They carried out salvage work as well as life-saving and pilotage, and the pilots used them regularly to board ships sailing south towards London through the maze of offshore shoals lining the East Anglian coast.
(Mersea Museum, John Leather collection)

Bittern, 1890

Length: 49ft

Beam: 9ft 6in

Depth amidships: 2ft 11in, plus wash strakes of 5½in, making a total depth of 3ft 4½in

Keel: 5 x 6½in American oak

Planking: ⅝in American oak

Top strake: 1in

Keelson: 5 x 5½in American oak, secured with galvanised screwbolts through 1in iron keelband

Timbers: 2½ x 2½in American oak or elm

Planking: copper fastened

Four grown floors at each end of boat

Gunwales: 2½ x 2½in American oak or elm

Bow wash strakes doubled to abaft fore rigging

Thwarts: 1½ x 7in English oak

Main thwart: 2 x 9 in English oak, all double-kneed with grown knees sided 1½in

Dowsings fore and aft secured with knees

Stanchions under thwarts

Oak bottom boards and red deal ballast boards

Bow and stern gratings

Three outside bilge pieces each side, through fastened

To row eight oars a side and rowlocks coppered

Hull finished complete for £95.

At the time Cooper wrote this, the *Bittern* had seen forty years of service and was going strong. She was a fast boat that performed well in the annual Yarmouth regattas. As a late example of the Southwold beach yawl, the *Bittern* lives on as a fine model in the Sailors' Reading Room high on the cliff where her beachmen used to scan the horizon. Her rudder stands sentinel outside the door.

The *Reindeer*, the schooner *America* and the end of the beach yawls

One of the beachmen's finest hours came in 1851 when the men of Yarmouth challenged Commodore Stevens of the New York Yacht Club. They had heard how his schooner had thrashed the assembled might of the Royal Yacht Squadron off Cowes and offered a stake of £200 for a match race between the newly famous *America* and their 72ft beach yawl, *Reindeer*. The *Reindeer* was then sixteen years old and was so huge that seventy-two people were aboard at her launching. She was blisteringly fast and the commodore, rather than take up the challenge forthwith, sent one of his gentlemen to check her out. This spy was so staggered by the yawl's performance that he advised against accepting the wager. It was suggested that the refusal be justified on the grounds that the yawl was not a proper yacht. Stevens was unhappy about this objection and instead came up with the cunning ruse of raising the stake to £1,000, a sum he knew the beachmen would never meet. The challenge passed over, but the *Reindeer*'s men had many a laugh about the affair in their beach hut over a bottle or two of contraband rum.

Notwithstanding their undisputable position as crew of the most charismatic craft in Britain, and quite possibly the whole of Europe, the ascendancy of the steamship, with its regular tracks and reliable pilot boarding points, tolled the knell for the beachmen. They faded with the topgallants of the oceangoing windjammers and the last billyboys sailing south with coal from the northeast. The dunes swallowed their yawls and the waves ate the low cliffs where their beach houses had stood. They had served their time famously and, when it was run, the sea swept away all evidence of their existence.

A Suffolk beach yawl

An eighteenth-century etching of an open beach yawl shows that these high-performance vessels had been developing for many years before the heyday of the beach companies in the late eighteen hundreds. *(Author's collection)*

Pilot cutters of the North Channel

As soon as Trinity House took over outer London pilotage in the first decade of the nineteenth century they began licensing pilots for the North Channel from Orfordness inwards. As in most places where compulsory pilotage held sway, unlicensed pilots continued to ply their trade illegally, and a mixture of pilotage was therefore on offer.

Initially, pilots boarded from beach boats as in the past, but it soon became clear that advantage could be gained by being further out to sea seeking ships, so licensed pilots grouped together into bands of four or five men and purchased cutters. Generally, these pilot boats seem to have been of the smack type, although few details of them survive. However, a number operated from Southwold in the days before the harbour silted up and drove the local pilots onto the beach. They included the *Abeona*, a deep-draughted (8ft) 19-tonner, built at Aldeburgh in 1825 for William Bokenham, which worked for twenty years before being sold to Yarmouth. Other pilot cutters included the *William and Mary* of 1845, also built at Aldeburgh, but for whom is unclear. Nothing is known of her save that her draught was 8ft, making her pedigree as a 'full-on' cutter beyond doubt, rather than one of the various beach yawls described in some records as 'pilot cutters'. William Easy commissioned the 27-ton *Amicitia* from Yarmouth much earlier in 1805, and twenty-five years later, the joyously named

British Tar was also laid down at Yarmouth for one Edward Palmer. This mighty 30-tonner carried a crew of ten, if the records are to be believed. Palmer was drowned on Southwold beach in 1844 when the 24-ton *Jubilee* was wrecked with ten crew. Others on the list include *Dolphin, Providence* and *Samuel.*

Apart from Southwold, some of these self-propelled North Channel pilots worked out of Harwich and Yarmouth, but Lowestoft remained a favourite. In addition to smacks and purpose-built pilot cutters, a number of pilot consortiums purchased pensioned-off yachts of about the right size. Around 60–70ft long with plumb stem and counter stern, these craft served the pilots well, though one must assume that these experienced seamen steered well clear of the dreaded 'lead mines', narrow-gutted monsters that the yacht rating rules were soon to create.

One yacht turned pilot cutter was Lord Brassey's famous *Cymba.* The *Will-o'-the-Wisp* was built as a yacht in Cowes in 1824 and served on the Yarmouth station until 1900. *Rapid,* built at Lymington in 1846, was half a century at Lowestoft. Another was the ex-Royal Cork Yacht Club *Cynthia,* who began a new life as a Trinity House pilot cutter from the dubious convenience of Southwold. Her life as a commercial vessel was not without incident and on 16 June 1894 two of her pilots, Robert and Earsley Crickmore, were drowned.

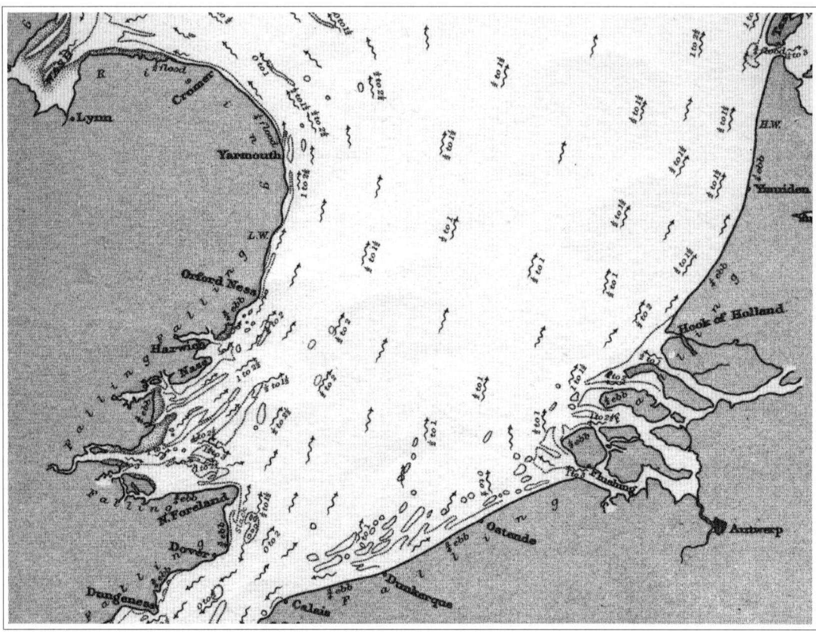

The Narrow Seas

In the days of sail and early steamers the southern North Sea was alive with shipping heading to and from the London River. The shoals of the Thames Estuary can be seen clearly on this chart, as well as something of the tidal streams which beset them, making guidance for ships' masters a critical necessity long before compulsory pilotage was heard of. *(From* Tidal Stream North Sea, *Admiralty publication 1899)*

All these yachts and others gave good service, though they were generally cut down in spar and sail from their 'Racing Clouts'. The *Cynthia* was sailed round from her old life to her new one by the pilots themselves. She was still 'fully dressed' as it were, and although they may well have enjoyed the trip, she ended up by giving them a fright. She luffed head to wind into the harbour at a remarkable rate of knots and, with her snowy canvas thundering, continued to shoot up through the bridge. She was half-way up Lake Lothing before she finally lost way amid considerable ribaldry from the longshoremen who, then as now, always seemed to turn up just when a skipper would rather they'd shambled off for a pint.

Examinations for the North Channel pilots were stringent and entirely oral. The pilot had to describe any buoy or beacon and give bearings from one to another, as well as cross-bearings throughout the area. Courses and distances were also required to be committed to memory.

Despite this tight control of their actual piloting skills, the administration of the North Channel men was never as regulated as their Dover colleagues. Even into the late 1880s, Trinity House had still not equipped them with cutters, preferring to let them charter or use their own. When Pilot Alfred Fisher was examined by Parliament at the important 1888 committee, he stated that in his earlier days as a pilot, back in the 1860s, there were sixteen cutters on North Channel station, all manned by a master and a mate, but that now there were only eleven.

In the old days, Pilot Fisher said, three cutters were designated to take off 'down' pilots while the other twelve 'cruised in the sea'. He goes on to state that by 1888, the 'taking-off' cutters were abolished and that two of the cruising cutters were now supposed to maintain station near the Sunk light vessel east of Harwich off the Naze.

Earnings were on the decline at this stage of the sailing service, for the usual reason that steamers were causing a decline in the number of ships and a corresponding reduction in the need for cruising pilots. The previous ten-year average earnings had been £205, but in 1886 only £126 was achieved; 1887 was little better with £134. Each man kept his own earnings and there was no pooling and dividing up. Fisher complained that while he and his colleagues had to make the same contributions to the Trinity as the other London pilots, they were far worse off because the expense of their cutters consumed up to 30 per cent of their income. These pilots were also now frequently under coercion by shipmasters to lower their fees, but were resisting these unreasonable and illegal demands by sticking together.

One of the main reasons for the diminution of pilots' income at this time was that they now rarely received what was known as 'distance money'. This was extra to their basic fees for the North Channel and was paid to a cruising pilot who boarded to seaward of the limits of compulsory pilotage. A North Channel pilot's licence generally took the bearer as far as the Dudgeon, forty-five miles north of Yarmouth, but Fisher pointed out that now steamers could move in a straight line, they no longer wanted a pilot before the Sunk, particularly since a lightship had been established on Smith's Knoll, a natural landfall point well out into the North Sea. From his tone, one can almost imply that he and his friends resented this improvement in shipping safety.

In 1876, eleven steamers and 138 sailing ships asked Fisher's cutter for a pilot. In 1887, they boarded 144 steamers but the number of sailing vessels was down to fifty-five. The writing was on the bulkhead for the traditional cruising pilot.

Another complaint of Pilot Fisher was that his income was eroded by hobblers rowing down from Gravesend in watermen's wherries. These, he stated, were often to be found as far seaward as the Gunfleet or Maplin Sands, where they 'hung about' looking for a hobble. It was easy for an experienced ship's master to slip past the cutters at the Sunk after dark and meet up with one of these unlicensed pilots further in towards London at daybreak. The practice was illegal, but when the pilots took offenders to court they received no satisfaction. This complaint was repeated to the same committee by pilots from the Dungeness station, who went even further and said they had disguised themselves to board ships and see whether there was a waterman working as pilot. Even with concrete evidence, they had had little fortune from the judiciary, because the bumboat men simply claimed that they had come aboard to help out with the ship handling. This was almost impossible to disavow, because to secure a conviction it was necessary to prove that the man had been assisting with the navigation of the ship.

The failure of the courts to pursue unlicensed Gravesend pilots was by no means typical. On the coast further north, just as in the Thames Estuary, it was normal for an unlicensed man to offer his services if he thought he could get away with it. These characters from the beaches were known as Brummagem pilots, a contemporary description implying inferior quality. If a licensed Trinity House man offered his services within the compulsory pilotage area to a ship that had quietly boarded an unlicensed pilot, the captain must accept him or face stringent penalties. The Brummagem pilot was then often literally stowed away until the licensed pilot had been taken off and the coast was again clear. Sometimes these 'criminals' spent their time in a spare bunk in a dark corner of the fo'c'sle. On other ships they were less lucky and it is easy to imagine the horrid holes into which they sometimes crawled to escape detection and the inevitable fine which would follow.

In 1915 the old sailing cutter *Vigilant,* acting as tender at the Sunk, was destroyed by a mine off the South Shipwash buoy with heavy loss of life. Trinity House brought in a steam-drifter also to be named *Vigilant* as a replacement, and that was the end of it all. The cruising pilot service was squarely committed to history.

Essex smacks as Trinity House tenders and salvage operators

For many centuries before the Trinity House involvement, unlicensed pilots offered their services as opportunity arose in the North Channel. Fishing was often their principal occupation, but if a ship were sighted flying a signal for a pilot, the unlicensed fisherman would board after a haggle on payment, perhaps taking the ship on into the mouth of the Thames. The smack usually followed the ship's wake to pick up her man when he left.

It must be understood that these Essex men were often experienced far beyond their home waters. They fished not only locally, but also at different seasons or for various reasons down-Channel, off the south and southwest coast of Ireland, the northern part of the east coasts of England and Scotland and the Dutch coast. As well as all this,

Pioneer, a deep-sea Essex smack, 1864

Built in 1864 by Harris of Rowhedge, *Pioneer* was originally a cutter of 57ft on deck, working out of Brightlingsea for deep-sea oysters. In 1889 Aldous of Brightlingsea lengthened her by 11ft, rigged her as a ketch and installed a wet well to facilitate working further afield. She was now a classic 'skillinger', a nickname developed from anglicising the name of the fishing area off Terschelling, whose rich oyster grounds were her second home. Finally decommissioned in 1939, she became a houseboat until, after blocking a land drain off East Mersea, she was towed away and ultimately sank. In 1998 she was dug out of the mud and transported to Great Totham by road to be restored by the *Pioneer* Trust. Relaunched at Brightlingsea in 2003, she is a monument to the men of Essex and one of the loveliest working vessels afloat. Like her sisters, she was primarily a fishing boat, but always ready for a spot of salvage and occasional pilotage.
(Mersea Museum, Tony Millatt)

they were also to be found around the Channel Islands and the coasts of Normandy. Because of their speed and ability to face very rough weather, they were also occasionally chartered to carry lobsters and crabs from Norway, or fresh salmon from County Sligo to Liverpool. Their main occupation, however, remained trawling for bottom fish, 'stowboating for sprats', and dredging for oysters and scallops off East Anglia.

Essex smacks were designed and built in small yards in the various lesser local ports. The seagoing versions were from 40–65ft in length (some up to 70ft), with a healthy beam and a draught from 5ft 6in to 8ft, the largest ones sometimes 9ft. They had plumb stems, counter sterns and straight keels. Their cutter rig consisted of gaff mainsail, foresail, a variety of jibs set on a long bowsprit supported by a bobstay, a selection of topsails on an elegant topmast, a light-weather foresail and sometimes a spinnaker. It was a powerful rig and the well-formed hulls were fast, weatherly and invariably well sailed.

A 40ft smack might have a crew of three or four for fishing, but a larger one could carry up to six hands living in a cabin aft, with bunks around its sides closed off with wooden shutters so the occupant was not thrown out at sea. The fo'c'sle was used as a store for gear, ropes, spare sails, etc. Decks were enclosed by knee-high bulwarks. A hand capstan stood amidships for handling warps when fishing, and a handspike windlass forward managed the anchor cable and the brutally heavy gear of the stowboat net.

In addition to transporting pilots, a further occupation which was a speciality of these 'first-class' smacks and their crews was salvaging, or rendering assistance to stranded vessels. This work extended over many centuries, but ended during the 1890s when steamships became commonplace

Hawthorn, CK 400

Hawthorn was a first-class, deep-sea smack, Colchester-registered and probably based at Brightlingsea. She is seen here drying her sails with her bowsprit and topmast housed.
(Mersea Museum, John Leather collection)

and navigation more certain. It generally meant putting part of the smack's crew on board a casualty to help pump ship or to handle extra anchors and cables. Sometimes, however, the salvaging smack arrived only to save the crew and any passengers, at great risk for themselves and the smack. Transfers were often made by the smack's boats in very bad weather and at night.

Once a ship was abandoned she became technically a wreck and the salvagers were free to remove anything from her. They could also attempt to float her. Sometimes they succeeded, but in most cases they were left stripping the vessel of as much cargo as possible. Depending on what this was and the conditions, they might also remove spars, rigging, equipment and fittings as fast as possible before the weather changed.

The salvaging smacks brought their plunder ashore at Harwich and Brightlingsea, where there were Receivers of Wrecks. The goods were auctioned and a proportion paid to the salvagers, but concealable items of value were often landed by night at the smack's home port. Bales of silk or tobacco, cases of spirits, coils of new rope, paint, cabin cutlery, crockery and the like were slipped ashore to be disposed of later, or kept for household use.

By the standards of the harsh social conditions of their times, the smacksmen could read and write well, had comfortable homes, and were proud of their seafaring skills and their fast vessels. They were among the world's finest fore-and-aft seamen and, from the late 1770s until 1939, men from their background and tradition supplied first-class crews for racing yachts.

When the Trinity House initiative of the nineteenth century made unlicensed pilotage illegal, a number of smacksmen continued to offer their services. With the vast numbers of ships trading, they were often still taken. Trinity House needed able vessels to recover their own pilots from outbound ships, particularly as the cruising cutters owned by the Trinity House pilots preferred to be out seeking inbound work. The Harwich pilotage station therefore chartered a number of smacks with their owners and crews to act as 'pilot tenders'.

Thomas Barnard of Rowhedge

Smack owner, fisherman, occasional smuggler, lifesaver and unlicensed pilot, Thomas Barnard was the archetypal 'Swin Ranger', named for one of the many shallow channels running out to sea from the Thames Estuary which he and his kind knew, night or day, as well as the names of their many children. His smack, *New Unity* was one of the fastest on the coast until she was lost on the Grain Spit in 1881. In his prime in the 1870s, Barnard and *New Unity* saved numerous lives. In one notable incident, while hired by Trinity House as pilot boat, he rescued the crew of a Spanish brig and was rewarded by the Spanish government. As a lad, Barnard stole some gear as a prank from the local Blacktail Beacon, was duly arrested and when told by the court that his action was endangering shipping, he went to what is described as 'considerable pains and some risk' to return it. Despite a successful outcome, he still served a formative week under lock and key.
(Mersea Museum, John Leather collection)

The duties consisted mainly of cruising to seaward of the Sunk sand, awaiting ships bound down from the Thames. The chartered smacks were rigged with a huge pennant to identify them. Because it was for the attention of ships bound down the Thames, this became known as a 'downie banner'.

The tenders with their downie banners kept on station in all but the very worst weather. Ironically, it was not the storm that drove them from their duty, but rather an ancient inclination to more profitable work. The piloting authorities frequently bemoaned the absence of one or more tenders from their station because their crews had sighted a ship ashore, often some distance away, perhaps seeing her rockets in the blackness of a winter night with a rising gale. Then the foresail was let draw and all hands settled down to fetch the wreck as fast as possible, to save life and lay hands upon any possible salvage.

After a time, yachts which the pilots were acquiring for use as cutters replaced the chartered smacks, but the question of taking off remained unpopular with the pilot vessels to the end.

Typical of those who chartered their smacks as tenders to Trinity House was Thomas Barnard of Rowhedge, smack owner, fisherman, unlicensed pilot, lifesaver, occasional smuggler and great-grandfather of the late John Leather, to whose work this chapter owes much. He spent his whole life in sailing smacks, from first going to sea in 1829 until he retired in 1881 after losing his largest smack in a winter gale. Like most of his contemporaries he was a good businessman and for a while was also engaged in the oyster and scallop business on the south coast. At the same time, he maintained his smacks at sea and at various periods he had four. His sons also were brought up in the fishing trade, serving with their father until purchasing their own bold cutters. The younger generation went on to become able captains of yachts in summer, but that is another story.

A colourful 'shop-floor' account of the demise of the North Channel sailing pilot service and its use of smacks is offered by Hervey Benham in his book, *Memories of a Scroper's Son*. Here, from his own encyclopedic knowledge of the East Coast and its seamen, he recreates the end in the words of his central character:

> The *Increase* was one of several craft the Trinity hired for pilot landing. First they closed down the stations at Yarmouth and Southwold and told the pilots to move to Harwich, which was a hardship to them to leave their homes, and in fact some never did. That was because the old sailing ships from Norway and Sweden and Finland and Russia was gone off the Suffolk coast.
>
> Then they decided to have just two cutters at the Sunk station and two at the Shipwash, and they employed our scropers to tend on them and land the down pilots. John Glover done that to the end. But that weren't much of a success. Scropers wasn't used to regular work, and as soon as there was a smell of a vessel ashore they'd humbug off and to hell with the Trinity. So in the end the Trinity said to hell with them and they used their own steam cutters.

The development of the cutter-rigged smack

The Essex rivers and fisheries demanded sailing craft that would tack tightly and surely when sailed shorthanded, yet still have powerful reaching performance and retain total manoeuvrability. Only the classic cutter could provide all these features, and the Essex smack developed into one of the finest examples of the type. The precise origins of the smack are lost, but it was well established in an early form by 1800, when several hundred smacks were operational. The majority hailed from Brightlingsea, a small but ever-lively port on a tidal creek in the mouth of the Colne. As time went on, the fleet subdivided into three general types. Specialists in inshore dredging and trawling rarely exceeded 35ft and 12 tons register; 50ft 18-tonners also tackled this work, but were more often used for general fishing at sea, while smacks at up to 65ft served in deep-sea fishing as well as salvaging, working with pilots and other varied forms of employment.

Eighteenth-century Essex boats were mostly of the smallest category. They were clinker-built with a transom stern, low freeboard and no cockpit, a feature which survived to the end. These bluff-bowed, chunky little craft had rigs not dissimilar to later versions, although the headsails and particularly the jibs were typical of their time, with a very low-cut clew and a sheet lead that appears to have been almost vertical.

A transitional type seems to be exemplified by the *Boadicea* which has chanced to survive to the present from a launch date of 1808. With her archaic 'cod's head and mackerel tail' hull form, she still works a dredge and is said to be remarkably handy.

Two or three decades after *Boadicea*'s keel was laid, a radical change in shape began to take place. Whether this was triggered by builders or their customers remains an evolutionary paradox, but some time around the 1830s smacks began to take on carvel planking and new lines. Entries lengthened and grew finer with a gently rounded forefoot, draught increased a little, beam shrank and flowing counter sterns replaced the transoms and lute sterns of their predecessors. Fifty-footers had bulwarks well over a foot high which scooped in the water aft where freeboard was low for handling gear, but their bold bows held them up to the hard driving to which their owners regularly subjected them. Rigs grew taller with sky-scraping topmasts, and by 1860 the Essex cutter was unrivalled in the North Sea for appearance and hard to beat for performance. She remained unchanged in all but a steady refinement until her final redundancy nearly a century later.

The facilities for the metamorphosis were in place soon after the French wars, since local yards were already building yachts to order with clean, sweet lines and powerhouse sailing characteristics. The Colne fishermen used to ship out on these craft as crew and captains in the summer months when oysters were out of season. It is not difficult to imagine a keen yacht hand coming home to his smack to find his homespun vessel frustratingly unweatherly and unlovely. Right on his doorstep were builders with the wherewithal to create a fishing boat that could work successfully and still satisfy his aesthetic and sporting instincts. What

The smack *Boadicea*

Launched in 1808 and probably the oldest sailing vessel in Europe that is still in use, *Boadicea* is an example of how the smacks of the Thames estuary looked before the influence of yachting took hold in the mid nineteenth century. Her transom stern and very wide beam of more than 10ft on a 30ft length are features from an earlier era.

(Mersea Museum, John Leather collection)

The yacht *Pearl*

Shortly after recovering from the loss of a leg at the Battle of Waterloo, the Marquis of Anglesey arrived in Wivenhoe on the River Colne in 1820 looking for a yacht builder. Philip Sainty was in line for the job, but not before the Marquis had arranged his release from jail. The result of their collaboration was the *Pearl*, so successful a yacht that many wealthy men followed Anglesey's lead and came to the Colne for their yachts. Perhaps even more significantly, the local fishermen whom he chose as his crew made such impressive yacht hands that almost all of them rose in due course to a yachting command of their own.
(© National Maritime Museum, Greenwich, UK)

is more, if he could gain prowess by thrashing all-comers in his smack, he was likely to attract the attention of a yacht-owner seeking to change his racing fortunes. Crack skippers were the heroes of the Essex towns, setting speed above everything, caring little for internal volume, headroom, or sometimes even whether a smack drew more water than was ideal for her work. And so was born a line of working craft that were halfway to being yachts.

One early example of yacht building in oyster-dredging country occurred at Wivenhoe, a village well up the Colne, in 1820. After taking stock on his return from the Battle of Waterloo, the Marquis of Anglesey decided he wanted a yacht of 130 tons. The Marquis was a phlegmatic character, hard to stop, as can be deduced from the anecdotal tale of his 'dismasting' in the great engagement. It appears he was astride his charger beside the Duke of Wellington when a French cannonball took off his leg. Without flinching, he turned to his general and remarked, 'By God, I've lost my leg!'

Wellington, no doubt with other matters on this mind, is said to have glanced his way and responded, 'By God, Sir, so you have!'

Quite why this old warrior came to the Colne for his yacht rather than Cowes or the Clyde is not told, but he clearly had inside knowledge, because on arrival he promptly demanded an interview with one Philip Sainty, the town's leading boatbuilder. Despite his name, Sainty was well-known locally for the stimulating criminal combination of smuggling and polygamy. When his patron arrived, he was doing time in Springfield Jail. The Marquis secured his release in return for a considerable sum, but Sainty refused to be 'sprung' until his brother and brother-in-law, also detained at King George's pleasure, were also set free.

The result of this infamous manipulation was the

Pearl, described by a reliable commentator as 'one of the finest vessels of its kind in the kingdom'. Her success was such that Wivenhoe steadily rose in status from the haunt of smugglers and fishermen into a fashionable yachting centre. Hardly a man in *Pearl*'s crew failed to become a yacht's master.

The rig of a typical smack

The smack rig is that of a classic gaff cutter simplified to the bare essentials and refined over a century and a half by world-class sailors. It can be seen to this day. Smaller smacks often work without topsails, though larger boats generally hoist topmasts which are generous in length, if not girth. When dredging, Tollesbury boats stowed these ashore in winter, substituting a short 'chock pole' from which a yard topsail could be set. Others kept them in the lowered position with the heel lashed to the mast, ready for hoisting in spells of light weather, their coiled topmast shrouds dangling like dowdy earrings from the temporarily redundant spreaders.

An average selection of three jibs enables something useful to be set from the bowsprit in almost any conditions. These long spars are innocent of shrouds but heavily bobstayed down. The desired angle is with the outboard end standing just a touch higher than the heel, although some are hove down below the horizontal.

Staysails are small and loose-footed, with a single sheet made back on itself through a shackle running along an iron thwartships horse. The sail is flattened by 'bowlines' set up from the shrouds either side, passed around the parts of the sheet, and used to heave the clew outboard and aft, thus flattening the sail and controlling twist for windward work. The bowline is also employed to 'back' the sail.

For reaching and running in light and moderate airs, a long-footed reaching staysail is set, sheeted directly to a cavil sited well aft. This more than makes up for any lack of power in the handy working staysail, pulling strongly on the reach and performing powerfully when boomed out on the run.

Smacks owned by racing skippers carried a single-luff spinnaker on regatta days, and so keen were these men to see off their rivals that it was not unusual to find a 38ft pole on a 40-footer.

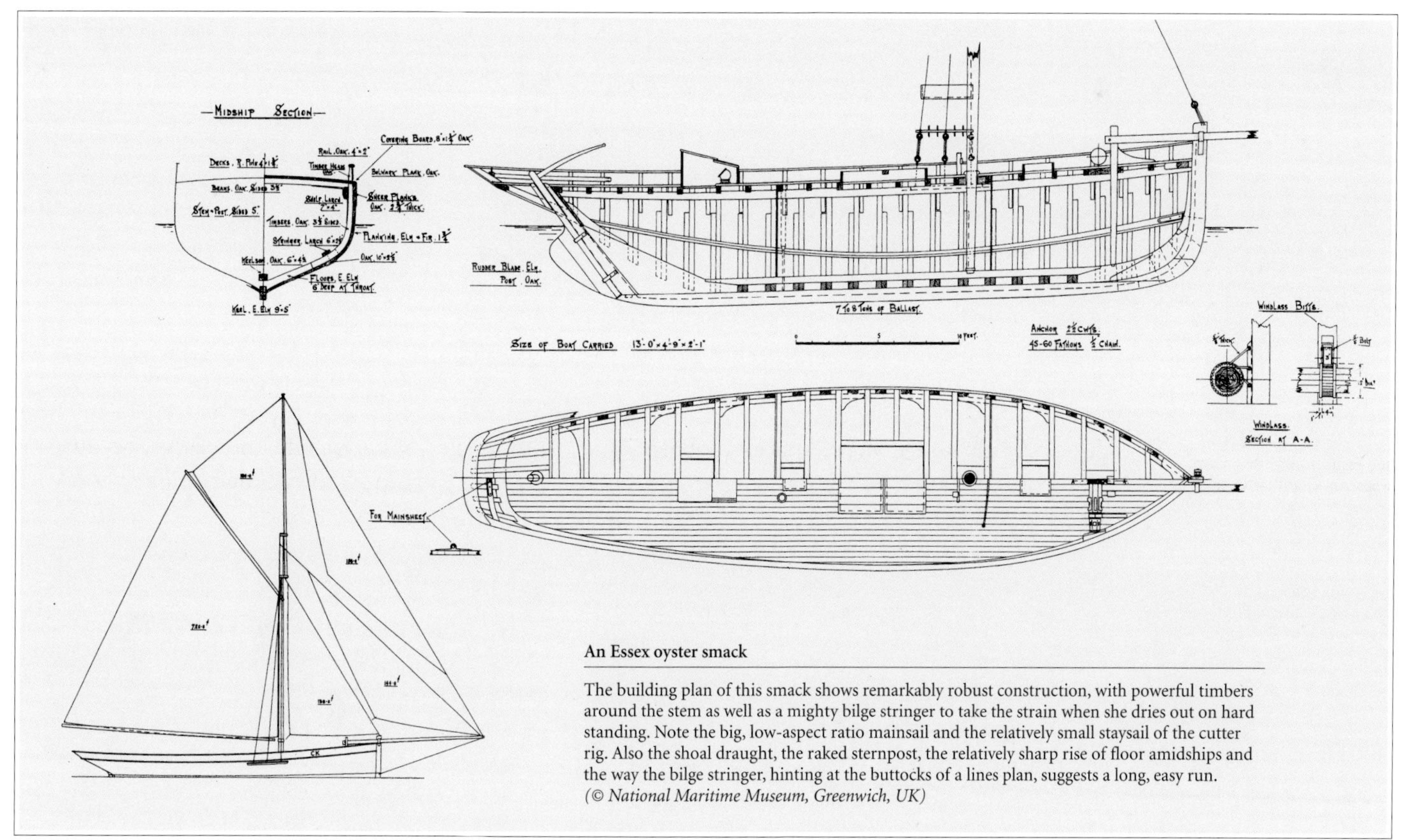

An Essex oyster smack

The building plan of this smack shows remarkably robust construction, with powerful timbers around the stem as well as a mighty bilge stringer to take the strain when she dries out on hard standing. Note the big, low-aspect ratio mainsail and the relatively small staysail of the cutter rig. Also the shoal draught, the raked sternpost, the relatively sharp rise of floor amidships and the way the bilge stringer, hinting at the buttocks of a lines plan, suggests a long, easy run.
(© National Maritime Museum, Greenwich, UK)

The proportions of the smack rig can be thought of as dictated by the length of the main boom, which is often around two-thirds the deck length plus an additional one eighth for overhang. There is no gooseneck, the boom heel having a simple jaw arrangement instead. The sail is hooped to the mast allowing the tack to be readily triced up for manoeuvring or rapid reduction of canvas. The main is, of course, loose-footed on the boom and the multi-part mainsheet stropped to the spar in preference to the expense and potential failure of ironwork. Only the largest smacks carried a trysail, but mainsails in working days could tie in a very close reef. It is said that some of the longer-haul boats rove chain reef pennants to stand up to the chafe endured on hard-driving reaches. Bearing in mind how even polyester ropes can suffer when a big gaff mainsail is left 'on the pennant' for a couple of days, it is easy to see how a manila or hemp reefing line would have been a cause for anxiety. The alternative solution of lashing the reef after heaving down the pennant would not appeal to a smacksman bent on maximum performance, since a degree of foot tension is inevitably lost as the pennant is slacked off after making the lashing. The resulting baggy sail would be an abhorrence to such seamen. Besides, nobody in their right mind wants to be hanging off the boom end on a dark night lashing a cringle unnecessarily while a low-freeboard boat is hammering along at 8kts!

A single topping lift is run from the lower mast-head and some larger smacks feature occasional running backstays. Race topsails might require long luff yards, but 'club' yards at the clew are generally absent. Topmasts themselves often appear to be bowsed forward to a crazy angle with no sail set, but such is the leech tension in the topsail once the sheet is cranked in, that the whole arrangement is forced 'into column'. The 'at-rest' state gives the boats a jaunty, uncompromising air which grows on an observer as he becomes better informed.

Wider horizons

The speed and sea-keeping ability of the Essex smacks made them well suited not only to fishing, and unofficial and semi-official pilot work, but to all manner of other profitable pursuits. While these do not relate directly to pilotage, a little study sheds much light on the sort of men who ran these boats, whatever they were doing for a job at the time.

As the Colchester Creek smacks gained in performance, the dreaded CK sail insignia was soon to be seen all around the coasts of Britain. Even across the Thames on the Kentish Flats, the Colne men taunted the local dredgermen, calling them 'stay-at-homes', as they helped themselves to young oysters that could have fed the Whitstable families.

This situation was typical, with the Colne smacksmen fishing out grounds in other parts of the country that had long provided a steady living for their natural incumbents. This created ill-will and sometimes physical resistance, but neither stopped the Essex men, who literally elbowed their neighbours aside in their zeal for profit. The ground near Bench Head at the mouth of the Colne was used locally as a store-room for culch. In the early 1890s, smacks from Burnham, a few miles to the south, began dredging this material for their own grounds. The local men from Tollesbury and West Mersea hurled all manner of threats at the incomers, culminating in a promise to run them down, but still the Burnham smacks turned a deaf ear. One day, four Burnham boats were dredging up their controversial harvest when three Tollesbury smacks approached, apparently innocently, with the usual two or three men on deck. One came alongside the Burnham smack *Emeline*. As the two boats ground together, the attacker flung open her hold and out sprang a dozen brawny Blackwater fishermen brandishing makeshift weapons. The *Emeline* capitulated after a token resistance. Two of the other 'southerners' also 'lowered their colours' in short order, but the fourth, the *Rose*, crewed by Messrs Rice and Andrews, proved a different kettle of fish. As a Tollesbury boat rounded up to board, Andrews produced a gun which he calmly loaded in full view of his assailants, offering to shoot anyone who put a foot over his rail. This led to an impasse, but did not help the other 'trespassers', whose crews now had to watch while their catch was hove over the side, together with any cabin stores the boarders could find. Items of value, such as tobacco, tea or coffee, were extorted on the spot, with the assurance that if any more Burnham craft came poaching, their crews would follow the culch back into deep water.

The smack *Neva* on race day

Neva was built by Harris of Rowhedge for Captain Lemon Cranfield and paid for with prize money won aboard the Fife-designed yacht of the same name, of which he was the highly successful skipper. Seen here in a smack race which, for once, she is not leading, two hands on the foredeck are in the process of hoisting, or perhaps lowering, the overlapping reaching foresail with a stiff breeze on the beam. Note the powerful, loose-footed mainsail and the running topmast preventer backstays which, unlike those on yachts of her day, are secured well forward of the helmsman.
(Mersea Museum, John Leather collection)

Eventually, a case for the capital offence of piracy was brought against the Tollesbury men, but the judge threw it out of court with some sharp remarks about wasting his time, and the gallows was returned to store.

As well as keeping a weather eye open for piloting opportunities, perhaps the most famous sideshow activity of the Essex smacks was 'salvaging' from shipwrecks on the numerous banks and shoals off their native coast. Ships were so often stranded on the edges of the Swin channel between the Barrow and the Maplin Sands that many of the smacksmen styled themselves with tongue in cheek as 'Swin Rangers'.

Craft from most outer Thames and Suffolk harbours undertook this opportunist work, but nine out of ten are said to have come from the Colne. Along with the profitable side, however, came great personal risk, and sometimes lives were saved with no possibility of commercial gain. Many a coaster operator considered the men of Brightlingsea and Rowhedge black-hearted sharks, while others of all nations owed them the very breath in their bodies. Too many Swin Rangers never came back.

Two incidents serve to illustrate this point: in 1856, a German ship bound for China and loaded down with barter goods, piled up on the Knock John Shoal in the outer Thames. A number of salvage operators boarded her, but the first was a Brightlingsea smack whose booty passed into legend. Amongst the numerous wonders that came

Smacks at Brightlingsea

At rest for once, it is interesting to note how many of these smacks have their topmasts housed. Today, topmasts are generally thought of as semi-permanent fixtures. Photographs of the smacks of Essex in their heyday indicate that housing them was very much a routine affair. If fitted with self-tumbling fids, the whole operation could be done from the deck. *(Mersea Museum, John Leather collection)*

off that ship were cases of fine drinking glasses, and for generations good fortune was toasted in 'Knock John glasses', passed down as mementos of that famous night's work.

A very different story was the rescue from the *Wesleyan*, a billyboy schooner wrecked on Beachy Head with a cargo of Portland stone, in a gale so heavy that the lifeboat could not leave harbour and the Dieppe steamer service was suspended. The smack *Wave*, possibly bound home after dredging Fécamp oysters or even some far-flung piloting exploit, hove alongside and offered to rescue the skipper. He refused to jump, saying he had 'something else' in the cabin. The smack skipper, Causton, clambered up and went below to find the man's wife with five children and a three-month-old baby 'as naked as he was born'. The water was above the bunk tops, and the family dazed with shock, but the oystermen dragged them out and somehow got them one by one aboard the smack. The captain had virtually lost his mind and refused to be taken off, saying he could not face going home to an empty house with his family, as the ship was all he had, so the smacksmen physically restrained him and cast him into their boat.

There was no salvage profit from the *Wesleyan* and Newhaven lay dead to windward. The spray must have flown over the gaff jaws beating in such conditions, but they arrived about nine o'clock at night after a difficult time with the captain's wife, who kept crying out that the smack would go down like her husband's ship. An impromptu collection of £5 was offered to the Colne men, who promptly handed it over to the unfortunate people off the *Wesleyan*.

On their return home, an audience in Colchester town hall are said to have wept as they heard the state of affairs in the ship's cabin described. Perhaps all was well that ended well, because Causton now received a bounty of £13 and his mate was awarded a gold medal.

One drawback of salvaging, even when it was apparently profitable, was that gear saved from the sea had to be reported and handed over to the Receiver of Wrecks. This official secured it for the crown and gave the salvors a modest percentage. To hand over their winnings to a brass-bound character snug in an office was unacceptable to men who had risked their lives out on the sands to turn a quick profit, so all manner of schemes were devised to outwit the system. One such method was employed at the wreck of the Norwegian barque *Nef* on the Long Sand on 24 September 1879. When found by Lloyd's, she had been stripped right to the door hinges, but the receiver was only handed the most meagre winnings. He knew full well that the smacks worked in unofficial companies, so that two

might go to the wreck while a third was very blatantly fishing. The three would meet up well offshore and the plunder was transferred to the 'innocent' fisherman, who spirited it home after dark. Meanwhile, the salvagers toddled up to the receiver's office to report some trifles that allegedly represented their total take. The authorities were aware of the system but found it difficult to counter, so that when a smacksman's wife turned up at church in a gown made from impossibly expensive fabric, there was nothing they could do about it, though they knew as well as everyone else that the contraband material was from a wreck.

Sometimes, even men themselves had to be spirited away so as not to be seen involved in a salvage operation. On one occasion, that famous Swin Ranger Thomas Barnard of Rowhedge, well known for his piloting work in addition to all his other salty callings, was smuggled home in a sack as part of a consignment of coal. The receiver never found out he was not still at sea until the transaction was completed.

Building, repair, and living conditions aboard

Almost all smacks were built locally, within the village from which they would work. Harris of Rowhedge, Aldous of Brightlingsea, and Harvey of Wivenhoe were among numerous successful yards. Some of these even built 'on spec', laying down a fast-looking vessel and finishing her for either pleasure or work once a buyer had declared his preference. Building was prolific, with the numbers of smacks in Colchester registration reaching a staggering 322 in 1872, including 132 of the charismatic first-class craft.

Smacks were constructed of inexpensive material that could be either obtained close by or cheaply imported. Framing and backbone were of oak or elm and planking was generally pine or fir, often imported from Eastern Europe rather than the more expensive pitch pine favoured by builders in other parts of the country. Nonetheless, many survived to great age. Fastenings were typically galvanised iron spikes and bolts. A heavy iron grounding band was attached to the wood keel, serving to lower the centre of gravity as well as protecting the smack.

At the time of order, a lines plan was drawn up for the owner's approval. This was a rough-and-ready affair, often followed by the carving of a half-model which was not used for lofting, but merely to assist planking up. The whole job might take around four months.

Smacks were often painted grey or blue. A new boat was the apple of her owner's eye and was kept in appropriate trim, smart and clean. Aldous looked after the souls of his customers by installing a Bible in every boat, complete with a built-in box in the cabin. First-class smacks had a forepeak for cable, abaft which came the 'mast room' which served as a pantry and housed the scuttlebutt. The hold occupied the centre third of the boat, while aft came the cabin, with four bunks. These were closed by sliding panels to give the sleeper the only privacy he could expect, sometimes for weeks on end. A rough-and-tumble 'double' under the counter known, for apocryphal reasons, as the 'Yarmouth Roads', offered home comfort for up to two apprentices, who must have had some disturbed watches below as the rudder groaned in its trunk and waves slopped beneath the counter, inches from their weary heads. Nor, when dragged from sleep to stoke the fire, could they expect what any mother would consider a decent cup of tea. The giant pot was kept permanently on the coal stove beside the kettle and was steadily topped up with fresh tea or water as circumstances demanded. It was never slopped over the side for a re-start until there was no longer space in it for six cups.

The lads were generally detailed off to cook. On a boat going to sea for a spell under the downie banner, the meat ration might consist of 1cwt (50kg) pork, 1cwt beef and a side of ham. Any unwanted fish taken were also 'up for grabs', with sole being a favourite for breakfast. One account has men putting away three or four weighing a pound apiece.

Apprentices were generally bound at the age of ten or twelve, and served for a minimum of five years. Some apprenticeships ran for nine years. They were paid around £10 per year and lived with their masters ashore, but were obliged to provide their own rig which, like their seniors', consisted of a 'cheesecutter' cap, an untreated canvas smock covering a thick Guernsey, and fearnought trousers worn inside leather seaboots with nailed soles.

Such was the life aboard a smack out at sea,

picking off pilots and looking out for a chance of profit elsewhere.

Like most working craft, smacks would from time to time require purging of vermin, and we are indebted to Mr Thurston-Hopkins for a first-hand account of this process.

> The cooking stove was roared up into a bright coke fire, then the companion hatch and all frames were closed and every chink and opening sealed up with brown paper and glue. Then three sticks of sulphur were purchased and a small bottle of mercury, all of which were bounded into a package with twine and brown paper. The package was then pushed down the deck chimney into the fire. After some hours of fumigation, the hatches were opened up and the harvest of dead rats and cockroaches were swept up.
>
> 'But why do they put mercury in the packet?' I asked …
>
> 'The brimstone is for the hinsecs [*sic*] and the quicksilver for the rats – it gives 'em the electric shock and kills 'em.'

The Gravesend wherries

The Gravesend wherry was around 20–26ft overall with a length to beam ratio of around 4:1. The narrow beam assisted easy towing as well as making the boat easier to row. A boomless standing lugsail and small staysail were set inboard in suitable conditions. Some even carried a small mizzen. The boats were generally black-leaded with a boldly picked-out sheer strake. If a wherry were painted white, as some were, the sheer strake was kept bright, oiled with linseed.

Gravesend wherries were used by local watermen for hobbling work, primarily for claiming an approaching ship then handling her lines for her. A favourite way of securing business was to hook on to an outward-bound vessel, perhaps one the waterman had been looking after, and tow out down the shipping lanes in search of the next customer. There are records of watermen not slipping their tow until off the Royal Sovereign lightship, almost at Beachy Head.

These are the men and the boats about which the North Channel pilots complained for picking up ships off the Gunfleet Sand that had slipped by the Sunk Light pilot cutters overnight. If questioned, the watermen would always insist that they were merely out looking for a 'hobble', and would have nothing to do with the navigation of their ships. This was believed by nobody, but proving their unlicensed activities as pilots was nigh-on impossible.

Yachting and village life

As we have seen, smacks would never have developed their full glory without the multiple careers of many smacksmen in their ancestral vocations down-Swin and professional yachting. One of the doyens of this breed was Captain Lemon Cranfield who made enough prize money skippering the Fife yacht *Neva* to have Harris of Rowhedge build him a 40ft smack named after 'his' famous yacht. The smack race was always the main event at village regattas, and with men at the helm whose priorities were more for racing than for their duties as Swin rangers, pilot carriers and deep-sea dredgers, it must have made a grand spectacle. Year after year, the *Neva* and 'Captain Lemon' would cream in first, with such flyers as *Wonder* and *Sunbeam*, built for Lemon's brother William of the Kaiser's *Valkyrie*, snapping at her heels. As she crossed the line first, ahead despite a handicap of one second per ton per mile, the local band would strike up some popular tune such as 'See the Conquering Hero Comes!' Cranfield's most athletic hand swarmed up the mast hoops to wedge the champion's gilt cock at the masthead, as his skipper acknowledged the applause of the crowd by raising his cap. Then he joined his crew in cheering the second and third smacks, who returned the compliment.

Some remarkable times were turned in at these regattas. In 1884, the records from Wivenhoe indicate that a course of almost twenty-one miles was completed by *Neva* in a few seconds over 2 hours and 23 minutes, an average of 8¾kts. The next two boats finished within a further 5 minutes. By today's standards these are phenomenal performances for gaff-rigged, heavy displacement 40-footers, but as Masefield remarked of a different set of seamen at the same period, these skippers 'mark our passage as a race of men.'

The spiritual life of the villages was actively provided for by the church, with harvest festival a major event. During the service, the church walls were draped with nets, contrasting their warm browns with the white and gold of lifebelts from yachts. Bright-varnished oars lined the aisle and the altar corners were defined by port and starboard lamps shining brightly over the healthy, rosy faces of the congregation. From the fisher lads at the back to the racing skippers crowding the front pews, all hands joined with full gusto in the traditional closing hymn, 'Eternal Father Strong to Save'.

CHAPTER 10

The Bristol Channel and its Cutters

FROM THE SEAMAN'S VIEWPOINT, the Bristol Channel is a geographic phenomenon. Its mouth extends forty miles north from Hartland Point in Devon, past Lundy Island, to the southwest corner of Wales. From this outer limit, the Channel narrows rapidly to a width of twenty miles or so between Ilfracombe and the Gower Peninsula, before stretching a further eighty miles east to Sharpness. Thereafter, deepwater navigation ceases and ships bound further inland take to the Gloucester/Sharpness canal.

The cul-de-sac nature of the Bristol Channel creates an exceptional tidal range, with heights up to 50ft in its upper reaches. The natural harbours therefore tend to dry out at low water, giving rise to a number of locked or dredged ports. The approaches to many of these have always been interesting to say the least, which, together with the mighty tidal streams that sweep up and down in the offing, led to an early need for reliable pilots.

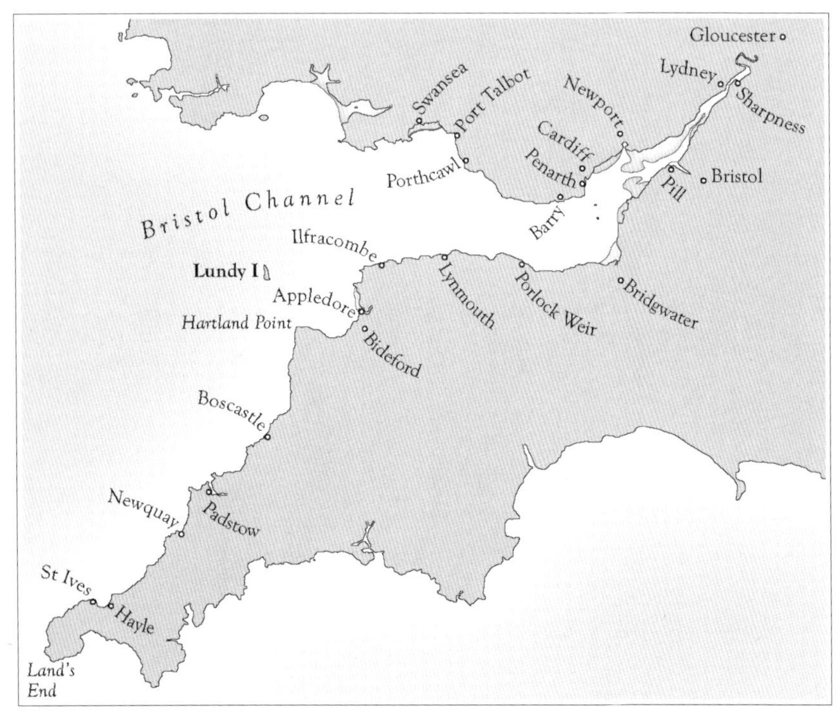

The Bristol Channel

The funnel shape of the upper channel in a region of generally big tides creates some of the world's largest rises with streams to match. In the prevailing southwesterly wind the powerful ebb currents enabled the pilot cutters to make good some prodigious distances in six-hour packages. The steep seas that necessarily accompanied this bonus had a direct effect on the final form of the local cutters.

From the beginnings of history, Bristol was a general trading centre. By the Middle Ages, merchant-adventuring and fast-expanding home markets were in full swing. The harbour lies eight miles up the River Avon, which virtually dries at low water, with streams running up to 6kts. The river had made Bristol safe from the natural dangers of the Bristol Channel and the old-time Viking plunderers but, as ships grew steadily larger, it began to cause real difficulties and resulted ultimately in the city-centre port becoming commercially unusable.

By the end of the fifteenth century, traders of up to 800 tons were arriving at Avonmouth for passage to Bristol. Such craft could not possibly negotiate the tortuously bending waterway with its winds distorted by the walls of the river's gorge, nor could they 'drudge' with the tide. Such methods were commonplace elsewhere, but the twists of the Avon made them useless. Instead, masters of oceangoing ships hired teams of hobblers whose lives were dedicated to the task of working ships up and down the river. These men traditionally lived in or around the village of Pill near the river's mouth.

The hobblers used oars, poles and small boats to keep the ship from swinging athwart the stream as the tidal stream carried her slowly but surely either up to the city or down to the sea. If they failed, so that the stem- or sternpost touched the mud of the steeply shelving banks, the ship would certainly 'stick' if the tide were falling. Stranded vessels were sometimes lost by breaking their backs or by capsizing on the slope of the dried-out river bed, so the hobblers and their art became crucial to the success of the growing port.

By the mid eighteenth century, ships were of such a size that even with the help of hobblers, only local owners would risk the passage up to the city. However, the port had become too commercially important to be abandoned so, rather than hazard the Avon gorge, other craft would anchor in Hung Road near the mouth of the river to have their cargoes lightered up to the city.

The problem of the Avon was never solved, and by 1800 it was clear that something must be done to make the port more attractive to ships. In 1810 the first major engineering work since medieval times was commenced, creating 30 hectares of deepwater harbour which was now entered on the

A seeking Bristol Channel pilot cutter

Like many others in this chapter, this lovely image is from the collection of Pilot Lewis Alexander. Some are hand-tinted glass-plate lantern slides and this one is so heavily retouched that it is difficult to judge whether it be photograph or painting. It is the former and shows a classic cutter of 50ft plus on deck. The topmast indicates that she predates 1908, after which almost all cutters had pole masts. She appears to be registered for Cardiff and Barry, although these would normally carry the legends 'Cf' and 'By'. Another unusual feature is her tan-barked sails. Virtually all pilots favoured white. Whether these anomalies are true or the imagination of an artist, the hull is glorious, with the high bows of earlier craft.
(Author's collection)

A job well done

A Barry pilot cutter waiting for a breeze in a West Country harbour. Perhaps she has put her pilot on the coasting schooner to bring her up to South Wales, or maybe she has just been brought in by her crew to wait for her pilot who has gone up-Channel on a ship and agreed to meet them at sea a few days later. We shall never know, but the old salt watching from the foreshore will be noting with approval the triced-up, loose-footed mainsail – no roller reefing on this boat – and the topsail, hoisted but not yet sheeted home.
(Author's collection)

tide via locks. Soon afterwards, the newly invented steam tugs presented large sailing ships with the possibility of moving against the stream, while powered cargo ships could propel themselves, given a tug to assist in manoeuvring. Both could now enjoy the option of leaving the locks an hour or two before high water, which improved steering and gave a second chance to any vessel unfortunate enough to run aground.

Despite these improvements, there was still no real choice but to relocate the main Bristol docks nearer to the sea. With the coming of the railways this finally became practical and a locked dock was constructed at Avonmouth in 1877. This and other docks which followed at Portishead restored Bristol's fortunes just in time. By 1908, Avonmouth had the largest lock in the country.

Among the other ancient ports of the Channel were Swansea, Cardiff, Gloucester and Newport. Port Talbot and Barry were opened in the late nineteenth century to keep up with the demands of shipping. By the heyday of Channel pilotage in the 1890s, Bristol was dealing in all manner of cargoes, while the South Wales ports specialised in exporting steam coal – the best in the world and the powerhouse of the growing empire – from the nearby Rhondda valley. Imports centred around ores for the new heavy industries. Such West Country harbours as Bideford, Appledore, Bridgwater, and numerous lesser ports including Lynmouth and Porlock Weir also flourished at this time of booming Victorian expansion, but remained outside the famous Bristol Channel pilot service.

Development of the Bristol Channel pilot service

According to tradition, the first Bristol pilot was a man by the name of George Ray, a barge master from the Avon. Ray is said to have piloted Cabot's ship, the *Matthew*, on her outward passage from Bristol at the start of her great voyage to the New World in May 1497. There seems to be no sound

Pill on regatta day

Pill, at the entrance to the Bristol Avon, was the ancestral home of Channel pilots. The word 'Pill' is synonymous with 'creek' in other parts of Britain, and this pill dries out completely, leaving the cutters upright, aground in the mud. The village of Pill was devoted to pilotage and many Bristol pilots still live there today. *(Author's collection)*

documentary evidence of this event, but the whole pilot community will affirm that it took place, so who are we to doubt it?

In his excellent 1953 paper on Bristol Channel pilotage, Grahame Farr states that from 1611 control of the Bristol pilots was vested in the Society of Merchant Venturers and remained with them for two and a half centuries. Evidence from this period relates to the fact that pilots were living at 'Crockerne Pill', 'Crockam Pill', or other variations of the name for the modern village of Pill on the Somerset bank of the Avon. To this day, the community remains a centre for Bristol pilots.

In 1798, the Bristol Corporation was constituted as the pilotage authority, not only for ports in the River Severn such as Gloucester, but also further west up to and including Cardiff. In practice, these powers do not seem to have been applied stringently. The five pilots operating from Cardiff at that time would have nothing to do with the regulations and answered to no special control. The only exception to this legislation was Swansea, apparently rendered independent by its own earlier Harbour Act of 1791, which gave authority to the port's trustees to appoint pilots for their bay and port.

The provisions of the 1798 act were clarified and modified by the Bristol Channel Pilotage Act, a more important statute which received royal assent in August 1807. This stated categorically that jurisdiction for all pilotage east of Lundy was vested in the 'Mayor, Burgesses and Commonalty of the City of Bristol'.

By-laws for the administration of this Act were drawn up by 1809 and expanded from time to time. There was now no doubt about who was boss, but the situation was not accepted without a fight. Cardiff in particular was active in trying to address the administrative nightmare caused by the edict, and unsuccessfully sought redress from Parliament in 1840. Twenty years later, the port was sending forty pilots to sea, almost as many as Bristol. They could no longer tolerate a 'foreign' master, so the Cardiff authorities joined forces with the equally disenfranchised Gloucester and Newport men to push a realistic bill through the narrow corridors of Whitehall.

In 1861, the new Bristol Channel pilotage laws were enacted. Under these, pilotage in the open Channel, beyond the limits of any port, became non-compulsory unless a ship were bound for Bristol. The Bristol port pilotage limits were initially set at Lundy, but were withdrawn after thirty years to the island of Flat Holme, only twenty-five miles to seaward of Avonmouth.

Pilotage for entering Cardiff, Gloucester, Newport and the lesser harbour of Porthcawl was set down as non-compulsory, but the other ports including Bristol and Swansea maintained compulsory pilotage within their own limits.

The 1861 Act also enabled suitably licensed Bristol Channel pilots (always known locally as 'Channel pilots') to bring ships into ports other than their own so long as they undertook the necessary examinations. While a ship in the Bristol Channel was not obliged to have a pilot unless bound towards Bristol, if she opted to take one, that pilot must be licensed. A licensed man could supersede an unlicensed pilot and claim the pilotage fee.

None of the pilots suffered under this legislation except the Pill pilots from Bristol, who had lost the unnatural ascendancy they had enjoyed under the previous rules.

The Pill pilots were now driven to work harder than ever before because if they did not offer their

Three Welsh pilot cutters beating seawards

This revealing image from the first years of the twentieth century tells us a lot. The first two boats appear to have roller reefing mainsails and both sails have hooked leeches which is doing nothing for performance. The third has a better cut mainsail, with standard 'points' or 'slab' reefing. The sail is setting beautifully with a clean run off the leech. All carry the outboard ends of their booms high, to give 'down' pull from the sheet to control leech tension and to keep the boom out of the water when running in a big sea. The third cutter has no bobstay. Many did not because its absence made reefing or housing the bowsprit easier, but one look at the spar 'skying' under the pull of the jib and the consequent sag in the jib luff tells any sailor that this boat is never going to be competitive to windward. Why this was tolerated to mitigate so minor an inconvenience is a mystery. *(Author's collection)*

services far down to the west, a licensed Channel pilot from some other port might take their ships as far as King Roads off Avonmouth, pocketing the lion's share of the dues. 'Channel' pilots, it must be remembered, could now bring ships up to the approaches for any port. A Channel pilot unlicensed for the ship's destination handed over to a local port pilot in the offing and the fees were divided.

Incomes in other ports did not fall as a result of the removal of compulsory pilotage. In fact, they rose. Pilots from outside Bristol flourished under the new arrangements and the competitive cruising for which the Channel cutters became famous kicked immediately into action.

The Bristol Channel had become wide open for pilots to indulge their capacity for hard work and big earnings. 'Channel Men' from Bristol and Cardiff, as well as hard-sailing pilots from Barry, Newport and the rest, were now regularly seen thrashing westwards to be first to offer their services to any rich ship that came along. In most ports, this was now the way of business for the next fifty years, though there was a bizarre hiatus at Bristol in 1880.

Throughout the world of pilot work, there has always existed a system known as 'choice pilotage', whereby a shipping company prefers one or more pilots out of those available. These choice pilots then take all the business offered by that firm. Such a system was often contentious and never put down roots in the Bristol Channel, perhaps because of the difficulty of finding your own pilot among the mass of cutters in the shipping lanes.

In 1880, however, the Great Western Steamship Company made the mistake of nominating three choice pilots for their highly lucrative transatlantic ships. At that time, there were forty pilots at Bristol and thirty-seven cutters. Bristol boats sailed with two westernmen, as pilot-boat crews were called, plus a boy. The Company's action meant a serious drop in earnings for a great many families and could not be tolerated. One of the choice pilots opted to walk home late to Pill from Bristol after leaving a ship, imagining this to be a safe alternative to risking a drowning accident in the hobblers' boat. His plan misfired, however, and he was ambushed by a gang of angry women who tarred and feathered him. Thereafter matters grew rapidly more unpleasant. In frustration one non-choice pilot tried to board

Barry Harbour

A Newport pilot cutter sails past the entrance to Barry with the tide well down. Ships are anchored in the offing and a local cutter is half in picture at the right. The paddle steamer is lying on the pontoon used by the pilots. The successor to this pontoon was still in place in 2009 and used by the modern-day pilots, whose pilot house remains at the top of its steps. *(Author's collection)*

A summer day in Ilfracombe

Ilfracombe harbour at high water in the early years of the twentieth century. The handsome cutter in the foreground is a yacht, but two pilot cutters are rafted up on the inside of the harbour wall opposite waiting their time to put to sea and pick up their pilots. Ilfracombe lies a convenient tide's sail westward from Barry and Cardiff. It made a perfect staging post for far-ranging cutters. *(Author's collection)*

***White Heather*, giving the ladies a day out**

White Heather was bought by Pilot Lewis Alexander with two other pilots in 1904 when he was first licensed. The boat had been a West Country fishing vessel, but he re-rigged her as a gaff cutter and sailed her with great success until he achieved his full Channel licence and commissioned the famous *Kindly Light*. The man sculling the cutter is Tom Morgan, who was Alexander's man-in-the-boat for many years. *(Author's collection)*

a Great Western steamer off Lundy on a winter's night, but was rejected. While he was below taking off his oilskins, his westernman set about ramming the choice cutter and would have succeeded had not the pilot scrambled up the companionway and knocked him from the heavy iron tiller.

On pain of losing their licences, the pilots could take no direct action in this matter. The westernmen were not so bound and in January 1881, they struck in earnest. Chains were stretched across the creek allowing no cutters in or out, and a meeting in the parish rooms declared that in future they would divide into two groups to cruise the approaches on alternate twenty-four-hour shifts until justice was done. When the Haven Master of Bristol demanded to be told what they were doing, the westernmen, all naval reservists, called back, 'You taught us to blockade the port.'

Any westernman, pilot or hobbler who refused to comply with the blockade was to be lashed to a cross and carried round the village with 'traitor' on his chest, before being dumped in a pond at the head of the creek. This dire retribution was in fact carried out on one blackleg.

Desperate to get to sea, one of the choice pilots now tried to shoot his way out of the creek with a revolver. He was disarmed by the men who then

Hard on the wind

A Cardiff cutter beats powerfully to windward. Although the image is not clear enough to be sure, the tight jib luff suggests that she has a bobstay set up. She carries the pole mast typical of later cutters and in order to regain the sail area potentially lost from her topsail, she is flying a large jackyarder. This picture is like a textbook on setting up a gaff cutter to work to windward. Taut headsail luffs lift her to windward while perfect twist in the mainsail and topsail uses the freer wind aloft to drive the boat ahead with minimal heeling.
(Author's collection)

imaginatively left him to the women. They tarred and feathered him, handed out the same treatment to his son, then beat them up on their way home for good measure. In due course, the strike was settled and choice piloting came to an end, but out of the affair sprang the United Kingdom Pilots' Association with its ringing motto, 'United we stand. Divided we fall.' The co-operative system operated during the crisis could be seen as the forerunner of the amalgamations which ultimately overtook all the Bristol Channel ports.

The Swansea pilots joined forces in 1898, with Gloucester following in 1903, reducing their number of cutters to four which they held jointly as a company. The rest kept on running their own individual boats until the years surrounding World War I. The 1910 Parliamentary report on compulsory pilotage made the general observations that

> the system of keen competition and privately owned sailing cutters is not only unsuited to modern requirements, but places upon its pilots a burden for which there is no justification. The direct result to pilots of this system is an enormous wastage of time, effort and, we regret to say, an occasional loss of life …We realise that some pilots are very naturally reluctant to change the conditions of carrying out their work … but the evidence … shows the need for some reform.

The report went on to recommend amalgamation. In 1913, the Cardiff pilots submitted to the inevitable. They were obliged to sell their cutters to the pilotage authorities who in due course sold them on to yachtsmen, small-time traders, fishermen – in short, to anyone with an eye for a weatherly, seaworthy vessel. The proceeds were invested in steam cutters to be kept on station at the Nash, Barry Roads and Cardiff Roads. The pilots worked on a rota and the game was over.

Barry followed suit in 1915, but not without stiff resistance. Pilot Lewis Alexander's son, Mr N Alexander, advised in the 1980s that when the war ended, his father and eight other pilots fitted out their old cutters and worked them for nine months. They pulled in huge wages because they had only to sail to seaward of the steam cutter to grab first choice of any ships. The commissioners, however, would have none of this. The 'wild-cat' pilots were pulled into line by the direct threat of having their licences revoked, and so ended the Barry sailing pilot service.

The last pilots to buckle under to amalgamation were those from Bristol, where the whole piloting business had begun so many centuries earlier. They amalgamated in 1918; in 1922, the steam pilot vessel *Queen Mother* sailed from the Avon. She was owned by a limited company of thirty pilots. The *EMC* and the *Pet* were retained for 'back-up' duties – the *Pet* had been a noted flyer in her day – but over a remarkably short period the remainder of the most famous cutters of them all beat away down-Channel and sailed into legend.

Perhaps the most appropriate epitaph for the cruising pilot was found on an otherwise empty sheet of paper on which an elderly pilot had set out to list his rational objections to amalgamation. He had written only five words: 'I shall lose my freedom.'

Cruising pilotage under sail

Traditionally, Bristol Channel pilots owned their own cutters as individuals, fighting out the daily battle for work, boat against boat, man against man. Exceptionally, two pilots would own a boat together, perhaps while saving up to invest in their own cutters. It was also understood that a young pilot who had not yet had the opportunity to earn enough money to buy a cutter needed a start, so an established pilot would take on such a man as his 'number two' for a short while until the less experienced pilot established himself. Surprisingly, no ports operated a system of finance for assisting in cutter purchase, although there exists a solitary ledger entry in Cardiff stating that this was done on one occasion. Most pilot groups ran a friendly system of mutual insurance, however, all paying into a common fund to help out any of their number unfortunate enough to lose his boat.

The cutters themselves were in the order of 50ft long and most sailed with a crew of two in addition to any pilots. The chief hand was known as the 'man-in-the-boat' on the Welsh side, or the 'westernman' on the English. His mate would either be a second man of the same calling, or an apprentice pilot, in his fifth or final year. Earlier in his time than this, the apprentice was an extra hand.

Pilots had their own systems of finding out what ships were due in the Channel. Some would make a point of 'looking after' shipping agents, others had an encyclopedic knowledge of what ships had departed, when they had left and whither they had been bound. Using this information, for steamers at least, their vast experience allowed them to predict with surprising accuracy when they would be back. As soon as the telephone became available, ambitious pilots installed handsets in their homes and received regular reports from contacts down west, who either knew or could see with their own eyes what was coming up. One Pill pilot is known to have made a private arrangement with the telegraph officers at the Land's End signal station.

At the other end of the technology scale, Captain Bartlett, a Newport pilot who served his apprenticeship in the old cutters, recalled in 1961 that his chief used to buy lists of ships expected in port from two shipping butchers' runners. The backhander for the runner was one shilling per list, with a bonus for a 'red-hot tip'. New ships were always marked, which was important because pilots who had put to sea the previous day would not know about them. It seems that the list from butcher Elliot was preferred to that of his rival, Ford, because Ford was reputed to copy his information out of the Liverpool and Cardiff journals, sources which the pilots all knew perfectly well.

Pilot Lewis Alexander had a man in Ilfracombe who received telegrams from home base in Barry, then put off in his boat to hand the insider information to Alexander as he sailed on westwards, already a tide ahead of the competition.

Once he knew a good paying ship was going to be off Land's End in a couple of days, it might serve a pilot well to press on all the way if he had a fair wind and could make it in time. Even if he failed, there was still a good chance he would be to the westward of his rivals. Many accounts exist of pilot cutters sailing up to Liverpool and Belfast to meet ships bound for their own ports while they were still in dock. Pilot Alexander took his wife on one such voyage to Northern Ireland, and the good lady consented to come along only if her feather mattress was shipped in the starboard quarter so that she could enjoy her watch below to the full.

Other accounts exist of pilots from the Bristol Channel sailing well up the English Channel to have first chance of a ship. The southwest of Ireland was also an established rendezvous for ships from North America, and many a pilot experienced a bad night or two hove to off Cape Clear.

Such zeal for action did not always guarantee success, however. A cutter might work all the way round to the Isle of Wight looking for a ship bound for Cardiff from some northern European port, only to have her offer of pilotage refused by the captain. Pilotage being non-compulsory, a skipper was at liberty to do this, and some preferred to take a pilot off Lundy, or even further in at Nash Point. The cutter had thus wasted her trip and could have had the ship far nearer home. Perhaps another ship would happen along, but pickings would be more spread out further from home.

While a ship retained the right to refuse a pilot, this liberty of choice did not work the other way round. If a ship requested a pilot, any Channel pilot was obliged to take her, whether he wanted her or

Aboard *Kindly Light* in 1918–19

This remarkable photograph shows three of the great men of the Channel in one boat at the same time. Furthest from camera is Pilot Lewis Alexander, complete with watch chain. Alexander was not a tall man, measuring up at around 5ft 3in. In contrast, Tom (Thomas) Morgan, sitting on the rail, was 6ft 1in, a champion swimmer and a well-respected athlete. In the foreground is Alexander's old rival and friend, Pilot Sam Davies, son of Horatio Davies of the *Wave* who had been Alexander's master in his time as apprentice. Not generally noted for sartorial splendour, he is putting a brave show on here for the camera, suggesting that he is not next to board. This picture dates from the days following World War I when Alexander and Davies continued sailing after the pilots had amalgamated until they were finally reigned in by the authorities, alarmed that they were making more money than all the rest put together. *(Author's collection)*

not. By popular consent, a pilot who had brought a ship up-Channel had the right to take her back down again. This meant that when a man arrived in port, he might well find one of his ships ready to sail within a day or two. If he were really in the money, she might be ready to drop down on the same tide that had brought him up-Channel. It therefore made sense for his cutter to wait for him down to the westward.

After boarding his pilot, the westernman would sail to some convenient port unless the pilot was expected back on the next tide, in which case he might simply heave to where he was. A favourite stopover was the North Devon harbour of Ilfracombe, where it was usual to see half a dozen or more pilot cutters dried out with men either scrubbing their bottom planking to maintain peak sailing performance, or sitting in the pub waiting for them to re-float. When his ship was ready to sail, the pilot would wire his men to be out and ready for him. In the days before telegraphy, careful arrangements with a wide contingency allowance were necessary, and these worked so well that it was rare for a cutter to miss her man.

When building a mental picture of Bristol Channel pilotage, it is important to understand that not all cutters were permanently in the habit of sailing down to Lundy and beyond. A number of ports also worked a rota in which every pilot was obliged to partake, fitting these duties in as best he could between cruises. In 1906, for example, a selection of Barry by-laws on the subject ran like this:

4 A rota shall be prepared by the secretary to the Board of Pilots ... so that there shall at all times, both day and night, be at least two pilots and their cutters under weigh, and stationed within port limits guarding the port. Any pilot who shall neglect to get and keep his cutter under weigh and on station duly guarding the port upon any day or night upon which it was his turn to keep guard, shall for the first offence pay a sum, according to the judgment of the Board, not exceeding £10.

20 a) The first pilot who arrives off Blackmore Point shall be deemed first on turn.

b) When two pilots are working together, the cutter must remain to the eastward of Blackmore Point until the last of the said pilots shall have been engaged, after which the cutter must be brought to Barry.

22 No pilot shall be entitled to more than one inward-bound vessel from the time he leaves Barry Pier Head until his cutter returns to Barry.

These regulations also give us a hint that in other aspects, the pilot's life was not as unfettered as we might imagine:

24 No pilot shall tow his cutter with a vessel further than the distance for which he shall have been engaged to pilot such a vessel, neither shall he join his cutter beyond the limits for which he has been engaged.

This can only have been an attempt to stop a pilot stealing a march on his rivals by having a ship drop him in the far west, the cutter having worked down to collect him while the pilot was away up Channel.

The *Hope*

The Barry cutter *Hope* was built in Porthleven, Cornwall, in 1899. Always a fast boat, here *Hope* is running before a light wind. She is showing a noble spread of canvas with an old-fashioned single-luff spinnaker that would not have disgraced a Solent racing yacht. It is more than likely that this hand-tinted image was shot by Lewis Alexander as his rival came running up to take *Kindly Light*'s wind.
(Author's collection)

Thomas Morgan, man-in-the-boat

Thomas (Tom) Morgan was the son of Pilot John Morgan of Cardiff. He sailed with Pilot Alexander aboard *White Heather* and later *Kindly Light*. He had the reputation of being one of the finest seamen on the Bristol Channel. Seen here as a young man with his fiancée, Rosa Ann Stoyle, he is wearing a necktie, but there is no ignoring his powerful hands, formed by being around the cutters from childhood. *(Courtesy Clive Roberts)*

Back with personal reminiscences, Pilot Bartlett mentions that in his day – in what might be termed 'the golden age of Channel piloting' – the Newport pilots could be loosely categorised by virtue of their psychology. First, there were 'cinchers'. These were men whose preference was to sleep in their own beds and to service docking trade from the harbour mouth. Occasionally, they might take their cutter to Bristol and see what was heading for Newport, or they might pick up the odd ship coming in from the west that none of the pilots down-Channel had wanted. More often, they came down the Newport River in a punt and boarded on the spot. Cinchers generally worked with a single apprentice.

The 'Crack of Dawn Boys' were Newport pilots who worked from Barry, mooring in that harbour overnight, then slipping out at first light to grab any ships that had slipped through the western pilot screen in the dark. They also picked up ships lying in Barry Roads with orders for Newport. Reading between the lines of Pilot Bartlett's narrative, one can tell that he had a low opinion of these men, 'tapping their barometers and predicting what terrible weather the pilots outside were going to have'.

The next and largest group were the modestly ambitious pilots who went some distance looking for work. It seems that many of these had an unstated individual limit as to how much weather they were prepared to put up with and how far they liked to go. Such a pilot might extend his unstated limits to work down below a rival, but if the other boat ran for home he would drop back to his usual hunting ground. He might well gamble on refusing a modest ship if he thought a bigger one was due; generally he worked hard and effectively.

The final group were the charismatic 'western-going' pilots. These were the famous men ready for anything in their search of profit. They specialised in big, fast cutters maintained to a tee and they tried hard only to bother themselves with steamers of the higher class. They sailed with two competent hands, and if one of these was an apprentice, he would be required to have enough experience to be totally able. Otherwise, there would be two men as well as an apprentice for some extra muscle. These craft had beautifully cut sails and were seen as far away as Dungeness in search of the right ship.

A good living

There seems little doubt that the Bristol Channel pilot service in the second half of the nineteenth century was among the highest paid of its time. In 1887, the net average earnings of Cardiff pilots were £324, a 10 per cent rise over the previous year. This was agreed by the commissioners and a Parliamentary committee to be a handsome income, but it pales into mediocrity compared with the remuneration of the best-paid Channel pilot of the same port, who took home £837 18s 5d. In other years, sums of £1,000 were not unknown, and this was after paying into the superannuation fund.

Such high incomes are easier to understand when one realises the energy and industry of some of these pilots. According to the pilot's younger son, Norman Alexander, Pilot Lewis Alexander's apprentice once recalled putting him aboard fourteen ships in a single week, a record for a sailing pilot cutter, and all the more remarkable when one learns that Alexander's religious beliefs would not let him sail on a Sunday!

By the early 1900s, pilot boat crews were paid £1 10s per week and received some share of the boarding money. They lived 'all found', and it cost around £5 to keep a cutter at sea for the same period. This included wages, insurance and normal wear and tear, but contained no contingency allowance for accidents. The pilots' insurance club paid out two-thirds of the agreed value of the cutter for total loss, the same proportion for repairs after a non-terminal stranding, but nothing for any other damage.

To put these figures into perspective, it should be borne in mind that a new cutter cost between £350 and £500, ready in all respects for sea right down to four sets of cabin crockery, while a second-hand one might be purchased for around £250.

The earnings of a successful Bristol Channel pilot far outstripped those on most other European stations, which may reflect the unusually high pilotage rates that traditionally prevailed here. The Bristol Docks committees received regular complaints from shipowners concerning excessive charges for the larger ships. The following examples comparing the approaches to Bristol with those of Liverpool are from 1888:

ss *Englishman* (4,708 tons)
Nash to Avonmouth (37 miles) £46 14s
Ormes Head to Liverpool (34 miles) £14 19s

ss *Celtic* (13,440 tons)
Nash to Avonmouth (37 miles) £122 16s 6d
Ormes head to Liverpool (34 miles) £18 4s

Some commentators blamed the cruising cutter system for these swingeing rates. It was claimed that a steam cutter on station would halve the pilots' running expenses without damaging their income at all. Whether or not this was true, the pilots were so horrified by the thought of amalgamation that it was thirty years or more before the recommendation finally came to pass at most of the Bristol Channel ports.

Another complaint from shipowners was that the numbers of pilot cutters sailing around the Bristol Channel was so great as to constitute a danger to shipping. While there is no doubt that on a busy patch such as the stretch between Nash Point and Barry Roads there were a great number of cutters, the view of the Cardiff pilot John Morgan, expressed in 1910 to the Parliamentary Select Committee on pilotage, would have been echoed by many. When confronted with this proposition, Morgan pointed out that the fleets of cutters were not a danger, but rather a safety factor in the Channel because of the number of lives they saved every year. And Morgan, of all people, would have known. In his time in the cutters he is said to have saved thirty-nine lives personally.

Apprenticeships and licensing

Being a Bristol Channel pilot was a career for life. John Morgan of Cardiff began with a five-year apprenticeship, followed by two years 'deep-sea'. He then sat a rigorous examination and served several years as man-in-the-boat until a vacancy on the pilots' list allowed him to be 'made Channel'.

In Morgan's day, the examining board for Cardiff pilots consisted of one experienced pilot who was also a commissioner, one gentleman with long experience of shipping and naval affairs, and a number of shipowners who had served at sea as captains.

A younger pilot from Barry, George Morrice, was apprenticed to Pilot Thomas Lewis in 1891 when he was seventeen. His indentures expired in 1896, after which he no doubt put in his deep-sea time. At this period it was usual to serve one year in sail and one in steam. He was licensed as a Barry pilot in 1904, and in 1911 came out with the brand-new 51ft cutter *Cornubia* (later the yacht *Hirta*), perhaps after being made up to 'Channel' status.

Despite being the general 'ship's dogsbody' and the inevitable butt of a good deal of banter, an apprentice's life was not all toil and tribulation. In a memoir describing his father's reminiscences as a pilot's 'boy', G Barrett Venn mentions that while lifejackets of monstrous proportion were theoretically supplied to wear during the hazardous business of boarding the pilot, actually putting one on was considered 'sissy' and almost never done. Thus the back-breaking labour of sculling the punt in a heavy sea with a single 10ft oar was exacerbated by increased personal danger. Despite this and other education in the school of hard knocks, the lads kept their spirits up in many ways and were remarkably well organised amongst themselves. In one port which is unfortunately unspecified, the apprentices are reported as getting together at low water springs and rowing out to an exposed sand bar where they would

***Kindly Light* in Belfast**

Pilot Alexander of *Kindly Light* was a lay preacher and a devout man. On this occasion, he took the boat north to Belfast in Northern Ireland to pick up a ship and offered his wife the trip as a holiday. Mrs Alexander agreed to come so long as she could bring her feather bed. The mattress was duly shipped and no doubt the lady enjoyed a fast, comfortable passage. According to the pilot's late son, the picture shows *Kindly Light* in Belfast Lough giving a treat to the members of the local prayer meeting.
(Author's collection)

join in a ritual football match. Time was called by the referee when the water rose to ankle height. All hands then repaired to the dock and the pitch returned to its more usual situation at the bottom of the Bristol Channel.

Pilot John Morgan

On 6 October 1896, Pilot John Morgan was in Padstow with the *Cardiffian* taking a well-earned rest, when a loaf of bread fell from its locker onto the cabin sole. He replaced it securely and once again it fell out. A gale was blowing outside, and Morgan, who was described as 'a psychic man', concluded this was a sign that he must go to sea. Somebody out there needed him, he said to his crew. They departed into a wicked night and saved six men from two barges which had come adrift from their tug. Morgan was awarded a silver medal by the RNLI. It was not his only act of mercy and when he died years later he was laid in an open coffin with his medals for all to see. *(Clive Roberts' family collection)*

The cutters

No pictorial evidence of pilot boats in the Bristol Channel seems to have survived from the eighteenth century or earlier. After exhaustive research in customs records and the early, incomplete national ship registries, Grahame Farr determined that pilot cutters from Bristol were of the following typical dimensions:

Length:	37ft
Beam:	10ft 4in
Draught:	5ft
Tonnage:	16

This was the *Bristol Endeavour*, built at Pill in 1791 and owned by 'James Buck, Pilot'. A number of similar-sized 'skiffs', as Bristol boats were known in the vernacular right up to the end (Welsh cutters were called 'yawls'), appear under the ownership of men described as pilots, but whether they were purpose-built or not is obscure. It seems likely that here, as in so many other areas, pilots of those days were also fishermen and that their boats were dual-purpose. We know that the *Fancy* began life as an open boat, but was decked and rebuilt before giving thirty years of service to Pilot James Parfitt.

By chance, the lines of the *Charlotte*, a skiff built for John Berry, pilot, have been preserved through the yard of Charles Hill & Sons, successors to George Hillhouse who built the boat in 1808. Her dimensions were:

Length :	38ft
Beam:	11ft 8in
Draught:	7ft
Tonnage:	19

The hull was of a bluff-bowed, non-extreme 'cod's head and mackerel tail' form. No sail plan exists, though the spar dimensions hint at an exciting rig:

The *Cardiffian*

Pilot John Morgan, on a holiday outing circa 1900. He and his wife Sarah Anne (née Woodward – sister of Giles and Abraham, both channel pilots) had eleven children. All the four sons became channel pilots. *(Author's collection)*

Patroness, Her Majesty, The Queen.

ROYAL NATIONAL LIFE BOAT INSTITUTION

FOR THE

Preservation of Life from Shipwreck.

(INCORPORATED BY ROYAL CHARTER.)

ESTABLISHED 1824.

SUPPORTED BY VOLUNTARY CONTRIBUTIONS.

Vice Patron.

His Royal Highness the Prince of Wales K.G.

President.

His Grace Algernon George Duke of Northumberland K.G.

Chairman	Depʸ Chairman
Sir Edward Birkbeck Bart. V.P.	Colonel Fitz Roy Clayton V.P.

Northumberland

President.

At a Meeting of the Committee of the Royal National Life Boat Institution for the Preservation of Life from Shipwreck held at their Offices, London, on the 12th day of November, 1896 the following Minute was ordered to be recorded on the Books of the Society, and to be communicated to Captain Pengelley, H.M.I.N.

Resolved, That the Silver Medal of the Royal National Life Boat Institution be presented to Captain John Morgan for gallantly assisting to save the crews–six men in all–from two barges, which had broken adrift from a steam tug in a gale of wind on the 6th October, 1896.

Charles Dibdin
Secretary.

Edward Birkbeck
Chairman.

Lifesaving certificate

The certificate awarded to John Morgan for conspicuous lifesaving to go with the medal he is illustrated wearing opposite. *(Courtesy Clive Roberts)*

Mast:	43ft (including 7ft 'head' above the hounds)
Boom:	32ft 9in (the same length as that on an 1890s' 50-footer)
Gaff:	20ft
Bowsprit:	34ft (of which a staggering 26ft stood outboard)

The measurements indicate the sort of long, low rig in vogue at that time. It suited the homely lines of the hull and would have moved her along well if performance estimates for Revenue cutters of similar form (though much larger) are anything to go by. The mast had a healthy rake and was simply stayed by two shrouds per side. The luff length of the mainsail can be calculated by subtracting from the full length of the mast a 7ft length from step to gooseneck, 7ft of the masthead, then a further 4ft or so for the gaff jaws to sit comfortably below the hounds. This still gives a luff in the order of 25ft, which would have been average for a far larger boat in later years – and the *Charlotte*'s successors were not slow by any standards. With her mighty boom and long, probing bowsprit, we can thus infer that she was something of a flyer.

To have been built from finely drawn plans, the *Charlotte* must have been a high-class vessel, because no such drawings survive of any of the classic Bristol Channel cutters from the mid nineteenth century onwards. These were built in the traditional way from a half-model made by the builder to a specification agreed with the owner. *Charlotte*'s lines are quite different from the Bristol Channel pilot cutter the world now knows; indeed, her midships section is more like an American pilot schooner than the *Marguerite*, *Baroque*, *Cornubia*, or any of the other surviving late examples of the type. Attempts to show a steady development from her to them would seem to be in vain. At some stage, therefore, the builders of the Bristol Channel and those of Cornwall and the other off-limits areas which supplied cutters, must have decided that the usual West Country form was, with some modification, superior for their purposes.

The only evidence currently to hand of an intermediate type is an ancient photograph of the Bristol pilot skiff *Trial* lying on the mud. *Trial* was run by Pilot T Vowles from 1847 to 1878 and the photograph, not reproduced here, is contemporary. Peter Stuckey, author of *Sailing Pilots of the Bristol Channel*, points out that the boat is clearly being used for fishing as well as pilot work. She has a hatch amidships which may be for a fish hold, while her pilot number is boldly painted on the high bulwarks. She is of the old, blunt-bowed hull form with a very short counter similar to that of the *Charlotte*.

By 1890, the following general dimensions were typical of the pilot cutters on the Channel:

Length:	50ft (sparred length with bowsprit at around 64ft)
Beam:	13ft 6in
Draught:	8ft
Tonnage:	35
Sail area:	1,400 sq ft

Most cutters had a fairly straight stem and a moderate counter stern, but there were a number of shorter boats of 35–42ft which carried their rudder on a transom. These mostly worked the inshore waters, perhaps servicing ships waiting to enter Cardiff, but some went seeking down-Channel despite their modest size.

The biggest of the classic, counter-sterned cutters ran up to 56ft long, although these were rare. The *Mascotte* of Newport reached an exceptional 60ft. At the lower end of the scale came the 45ft *Mischief*, which found fame in her old age sailing to the ice under the ownership of Major H W Tilman, or *Madcap*, built in 1875 by Davis and Plain, also still sailing to the far north and one of the shortest cutters to have a full counter stern.

There were many established builders of pilot cutters on the Channel, all with their own trademarks. Hull forms varied considerably and there was no rule of any sort apart, ironically, from the paint job. This was laid down by statute as black with a white strake under the capping rail, the pilot's number on the side and port logos on the sails, but even these regulations were interpreted with a large grain of sea-salt by the individualistic pilots.

Rowles of Pill built many skiffs for Bristol pilots, a number of which found their way to South Wales, including the *Marguerite*, who won fame in the ownership of Pilot Frank Trott of Cardiff. Trott had a fancy for racing and triumphed in so many

Pilot cutter builders

The men of Slade's yard at Polruan by Fowey which built Pilot Morrice's *Cornubia* in 1911. Taken somewhat earlier in 1897, the men are identified as follows:

Back row: Frederick Salt, Matthew Salt, Frederick Johns, Harry Braddon, Ned Dean, Tom Wyatt, Bert Luxton.
Middle row: Charles Wakeham, Albert Pearn, Harry Rogers, Jack Welsh, Sam Slade, John Slade, Nathaniel Toms Hunkin, Mark George, Joseph Slade.
Front row: Ernest Slade, William Welsh, Benjamin Moss Tregaskes.

Ernest, James and Joseph Slade, grandsons of Jane Slade who was the 'J' in 'J Slade and Sons', probably actually built *Cornubia*. The yard served as the template for Daphne du Maurier's excellent novel, *The Loving Spirit*. It continues to build wooden boats into the third millennium under the name of C Toms and Son Ltd. (*Author's collection*)

Sea trials in Fowey Harbour

Just launched from the yard of J Slade and Sons in 1911, Pilot George Morrice's *Cornubia* is undergoing sea trials. The flags will be her Lloyd's number. The tiny topsail is a working sail that one man could set and hand with ease. It makes a surprising difference for so modest a rag of canvas. *Cornubia* was sold out of the Barry pilot service in the early 1920s and by 1930 was in the ownership of the Earl of Dumfries who renamed her *Hirta* after the main island in the St Kilda group which he owned. Said to have crossed the Atlantic in the 1930s, she remained in Scotland for most of her life until purchased by the author, who sailed her to Greenland, Newfoundland, the Caribbean and Russia amongst other places. Now completely restored, she has reverted to her original name.
(Author's collection)

regattas with this big, husky boat that in one year he managed to dress her overall with his prize flags. Rowles's cutters had a slightly raked stem with a curved forefoot and were noted for broad counter sterns and large internal volume. They were comfortable at sea and generally performed better than average.

Many of the other Channel ports had their own builders such as Hambly at Cardiff, Mordney Carney of Newport, and Bob Davis at Saul in the Sharpness Canal, who was responsible for the powerful Gloucester cutters *Berkeley Castle* and *Alaska*. In addition to these local builders, there were a number of yards in Cornwall favoured by pilots with an eye for a shapely vessel. Slades of Fowey built *Cornubia* in 1911 for Pilot George Morrice of Barry. Slade is also said to have built the *Clarice* for an unknown pilot the previous year. Bowden from Porthleven was responsible for the beautiful *Olga* of 1909. Both these boats had a lovely curving variant of the Cornish plumb stem. This swept back into a raking keel which only ran truly straight from the mast aft to the sternpost. They had slack sections forward like a Rowles boat, but a finer counter and run. This, together with notably well-balanced sections, promised well-mannered sailing performance at the expense of less room below decks.

In 1904, one of the fastest cutters on the Channel was built by Liver and Wilding at Fleetwood, Lancashire. The *Alpha* was constructed on the lines of a deep-draughted, over-sized Morecambe Bay prawner. Prawners were an entirely new hull form, drawn on yacht-like lines late in the nineteenth century to service the Victorian craze for shrimps. They had to operate in narrow, drying channels and needed to be extremely weatherly and handy. Rarely over 35ft on deck, these craft were of extreme shoal draught. When the chance came to build a 50-footer with no draught restriction, the yard produced a very slippery vessel indeed. In due course, Pilot Alexander decided that he must have an even faster boat and, although *Alpha*'s owner was 'close' about where she had come from, he worked out that it must be Fleetwood. This energetic pilot found the master builder, a local man by the name of Stoba, who was now working for Armour brothers, and asked for a cutter to beat the *Alpha*. The old man said this was not possible, but that if Alexander chose, he would build him a similar boat, only bigger, which might do the trick by virtue of waterline length alone.

And so the 53ft *Kindly Light* was built for £525. Probably the fastest of them all, her lines were so fine and radical that she romped out ahead of almost all the opposition. She was wet, tender and reputedly found it difficult to heave to on station, preferring to keep on going 'as straight as a gun-barrel'. She made Alexander a very good living indeed, and when the Barry pilots turned back to sail in 1919, she and her owner were among the ring-leaders of the short-lived but glorious revolt against amalgamation.

The first of one or two defections from the time-honoured method of building from models was the Barry pilot cutter *Faith*. She was designed by Harold Clayton on paper, and a fine-looking vessel she was. It would be hard to imagine a better cruising yacht. The only thing missing is the vital deep forefoot that would have given her the edge in heavy weather, but at this time a number of pilots, including Trott and Alexander, were opting for 'model-designed' pilot boats with equally cut-away bows. One thing is sure, however: *Faith*'s lucky owner would have appreciated his noble accommodation. His was the only cutter on the Channel to have a real owner's cabin.

Bristol Channel pilot cutters were flush decked with bulwarks. English boats favoured these at 18in high, or even more, while those of the Welshmen were often as low as 10in. The boarding punt was brought in over the rail of a Welsh boat, but in Bristol a gate was built into the bulwarks so that the tender could be handled even more easily. All the boats had a tiny, offset forehatch with the bowsprit running in on the other side. A basic windlass and a mighty set of bitts capable of withstanding the terrible forces developed under occasional tow made up the simple foredeck.

The punt stowed in chocks amidships or slightly to port, and the cutter was sailed with a tiller – usually iron – from a small, deep cockpit of pleasing proportions. All joinery was of teak where possible, and the cockpit sole was watertight, self-draining through four 1in lead pipes which pierced the planking just above the waterline, and were peened over into a simple skin fitting. These pipes lasted the life of the boat. Such cockpits were a standard

fitting on all cutters. Access to the accommodation was via a companionway at the forward end with a sliding, radiused hatch.

Life below deck was primitive but practical. Immediately inside the companionway was a passage called 'the runs' in Welsh boats, where rope and other spare gear was hung. Needless to say, in winter this could be a dank and gloomy place. At its forward end was a door into the full-width main saloon up to 12ft long and reaching to somewhere around the mast. This had comfortable benches along both sides and two or more bunks outboard with excellent facilities for keeping the sleepers in place at sea. A 60-gallon iron water tank was set on the cabin sole beneath the saloon table because its logical home, the bilge, was full of ballast. This tank was filled by the apprentice with water he carried to the cutter aboard the punt in small wooden barrels, or 'breakers', from the nearest source. It was a tedious job.

Beyond the mast was the forecabin with a coal range and two more bunks. In here slept the apprentice and sometimes the westernman, depending on his relationship with the pilot. The forepeak contained the bitts and not much else, it being a fetish to keep weight from forward and give the boat her best chance to rise to a sea.

There were no official washing facilities and rarely a head, or toilet. Like the old man in the Hebrides whose house was kitted out with a bathroom by a

The *Frolic* in yachting trim

Frolic is a big pilot cutter at 55ft, built in Bideford for Pilot Alf Edwards of Cardiff. Her underwater shape was radical, having a relatively shallow forefoot and considerable drag aft to her deep sternpost. She was a notable performer and, in yachting trim, won the 'Cock of the Channel' race in 1936. She was helmed all the way round by retired pilot Frank Trott. In this photograph, she has obviously been sold for a yacht. Her sail covers are immaculate, she has no number on her bulwarks, and the fact that she has been fitted with running backstays is the real giveaway. No pilot would have countenanced such a thing. *(Author's collection)*

A transom-sterned Welsh pilot cutter

Whilst the overwhelming majority of pilot cutters on the Channel were of the counter-sterned variety, a number of smaller craft with transoms were in service. This one is from Cardiff. She and most of her sisters only boarded ships close to the port in the lee of Penarth Head, but some worked the broader waters of the Bristol Channel.
(Author's collection)

film company to accommodate a lady star on location, pilots would have deemed such luxuries sinfully superfluous, 'when God has given us the biggest bathroom in the world just outside.'

Hulls were heavily built of pitch-pine planking, sometimes with an elm bottom, on double oak frames. A few were copper or bronze fastened, but most used cheaper, stronger, shorter-lived iron. Ballast was almost invariably internal and was of the densest material affordable. Typically, it consisted of scrap iron set in cement, but anecdote has it that an unexploded ordnance shell was discovered in the concrete of the Bristol cutter *Pet* while she was being broken up. Nothing to do with stability but of equal interest is that the *Pet*'s pilot was so anxious not to leave the helm while seeking a ship that he had a commode built into his cockpit seat.

An insight into the pilots' interest in performance is that in many cases, the concrete was swept through to the ends to ensure a clear run for bilge water, but was laid over champagne bottles or some other light, airy material such as cork at bow and stern. This was to keep the weight low down and out of the ends of the boat, a requirement for all small sailing craft which confers stability without imparting a tendency to pitch heavily. Frames were generally single in the ends as well, perhaps for the same reason. So important did the pilots believe this question of weight distribution that anchors and cable were stowed in way of the mast rather than in the eyes of the ship. One noted speed merchant, 'Slippery' Tom Williams of Cardiff, used to ship an anvil aboard his flying cutter, the *Polly*, on regatta days, chocking it off on the middle of the cabin sole, and if anybody was misguided enough to hang even an oilskin coat forward of the bitts, heaven help him.

Rigs in these craft were small by the standards of the yachts of their day, but one must be mindful that they served the boat in all seasons and in all weathers. Generally speaking, a 50-footer could carry her working topsail on the wind well into force 4. One reef would be tucked in at force 5, with the working jib being substituted for one of a choice of smaller sails, and so on. The same boat was eminently capable of beating into a 40kt gale and she could maintain her position off a lee shore in almost anything by the simple expedient of heaving to.

A Bristol Channel pilot cutter heaves to as well as any vessel afloat. With her headsails aback, the main idling just off close-hauled and the tiller lashed to leeward she will drift slowly across the wind making little or no leeway. In force 9 and a serious seaway, a cutter hove to under minimum mainsail and deep-reefed staysail will still lose no ground. This feature of their performance was of great utility since having fought the weather to the westward, it was very pleasant to know the boat would not be driven back, come what might.

Before about 1900, masts were extended by a short topmast from which a topsail or pilot flag could be carried. Thereafter, more and more pilots turned to slightly taller pole masts for extra security and lower maintenance. The jib halyards could be attached higher on such a rig, which made the luff more vertical and thus conferred an advantage in windward performance, but still the boats sailed without running backstays. Instead, the jib luff was hardened against a third shroud attached at the same point as the halyard. This shroud was set up with a lanyard and dead-eye arrangement as were the others, but was further aft than would otherwise be the case. The extra shroud, or swifter as it is sometimes called, did not materially impede the boom off the wind, because by the time it was eased off that far, the gaff was square across the boat. To give any more sheet was thus counter-productive.

Mainsail reefing was originally worked by conventional points with a loose-footed main set on a boom. Later, many pilots preferred a roller reefing arrangement of the type known as an Appledore gear. This undoubtedly made shortening down easier, but did little for the set of the mainsail and caused some broken booms. It also limited the length of the boom to the stern of the boat, because the sheet bail had to swivel and therefore had to be on the extreme end of the spar. If this were abaft the bottom mainsheet block on the counter, the system 'hung up' with the friction and would not turn. Another requirement was that the boom was absolutely symmetrical with no sag at all. This was not easy to achieve with a grown spar, so some pilots, including the redoubtable Frank Trott, now sailing a new boat with a seriously cut-away forefoot, the *Frolic*, experimented with iron piping by way of a boom.

It has been averred that main halyards were led aft through open-cheeked turning blocks on the fife rail and belayed on posts by the cockpit. The sail was certainly far too heavy to hoist from this position, demanding the weight of a man standing beneath the halyard falls to deal with it, so it is not easy to understand why this was done. The open-cheeked fife-rail sheaves were certainly used, because they are confirmed by photographic evidence and were still in existence on *Hirta* in the 1980s, yet any requirement to be suddenly rid of the main would be uncommon, and single-handed reefing could only have been easier with the halyards belayed near the gooseneck. The falls of the halyards would have been a nuisance to stow down aft and the peak halyard running well inboard down the port side deck would have interfered with the punt. The only obvious advantage is that a single-handed helmsman would be able to drop the peak to scandalise the mainsail and so lose sail area instantly, but this seems hardly worth the trade-offs. Why this unusual arrangement was adhered to remains a mystery, at least, to this author. *Kindly Light* has recently been restored with full gear, however, so we must look to her for future enlightenment.

The perfect seagoing cockpit

The cockpit of the Barry pilot cutter *Hirta* (ex-*Cornubia*), photographed in the late 1980s. The wheel steering was fitted in the 1950s with gear lifted by Mark Grimwade from what remained of the Bristol Channel pilot cutter *Saladin*, a pioneering ocean racer. The lights (windows) in the companionway sides were also installed at that time. Otherwise, this cockpit and companionway was original. It featured the 1911 bilge pump with elegant iron lever, and the lead pipes for self-draining were still working. The whole was constructed entirely of teak and was a thing of unusual functional beauty. Virtually all Bristol Channel pilot cutters had similar arrangements. In the opinion of the author, they have never been bettered.
(Tom Nitsch)

All sheets were led to the cockpit and generally the boat was sailed like a modern yacht in this respect, making it easier for the westernmen to achieve some of their remarkable feats of boat-handling.

Some cutters sailed adequately with just a main and staysail when they were not in a hurry. Others would always demand a rag of some sort on the bowsprit to keep the head down and balance the helm. For this reason, one sees photographs of the tiniest scraps of canvas imaginable set from these spars in hard weather. Even in decent going they would sometimes settle for a very small jib to ease the workload while on station waiting for a ship.

Many pilots refused to use a bobstay to support the bowsprit from below. This made life simpler when reeving the spar on entering harbour, but it must have destroyed the vessel's pointing ability. A cutter with a sagging jib luff is a sorry sight and there are plenty of pictures of pilot cutters exhibiting just such a horror. It is hard to speculate why any pilot would have put up with this, since a running bobstay is simple to arrange and many boats were rigged with them.

The number one sees on the bulwarks of pilot cutters in period photographs is the pilot's own number, not his cutter's. The boat was also supposed to carry his name and the port for which he was registered under her stern. The name of the cutter herself was painted on the bulwarks in way of the quarters. Bristol boats had their pilot's number on the sails, which bore no other logo.

From a great distance, the white sail was a give-away that a cutter carried pilots. Billy Prethero, a crafty old operator, used to ship a tan-bark topsail to set while hiding amongst a fishing fleet when he was to windward of his rivals. The old, brown cloth did not stand out amongst the fishermen and for a while he escaped detection by the ruse. As soon as he spotted a ship, he would drop his false colours and hoist his biggest, flattest, whitest topsail and go hell-for-leather for the prize. One wonders how many times he got away with this before the rest grew wise to his game.

Like most working vessels, the Bristol Channel pilot cutters have had a number of extravagant claims made for their performance by enthusiasts. However, we must remember the facts of life. These were heavy boats with a small sail area and a typical waterline length of around 44ft, so those who warble about 12kts are definitely out on a seafaring picnic. What is far more important is how effortlessly a pilot cutter with a clean bottom and a good suit of sails can achieve 7kts on a reach. This is what gives them the capacity to make fast passages, for which they were well-known by the cruising yachtsmen of the twenties and thirties who bought them from the pilots.

Close-hauled on a good breeze in flat water, a well-rigged pilot cutter with a decent suit of sails can expect to make something over 6kts at an angle to the true wind of little worse than 45°. Substitute worn-out canvas, the propeller of an auxiliary engine dragging her back with a little bottom slime thrown in, and a knot comes off that straight away, together with 5° or even 10° of close-windedness. Like any sailing boat, a pilot cutter must be treated with total respect if she is to deliver the goods. Off the wind, a 50-footer in original order can make 9kts and perhaps a bit over if driven hard by a dedicated crew. She might manage more in the most exceptional circumstances, but only for very short distances.

We cannot finish a study of the form of the Bristol Channel pilot cutter without quoting from Douglas H C Birt, writing in the *Trident* magazine in 1951. Birt was one of the great yachting correspondents of his generation, a man who understood the sea totally.

> We shall be forgetting half their glory unless we recall that they were built by poor men for poor men, suffering from the two great spiritual evils of poverty – ignorance and prejudice. That they still produced fine boats is to the glory of natural man, who, living close to elemental things, develops an instinct for the earth or the sea which passes sophisticated understanding.

Boarding

Boarding was always done from the boarding punt. Research by Malcolm McKeand of *Kindly Light* indicates that a punt from a cutter was generally 12ft overall with a flat floor amidships for stability, a healthy beam, and a rather shapely transom. Some were a little longer and often a foot or so shorter. The clinker-built boat had two rowing positions

Boarding in the Bristol Channel

Here, the pilot from *Kindly Light* is about to board the ship from which the picture is taken. The ship is hove to across the wind to create a lee. The cutter has launched her punt and the pilot is in the bows manning the painter. The apprentice is ready to scull him across to the Jacob's ladder hanging from the ship's side as soon as the pilot casts off. The manoeuvre called for boat handling of the highest quality and the price of getting it wrong was sometimes counted in human lives. *(Author's collection)*

with the most appropriate being selected by the westernman or the apprentice who was ferrying the pilot across. Welsh punts were invariably sculled with a long sweep for boarding purposes, while the pilot hung on in the bows. Techniques varied with conditions, but the scenario often went like this.

First, the cutter ran alongside the ship and called up to the bridge with her speaking trumpet. If a pilot was required, the ship would heave to half-across the wind, giving a lee for boarding. The punt was now launched, the pilot and the boy climbed aboard and the cutter sailed downwind of the ship towing the punt as close as she dared into the lee. When she was handy to the boarding ladder, the punt was released and the lad heaved mightily on the sweep, bringing the cockleshell alongside the ship as soon as possible. The pilot jumped for the rope ladder and the lad sculled back to rejoin the cutter which by now was well out of the way.

The difficulty was that a ship laid across the wind causes a back-draught into her lee. If the cutter sailed into this she could be becalmed or even sucked in towards the ship's plating. The ship herself would also be drifting bodily to leeward, particularly if she were floating high on her marks in ballast, with the result that the cutter might be unavoidably drawn into a dangerous collision. The cutter's crew had to tread a fine line between leaving the boy with an impossible distance to scull, or endangering everyone by coming in too close. Getting this balancing act right required great skill and a good deal of experience. Sailing the heavy cutter through this manoeuvre, perhaps single-handed, demanded seamanship of the highest order, but for these men it was all in a day's work.

In really hard weather, the pilot would sometimes scull across to the ship single-handed, then kick the punt off for the cutter to pick up after the ship had got under way. Occasionally, the small boat was dragged aboard the ship and landed with the pilot.

Punts were launched by manhandling them over the side of the cutter to leeward. For two strong men this was easy. Recovering the boat was generally achieved while hove to. First the punt was brought into the cutter's lee then, if she were heeled far enough, it was simply dragged aboard – a readily achievable job for two fit men. If the cutter were more upright, a 4:1 'punt burton' was kept slung from the hounds. Hooked onto a wire strop in the punt, this made short work of the business.

Few pilots' men would have attempted the running gybe to flip the punt over the rail as suggested in Surgeon Commander Muir's book, *Messing About in Boats*. Muir made a few trips aboard a Bristol pilot cutter and generally wrote well about the experience. The cutter's short-term westernman, when left alone on board, boasted that he could get the punt on board easily single-handed. He went on to demonstrate by attaching it to the boom on the lee side, then literally gybing it onto the deck. The man made a point of the fact that this was never done with the pilot present for he, of course, owned both punt and cutter and would have no wish to chance his investments. Reading between the lines, what took place was clearly an act of bravado. It is unfortunate that Muir has been quoted from dawn to dusk in the waterfront pubs of the world by his readers, many of whom aver that this was the way the job was done as a matter of course. Muir suggests no such thing, and men who worked the cutters all had a chuckle over this legend, because bringing the small boat aboard was no real problem in any case, and the risks would have been far too great. A cutter with a damaged punt was disabled, and as the men all had some share of the take, nobody would want to risk it. When pressed on the subject, Mr L 'Kip' Alexander, the son of Pilot Lewis Alexander, who had sailed on the cutter with his father, suggested to this author that perhaps the myth had come into being because some crews might have attached the painter to the boom with the cutter hove to and the boom pinned just to leeward of amidships. If she were now gybed round, the boom would flop gently across a couple of feet or so, giving the men a start at heaving the bow of the punt over the rail. It must be said, however, that he was unwilling to accede that even this was common practice and actually asked the author to write an article debunking the whole business.

It is easy to take up the idea that boarding a pilot was invariably a dramatic business with a stiff breeze and a big sea, but this was by no means always the case. Pilot Buck, a retired Bristol pilot, recollected that as an apprentice he once put two pilots aboard on successive nights by rowing long distances to ships in the punt. On the first evening, the cutter was becalmed off the Wolf Rock near the Isles of Scilly when a steamer they thought might be the one they were expecting hove in sight. The sea was mirror-calm and the stars reflected in it as brightly as they shone in the sky. All around they could see the loom of the lighthouses of the islands and Land's End. The ship was passing well north of them. They launched the punt and began pulling two-handed until the ship was as close as she was going to get, but still well distant. The pilot and the boy shouted out and showed a flashlight, but had given up when suddenly the ship turned and showed her port light. It was the one they were after and the captain told the pilot later that he had been lying in his bunk when he heard the distant hail, 'We are the Bristol pilot!' The watch on deck had not heard their calls.

The following night, there was still no wind and other than drifting up and down on the tide, the cutter had gone nowhere. This time, the boy and the number two pilot had a longer row, pulling together with some urgency. When the ship had been boarded, the lad hoped for a tow back to the cutter but it was not to be. The ship had a damaged propeller and was saving her time. The cutter's light was lost among the stars and the young boy kept on rowing without finding her. By the time she finally was in sight, it was almost dawn and he was singing songs to keep up his spirits.

This was not the end of Buck's tribulations in the punt, however. The little boat was once lost after boarding a pilot. The lad had made the deck safely but the punt had filled while he and the westernman were trying to bring her aboard. They let her go in the dark, then hove to on successive tacks, half an hour per tack, to maintain their exact position relative to the wind and the punt. The following morning, never thinking they would find her, they ran off dead before the wind. Half an hour later they discovered the boat and dragged her aboard with a jib purchase. They made light of the matter, but it was a very nice piece of seamanship.

Buck's fourth bad experience could have cost him

After the review

After the annual review, the Cardiff pilot cutters went to sea in an impromptu race, vying to be furthest to the westward by morning. Here, they are rounding Penarth Head setting every stitch, many with big jackyard topsails. All have their pilot flags aloft and some are carrying name pennants from the gaff end. *(Author's collection)*

his life. Cast adrift from a steamer after boarding the pilot, a snowstorm shrieked down and cut the visibility to nothing. He did the only thing he could, which was to keep the little boat's head to the mounting sea and stay put, hoping to be picked up. His strength was fading when he suddenly saw a glimmer of light close by and threw the punt's long painter at it. His luck held and the painter hit his father in the face. After the shock, the man grabbed the line and pulled. There on the end of it was his son, looking like a snowman, frozen half to death. The father's first words were, 'I thought I had lost you,' but he hadn't, and Buck went on to become a licensed Bristol pilot who worked until long after the punts were only a memory.

Life and death in the cutters

All the pilots and their men maintained encyclopedic knowledge of the other cutters and would keep up a steady commentary on the activities and performance of their rivals. In the first decade of the twentieth century there were between one hundred and one hundred and fifty pilot cutters working the Bristol Channel. All were readily identifiable by their big pilot flags in the daytime and their flares at night. Cutters rarely used the sidelights required by the law, preferring the all-round white masthead light of the sailing pilot vessel. Each port had its own flare code for when it was too dark to see the sail logos. Cardiff employed the pattern, one long and a short every fifteen minutes. Bristol was two shorts and a long, while Barry had a long and three shorts. The flare itself was a clout of cotton waste on a stick dipped in a can of paraffin.

One of the greatest dangers to pilots was that their cutters would be run down, either by accident or during the boarding process. One night in March 1918, Buck, now a westernman, and his crew were run down in the cutter *Greta* by a steamer off the Breaksea lightship. Buck and his mate grabbed onto the ship's port anchor as the cutter sank beneath them, but they thought Pilot Chiswell was gone. To their relief he soon reported that he was out of sight hanging onto the starboard anchor. After a while a face appeared the ship's rail looking down at the bizarre sight of two characters on his port hook, and soon the young men were up on deck. Nobody had rescued the pilot, however, and he was in dire straits hanging on by his arms only. Since he was

The *Spray* in racing trim

Seen here on race day 1907 going like a train, *Spray* shows that the Bristol Channel pilots took competition seriously. Races were often associated with the annual review, and the only parts of the rig that measure up with those seen on the same boat on the opposite page are the mast and bowsprit. The racing boom is carried well out over the stern, while the gaff is supported by three sets of gaff spans instead of the usual two, with the halyard dead-ended on one of the spans. The tow foresail and jib topsail could have been used when working but the huge jackyard topsail would be for race days only.
(Author's collection)

over sixty, this was not good and Buck immediately sent him down a loop of line to put a foot in while the crew went for a ladder. In due course the 'old man' made the deck, but many years later he averred that to his dying day he would never forget hanging onto that anchor. He weighed 15 stone!

Pilot cutter crews rarely used the compass they were obliged to carry by the regulations, and a chart was almost unheard of. Under interrogation by the 1910 Parliamentary Select Committee, Pilot John Morgan made the point that:

> the difference between a pilot navigating a ship and the captain navigating a ship is that the ship-master navigates in miles and that a pilot navigates in feet. ... I have been on board many a ship where the captain has said, 'Bless my life, we shall strike that!' At the same time I have known that we shall not strike it. The reason is the difference in appearance at sea and in narrow waters.

Heavy weather

A very different view of the cutter *Spray*. Here, she is entering Ilfracombe in a gale. Her main and staysail are both heavily reefed and her bowsprit is hove well inboard with a tiny spitfire jib to balance her. One might imagine that in such conditions, sailing under main and staysail would answer well enough, but the difference even a scrap of canvas outboard of the staysail makes to the liveliness of the cutter, particularly when close-hauled, is surprising. Approaching harbour at hull speed, one man is at the helm, another by the mast preparing the halyards so that nothing fouls at the crucial moment. *(Author's collection)*

On station

This beautiful hand-tinted glass lantern slide shows a Cardiff cutter under easy sail with the whole Atlantic open to windward. The mainsail is roller-reefed with never a crease to compromise performance. The staysail is sheeted half to weather so that the boat is slowed right down and is quietly fore-reaching. The tiny spitfire jib serves to balance the sail plan. Note the mast hoops on the upper part of the luff of the mainsail. The lower half was usually either unsecured or loosely laced to allow for easy single-handed reefing. With her punt on deck and only the hand in the cockpit, she is almost certainly waiting, either to board a ship she knows is due, or to collect her pilot as he comes down-Channel from Cardiff. The image is serene, creating a powerful feeling that this boat and the man at the helm are entirely at one with the ocean. *(Author's collection)*

The westernmen sometimes had a different philosophy, yet they kept out of trouble in their own way. Pilot Bartlett remembers a night at sea with his mentor, Billy, early in his career. Billy left him in charge of the cutter with the order to keep her straight before the wind.

> If I let her gybe [wrote Bartlett], he told me I should have the mast out of her, and if I let her swing the other way she would go on the rocks and we should both be 'chewing gravel' by morning, which was his delicate way of saying we should be drowned. I asked him where we were and he replied, 'Between Trevose and Lundy.' I followed this by asking how far offshore we were, to which he replied, 'A tidy distance.' Having thus reassured me on the dangers besetting us and the pinpointing of our position, he went below ...

Every year the pilot boats gathered in their home ports for the annual review. The commissioners inspected each vessel to ensure that her safety gear was in order and that she was sound, well fitted and able to carry on her business. Needless to say, the pilots and their men were casual in the extreme over such matters as life jackets. These were almost never worn, even when boarding in a winter gale, so boats were short of them. Often, the life jackets would be handed out of the forehatch after inspection, passed across to the next boat, and so on down the line. The pilots were deadly rivals afloat, but ashore they stood together. As soon as the review was over and the fleet was released to the freedom of the Channel, an impromptu race invariably began, with the keener competitors sailing ever westward to be the furthest down-Channel. Many a profitable job was let pass for the slower boats as the flyers hammered out to windward, sometimes neck-and-neck all the way to Land's End and beyond.

Towing behind a ship had its own dangers for the cutters and was rarely popular with the men. On one occasion, the *Kindly Light* was in tow alongside a ship. The pilot's son was the boy onboard and the man-in-the-boat was growing restless.

'Getting dangerous, this is,' he observed as the youngster fought the tiller to keep the cutter off the ship's side. Suddenly, the man grabbed the fire axe. 'Late back or not, we're having no more of this,' he muttered. The axe fell with a thud, the line parted like a gunshot and the *Kindly Light* surged free, preserved to swim for another hundred years.

The *Lead On* was not so lucky. One dark night she was under tow after boarding her pilot, Zacariah White. Nobody had noticed that her masthead light had gone out. Shortly afterwards, the *Gwladys* came alongside the ship, not realising that there was already a pilot on board. On learning that she was not required, she bore away under the stern of the ship and rammed the *Lead On* in the darkness. Both cutters sank immediately and all five men scrambled aboard the one surviving punt. All night they drifted in a strong wind, and the following morning had more or less given up hope when they were sighted and rescued by a Norwegian sailing ship, the *Consuelo*. Their saviour was probably out of Archangel with timber, and by the time she had made it to Cardiff, the five were posted as drowned.

So great was the relief as the dead men stepped ashore that Captain Rasmussen of the *Consuelo* was awarded a fine telescope and a watch worth £45. He was also given a diamond brooch to take home for his wife and, lest the good lady suspect any other motive, a Norwegian Bible as well.

This story, as told on the Bristol Channel, says only that the men were picked up by a 'Dutchman', but it should be remembered that in those days all Scandinavians were referred to as Dutchmen by certain elements in the seafaring world. The evidence concerning the *Consuelo* comes directly from Norway where the events were recorded in the press of the day. The only discrepancy is that Captain Rasmussen said there were seven men in the punt. Perhaps there were. Who are we to question the hero of the day? But whatever the ultimate truth, there is no doubt that the unfortunate *Gwladys* and the lovely *Lead On* now lie on the bottom of the Bristol Channel.

Despite their fierce competition, the pilots were always generous to one of their number who was down on his luck. This is the story of how a pilot, who was successful enough to employ two grown men as crew in addition to the boy, tried to help a broken-down fellow pilot who had drunk himself onto the scrap-heap of the service. It was Friday the 13th, and Pilot Alexander had decided not to go to sea because the day was inauspicious when he heard that the drunk pilot, who had no cutter of his own, needed to go out to find a ship. The man had no money left at all and had sent his wife out to borrow 10s. He had not been to sea for three months.

Alexander went across to where he stood and touched him gently on the arm, 'I'll take you, Bill,' he said, 'I'll take you to sea.' The man accepted immediately and Alexander's men agreed that they should all leave on the tide that evening.

The night was foul and stormy. Two other cutters were sighted to the westward, but the *Kindly Light* outsailed them and by the following afternoon she lay to windward of all the other boats, so they hove to for what they called a picnic tea. They opened a can of tongue, cut some bread and butter, and made a big pot of tea. The boy laid the repast out on the table in the fo'c'sle together with four new mugs and went to keep the watch, leaving the men to eat first. As they poured the tea, one of the earthenware mugs began to whistle with an eerie, hissing sound. One of the men, Tom Morgan, the son of Pilot John Morgan who was a spiritualist, exclaimed, 'I'm not drinking out of that mug, if you don't mind!' His brother Ernie eyed the flawed mug with distrust, 'Not me, neither,' he announced firmly.

The second pilot, Bill, who had sobered up after twenty-four hours beating to windward, reached out and took the mug, which was still singing. 'I'll take it, boys,' he said easily, 'I may have been a bit of a drunk, but I was never superstitious,' and he swigged the tea off in one gulp.

Shortly afterwards a ship came down on them bound towards Barry and it was agreed to put Bill aboard. Tom Morgan sculled him away through the mountainous seas in the little punt as Alexander put the *Kindly Light* before the wind to gain sea room. Suddenly he was horrified by Ernie Morgan's shout, 'Good God, Skipper, they've gone and we're going too!'

The ship was thrown half down by a breaker like an avalanche. The punt was capsized and seconds

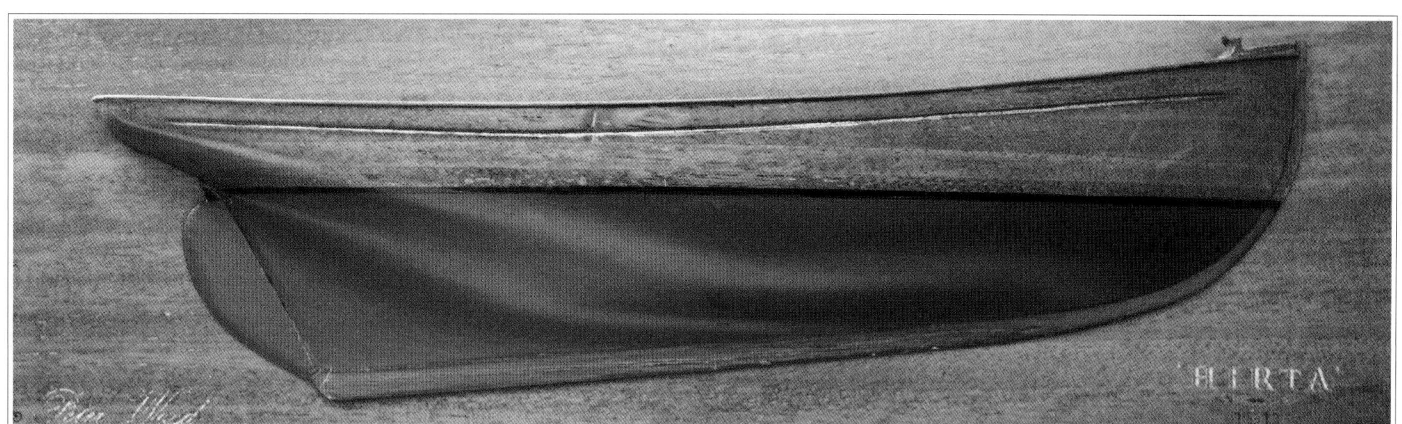

Half-model of Barry pilot cutter *Hirta* built by Slade of Fowey 1911

Hirta was built originally as *Cornubia* and restored under that name in the last few years. The restoration has lengthened her stern a little and in her original form, as seen here, she was a foot shorter than she is now. Other dimensions also vary slightly. The original measurements were 51ft length on deck, 45ft length waterline, beam 13ft 6in, draught 8ft. Displacement around 30 tons. This fine half model was built by Peter Ward to lines taken off by Malcolm McKeand in the late 1980s.
(Author's collection)

A pilot cutter in tow

When a pilot boarded a ship and did not have another in harbour waiting to be brought down to the sea where he could rejoin his cutter, he would sometimes direct the ship to tow his boat home. The practice was potentially dangerous, often uncomfortable and crews hated it. On a good day, a cutter could outsail an early 6kt steamer and it was not unknown for the man-in-the-boat to axe the towline. This lad looks relaxed about it all, but there is a sea running and he may change his mind after a few more hours. *(Author's collection)*

later the *Kindly Light* was overwhelmed by tons of angry sea. By the time she had shaken it off she had taken a lot of water below. Morgan and Alexander immediately set about trying to rescue the other two men. As Alexander said afterwards, 'Those two were old hands in the water,' so going for a swim cannot have been too rare an occurrence in the service, but on this occasion the seas were so terrible that soon the pilot was floating face down and they could see that he was drowned.

Despite being half full of water, the *Kindly Light* still handled well enough to pick up Tom Morgan and the body of the pilot. They laid him gently on the deck and, as the saying was, went hard up for home, arriving sadly the following morning.

The pilots were so moved by this story of a man flying bravely in the face of the portents that, although the drowned man had brought disgrace upon himself and the service by his drunkenness, he was forgiven and his widow was awarded a pension with which to make the best of her tragic loss.

Meanwhile, the nitty-gritty of life went on. Like all free-living communities largely in charge of their own destiny, the pilots and their men were great characters. Some were religious. One was a lay preacher and even had 'God is Love' sewn into his topsail. While this was arguably the case, the commissioners decided that using a pilot cutter as a wayside pulpit was too much and he had to remove it before she was allowed to sea again.

Other pilots were more inclined to what their pious brothers might have seen as wickedness. Smuggling goods ashore from ships was a common occupation and some pilots made something of a business of it. Unless it became too blatant, the authorities tried to turn a blind eye, but occasionally they were left with no choice but to suspend a recurrent malefactor.

Certain of the less godly pilots submitted to temptation and topped up their food lockers from the land. There are apocryphal tales of sending the apprentice ashore on a moonlit Somerset night to grab a lamb from the field for the pilot's Sunday lunch.

Pilots were traditionally close with money, preferring to trade than to buy, and coils of rope, drums of paint, food and liquor often came down the pilot ladder with the pilot as he was taken off a ship. Coal was never purchased for the galley stove. It always came from one ship or another, sometimes in exchange for condensed milk. Up went a dented can, down was lowered a hundredweight sack of finest steam coal.

Tugs were in the habit of offering a bonus to pilots who recommended them. The Christian pilots would have none of this dirtying their hands with money, but were more than happy to accept coal in lieu of cash.

Being well into pensionable age mattered nothing to many pilots of the Channel who continued beating down to the westward regardless of what must have been some creaking joints. One case which illustrates the energy of these men is that of the brothers Cox. Both were sons of Pilot Charles Cox of Bristol. Born in 1807, Cox the elder transferred his duties to Newport when the dock was first opened. His bold enterprise prospered and all five of his sons followed him into the profession. The two in question were Thomas, licence number 27, of the cutter *Mascotte*, and Elijah of the *Leader*.

Thomas Cox appears to have been an irascible man who was not popular among his fellows or, indeed, with anyone else. We will never know who gave way to whom when the brothers crossed tacks off Flat Holme, but one thing is sure. Elijah was high on the list of those who wished Thomas something other than fair winds through life. So bad did matters become between them that one fine day the sprightly pair were reported for brawling on Newport quay. Such behaviour was considered likely to bring the pilot service into disrepute, so the incident appeared on the agenda at the next meeting of the commissioners. A newspaper report of the proceedings which cannot now be confirmed would have us believe that the punch-up started over a dispute regarding Elijah's wife. Perhaps it is because Thomas was sixty-three years old and Elijah was pushing seventy-one that the commissioners decided to take no further action.

Pilots liked to dress formally when boarding, preferring a waistcoat, watch and chain, and a smart shore-going hat. The wide-brimmed 'Holy Joe, as worn by persons of quality' was a favourite amongst those who fancied themselves.

Many of these short reminiscences are thanks to Lewis Alexander junior, who went to sea with his father in the apprentice's berth during the 1919 Barry pilots' revolt. His final word gives an unusual perspective on these remarkable men: 'It was a noble sight to watch a big cutter sailing home with the pilot standing proudly on deck, the lee side of his hat brim beating to the wind in time with the foot of his mainsail.'

While Mr Alexander recalls the colour of the scene, we should return to Captain Bartlett for the final word. His elder brother, a western-going pilot who stood 5ft 2½in tall and was deterred by nothing, sailed an old, leaky boat that was by no means fast. When the wind blew hard from the Atlantic and the grey seas piled mountains high, he would narrow his eye and outstare the storm. 'Bad weather is our chance,' he would say, 'That's when ships want pilots most.'

Footnote

Because of their numbers, availability, suitable size, handy performance and first-class sea-keeping abilities, the Bristol Channel pilot cutters were sought after by cruising yachtsmen at the end of their careers. Many were thus disposed of for prices in the order of what the pilots would have liked to believe they were worth: £250 to £350 was not unusual.

Typically, after sale a boat would be 'tarted up' and fitted with heretical devices such as running backstays and wheel steering. A few of these changes were real improvements, others imaginary. One or two boats survived without major alteration. Many of these fine craft are still sailing into the new millennium and the majority have now been fully restored.

Some boats have become famous, such as Major Tilman's *Mischief*, of high-latitude fame in both north and south hemispheres. Another is *Theodora*, ex-*Kindly Light*, with which Christopher Ellis and Chris Courtauld founded that great British institution, The Ocean Youth Club, now the Trust of the same name. Renamed *Kindly Light* once again, she has been totally restored by Malcolm McKeand with David Walkey as shipwright to a remarkably original state. She even has no engine, an act of great faith and more than a little courage in the year of her relaunch, 2011. *Hirta*, *Madcap* and *Dolphin* have all made high-latitude voyages of note. Others such as the *Jane* have quietly looked after their amateur owners out of the glaring light of publicity, but all have performed mightily. They have generated some fine maritime literature, and have introduced young people to the sea in a way that a modern yacht can never hope to emulate.

CHAPTER 11

Norway and its Pilots

A THOUSAND YEARS AGO, the Norse peoples were world leaders in seafaring. Although the Scandinavian nations were as yet ill-defined, the Danes had voyaged south and east to make the most of the power vacuum never properly filled after the disintegration of the Roman Empire; Swedish Vikings had penetrated the eastern Mediterranean via the great rivers of Europe, portaging their ships into systems that drained into the Black Sea, while the Norwegians had colonised Iceland, Greenland, and even established a toehold in North America.

The ships used for the Atlantic voyages were not for the most part the warlike longships of Viking fable. They were fuller-bodied merchant vessels called *knarrs*. Both types, as well as numerous smaller craft, were in use around the coasts, however, and the classic 'Viking ship' of history had much to do with the boats of the Norwegian coast communities until very recently.

The medieval Norse conducted their seafaring entirely without charts. They had a basic conception of comparative latitude, understanding that the Pole Star stood the same height above the horizon at Bergen as it did at Cape Farewell in southern Greenland, but they did not use longitude as such, or any workable equivalent. For much of their time, no compass was available to them, but they were past masters at observing the movements of the sun and the other heavenly bodies. They knew the west, east, south and north and they had a clear idea of distance based upon the 'day's run' of a ship. The voyaging Viking stayed within sight of land as far as he was able. This elongated his passage times, but made his ultimate arrival more certain. To run the various distant coasts along his route, he made use of pilots wherever possible.

Often, a Norse pilot would be a seaman who had made the passage before and who was shipped from home as part of the crew. There are a number of saga references to such individuals, but it is known that 'local knowledge' pilots referred to as *leidsogumadr* were also employed. Once a ship had sailed beyond her home waters, it would have been virtually indispensable to take on these men from time to time in the almost infinite rock-strewn complexity of the *skjaergaard* (skerries), with which most of the Scandinavian coast is surrounded. Presumably, voyage pilots were paid shares in a trip along with the other men, rather than any fixed pilotage fee. One can well imagine the short shrift that would be meted out to any pilot who got things wrong in those days of direct action.

It is not clear whether there were any full-time pilots in saga times, but by 1687 laws laid down by King Christian V leave no doubt that the profession had become established in Norway. Like many of the Laws of Oléron, which must have been known to the King's draftsmen, these concern themselves with the punishment of pilots who fail in their duties. If a pilot were found guilty of damaging a ship or her cargo, he was to be liable for any loss incurred. If unable to meet the bill, he was deprived of his livelihood.

In pre-industrial times, the Norwegian coast was furnished with small communities. Many engaged in modest trade both with one another and with the outside world, notably Britain and Holland. The mainstay of this traffic was timber carried in ships of modest tonnage. In the south particularly, insignificant tidal rises coupled with a multiplicity of sheltered waterways and deep sounds made the establishment of tiny ports a comparatively simple matter. Further north, the tides increase and communities thin out, yet similar population patterns existed even north of the Arctic Circle, in waters which, offshore at least, were kept ice-free by the Gulf Stream.

The effect of having so many harbours was that, with the exception of a few trading centres such as Bergen or Oslo, many more pilots were needed for a smaller volume of local business than was common in other countries. Thus, there were more 'pilots per ton' of commerce than was generally the case, and the rewards were correspondingly meagre.

Pilot boat in a high sea

This evocative image, painted in 1875 by Hjalmar Johnsen, shows a classic sprit-rigged Norwegian pilot cutter, shortened well down in heavy weather. The sprit rig was much used until gaff superseded it late in the nineteenth century. The distinctive red stripe on the mainsail stayed with local pilot craft to the end of sail. *(Norwegian Maritime Museum)*

A second cause of poor income was quite simply the weather. Conditions off the Norwegian coasts in winter can be shocking. Sometimes whole island communities such as Grip near Kristiansund were swept off their rocks by the seas accompanying great gales. Furthermore, any ships trading with the Baltic were laid up from autumn to spring because their main routes froze over.

The bad weather was not all loss from the pilot's point of view, however. Along the south coast especially, there were many fine storm havens suitable for ships running from heavy weather in emergencies, usually southerly gales. These vessels desperately needed pilots in conditions when small craft would want to be anywhere but at sea, yet their needs were usually serviced. In later years, this work was carried on in conjunction with the famous Rescue Ships (*Redningskoites*) developed by Colin Archer, although such activities became less crucial with the arrival of steamships, owing to their increased ability to keep the sea on a lee shore.

Despite these possibilities for work, Norwegian pilots in the old days were often under-employed and were poorer than in other parts of the world. In the mid nineteenth century, more than seven hundred were registered in the southern half of the country alone, together with almost the same number of boats. At Færder near Oslo, an individual pilot averaged forty ships a year in 1880. According to Storm, a commentator of the time, even if a number of pilots pooled their resources and shared a boat and a 'pilot lad' to handle it, their income was unlikely to exceed the following:

Gross income:	Kr 1248
⅓ to pilot lad:	Kr 416
Boat share:	Kr 350
Nett income:	Kr 482

Pilot cutter from Langesund

A local pilot cutter from Langesund in southern Norway named after her home port and operating from 1880–1890. She was built in the town to service the heavy sailing-ship traffic coming into the skerry channels from outside the Skagerrak port of Langesund. Although apparently not a Colin Archer boat, this fine cutter has many of their attributes including the bulwark capping rail, the low coachroof, the aft cockpit and the mainsheet horse.
(Langesund Seamen's Club)

Even in 1885, this was thin pickings, and hunger often knocked at a pilot's door. To offset the shortfall, many also worked as fishermen, particularly drift-netting or trolling for mackerel when the fish came flooding north in spring. This helped, but hardship was their constant companion. Storm concluded that it would be better for pilots to amalgamate into groups, but few were those who took his advice.

The development of the Norwegian Pilotage Authority

In 1720 a young lieutenant commander from the Norwegian Admiralty called Gabriel Christiansen spearheaded a review of the pilotage situation throughout the country. He submitted a report to his superiors which was far from encouraging, pointing out that all manner of people, such as farmers and even 'female persons', were in the habit of carrying out pilotage jobs. Such a denouncement could not be ignored. A decree was therefore passed which provided instructions for pilots. It also established a system involving intermediate officials known as pilot masters, and two senior pilots. The senior pilots were appointed to look after the affairs of the two pilotage districts, North and South, into which the land would now be divided. Christiansen himself was appointed the first senior pilot for the South. His bailiwick extended from Halden to Ana Sira.

Senior pilots took on the task of ensuring that their subordinates were competent. They also administered survey work, cartography and fixed all pilotage dues. On the whole, the new arrangements were not well received, though the pilots themselves cannot have found them onerous, since they provided for compulsory pilotage whether a vessel had taken a pilot or not.

Many ports had a vantage point where the pilots would wait, spyglass in hand, for the arrival of likely shipping. This was a comparatively efficient way of getting work, but sometimes pilots would sail far off to sea, hoping to come across a ship requiring their services. Ships recognised pilot cutters by their white canvas with a fully tanned stripe down the centre of the mainsail.

Presumably, pilots were not above avoiding contact with ships they did not fancy, because in 1725 a law was enacted reviewing the original one and placing the onus firmly on the pilots to service any ship showing a 'pilot required' flag, enforced by threat of the courts.

Under the 1725 decree, any communal system the pilots may have been operating for inbound ships was rescinded. Each pilot thereafter kept what he earned, subject always to handing a share to the senior pilot and the pilot master. While outlawed from pooling inbound fees, communes were still permitted when it came to taking ships to sea. The law also backed off to allow any competent individual, including farmers, fishermen, or even 'female persons' with sufficient local knowledge, to pilot a ship if no professional pilot were to hand. The result of this was a 'first there, first served' system for official pilots and their unofficial rivals. The competition this engendered was fierce and continued for almost two centuries.

In Christiansen's time, there were 340 pilots and pilot masters in the southern half of Norway. After a peak in the mid nineteenth century, the number fell away to two hundred or so by around 1910.

Gabriel Christiansen met a tragic end that seems as ironic as it was undeserved. He was at sea between Flekkero and Kristiansand when his boat hit a rock, colourfully known locally as *Grisrumpen* ('The Pig's Backside'). Christiansen was drowned, although the weather was crystal clear, and he had four qualified pilots as shipmates.

In 1858, there was a tightening up of pilots' areas along this complex coastline when tests began for pilots on their local patches. Two years later, the senior pilot noted that the men still appeared to know less than he thought they should, so it was doubtful whether the arrangement had helped at all. No pilots had asked to be retested for neighbouring sectors, although considerable overlapping was inevitable; there was definitely an anarchic edge to the goings-on.

As steamships of increasing size began to appear on the scene in the 1870s, complaints were made by shipowners that some of the pilots were out of their depth when it came to ship handling. Similar criticisms were being heard in other parts of the world, and it certainly seems rational that a 2,000-ton steamer would be outside the experience of a pilot who had cut his teeth on small sailing brigs. Accordingly, the senior pilot undertook a survey.

Signalling for the pilot

This barque has struck lucky in her timing. Not only is the pilot cutter on hand to board her, a tugboat is also out touting for business. The scene is a perfect one for the Norwegian coast, with fringing skerries and a small lighthouse on a rock. These lights run all the way up the coast and it is possible to navigate the skerries by using only their coloured sectors on the long winter nights. *(Langesund Seaman's Club)*

As far back as the early 1800s, a pilot had to have eighteen months at sea before appointment and nobody was taken on unless he had at least achieved the rank of able seaman. Pilots were also required to know all the buoyage, reefs and courses in the area for which they were licensed and it was up to the senior pilot to ensure that this was so. The senior pilot took all this into account in 1880 and reached the conclusion that the education of pilots could be improved, but that as the old order seemed to function without too many real problems, it might be better to let things be. So, for twelve years, the system limped along.

A further problem arising out of the increasing number of steamers was that while the pilots themselves were learning by experience and were more than capable of trying out a ship's handling characteristics as they brought her in, the lads were missing out badly. In the old days, after the pilot had boarded a sailing vessel, the lad would bring his cutter home. In fact, he would follow in the wake of the ship if her sailing qualities made this possible; otherwise, he would manage as best he could. As a result, pilot lads came to know the waters in their own right, developing great skill at working their small boats which could later be translated into ship-handling ability. With steamers, a pilot would often tell the lad to wait out at sea or in the skerries, until he came down on another ship.

Various half-hearted attempts were now made to institutionalise the training of pilots, but none was a roaring success. In 1892, it was recommended that a teaching establishment be set up to provide four-year courses for nineteen-year-olds to obtain a commission. At that time, a new pilot had to be between twenty-three and forty-five years old. Typically, the independently minded pilots resisted and the plan never came to fruition, though in 1908 the pilots of Færder did institute an arrangement that was not entirely dissimilar. Along most of the Norwegian shoreline, the traditional system of apprenticeship, often a father/son arrangement, was preferred right into the 1920s when power took a firm hand in the proceedings.

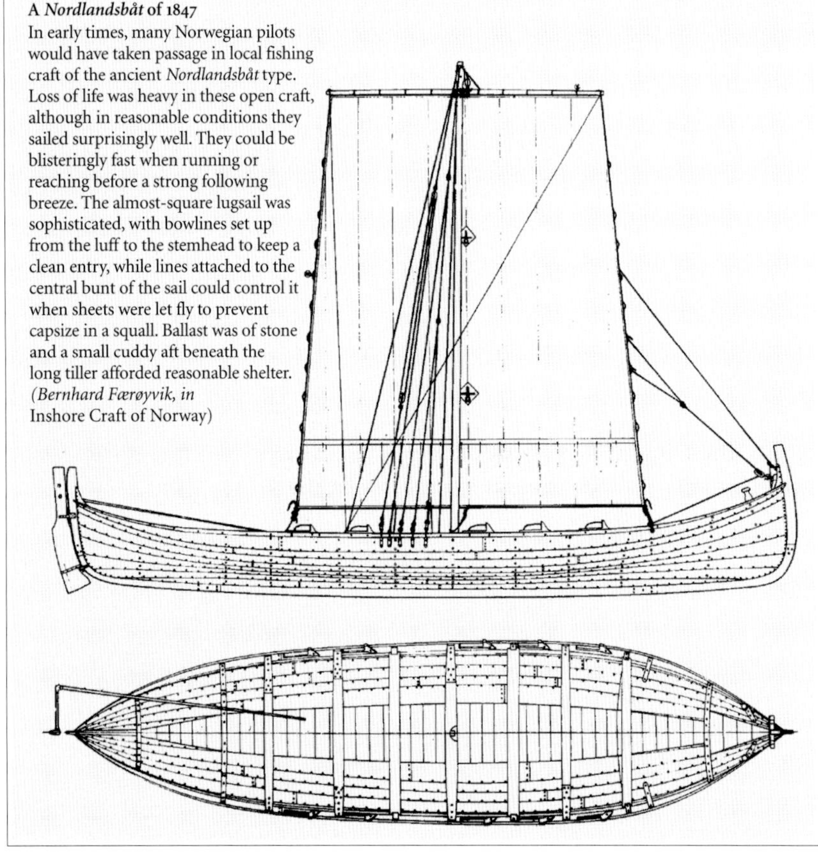

A *Nordlandsbåt* of 1847
In early times, many Norwegian pilots would have taken passage in local fishing craft of the ancient *Nordlandsbåt* type. Loss of life was heavy in these open craft, although in reasonable conditions they sailed surprisingly well. They could be blisteringly fast when running or reaching before a strong following breeze. The almost-square lugsail was sophisticated, with bowlines set up from the luff to the stemhead to keep a clean entry, while lines attached to the central bunt of the sail could control it when sheets were let fly to prevent capsize in a squall. Ballast was of stone and a small cuddy aft beneath the long tiller afforded reasonable shelter. *(Bernhard Færøyvik, in* Inshore Craft of Norway)

Norwegian pilot boats

It is probably true to say that in the eighteenth and nineteenth centuries, Norwegian sailors were among the world's finest handlers of open boats at sea. As a race, they had certainly had plenty of practice, with seafaring in large undecked vessels going back so far in their history that the skills involved must have become embedded in their genes. Notwithstanding this, the loss of life among pilots and fishermen was dreadful.

Whole northern fishing communities and the associated pilots, which in other lands such as Britain would certainly have used decked craft kept afloat in harbours, went to sea in open clench-built boats of the *Nordlandsbåt* type. All but the largest of these were generally dragged up the rocks at the end of each trip, which inevitably placed a limit on their size and hence their seaworthiness. These direct descendants of Viking vessels rowed well and sailed blisteringly fast downwind, virtually planing in a hard breeze under their almost-square lugsails, but they were extremely dangerous. They were constantly at risk from capsize and sinking or from the simpler perils of swamping.

Further south, things were little better.

Sølling's boats

In the late seventeen hundreds, a young ship's officer called Peter Norden Sølling was driven into a coastal harbour to shelter from hard weather. During a prolonged stay near Mandal he was horrified to discover how severe the poverty resulting from lost boats really was. The following shocking statement is typical of the sort of thing he found. In 1802, the neighbouring villages of Svenør and Nesset in the Vest-Agder district housed thirty-one pilot widows with a total of seventy-one children between them. It would be a century and a half before welfare and social security were established, and the situation of such courageous women cut Sølling deeply.

Sølling joined the navy shortly after this experience and soon rose to captain's rank. He now set himself the task of dealing with the conditions he had witnessed as best he could. Given leave from his post, he travelled to England and seems to have been impressed with the smacks of the southeast, many of which were by this time at least partially decked. He produced designs for a Scandinavian 'decked cutter' which clearly owes some of its inspiration to a Thames bawley.

The cutter designed by Sølling for the Norwegian pilots had a fairly traditional round bow and was wide-beamed by general British standards, though typical of the bawley. Its radical features were a square stern and a 'full-on' gaff rig, complete with occasional square sail, to replace the preferred spritsail. The new stern showed some resemblance to the 'lute stern' favoured by beach boats of the eastern English Channel at that period. The boat was to be clinker-built out of oak and various sizes were offered from 30 to 35ft on deck. Ballast remained internal, consisting of 9,000–10,000lb of the plentifully available iron ore, or stones.

Permission was finally granted by the King to build three of these boats. One might imagine that so obvious an improvement would have been embraced by a grateful pilot community, but this was not the case. In fact, Sølling's adversities only now began in earnest. As he sailed the coast promoting his innovative vessels, he discovered a home truth about seamen which perhaps by that time of his life he should have realised. Two thousand years of hardship and disappointment have made them a conservative crew, and Norwegian pilots in the early nineteenth century were no exception. At the outset, Sølling's potential beneficiaries would have nothing to do with his newfangled ideas. In desperation, he successfully put to sea in a storm when open boats had to stay at the wharf, but it made no difference. Returning disconsolate, he wrote, 'The pilots will no way use it. Each would prefer his open boat – how I was discouraged by this event I cannot describe – captains and pilots laughed at me and made fun of me behind my back.'

Rather than give up, however, Sølling now reverted to stealth. He would wait for a pilot to go to sea, then visit his wife with gifts of luxuries such as real coffee which he knew she could not afford. The implication was that if the 'old man' would recant and buy a decent boat, such joys would come to the house on a regular basis. Finally, in January 1802, the first 'Sølling' pilot boat, *Anker* was stationed at Svenør. The pilots were ordered to pay 3 riksdaler per year until the bill was settled, an initiative which was highly unpopular. They wrote to their pilot master saying, 'We want absolutely nothing to do with these pilot sloops. We have, thank God, pilot boats good enough to carry on our business and better to handle in good weather or bad.'

Two years later the Svenør pilots had changed their tune, writing to their boss that, 'We assure your highness that the named pilot boat or sloop is as good for pilots' use as we could wish and we humbly enclose our dutiful thanks to the superior men who decided we should have this.'

Such a turnaround can only fuel speculation about what went on behind the scenes. There is no doubt that Sølling himself was not above overselling the fruits of his product. Maybe he had something to do with this uncharacteristically sycophantic communication.

As time went by, Sølling's boats became more prevalent along the south coast of Norway, but they never achieved the total acceptance that might well have proved a good thing. Their creator certainly either suffered from tunnel vision or was severely misled when he wrote on the back of a painting of *Pilot Boat No 1*, 'Of decked pilot boats quite like this one I found 600 in 1826. Southern Norway and Western, and the open coffins – ousted – abolished.'

Peter Norden Sølling 1758–1827

Commander Peter Sølling was the first to attempt to introduce safer, more seaworthy boats for the pilots of Norway. Ridiculed at first, he persevered until his cutters were accepted. He died a well-respected man.
(Norwegian Maritime Museum)

Whether or not he really did find six hundred decked pilot craft or was carried away by his own enthusiasm may never be known. What is sure is that most of his ideas, while apparently sound, soon fell into the waste basket of history, because in the 1870s a man named Colin Archer began a second and this time successful assault on the dubious craft in use by pilots. By now, the pointed stern was virtually universal once more and, with a few exceptions, the sprit rig had again taken over. Nevertheless, it is at least possible that a series of deeper, rounder boats built in East Agder in the nineteenth century were to some extent influenced

A Sølling boat

Another image of one of Sølling's pilot cutters. These boats also ran mail between Norway and its ally, Denmark. A number were sunk by the Royal Navy during the wars in which England and Norway ended up on opposite sides. This picture shows some interesting detail. The crew are fishing and appear to be drying their catch on a lowered square yard. A lug topsail with a head stick is lowered and the main tack is triced up to keep it away from the action.
(The National Archives of Norway)

by Sølling. Gaff rig also took an early foothold in this area, perhaps for the same reason, but regardless of Sølling's ultimate success or lack of it, he was without doubt a true altruist who well deserves the kind remarks by 'a friend' on his tomb at Holmen in Copenhagen. They read like an old Norse poem from the sagas and are loosely translated thus:

In word and deed a man of honour
A true spruce from Norway's mountains
His kind and bright intellect
Helped the hero to slay life's sorrows
His pilot boat saved life and goods
His 'bombbox' is lifted proudly
He left it and Norway's pilots
His dust rests; his memory lives.

The Lister boats

Traditionally, the inhabitants of timber-free Lister had to buy their boats from neighbouring provinces. Inshore craft were available in Flekka just 'around the corner', but when a serious sea boat was required, such as a pilot or offshore fisherman might demand, they found themselves in an interesting dilemma. To the east, the builders of Mandal could supply strong, heavy boats that were not notably quick, especially in light airs. Lister men could also go up north to the Hardanger Fjord where light, fast boats of less able sea-keeping qualities were in vogue. An honest Lister pilot who had selected his vessel in order to stay alive therefore often suffered the irritation of seeing his prize snapped up by a 'chancer' in a lightweight flier.

In 1830, a boatbuilder called Gjert Gunnersen moved from the well-known boat centre at West Agder to Lister. Gunnersen was originally from Jondal up north in Hardanger and he now set to work combining the best of both worlds. A local commentator, Eilert Sundt, described Gunnersen as a man of few words who refused to take on an apprentice, but his boats were so useful that people soon started to make their own copies to his model, with Ole Stave a prime mover.

At that time, local boats were measured in 'tuns', or the number of barrels of corn they could carry. According to one authority, a typical Lister boat of 25 tuns had the following dimensions:

A *Listerskoite*

The term 'skoite' is a generic word meaning a decked, beamy double-ended boat. The *Listerskoite*, so-called because she hailed from the port of the same name, is seen here at a regatta off Ålesund in 1898. Although well-suited to pilot work, she bears little if any resemblance to the clinker-built Lister boats favoured by Lister pilots from many years earlier. *(Norwegian Maritime Mueum)*

Length between stem- and sternposts:	27ft
Beam:	9ft
Depth from keel to gunwale:	4ft

Lister boats had a pronounced sheer and were remarkable for their use of 'washboards' – extra boards above the gunwale to help keep heavy seas out. A study of photographs also shows that they carried a plank laid inboard of the gunwale almost like the covering board of an embryonic deck. All this undoubtedly made the boats more seaworthy but such innovation was, of course, criticised by the pilots. They said that it would make the boat dangerous because she would be less likely to tip out her ballast if she capsized!

The boats were clinker-built of pine on oak frames with an oak backbone. They were fastened with wood trenails according to eastern practice, instead of the iron clench building fashionable on the west coast. Sprit rig was carried by most Lister boats and this, at least, can have caused no controversy. Any Lister boat with pretensions to performance carried a well steeved-up bowsprit which people from the east said spoiled their looks. Some owners specified gaff rig, complete with most of the trimmings, but they remained in a minority. Lug topsails were carried by many and the mast had a system of unstepping which was useful for herring drifting.

Although the Lister boat gained little ground with pilots on the south coast to the east of Mandal, the type spread piecemeal to the north and west. Many ordinary folk in Lister built their own copies and sold them out of the area, some as far off as Lofoten. Some were decked, others open. Some were fine copies of Gunnersen's originals. Others were not and by no means all the customers were happy with the deal.

The Hvaler boat

Despite the efforts of Sølling and the influence of the Lister boat further west, the most popular pilot boat in southern Norway in the nineteenth century remained the Hvaler boat. These traditional craft originated from Hvaler (Whale Island). They were around 28ft on deck with a great beam of 10ft and the shallow draught of only 3ft. Clinker-built, and lightly constructed, they were usually decked over and while some were well maintained, many were apparently not, being kept in service as long as they would float.

The generally sprit-rigged Hvaler boats favoured the 'cod's head, mackerel tail' hull form and carried exceedingly flared sections above the waterline. This gave huge reserves of buoyancy, but rendered the

Hvaler boat

The typical form of these vessels is clearly shown here. The heavy clinker building, wide beam and relatively shoal draught with a fine springy sheer are dominant features, along with the elegant out-hung rudder and tiller steering. The simple sloop rig made for easy handling. *(Photographer unknown, Østfold fylkes billedarkiv)*

boats sometimes difficult to handle. Away from their home waters, they were not renowned as good sea boats; by the 1860s at least, some pilots were beginning to acknowledge that the western boats were able to keep the sea in worse weather. Furthermore, any attempts by pilots to obtain loans to build new ones were systematically rejected. They were overdue for replacement. With the wisdom of hindsight, one can say that the only feature that would be truly missed was that these boats had a charisma all their own and, if well turned out, could be extremely pretty.

Colin Archer

Like most initiatives in the development of the Norwegian pilot cutter, that of Colin Archer was motivated by humanitarian concern over loss of life. His early work on pilot boats began around 1870 and certainly in those days there was little relief from the horrific losses that had so moved Sølling half a century before. *Skillings Magazine* no 44 in 1869 notes that there were a number of ports where no pilot had been buried ashore in living memory. Sooner or later, all succumbed to the sea.

That such claims are not exaggerated is borne out by recent anecdotal evidence. In the 1980s, the writer met with a young woman on the northwest coast whose forebears were pilots of Hustadvika near Kristiansund, one of the worst places on this awesome shoreline. This charismatic lady's great-grandmother had been married to not one, but five different pilots, each replacing the other as his colleague was drowned. So rapid had been the turnover at one stage that there was some doubt about which deceased pilot had actually sired the young woman's line of descent. She herself was owner of a large fishing boat, so it seems that hope still triumphs over experience in that supremely dangerous place.

Confronted with statistics like these, Archer was stirred to action. Colin Archer was born in Norway of Scottish parents who had emigrated from a failing family timber business in Fife during the depression which followed the Napoleonic Wars. The Archers set up house at Larvik on the south coast, just outside the entrance to the Oslo Fjord. Here, Mr Archer senior began a successful lobster exporting business which later expanded to include timber once again.

One of a large family of brothers and sisters, Colin spent some years of his early life adventuring in Australia, but when his father died he returned to the family home in an old customs house at Larvik known as Tolderodden. It seems that the business worked well enough to support him without undue effort, because for a while he lived a life of active leisure. After a few years, however, this popular and capable man began to look around for useful ways of employing his time. He had always been interested in small boat sailing, and the proximity of his home to the main shipping routes into Oslo gave him ample opportunity to consider the pilot service. Speaking of his ancestor, James Ronald Archer notes, 'Here was employment, not only highly congenial, but which might be instrumental in mitigating the hardships and removing some, at least, of the many dangers of their callings.'

Boarding Norwegian-style from a Hvaler boat

An early Hvaler-boat pilot cutter approaches the lee of a ship to board her pilot. In fair weather, she would range alongside, keeping damage to a minimum with fendering and even a sacrificial strake. In heavy seas, rather than risk his cutter, a pilot might well pass within a line's toss and heave a rope across. When this was secure on the ship, he would pass a bowline around his waist and leap into the sea to be hauled aboard in short order. *(Author's collection)*

Archer had no formal training in naval architecture, so he began studying the subject privately at home, with no more background than the maths he had picked up at the local school many years before. In 1865 he began boatbuilding, and in 1867 opened his boatyard in Larvik. This consisted of two slipways at the back of Tolderodden. A year later, Archer's commitment to the area was sealed when he married a local girl and built a new home, Lilleodden, in the grounds of the old custom house.

Archer's innovations in pilot boats centred around the obvious need for better construction,

The Tenvik boat

A model of the Tenvik boat, built for pilot work in Tenvik in Vestfold County close to Colin Archer's home and yard was, from many accounts, an inspiration to him as he sought to design and build an improved pilot-boat type.
(Norwegian Maritime Mueum)

Colin Archer pilot cutter

The perfection of a Colin Archer pilot cutter.
(Author's collection)

larger size, properly secured ballast or even a ballast keel, comfortable accommodation and carvel planking. This latter requirement served to reduce skin friction as well as cutting down damage when the boat went alongside a ship in rough weather.

Unlike Sølling, Archer began quietly. His first seven pilot boats were clinker-built because, as always, the pilots refused to countenance any new ideas. After a short interval he was able to persuade one or two far-sighted customers to accept a strong plank-on-frame construction. From this was developed the heavy-framed, trenail-fastened construction for which he became famous.

In 1873, one of Archer's boats won first prize in the prestigious Jomfruland regatta. Her owners, the Josefsen pilot family of Nevlunghavn, were delighted and the rest of his world was suitably impressed. Orders now began to flow steadily and Archer was able to whittle away at the bad features of the pilot boat. Extreme flare was removed, the midships section slid aft to a more central site leading to a better balanced hull. Draught and size generally increased so that pilots could at last stand up down below. The most radical improvement was the addition, very surreptitiously and bit by bit, of outside ballast. By 1875, an Archer pilot cutter carried up to one-third of its ballast outside. The remainder continued to be iron ore, but in his boats it was properly secured under the cabin sole. Extreme beam was also slowly but steadily reducing.

In the 1884 edition of his *Manual of Yacht and*

Boat Sailing, the English writer Dixon Kemp gives Archer a section in which to describe his pilot boats. Kemp was clearly impressed by them, noting that, 'if the flare of the bow were reduced, the forefoot rounded up a little, a lead keel added, and a suitable sail plan, we think that a very fast and weatherly yacht could be built from these lines.' Kemp obviously had the same eye as Archer, because these were exactly the innovations the Norwegian was trying to bring about.

At the time of the Dixon Kemp book, Archer's boats had no shrouds, only a forestay and were still sprit rigged. They were extremely easy to handle and very quick in stays which, as Archer pointed out, were crucial features to their task. Later, Archer brought in universal gaff rig with a short mast set well into the boat. This made for a short boom and a large staysail, both of which make for ease of handling with a small crew. A readily shipped bowsprit was also a feature.

As early as the 1880s, Archer's pilot boats had appeared up and down the whole coast of Norway as far north as Ålesund and had been exported to Denmark and Sweden. The pilots had finally been led to accept the truth and when his boats swept the board at the Arendal regatta, his name was cheered. 'Archer. *He*'s the man, *he* is,' was the verdict of one hoary old salt.

When the Færder pilots' committee was formed in 1899, Colin Archer was invited to sit on its management board. With this official acceptance came the freedom to develop his boats, and five years before the turn of the century, Archer's pilot cutters had achieved a degree of seaworthiness, good looks and performance which have never really been surpassed by any deep-keeled working vessel. For the pilots at least, his task was complete. He was a true genius whose boats speak for him more loudly than words ever could.

Colin Archer also built yachts, some of them almost pure pilot cutters. Ultimately, he created the famous rescue boats which revolutionised the life of the fishing fleets, and endure to this day as the yardstick by which ultimate seaworthiness in small craft must be measured. He remained a philanthropist all his days, subsidising the price of his early pilot boats to help his customers make up their minds; indeed, it seems doubtful whether any of his pilot boats made a profit for him. Nonetheless, they have been copied and used as pro formas for many late designs. Many of these replicas are excellent, some are not, but the designs are so timeless that it seems they will be built for ever.

Colin Archer's selfless work was acknowledged by all to be of enormous value to Norway and, for it, he was honoured by the King. He died at a great age, loved not only by his family, but by the whole seafaring community in the land of his birth.

The life of the Norwegian sailing pilots

When studying the world of a pre-Colin Archer pilot on Norway's south coast, one is presented with conflicting images, but it does seem that, while the boats were a pretty sight from a distance, close-up on a winter's night they presented little charm. It would not be right, however, to dwell on the horrors of a pilot's existence without seeing the idyllic image of regatta days in high summer, when the blue Skagerrak laps around peaceful islands and the skerries seem to dance in the haze of the sun's heat. C Schollert wrote a small book about the Færder pilots during the transitional period from Hvaler boats to their Archer-inspired successors.

> It is a lovely sight to watch the whole fleet stand out to sea under a stiff breeze. Among the boats are some of the best sailers along the coast. They are so burnished up that they actually shine, and the rigging has been carefully overhauled as if they were racing craft. Under the press of sail carried they heel over down to their gunwales, and their lee bows are hidden by the wave of foam churned up. The pilot's family watches the race from the harbour and a smile of satisfaction flits from face to face as a boat forges ahead to windward. It is their father's boat.

A few years earlier, in the unimproved Hvaler boats it had been a different story. In the old days, a pilot had no oilskins and no creature comforts aboard of any sort. Heat and cooking facilities were provided by a battered tub lined with stones in which a fire was kindled. The smoke had to escape as best it could, sometimes through a hole in the leaking deck, whose production of water would extinguish the fire as often as not. There was no bedding on the

110

wooden bunk boards, save perhaps a sack of seaweed and maybe a half-frozen jib as a pillow.

Winter sailing in these latitudes frequently involved the boat becoming beset with ice that built up from precipitation and spray, not only rendering life unpleasant in the extreme, but also eroding stability. Inshore waters away from the direct influence of the Gulf Stream might also freeze over, making passage through the skerries extremely dangerous. As if this were not enough, boarding techniques were potentially very hazardous indeed.

Anyone who has tried to come alongside another vessel in a seaway will understand that it is a procedure fraught with peril. A pilot vessel displacing 5 tons, or considerably more in later days, grinding up and down a ship's side is a lively business which can easily result in heavy damage. Bringing the boat alongside is one problem, working her off again is another. The only safe way under sail would be to keep as much way on as possible, regardless of the point of sailing, and have the pilot jump for it at the right moment. Ideally, this would be accomplished without the two vessels ever coming into contact, but pilot boats carried an impressive set of fenders just in case. The outside of the covering board sometimes stood proud of the hull as a sort of rubbing strake which was often a sacrificial piece not structurally part of the deck itself. If there were a mishap, it would carry away without further damaging the boat. An additional refinement relied on the plentiful deck space enjoyed by these beamy craft. This enabled the bulwark rail to be set well in from the deck edge, providing a safe and comfortable footing for a pilot hanging onto the shrouds waiting to jump across to his ship.

Risking the boat alongside a ship like this was, surprisingly, the soft option for a Norwegian pilot. If things were really rough so that ranging alongside would mean certain disaster, she was sailed close up on the weather side while a line was hove to the ship's crew. When they had a good turn round a solid pin, the pilot looped his end around his body and jumped into the sea. The cutter then veered off to safety and the ship's crew heaved on the rope to drag their saviour aboard. No further comment is required on this common practice, except that it often led to arthritis as surviving pilots gained in years.

A later pilot cutter in action

This superb image is full of fascinating detail. The cutter, if not an Archer, is certainly inspired by his work. In addition to the fendering, note the helmsman's cockpit, the characteristic bulwarks, the mainsheet horse with its elegantly bent outboard ends, the simple standing rigging with only a forestay and two shrouds a side and the low coachroof with its oblong lights. The bowsprit has been run in for manoeuvring. This was often done and it was particularly simple on these boats. All that was necessary was to drop the jib and ease the bobstay tackle, then shove the spar forward out of its socket on the samson post and lift it clear. Gravity and the laws of physics did the rest. *(Norsk Folkemuseum)*

After the pilot had boarded a ship, the pilot lad was left alone to bring the boat back, or at least to fend for himself. In his book, Pilot Master Storm describes how one young lad put his pilot aboard a ship on the morning of 7 December 1870, four miles outside Færder. The weather was coming on thick with snow and a northeast gale, which now deteriorated into storm-force conditions. The unfortunate lad had to reef down so far that he could no longer make effectively to windward. Stiff with cold after many hours of tacking to and fro in the snow-driven darkness with the boat half-full of freezing water, he thought himself lost.

Fortunately for the lad, the pilot and his ship had also been making heavy weather of things, and both had been out all night. The following afternoon, to his amazement, the boy saw the ship heave into sight through the mist of spray and the densely flying snow. He pulled himself together, bore down on her and was hauled aboard. Fifteen minutes later, the pilot boat, now presumably in tow, sank to the bottom.

Nowadays, strong drink is very expensive in Norway. This was not always the case. In the days of the Hvaler boat, the sparsely sited 'State wine

A Colin Archer-type cutter putting to sea on 4 July 1901

Unfortunately no information has come to light about this image. However, sailors will note with curiosity the light running rigging. There appears to be no bobstay, hence the rather 'skyed' bowsprit. The single gaff span with only a two-part peak purchase must have demanded a hefty heave to hoist the sail and caused concern about gaff damage due to lack of the more usual load-spreading effected by a pair of spans. *(Norwegian Maritime Museum)*

Saari

The Colin Archer-designed 32ft *Saari*, built by Abö Batvarf in Finland around 1920, apparently for a Finnish pilot. Her construction was classic Archer – big sawn larch frames and futtocks fastened with trenails, with alternate steamed oak timbers, riveted with Swedish iron. In her the author and his wife sailed to North and South America. Her whereabouts is now unknown. The image shows her outbound for Brazil from the Solent in 1975, deep-loaded with stores and with two reefs down. *(Photograph by Jeppe Jul-Nielsen)*

Colin Archer yacht *Venus*

In addition to pilot cutters and rescue ships, Colin Archer also built a number of 'skoite'-style yachts which owed their ancestry to his pilot cutters. One such is *Venus*, built as a yacht in 1889 and still going strong.
(Are & Thoralf Qvale, through Norwegian Maritime Museum)

monopolies' which corner today's market with exorbitant prices did not exist. Licensing laws were as liberal as prices were affordable. All along the Kristiania Fjord, for example, were 'distilled spirit stations' where pilots and other thirsty mariners could fend off the miseries of reality for a modest fee. Booze was also available in bottles to take away, and many a pilot eased the grim nights hunkered down on a pile of rags and seaweed with a drop or two of the right stuff.

Tragically, but inevitably, chronic drunkenness was the result for many a good man, and many were the lives consequently lost in this unforgiving environment. But it was not all gloom. There were happy endings as well, such the one which befell two pilots and their lad homeward bound from Kristiania Fjord to Sandosund after a successful job. To ease their minds in the fresh northerly wind and driving snow, they had stopped to load up at the grog shop.

The wind and their humour rose together and just before reaching the land, one pilot tumbled over the side. So deep was the darkness and so high the spirits of his shipmates that neither of them noticed him go, but mercifully, he managed to grab a rope untidily dragging astern. He hung onto this tattered end all the way to the berth, where his partner and the apprentice, now thoroughly 'lit up', were surprised to hear his voice coming to them from the water rather than the cockpit.

The improvement in quality of life for the Norwegian pilots brought about by Colin Archer and the work of those boatbuilders who followed his example cannot be overstated. Warm, dry accommodation, a boat that would live in virtually any weather and not be cast upon the first lee shore that threatened her in a storm of wind proved all that these men needed. They were toughened beyond modern comprehension by their calling, through their own life experience, and through the expectation of hard times instilled by preceding generations. When things finally came right for them, they were among the finest pilots in the world. The phenomenal skill that enabled them to work the intricacies of their ironbound coastline under sail through twenty-hour winter nights will remain a wonder to seamen as long as the sea is salt.

CHAPTER 12

Pilot Cutters in the New Millennium

THERE IS NO DOUBTING the success of the pilot cutter as a working vessel, but many other craft of the era fulfilled their own purposes equally well. Nevertheless, with the twenty-first century well under way, it is the pilot cutter above all generic types that is being replicated in increasing numbers. Other traditional boats inspired by the pilot cutters are proliferating, and the original survivors which have reached great age intact are almost all now totally restored. One need not look far to discover the reasons for this revival of interest because, in truth, the virtues of the pilot cutter have never been totally lost from view. Merchant seamen recognised them from the outset, but it was not among the professional community that the cutters were to achieve their greatest fame. When the boats were paid off in the years leading up to the Great War, many were laid up for the duration. As 1920 rolled around, yachtsmen not wealthy enough to commission a new cruising yacht – or indeed, an ocean racer – began searching for alternatives. Thus, the buyers came looking just as the fleets of 'instant offshore yachts' became available at affordable prices. Amateur sailors bought them, they sailed them to some remarkable places and they took part in many of the early ocean races. Most importantly, they wrote books about them. The printed word, so ably executed by the generations between the wars, established the legend; history lived on in the ageing timbers of the boats and the pilot cutter became the definitive stuff on which dreams are made.

Books by E G Martin, the 6ft 7in giant who bought the Le Havre classic *Jolie Brise* out of France and went on with her to found what became the Royal Ocean Racing Club, inspired a generation. They still inform those wise enough to read them. Less ambitious volumes such as Ellen Barbara Flower's *Under Jane's Wings*, and, of course Frank Carr's *A Yachtsman's Log* are delights which kept the flame burning for the Bristol Channel, while the swashbuckling adventures of Erling Tambs in his Norwegian Colin Archer pilot cutter *Teddy* have inspired many a young man to go to sea, including myself.

In the 1960s, the most famous books of all were written by the mountaineer/sailor H W Tilman. Tilman was a one-off who made numerous voyages to the Arctic and Antarctic in several Bristol Channel pilot cutters. A survivor of two very active world wars, he climbed the Himalayas in his middle years, which fell between the conflicts, before finally admitting to himself that he was becoming a little elderly for high altitudes. With *Mischief*, *Baroque* and *Sea Breeze*, he sought unclimbed mountains of more modest size that could only be reached by sea. His books are among the greatest literature of the oceans and are made all the more readable by the fact that, to those with the wit to see it, there is a laugh on almost every page.

These are the people to whom the modern pilot cutter world owes its debt. The writers of this extraordinary period joined with the original pilots to motivate visionary men such as Luke Powell in Cornwall and the builders and sailors of West Norway to construct new boats, sometimes on spec, simply because the world needs to be reminded of the things that really matter at sea.

This chapter is dedicated to the new boats, the survivors and the restorations that keep the traditions alive. Space precludes me from including

Hirta in Douarnenez

(Author's collection)

all I would like, so I have selected what I hope will be seen as a small representative group. I have started with a few brief reminiscences of my own from the interim period when the old boats were still largely unrestored and the new ones were not yet a glimmer on the horizon.

Douarnenez 1986

The Bretons have always known how to put on a good party. In 1986, the fishing town of Douarnenez, motivated and organised by the remarkable sea journal *Le Chasse-Marée* showed the world how it is done. Douarnenez snuggles in the sheltered southeast corner of the great bay between the infamous Chenal du Four and the even more dangerous gap in the rocks leading directly into Biscay known as the Raz de Sein. Historically, it was the home of great fleets of sailing tunnymen and sardine luggers. Today, it is a major commercial port for state-of-the-art deep-sea trawlers, but it has not forgotten its past. In the summer of '86, the town barricaded off the streets leading to the old port of Rosmeur for a week and declared a free-for-all to every traditional boat that could spread canvas or be propelled by oars. All that was needed was to get there, somehow. The public paid good money to enter the town and the boats pitched up in hundreds. The scene for the sailors was set on the first night at what was billed as a 'reception for crews'. This event was simply the best bash the author has ever been a part of, and it is confessed openly that he has attended many. A thousand folk of the sea gathered in the *criée* – the wet fish market where the catches are landed. The food was passed round in plenty, on time and of a quality which in those days only France could offer. When one of my crew asked a passing fisherman where he could replenish his glass of wine, the hard-bitten man of the sea held up a finger to wait a moment. Two minutes later he returned with a case of the finest and bashed it down on our table.

'*Voilà*!' And away we went. The buzz of human

voices was unsullied by muzak; only the roar of a chantey well-sung by one team or another broke the sound of conversation and laughter. Out on the water, the spirit of the event continued. Boats had come from Spain, Portugal, Ireland, Norway and Britain. Some had even road-trailed up from the Mediterranean, yet the meeting was not international as such, for we were all brothers and sisters that week. The ocean was our country.

Boats and small sailing ships of all types were represented, but there is no doubt that the show was stolen by four pilot cutters from the Bristol Channel. In those days, nothing was organised for such craft and it is not unlikely that we represented the biggest gathering of the faithful since World War II. We had made no communication with one another. We were just there. Rafted up against the high wall of Rosmeur, we made a fine sight and I suspect it was then that the world saw the start of what has since become a movement. None of the boats was officially restored, although *Peggy* from Bristol had been soundly rebuilt. She sported a new, light rig of great altitude which made her a tough boat to catch. Tilman's old boat *Baroque* lay next door, her sheer in some doubt, but her prestige unassailable after her Arctic voyaging. Next came *Madcap*, built in 1875, in relatively good shape after some serious work, her own Arctic voyaging still to come in another life. Last was *Hirta*, my own boat, recently home from Greenland via America and the West Indies. She had no restoration at all, except for continuing remedial work, much caulking and refastening by our crew, and a new deck in the 1960s.

Le Chasse-Marée were so impressed by the cutters that they ran a number of features on them and the word went out: pilot cutters were still around. They made the best sea boats, and in a world turning increasingly to plastic, their charisma was higher than ever.

Similar events with a strong Scandinavian flavour were being organised in Risør up in Norway. *Hirta* attended one of these a year or two after that first Douarnenez festival, and it was clear that Colin Archer, his rescue ships, and in particular his pilot boats, were captivating the crowds. The scene was set. It only remained for builders and restorers to sharpen their tools and remember.

Restoration – Bristol Channel pilot cutter *Kindly Light*

Kindly Light's history is typical of a surviving pilot cutter but, as with everything else in her life, it is somewhat more spectacular. Built in 1911 for Pilot Lewis Alexander of Barry in the Bristol Channel (see chapter 10), this 54-footer was among the most radical of them all. Said to be faster than anything else on the Channel, she earned her pilot a notable living and was one of the small group of cutters which operated after World War I in the face of the pilots' official decision to amalgamate and work turn-about from a steam vessel.

Later in life, *Kindly Light* was owned by Christopher Ellis under the name *Theodora*. In this guise and sporting a square yard, no less, she crossed the Atlantic to New York where legend has it a harbour policeman handed her a ticket for exceeding the speed limit under sail. Ellis and a friend, Christopher Courtauld, used '*KL*' and Courtauld's gaff yawl *Duet* to found the organisation which is now the Ocean Youth Trust. This, and the Ocean Youth Club which preceded it, have taken literally thousands of young folk safely to sea as working crew. Without *Kindly Light* it is probable that this tremendous success story would never have happened at all.

In due course, Chris Ellis handed *Kindly Light* to a museum in Wales, where she fell upon hard times. After sailing in on her own bottom with a crew which included Pilot Alexander's son Norman, her condition deteriorated seriously. She was saved from an uncertain fate by Malcolm McKeand, who had sailed with the author aboard *Hirta*. McKeand transported the boat to Gweek in the far west of Cornwall by road. Here, over a leisurely period, she underwent a total restoration in the hands of McKeand himself and David Walkey, master shipwright.

The restoration of *Kindly Light* reads like a textbook on how to get things right. McKeand, a craftsman of world renown in a different discipline, insisted on the fullest research and no compromise whatsoever in his quest for a real pilot cutter, just as she was on her launching day in 1911. This 'zero tolerance' approach means that *Kindly Light* is without power of any sort other than her sails. Even her punt is a fully researched replica of Pilot

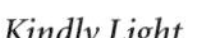

Kindly Light

(Ros Cunliffe)

Alexander's own 12ft *Lead On* with an 11ft 6in sculling oar to drive her.

Relaunched at Cornwall's National Maritime Museum in Falmouth in 2011 on her hundredth birthday, she will be sailing by the time this book goes to press.

Length on deck:	53ft 11in
Beam:	14ft 6in
Draught:	8ft 6in
Displacement:	33 tons

Restoration – Le Havre pilot cutter *Marie-Fernand*

Marie-Fernand, one of only two surviving Le Havre pilot cutters, was built in 1894 by Le Marchand for Pilot Eugène Prentout, who named her for his two children, Marie and Fernand. H23 proved a fast boat from the outset and within a month of her launching in June had won the Pilots Race organised by the Société des Régates du Havre. She worked the Channel waters until, in 1917, she was sold to a fisherman. The same fate befell her more famous cousin *Jolie Brise*, and the parallels did not end there. In the early 1920s, *Marie-Fernand* caught the eye of British yachtsman E G Martin, who would have bought her, but for a chance which showed him a half-model of *Jolie Brise*. Infatuated by the bigger boat's lines, Martin sought out '*JB*' and that might have been the end of the matter, except that another British sailor snapped up

Marie-Fernand

(Valetoux collection)

Marie-Fernand and brought her to the UK. Here she remained, renamed *Leonora*, until Peter Gregson of Wooden Ships Brokerage in Salcombe, Devon, recognised her importance in 1984 and contacted Le Havre.

Now the rebirth of the real pilot cutter began. In typical northern French fashion, a number of dedicated enthusiasts got together as L'Association de l'Hirondelle de la Manche. Their patron was no less a sailor than Eric Tabarly himself and, under their guidance, a noble restoration has been completed. *Marie-Fernand* has been classified among France's *Monuments Historiques*. Today, she sails with the Association and can be seen in her glory at the festivals of traditional sail as well as making a presence for *patrimoine* at some of the spectacular French-based ocean race starts and finishes.

Length on deck:	52ft 2in
Beam:	4.25m
Draught:	2.5m
Headroom:	2.1m

Restoration – Norwegian pilot cutter *Frithjof*

Frithjof was built in 1896 at Porsgrunds Baadbyggeri by Thor Jenssen, formerly chief craftsman at Colin Archer's yard. Her designer was most likely Fredrik Johannessen. She is oak planked on heavy double pine frames after the fashion of Colin Archer. She was commissioned by Pilot Thor Andersen at Ula in Vestfold, who started his career as a pilot lad at the age of nine. He was the son of a legendary pilot, and by the time of *Frithjof*, he had held his own licence for thirty years.

Frithjof was considered one of the largest and most modern pilot vessels of her day and in her early years she was successful in the extensive competitive piloting then in common practice. When these days came to an end in 1911, she joined others in sailing specified waters on a repetitive schedule. In 1915 she was sold by Andersen's sons to three pilots for patrolling outside Færder at the mouth of the Oslo fjord. She kept her original appearance but more berths were added. She worked four to six days on and three to six days off, although this routine was interrupted by some dramatic rescue operations. A typical example came in 1928, when she saved a Dutch schooner with four men from total loss in a heavy storm.

After World War II, classic pilot boats like *Frithjof* were outdated and she was sold to three friends from Oslo who converted her to a yacht and cut down her rig. Becoming a ketch did her no favours, but things looked up in 1954 when Einar Salvesen took over. For the next thirty years, she sailed as the *Cara* and was a pioneer in the growing interest for veteran double-enders in Norway.

When she came up for sale in 1984 she was bought by a foundation in Larvik specifically formed to bring her back to her home waters. The

foundation now runs the finance and formal ownership, while the daily management of everything from crew training to editing a membership magazine is by the Friends of *Frithjof*.

Frithjof was restored to her original form in 1986–88. As time has passed, further work on the hull has been required, all of which is carried out by volunteers, but she sails every summer and took first in class and first overall in the Newcastle–Bergen and Stavanger–Gothenburg Tall Ships Races in 1993 and 1997.

Frithjof is regarded as one of the best preserved pilot boats in Norway and is on the national list of specially protected vessels.

Length on deck:	12.75m
Beam:	4.6m
Draught:	2.1m
Sail area:	221m^2
Ballast:	all inside

Frithjof

(Private collection)

Bristol Channel pilot cutter replica – *Morwenna*

Morwenna is a replica of *Mischief*, the pilot cutter made famous by H W Tilman in his books on the old boat's Arctic and Antarctic voyages. Launched in April 2009, she was traditionally built at the Underfall Yard, Bristol, with larch planking on English oak frames to designs worked up by Ed Burnett. Her Douglas fir mast and boom were grown in the forest at Longleat, Wiltshire, and while *Morwenna* looks like a truly traditional vessel from the outside, she is fully powered with an auxiliary diesel and is equipped with up-to-date electronics. The design of her cockpit and her small coachroof do not strictly replicate the original, but are well thought out for her purpose in today's world. This, in true harmony with her predecessor, is entirely professional, although rather than transporting her pilot, she is now crewed with trainees and charterers.

Morwenna is called after a Cornish saint born in the fifth century whose name, literally translated from the Cornish, means 'white seas'. Morwenna lived out her days in a small hermitage overlooking the Atlantic on the cliffs near Bude at a place called Morwenstow.

Length on deck:	45ft
Beam:	13ft
Design draught:	8ft
Displacement:	30 tons

Morwenna

(Traditional Sailing)

Scillonian pilot cutter replica – *Agnes*

Luke Powell was among the first, if not *the* first to build replica pilot cutters in Britain. His inaugural boat *Eve of St Mawes* set the bar high and he has since gone from strength to strength. He is an expert on the pilots of the Isles of Scilly and his boats reflect what he has discovered about these somewhat apocryphal vessels.

After extensive research, the 46ft *Agnes* was built to lines of the original *Agnes* of 1841, the top pilot cutter from the Isles of Scilly. The old boat was lengthened twice in her life but Powell sensibly opted for the first form. She is unusual in her lute stern, a type not built since the 1850s. There are no living examples of this hull form, so the mysteries of the framing and proper shape were sourced from contemporary models, engravings and paintings of Revenue cutters found in the Science Museum in London and elsewhere.

Agnes' forefoot was also controversial and doubters lined up to announce that, being so deep and square, it would cause her to gripe in a quartering wind and refuse to tack when asked, two vices prophesied to be exacerbated by her narrow, old-fashioned rudder. A well-known naval architect actually queried Powell's sanity in building a shape that had long been superseded.

Powell stuck to his guns in face of the storm of criticism; he relied on what those who know him understand to be one of the best eyes for a boat in the business, and *Agnes* was born again. Flush-decked aft with no cockpit, she is constructed traditionally, without compromise, on sawn frames with caulked planking.

The original *Agnes* was the last cutter to work out of the Isles of Scilly. Her final captain was Stephen Jenkins, and the Powell yard was honoured when his grandsons Alf and Barry came to launch the new *Agnes* in May 2003. She has proved fast and, unlike many pilot cutters, is surprisingly light on the helm. As she powers to windward in a big, awkward sea and heaves to like a swan, she has shown the prophets of doom exactly what their book-learning is worth when pitted against men who absorbed the lore of the sea from their fathers before they could read or write.

Agnes' first job was to cross the Atlantic, but she is now once again berthed in the UK. Powell and his firm, Working Sail, use her to show potential customers something of the world they are about to enter. In the summer months she is often seen in European festivals, flying the flag for pilot cutters and racing with considerable success.

Agnes

(Luke Powell)

Above all, Luke Powell's boats are beautiful. It could be said with justification that here is a man with artist's fingers working with a sharp adze in powerful hands.

Length on deck:	46ft
Beam:	13ft 3in
Draught:	8ft 6in
Displacement:	26 tons

Traditionally built replica based on a Bristol Channel pilot cutter – *Merlin*

Merlin's lines are extrapolated from the original Bristol Channel pilot cutter *Peggy*. With her lightweight, oversized rig, *Peggy* has always been a noted flyer and Cockwell's of Falmouth had already built the replica *Polly Agatha* when they were approached again. *Merlin* follows *Peggy*'s lines, but has been stretched 3ft to give a bigger saloon and allow space for a workshop.

Merlin took almost two years to build in the traditional way, with 6in x 3in oak frames and 1⅝in larch planking, all cut from the round in Cockwell's previous yard at Ponsharden.

Like many replicas and near-replicas, *Merlin* is fitted with the Appledore roller reefing gear favoured by pilots in the last years to ease single-handed reefing at some cost in mainsail shape and boom integrity. She also carries a boomed, self-tacking staysail which facilitates the tacking process considerably when short-handed. Any cutter based on *Peggy* will almost certainly need to support her extra-tall mast with the running backstays which the pilots never used.

Merlin's deck is composite, with teak laid on ply with an epoxy-glass protective layer in between. As well as guaranteeing dry bunks, which many a pilot would have been delighted about, the ply strengthens the deck laterally, whereas traditional craft had only lodging knees. Most of the deck fittings were custom cast in bronze and she boasts a fine, yacht-quality interior of English oak.

Length on deck:	48ft 9in
Beam:	13ft 6in
Draught:	7ft 6in
Displacement:	28½ tons

Composite cutter inspired by the pilot cutter form – *Westernman*

Westernman comes at the end of this chapter because, while she represents an honest departure from any suggestion of replication, she is solidly based on the ethos of the pilot cutter. She was designed for the author by Nigel Irens, an architect better known for his world-beating multihulls than for the long-keeled traditionally inspired craft which hold a special place in his heart. Whichever way you look at *Westernman*, she appears to be the real thing, except perhaps for a touch of rocker on her keel, and her rig. This is taller and narrower than a traditional gaff cutter, yet by employing the additional shroud starting at the jib halyards aloft and landing abaft the rest – as favoured by the Bristol Channel pilots and others – she has carried her spar without the plague of running backstays since her launch. Her jib luffs are kept taut directly against these shroud/backstays by virtue of an 8:1 final purchase, and she points up like a modern yacht.

Being heavily built of wood epoxy, *Westernman* is essentially monocoque in form and can therefore readily support outside ballast. The old cutters all

Merlin

(D Cockwell)

Westernman

(*Author's collection*)

carried theirs inside, making them less powerful but more comfortable. On a dry displacement of around 21 tons, *Westernman* has between 7 and 8 tons of lead on the keel and a further ton or so of lead trimming ballast inside. With the exception of her boom, which I believe should be as heavy on a gaffer as it can be made, all her pine spars are hollow. This gives her phenomenal power to carry sail, but the trade-off is less comfort downwind than with a more traditional vessel. Her running gear is based on the original *Hirta*, which, when she was in my ownership, was as near original as it was possible to get, except for two things. One was the addition of a Wykeham Martin jib gear which enabled us to change jibs single-handed in bad weather; the other was that I never replaced the Appledore roller reefing gear which some well-informed sailor had removed much earlier. I am glad he did because, although roller reefing makes the sail easier to shorten, it does not give a good shape. I am, above all, a man who loves to sail, and am prepared to put up with minor inconvenience in this area, in exchange for seeing my boat eat up to windward like the thoroughbred she is. Earlier Bristol Channel cutters used 'points' reefing, and so did I! Her gear is a joy to handle and, like *Hirta* before her, she can easily be sailed by two men in any weather at all.

Westernman was built in North America. She sailed home in fine trim from Cape Cod to the English Channel, then gave me thirteen more years of glorious cruising throughout Europe. She won an embarrassing number of races and was as well-appointed and comfortable a home at sea or in harbour as anyone could desire. Several more boats were built to her design and I am confident that modern materials will be used more and more by those who wish to keep the flame burning but must make some compromise with the ever-changing world around us.

CHAPTER 13

Pilot Cutter Seamanship

To capture the real feel of a full-sized pilot cutter, try to move your mind back to 1911, twenty miles to windward of Lundy Island. A Bristol Channel boat is hove to on the port tack, deep-reefed and shouldering the seas, as a winter gale roars over her. Just before the day dies, the companionway door opens and a small, cloth-capped figure appears carrying an enamel teapot. He primes the bilge pump and works the handle steadily. The water flows over the deck and is washed away by the sea. After a few minutes the pump sucks dry. He dumps the tea dregs over the side, takes a last look to windward, then eases the weather sheet of the double-reefed staysail and takes up the slack firmly on the lee sheet, leaving the clew pinned firmly somewhere around amidships. Adjusting the helm, he notes the boat beginning to jog ahead, self-steering gently to windward. After satisfying himself that her progress is slow, safe and stable, he goes below for a fresh brew before turning in. He's waiting for his pilot, who boarded a ship last night and who expects to bring a steamer down from Barry the following morning. The orders to the man-in-the boat were to stay upwind and be on the outbound track towards Liverpool and points north around low water.

It's not his first storm, nor will it be his last. Soon the Great War will put a stop to the cruising pilot service as he knows it, but many of the boats will live on. So long as those of us who sail them listen to that man's spirit, we won't go far wrong.

Bristol Channel pilot cutter *Hirta*

I owned the 1911 Bristol Channel pilot cutter *Hirta* for fifteen years between 1981 and 1996. In that time I sailed her from Europe to North America, Greenland, Russia, the Caribbean and all sorts of holes in between. She was 51ft on deck and, in the early years of my tenancy, she carried a flax gaff mainsail on her solid 30ft boom which two young men could barely lift. Her working rig was completed with two headsails and a topsail which set from a 15ft solid pine yard. Rigged in 1911 for all weathers by Pilot George Morrice of Barry (Channel licence number 25), she had been little changed when I bought her to the extent that she still had no electric lighting. Any alterations I made brought her closer to the pilot's intentions. She still had her original pitch-pine mast and boom when I sold her, and her rig had never been compromised by the usual yachtsman's addition of superfluous running backstays.

Hirta's sail area in this all-year working trim was a modest 1,450 sq ft, and there were no winches. We learned, as did the pilots before us, to handle her with a small crew. Sometimes in the latter years this was only my wife, my then-teenaged daughter and myself. *Hirta* was gentle and predictable and even when I asked her to do something she didn't wish to do, she wouldn't behave erratically. In truth, she was the best-mannered boat I ever sailed in forty years of professional yachting, but she had to be treated with respect. Given the power and weight involved, there was only going to be one winner if I got into a fight with her, and that wouldn't be me.

In their day, pilot cutters kept the sea under shortened sail in all manner of weather. Reefing and heaving to were so routine that the hull shape and rig configuration evolved to meet these needs as well as serving the over-riding demand for tolerably good performance. This means that, unlike a modern yacht, a pilot cutter will stop as well as she will go. Like all sailing craft of the pre-auxiliary-engine era, however, there had to be sufficient sail area for light winds.

Today, things are different, and in my time even *Hirta* had an engine. She also had a feathering propeller in my later years, and I used to get a huge kick out of sailing her as she was born to be sailed, sometimes beating to my mooring far up the narrow Beaulieu River and picking it up under sail. Such boat handling has to be seen as something of a mutually agreed-to situation wherein the boat does what the skipper asks, but always in her own sweet time.

The scope of this book renders a complete exposition of pilot cutter seamanship out of the question. However, with so many miles under my belt in these remarkable vessels, it seems a shame not to allude to some of the lessons learned from

A ship for all seasons

The 51ft Bristol Channel pilot cutter *Hirta* (ex-*Cornubia* – Pilot Morrice of Barry) in 1986, while in the author's ownership. The image shows her shortly after completing an Atlantic cruise which took her to Greenland, New York and the Caribbean, still under a flax mainsail. In the lower image,she is beating out of Brest at the first Festival of the Sea. At this time in her life, she was still unrestored. Her rig was as it was in 1911 with the original mast and boom still giving good service despite some extreme weather on her recent passages.
(Top, Kos; lower, author's collection)

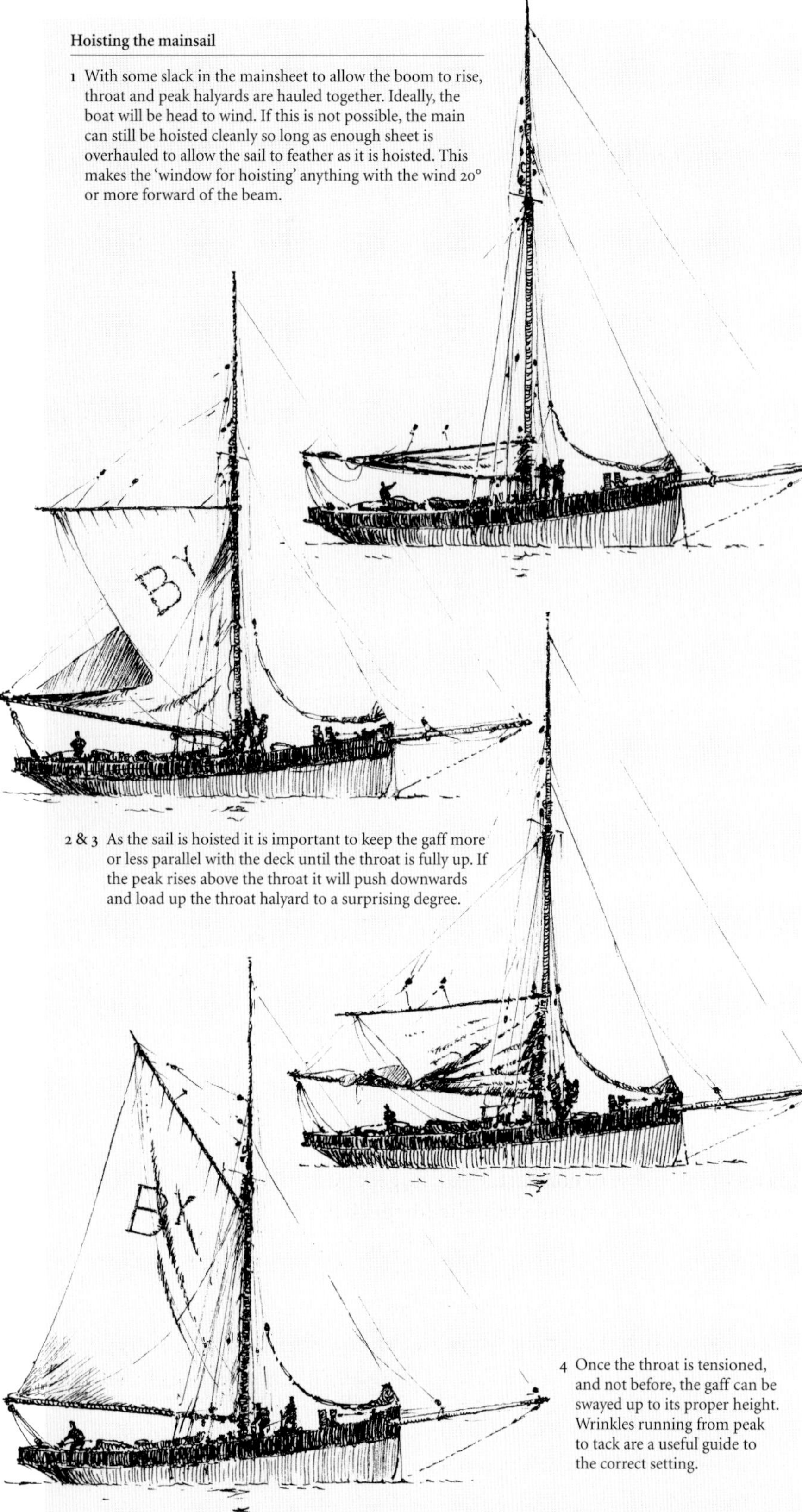

Hoisting the mainsail

1 With some slack in the mainsheet to allow the boom to rise, throat and peak halyards are hauled together. Ideally, the boat will be head to wind. If this is not possible, the main can still be hoisted cleanly so long as enough sheet is overhauled to allow the sail to feather as it is hoisted. This makes the 'window for hoisting' anything with the wind 20° or more forward of the beam.

2 & 3 As the sail is hoisted it is important to keep the gaff more or less parallel with the deck until the throat is fully up. If the peak rises above the throat it will push downwards and load up the throat halyard to a surprising degree.

4 Once the throat is tensioned, and not before, the gaff can be swayed up to its proper height. Wrinkles running from peak to tack are a useful guide to the correct setting.

(All drawings in the chapter by Martyn Mackrill)

sailing *Hirta* and her successor, the Nigel Irens-designed *Westernman.* This was a 22-ton transom-sterned 40-footer inspired by the real thing. Her first significant passage was an out-of-season North Atlantic crossing from Cape Cod to the Bishop Rock.

All the manoeuvres and techniques described below are discussed from the assumption that the boat has no engine, or that the skipper has opted not to start it.

Day-to-day sailing

Hoisting sails

Mainsail

As on any fore-and-aft rigged boat, in a set-piece situation with no tide, or with wind and tide together, the vessel will be lying head to wind if moored or anchored. The mainsail is therefore hoisted first. Provided the boat is rigged with twin topping lifts, as many pilot cutters were, and has the hauling parts of the halyards led so they can be hoisted as one, setting a mainsail of 800 sq ft or so should present no difficulty. Twin topping lifts are a 'must', because a single lift will always be tight when the sail is being hoisted, lowered or reefed. Unless the boat is motored head to wind or she is moored in no tide, the lift must be to leeward of the mainsail half the time. When it is, it will press against both gaff and canvas, making the sail reluctant to hoist, drop, or reef. If, on the other hand, the boom is supported by the weather lift of a pair, the lee topping lift can be slacked away, eliminating the issue and ensuring the sail has an undisturbed passage up or down.

Working pilot cutters rarely, if ever, carried boom crutches or permanent gallows. My earlier experience with gaff-rigged craft had involved these and when I took delivery of *Hirta* I was concerned about not having any. I need not have worried. It soon became clear that the gallows had been getting in my way for years, and while a crutch is a useful system for taking load off the mast when the vessel is at rest, with a hard-working craft out most days, rigging it is an additional job the crew don't need. On the rare occasions when the boat was rolling at anchor and snatching at her boom, rigging a quarter-tackle from the boom end snugged things down easily.

The question of how hard to set up the main halyards is often asked. The two halyards should be hauled together as one until the throat is all the way up. With a Bristol Channel boat, a strong man ought to be able to manage this alone on a quiet day. If he can't, something is wrong with the halyard system or the gaff is too heavy. A bigger cutter such as the 55-ton Le Havre cutter *Jolie Brise* needs two, unless time is not of the essence. Back with the one-man job, if you can't manage both halyards together, hoist the throat five feet or so, make fast, then follow with the peak until the gaff is a little above horizontal. Now go back to the throat, the peak, and so on until the throat is almost fully up. The gaff should be more or less parallel with the deck.

The luff is tensioned using a purchase. Typically, a five-part purchase is permanently rigged on the standing end of the throat and peak halyards. Because its effort is a multiple of the main halyard set-up, it gives a velocity ratio of 20 : 1. This is adequate in all conditions for a single person to do everything he or she needs. Heave it up tightly, but not so hard as to distort the sail with a reverse curve immediately abaft the luff. If the boat has been rigged without a purchase, the crew are going to have a tough job swigging up the tension.

With the throat up and belayed, all attention can be turned to the peak halyard. This is hove up until the sail looks as it should and is just beginning to make a wrinkle between the peak and the tack. The wrinkle signals the correct tension, so the halyard or purchase, if used, can be belayed. If all is well, these wrinkles will disappear when the topping lifts are eased and the sail fills with wind. The great East Coast skipper, Jimmy Lawrence, once told me that the wrinkles should reappear as the boat tacks and the sail spills its wind, to vanish again as it fills on the new tack.

One unexpected beauty of rigging a permanent peak purchase is that it allows minor adjustments of the peak without dropping the whole coil of the halyard on deck and having to cope with the full weight. Using the purchase, a child can sweat up the peak on a 35-tonner to flatten the sail a little when she comes onto the wind. To ease it away in order to power up on a reach is a matter of a few seconds.

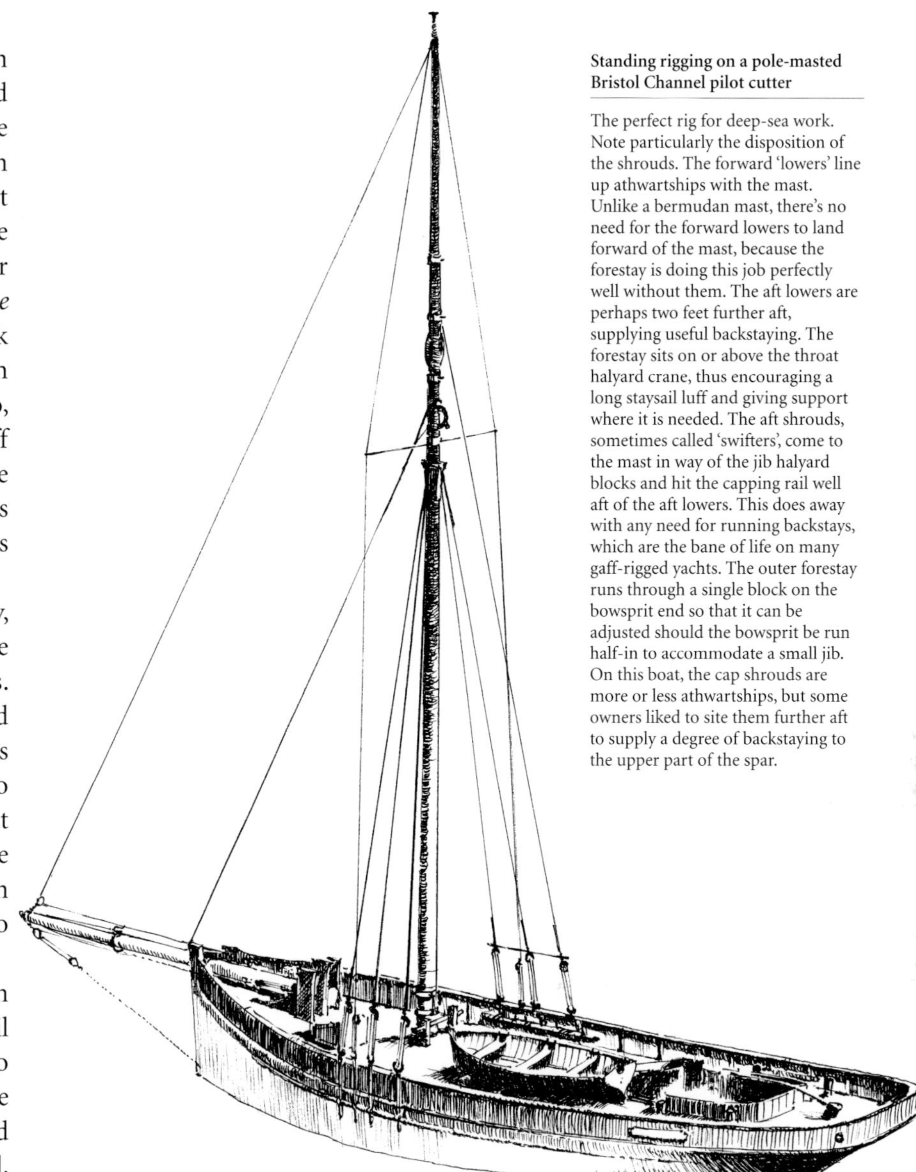

Standing rigging on a pole-masted Bristol Channel pilot cutter

The perfect rig for deep-sea work. Note particularly the disposition of the shrouds. The forward 'lowers' line up athwartships with the mast. Unlike a bermudan mast, there's no need for the forward lowers to land forward of the mast, because the forestay is doing this job perfectly well without them. The aft lowers are perhaps two feet further aft, supplying useful backstaying. The forestay sits on or above the throat halyard crane, thus encouraging a long staysail luff and giving support where it is needed. The aft shrouds, sometimes called 'swifters', come to the mast in way of the jib halyard blocks and hit the capping rail well aft of the aft lowers. This does away with any need for running backstays, which are the bane of life on many gaff-rigged yachts. The outer forestay runs through a single block on the bowsprit end so that it can be adjusted should the bowsprit be run half-in to accommodate a small jib. On this boat, the cap shrouds are more or less athwartships, but some owners liked to site them further aft to supply a degree of backstaying to the upper part of the spar.

Jib

When leaving a mooring or weighing anchor, it makes a lot of sense to hoist main and jib, get under way, then hoist the staysail when the foredeck has been cleared away. A gaff cutter balances better under main and jib than main and staysail because the jib has more leverage on the centre of lateral resistance. What's more, the foredeck is free of clutter, visibility is better and there is only one set of sheets to attend to. For these reasons alone, most manoeuvres are best dealt with under main and jib.

One of the distinguishing features of European gaff cutters is the way their jibs are set flying, rather than hanked to a stay as they often are in the

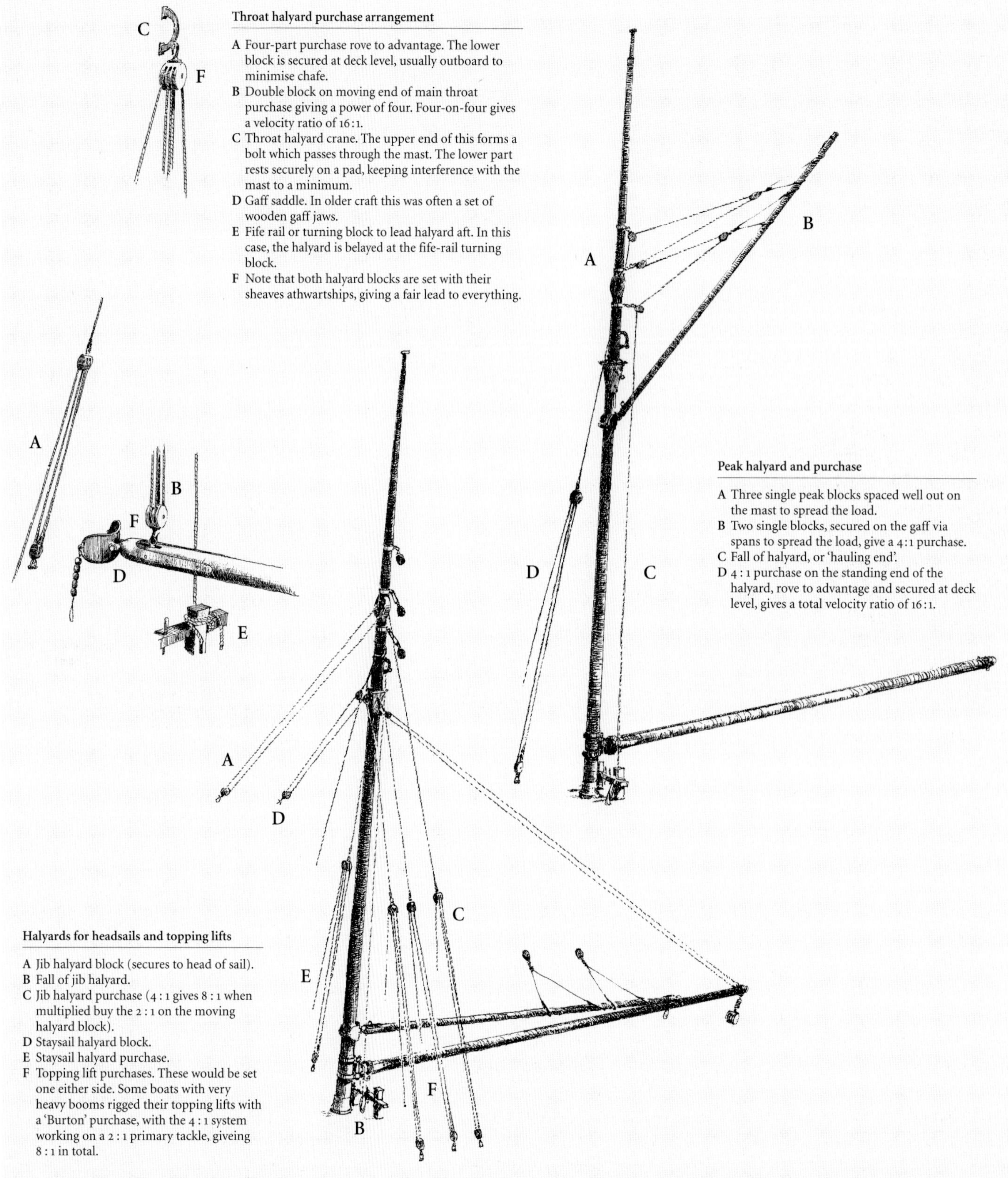

Throat halyard purchase arrangement

- A Four-part purchase rove to advantage. The lower block is secured at deck level, usually outboard to minimise chafe.
- B Double block on moving end of main throat purchase giving a power of four. Four-on-four gives a velocity ratio of 16 : 1.
- C Throat halyard crane. The upper end of this forms a bolt which passes through the mast. The lower part rests securely on a pad, keeping interference with the mast to a minimum.
- D Gaff saddle. In older craft this was often a set of wooden gaff jaws.
- E Fife rail or turning block to lead halyard aft. In this case, the halyard is belayed at the fife-rail turning block.
- F Note that both halyard blocks are set with their sheaves athwartships, giving a fair lead to everything.

Peak halyard and purchase

- A Three single peak blocks spaced well out on the mast to spread the load.
- B Two single blocks, secured on the gaff via spans to spread the load, give a 4 : 1 purchase.
- C Fall of halyard, or 'hauling end'.
- D 4 : 1 purchase on the standing end of the halyard, rove to advantage and secured at deck level, gives a total velocity ratio of 16 : 1.

Halyards for headsails and topping lifts

- A Jib halyard block (secures to head of sail).
- B Fall of jib halyard.
- C Jib halyard purchase (4 : 1 gives 8 : 1 when multiplied buy the 2 : 1 on the moving halyard block).
- D Staysail halyard block.
- E Staysail halyard purchase.
- F Topping lift purchases. These would be set one either side. Some boats with very heavy booms rigged their topping lifts with a 'Burton' purchase, with the 4 : 1 system working on a 2 : 1 primary tackle, giveing 8 : 1 in total.

Americas. It means that nobody has to go out on the bowsprit to set or furl the sail. Not only is this safer, it also allows the main forestay to be attached at or near the stem head on solid boat rather than set up on a bowsprit end. The latter arrangement makes the security of the whole rig dependent on that spar and its bobstays. In a European cutter, if the bowsprit goes by the board, it's a nuisance. For an American gaff sloop, it may well spell goodbye to the whole rig.

To set a jib, the tack is hooked onto the traveller ring. This slides along the bowsprit and can be pulled out to its end by an outhaul. There is generally no need of an inhaul, because the natural tendency of the sail is to pull aft with the sheets and, as in all things, the fewer the ropes, the better. The leathering on the iron traveller creates considerable friction if left to itself, but a liberal application of tallow makes a surprising difference to its operation.

Once the tack is hooked on, the halyard and sheets are attached, making sure that the sheet coming from the side of the boat opposite to where the sail is lying on the foredeck is led outboard of the forestay.

Timing is now of the essence: the traveller ring is hauled out to the end of the bowsprit and the outhaul made fast. In calm weather, there's no hurry before the next stage, but if it's blowing half a gale, there is not a moment to be lost, and the halyard must be hauled up quickly. If you are slow with the halyard, either the canvas will slump nastily overboard, or the sail, which is effectively out of control until the luff is set up hard, will flog the halyard out of your hands.

One way to keep the sail on deck rather than under the boat during the hoist is to lay it out to windward rather than to leeward of the forestay. This way, even if the wind catches the sail while most of it is still on deck, it will blow harmlessly against the forestay and rarely, if ever, foul it on the way up. The only danger is that the halyard block at the head of the jib may be blown through the foretriangle and get jammed between forestay and mast. You can avoid this by keeping the sail bunched in your hands as it goes up; then, at just the right moment, give its luff an almighty flick to carry the block around the forestay.

If a boat has bulwarks, the jib can be stuffed in behind them and hoisted on the lee side after the traveller ring has been run out, but with this scheme you run the risk of the wind catching the bight of sail out there on the bowsprit and blowing the whole thing away before the halyard man has things under control.

Once the jib is hoisted, it's a good idea to trim one of its sheets to tame its flogging before setting the luff up taut with a pull on the halyard purchase. A jib simply must have a purchase on the halyard. On a full-sized, short-handed pilot cutter, a final ratio of 10 : 1 works well. This is achieved by a five-part purchase on the typical two-part halyard running through a single block on the head of the sail. The hauling end is led to one side with the standing part coming down on the other. The purchase is permanently rigged between this and the deck.

The tension for the jib halyard clearly needs some sort of opposite number pulling aft as the sail luff pulls forward. Pole-masted Bristol Channel boats solved this without the need for running backstays by carrying a permanent upper shroud sometimes known as a 'swifter'. This began on a mast band, in way of the upper jib halyard blocks, and came to the deck abaft the aft lower shroud. It triangulated perfectly with the jib halyards and supplied all the backstaying the spar needed.

The hoisting and lowering of flying jibs can be

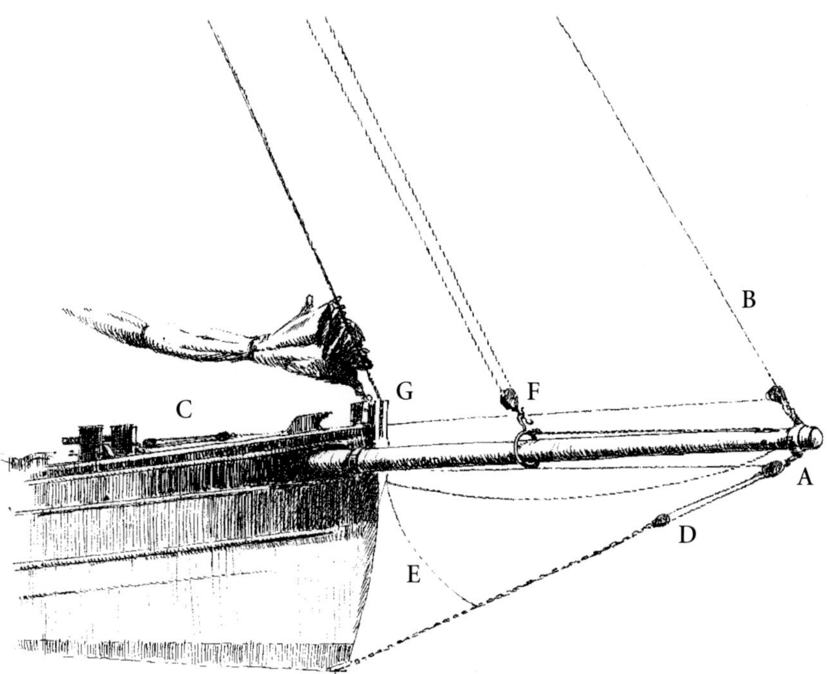

Headgear

As in so many areas, headgear would vary from boat to boat. This is a typical setup which I inherited on *Hirta* and used with success on *Westernman*.

A Cranse iron – a driven fit on the bowsprit end.

B Running outer forestay.

C Tackle to set up outer forestay.

D Bobstay with 2 : 1 wire tackle, set up on deck with a 4 : 1 tackle between the hardeye on its extreme end and the bitts, given 8 : 1. Any less purchase is probably too little for this important job. 'Spectra' core makes a useful alternative to wire for the 2 : 1 in today's world.

E Tricing line for heaving the bobstay up and clear when the purchases are let off, so that the anchor cable or mooring does not chafe on the bobstay.

F Bowsprit traveller with jib halyard stowed on it. Note the single-part outhaul. Some boats rig an inhaul, but this is really superfluous as the sail is trying hard to run in most of the time.

G Forestay passing inboard through the stem head to be set up with a powerful lanyard or rigging screw on deck. This technique allows the whole stem to take the main strain of the stay and also allows the staysail to be snugged right down close when it is lowered. A rigging screw or heart lanyard leaves the sail two feet up in the air which is undesirable for obvious reasons.

defused to excellent effect by running downwind and hiding the foredeck in the lee of the mainsail. However, shortage of sea room or lying to a mooring may render this convenience a non-starter, so it cannot be relied upon as a primary tool.

Staysail

The staysail can be hoisted or lowered easily on any point of sailing. It is usually rigged with a simple double-ended halyard similar to the jib halyard described above, giving 2:1 for hoisting and 8:1 for tensioning. This amount of 'grunt' available on a halyard means that the luff can be tensioned to keep the sail's camber where it should be even while the sail is drawing. Any lesser arrangement means the sheet must be let fly in an unseamanlike manner that any westernman worth his share would have hated.

Trimming sails

It's been said with justification that a bathtub with a board over the side to cut leeway will reach quite well under a nicely set towel. A haystack would run downwind if it could be persuaded to float. The crunch comes when trying to make to windward, which most pilot cutters had to do on a daily basis, so this is the area which we will consider.

Even though the procedure is more of an art than a science, a few guidelines can be set down, along with one golden rule. When working a pilot cutter to windward, never, ever, oversheet the jib.

Given the fact that oversheeting the jib is catastrophic to performance, where does one start trimming? After all, in a modern yacht, this begins with the genoa because it alone is cutting clean air. The main is then set up in the airstream the headsail is creating. Beginning with a pilot cutter jib is a bad plan, because if it is under-trimmed, it will not allow the boat to point as high as she can and, if sheeted in too hard, it can leave her dead in the water.

Start instead with the staysail. Given a decent sailing breeze on a normal close-hauled heading of 50° or so from the true wind, sheet this in as hard as you can without flattening the life out of it. The mainsail can then be set up so that the staysail begins to backwind its luff, then trimmed in just far enough to put it to sleep – that is, to stop the luffing. If you've just tacked and sheeted the headsails in hard before they were filled with wind, the boat will be sailing like a dead body because the jib is probably overtrimmed. Now comes the magic moment. The jib sheet is carefully eased, inch by inch, until it stops backwinding the staysail. You may find it needs letting off a surprisingly long way, but as the sheet is cracked, the boat will literally leap into life.

For best windward performance, keep the luffs of the headsails tight, but not so tight as to distort the sail shape.

When it comes to finding the ideal leech twist for the mainsail, there is no simple answer, but excessive twist is certainly undesirable. With too much twist in the mainsail, the topsail above it (if one is set) will begin to luff before the jib – hopeless! A little twist is a good thing, however, because the air aloft is flowing faster than the air at deck level. Also, the wind aloft hasn't been bent forward by the headsails so, one way and another, the apparent wind is at a wider angle and the upper part of the sail can be set a little freer for more forward drive. Getting all this to work properly is best achieved by having some control over the leech tension of the sail. A double-ended mainsheet will help, and setting up the peak purchase will certainly take out some twist, but the most effective way is to govern the movement of the mainsheet block on a horse or traveller. For more twist, pull the sheet block closer to amidships, ease the sheet and allow the boom end to rise a little; for less twist, let the sheet block slide to leeward so the boom is over the quarter, then haul the sheet down hard. This sort of finesse, while available on Colin Archer's boats and regularly practised by sophisticated cutters such as Falmouth working boats, is rarely seen on English or Le Havre pilot cutters. Short of rigging a vang of some sort, one is left with the peak purchase, a double-ended mainsheet, or nothing.

Steering to windward

Once the rig is set up, it only remains for the helmsman to present the whole carefully arranged aerofoil at the correct angle to the wind, a situation best arrived at by bringing the boat closer and closer to the wind until the jib starts to show signs of luffing. As this point is approached, you will also feel the boat coming upright and losing drive. Bear away a degree or two until all sails draw sweetly, she heels steadily once more and the seat of your pants tells you all is now well. If the sheeting position for the staysail is correct – and remember, this is what the other sails are trimmed to – you will find that this allows a close-hauled angle of around 50° or, given a decent set of canvas, a little better. All gaffers will point higher than they will sail by oversheeting the jib, but the boat will travel much more slowly and make more leeway. The net result is fewer miles made good to windward.

In a flat sea and a strong wind, *Hirta* used to sail as close as 45° to the true wind. In lighter going I had to let her off a bit to generate more power. In rougher seas, trying to point too high was invariably counter-productive. The secret was to accept that it was going to be 55°, and let her rip. I'd then get 6kts plus through the water and not a lot of leeway. The result was 'Vmg' (velocity made good to windward) in plentiful supplies. So plentiful, in fact, was this rare commodity that on one memorable day off La Trinité in the Bay of Biscay, we beat the Fife yacht *Pen Duick*, skippered by no less a seaman than Eric Tabarly, on a straight beat upwind. It was blowing only a little short of a gale and we were the only two boats on the race course. All the others had gone home and *Hirta* acquitted herself so well that the great man came aboard afterwards, accepted a glass of rum and gave her a resounding 'thumbs up'.

Tacking

The successful handling of any large boat depends on having powerful running gear that falls readily to hand, and using wind and sea to help lighten the load. Even the largest pilot cutters benefit from headsails considerably smaller than those of comparable Bermudan rigs. Even so, in a strong breeze, a headsail without a winch can rarely be pulled in hard enough using a purchase alone. The way to get headsails trimmed in for close-hauled work is to whack them in bar tight as the boat comes through the wind; once she starts to pay off, if you haven't got the sheets in, your only chance is to let the boat get some way on, then luff up above a close-hauled course and sweat the slack in as the sail begins to luff. The long-keeled pilot cutter with her deep forefoot comes through stays so slowly and deliberately, however, that there should always be plenty of time to get it right the first time. Taking things steadily, it ought to be perfectly possible to tack a properly rigged 50-footer single-handed, because this was what was done 'back in the day'.

If you have to leave the staysail aback in order to force the boat through the wind onto her new tack (and if she is well designed and set up, this should be an exceptional circumstance), the timing for releasing the weather sheet and trimming in the lee one is crucial. With care, however, it can be done before the sail fills.

As we have seen, after the boat starts sailing on the new tack, the jib sheet generally needs easing because if the sheet hands have been doing their job right, it will almost certainly have been over-trimmed while tacking. Whatever the point of sail, however, the jib clew should be allowed to lift so that the curve of the leech follows that of the staysail. If the leech is harder than that of its partner, it will tend to drag the boat sideways instead of lifting her ahead. On a big boat, it's handy to station a man at the forestay to call the shots to the person easing the sheet. If all this is done by a well-drilled crew, the boat will go through stays with a beautiful certainty, then rapidly fill away on the new tack with no lee helm and little loss of way. The crucial things are timing and arranging the deck so that those tending the sheets have room to work. Fortunately, a pilot cutter has ample deck space to allow her crew to throw their weight into the task.

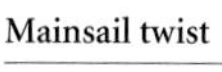

Mainsail twist

A little twist correctly controlled makes the boat go faster, heel less and carry less weather helm

Lowering Sails

Headsails

When a solo deckhand drops any sail on a biggish boat, it's best if both arms are available to smother the canvas. If the halyard is simply let go, it may escape and be carried aloft out of reach, so it pays to secure the bitter end before taking the bight off the pin. Make fast the end away from the pin and lead it cleanly from under the coil so there's no risk of snagging, and joy will be yours.

Under normal weather conditions, with the boat approaching a mooring or anchorage, the staysail will be lowered in good time to get it out of the way. It presents no special problems. If a topsail is set, that will go first, of course. Once the boat is moored, the jib must be tackled, unless it is decided that conditions are so 'hairy' that it would be better to lower it on a run behind the main while still in the offing. This way, it is quite safe to cast off the outhaul before the halyard and pull the sail inboard as it comes down so it doesn't fall in the water. Running off is generally a safe option, but it needs ample sea room and it does mean putting up with the poorer handling of the boat under main and staysail on the final approach.

When dropping a flying jib, preparation and good decision-making is all. It's unwise just to let go the halyard and hope for the best, because if the sail is full of wind and the foredeck hand grabs the sheet in an attempt to get it down onto the deck, he's likely to be left with two ugly alternatives: either letting go after skinning his palms, or hanging on too long and being flicked overboard like a rag doll.

Easy on the helm

All trimmed to a nicety with the jib well off, this cutter is sailing close-hauled to perfection

On the mooring, or with the boat head to wind in general, it is better to ease the halyard away smartly and grab the sail as it blows inboard, before easing the traveller outhaul. If this is let go with the sail at full hoist on a windy day, the luff may start to beat around like washing on a line, with potentially dire consequences. Once the head of the sail is in hand, the rest is docile and the tack can be brought aboard in relative tranquillity.

When the jib has to be lowered at sea – perhaps to change down for a smaller one – another way to douse it is to tack, leaving both headsails aback, as though heaving to. The foredeck hand can now grab the weather jib sheet, leaving the outhaul belayed. The halyard is slacked away carefully and as the luff begins to sag, the sheet is pulled so that first the clew and then more and more of the sail above it is blown flat against the backed staysail, effectively neutralising its antics. When, and only when, you have the sail lowered and its halyard block in hand, you can let off the outhaul and bring the tack aboard. If the outhaul is let off too soon, the traveller ring will zip inboard at the speed of light, the luff will collapse and the sail will blow away to leeward like a spinnaker.

Mainsail

Dropping any gaff mainsail can be a pleasant exercise while lying head to wind, so long as the peak of the gaff is kept well above the throat so that the weight of the spar pushes the whole unit down. Let the peak go first and nothing will persuade it to drop. Controlling the sail once it is on deck is important, and this is where lazy jacks come in. How elaborately they are rigged is a matter of personal preference and depends somewhat on how short-handed you are, but at least one pair running from twin topping lifts to a point on the boom just inboard of the end of the lowered gaff will keep that spar under control until it is secured to the boom with a gasket. Without these, the gaff is free to roam and can become a lethal weapon when first lowered. A lightweight pair of lazy jacks isn't strictly traditional, but they will repay their windage and any nuisance factor when hoisting sail many times

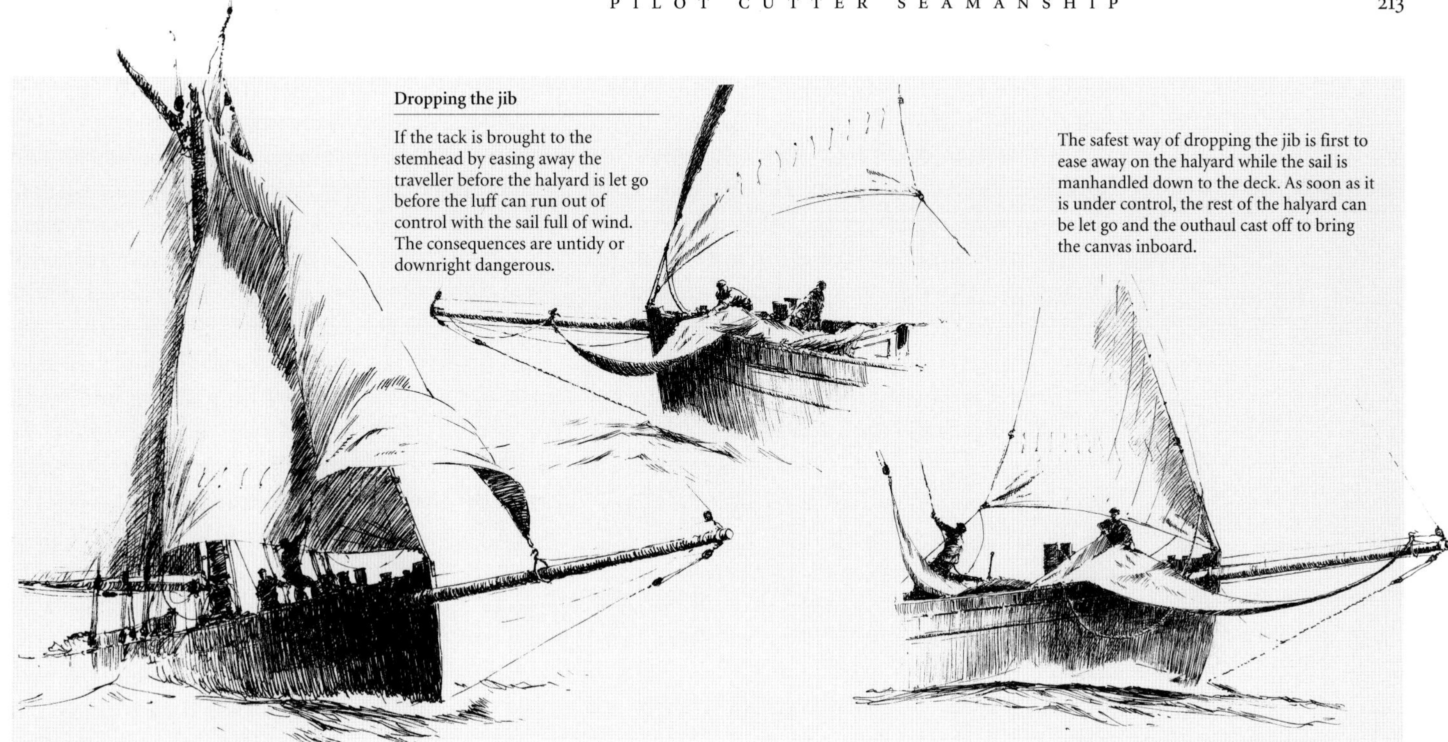

over, even on a fully crewed boat. Using more than a pair will smother the sail handily but, on the negative side, the sail tends to hang up on them as it falls (unless the boat is dead head to wind); they must be adjustable if they are not to cause chafe; they interfere with a fine harbour stow, if that is important to you, and they add windage. Lazy jacks can be lifesavers on a 30-tonner sailing with a crew of two or three, but they should be seen in perspective. They are not all things to all men.

One final point. If the sail is loose-footed, rig the ties around the gaff, not the boom, and allow the gaff's outboard end to run down a little towards the end of the boom, creating an elongated, very shallow 'V' shape. Now top up the boom, peak the gaff up a little less to create a racy angle, and you have stow to be proud of. Nothing else will do.

Heavy weather

When the gales blow hard in open water, the pilot cutter really comes into her own. Not for nothing did the old Bristol Channel pilot say to his mate, 'Bad weather is our chance'. So long as her gear is good and her crew can snug her down, she will ride out the worst of deep-water storms and look after herself with no further assistance from them. I have sat out many a mid-Atlantic storm in *Hirta*, *Westernman* and also in *Saari*, a much smaller Norwegian pilot cutter I once owned, designed by the great Colin Archer. They gave a sense of confidence I have rarely found in modern yachts, and they allowed me time to regain my strength when the conditions had left me exhausted.

Reefing

Roller booms

Later examples of the Bristol Channel pilot cutter were famous for their roller reefing booms. In many ways, these were a mixed blessing. The sail certainly did not set so well as one reefed with conventional points, and the leech of the reefed sail imposed a huge point-loading on the boom, leading to many a broken spar. However, the over-riding advantage was that in these short-handed craft, a reef could be rolled in easily by one man.

The technique was simple. The boat was hove to, ideally on the starboard tack, because that placed the throat halyard, which was always rigged to starboard, on the 'uphill side'. Topping lifts and mainsheet were secured to a boom-end fitting which allowed them to remain in place while the body of the boom rotated 'inside' them.

The weather topping lift was set up to take the weight of the boom and the throat halyard eased away. Bit by bit, the Appledore 'worm' reefing gear was cranked as the sail rolled around the rotating boom. If the geometry were correct, the equivalent of two conventional reefs could be rolled in before it became necessary to ease the peak halyard. When enough sail had been reefed away, the pawl or pin was applied to lock the reefing gear and the halyard was set up to tension the luff. Alternatively, the halyard could be belayed and the gear cranked round until the luff was tight. Any minor adjustments could then be made using the peak purchase, the topping lift was eased off and the reef was in.

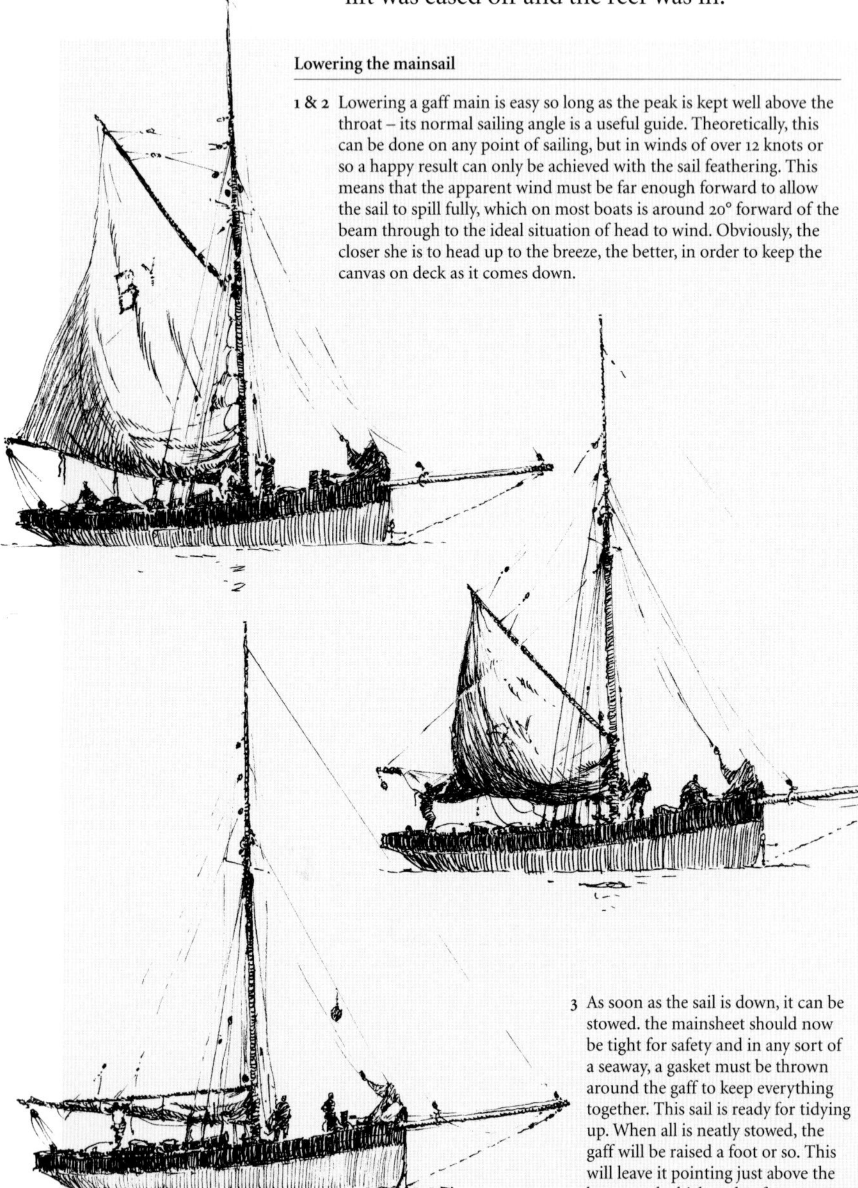

Lowering the mainsail

1 & 2 Lowering a gaff main is easy so long as the peak is kept well above the throat – its normal sailing angle is a useful guide. Theoretically, this can be done on any point of sailing, but in winds of over 12 knots or so a happy result can only be achieved with the sail feathering. This means that the apparent wind must be far enough forward to allow the sail to spill fully, which on most boats is around 20° forward of the beam through to the ideal situation of head to wind. Obviously, the closer she is to head up to the breeze, the better, in order to keep the canvas on deck as it comes down.

3 As soon as the sail is down, it can be stowed. the mainsheet should now be tight for safety and in any sort of a seaway, a gasket must be thrown around the gaff to keep everything together. This sail is ready for tidying up. When all is neatly stowed, the gaff will be raised a foot or so. This will leave it pointing just above the boom end which makes for a seamanlike result.

Conventional reefing

Reefing the mainsail with points on a boom 30ft long or more in a serious breeze can present problems. Since the boom on a cutter extends at least to the stern, it has to be sheeted in close during the reefing operation so that you can get at the pendants and the reef points. Because of the size of the sail, reefing is an impossibility if the boat keeps on a close-hauled course and the sail has any weight of wind blowing into it. The only sensible action in a strong breeze is to temporarily heave to (see below). Pilot cutters have a happy way of pointing well up when hove to, so the mainsail will spill wind nicely from time to time while you reef it and, because the helm is lashed, all hands are freed up for the job.

First, the weather lift is set up and the coil of the throat halyard dropped on deck. Before slacking off the throat halyard, its purchase must be overhauled to its full length. The throat is now eased carefully, just far enough to pull the tack down to its reef cringle. With the tack lashed down, the luff can be easily set up using only the halyard purchase.

As with a roller mainsail, the geometry of the rig may well allow putting in at least one reef without taking down the coil of the peak halyard, so there's probably no need to ease this.

The next job is to rig the reefing tackle under the boom and hook it onto the reefing pendant; 4 : 1 rove to advantage is a good ratio for the tackle. It sets the double block at the aft end of the purchase which not only supplies full power, it also places the person pulling it safely by the mast. A good policy is to keep the reefing pendants rove all the time, because trying to reeve them up with the sail set in a seaway is downright dangerous. The reef cringle must now be hove down until it is on, or very close to the boom. If this is a struggle, the leech of the sail must be eased somehow. The choices are to slack off either the mainsheet or the peak halyard; the clew can then be snugged down without difficulty. If you can, ease the sheet rather than the peak halyard, because it is far easier to slack it off and pull it in again than it is to drop the peak halyard coil, overhaul the purchase, ease the halyard away, and then have to reverse the actions and recoil the halyard afterwards.

Unless you propose sailing across the Atlantic

with a reef down, the clew can safely be left 'on the pendant', which does away with the inevitable danger associated with trying to lash the clew cringle down to the boom.

With tack and clew pulled down to reefed position and secured, tying off the reef points to secure the bunt of the sail is the next operation. The first thing to be said about reef points is that they must be long and of a substantial, non-slippery material. If slippery rope has been used, the first overhand knot will slide out before you can put in the second. If they are not long enough, you'll be struggling to get the deeper reefs around the bunt of the sail.

A loose-footed mainsail is a joy now. Anything laced to the boom is by comparison problematic, and it's points you need, not lacings. Even though there are some benefits to using lacing lines instead of reef points (better airflow across the sail; even loading on all the eyelets as the lacing takes up its natural position and ease in shaking out the reefs), reef lacings, in my opinion, have no place on the offshore gaff sail. Anyone who has struggled to reeve a lacing line through the correct eyelets on a dark night with the bunt of the sail thrashing around in the breeze will assure you that whatever its advantages, a lacing line is not worth it in the real world. If a mainsail was built for lacing with a neat row of brass eyelet holes across it, rather than reef points, it is a simple matter to add permanent reef points by reeving them through and tying them off on each side of the eyelets with a stopper knot. Conversion should take no more than an afternoon, including whipping each point at both ends.

Hirta's flax mainsail has been justly criticised because of its bulk and weight as compared to modern synthetics. This is undeniable. I did in the end order a polyester replacement and was not sorry I did. However, on a long passage, the flax was lovely because its stitching bedded into the canvas and seemed impervious to the chafe which bedevils modern materials. It also sat quietly on the boom while it was being stowed, rather than slipping and sliding all over the place as did its replacements and when flopping from side to side in a calm it made a far nicer sound than the frantic scrabbling of a polyester sail. Reefing, we compensated for the weight of the flax with long, stout reefing points. We started at the tack and clew, and worked toward the middle. By far the most difficult part is the central 30 per cent of the sail, and by working up to this from the ends, the wind is gradually spilled.

If the sail is loose footed, you can enjoy the comfort and security of standing between the boom and the sail while tying off the points. One word of advice, though: first make the mainsheet fast yourself, and keep an eye on any of your enemies who may be loitering around the mainsheet cleat.

If, despite all your efforts, you still can't get the bunt of the sail snugged down in a blow, the final solution – provided you have extra-long reef points – is to tie a tiny bowline very close to the attachment point in one end of the points. The other end is passed through the bowline, giving you a two-to-one purchase like a trucker's hitch. Heave down on this and tie it off with a slippery hitch. The reefed sail may not look pretty enough for the Solent, but in a midnight Arctic twilight and a 30ft sea, it looks just fine.

Waiting around and gale survival

Heaving to

One salient feature of all pilot cutters was, whether waiting to board a ship or take a pilot off a ship, the boat had to be able to heave to. This was universally achieved by backing the headsails – or a single headsail in heavy weather – and balancing these against the mainsail and rudder.

In the hove-to state, the headsails are trying to push the bows to leeward. At the same time, the mainsail, acting abaft the boat's pivot point, is doing mighty work attempting to swivel the stern downwind and the bow upwind. The rudder is set to steer hard to windward (tiller 'down' to leeward), thus assisting the mainsail. Rudder and main, left to themselves would encourage the cutter to gather way and, as she did so, to swing up head to wind. She might even tack herself but the headsails do not allow it. Instead, she settles down at an easy equilibrium, pointing at anything between 30° and 50° from the true wind.

Heaving to is most easily achieved by sailing close-hauled, shoving the helm to leeward and, as the boat tacks, leaving the headsail sheets made fast. Once through the wind, the helm is reversed, and that's it. Job done.

In this condition, with two reefs in the mainsail and a backed, reefed staysail, *Hirta* would drift square across a force 8 gale, making no leeway at all. She would be pointing at around 45° to the oncoming seas, taking them on her shoulder, where she liked them best. At this angle, a boat of her displacement had no more chance of being knocked down than a corporation bus in a garage, and she felt equally safe. Should the gale harden, she still had a reef in hand for the main and one to spare for the staysail. When things got really serious, we could drop the main and substitute a jib-headed trysail as we did in Hurricane Klaus in 1984. *Hirta* pointed up, she took what was coming like the trooper she was, and we never had a moment's doubt for our security.

Dropping the main at sea

It must be said that dropping the main in these sort of conditions was a serious challenge and perhaps a description of the technique we adopted may prove useful to others. Much has been said over the years about the benefit of being able to drop a gaff sail on any point of sailing. While this is true in moderate going, in a solid 50kts of wind far out at sea it doesn't really hold water any more. Somehow, the boat must be manoeuvred from the hove-to state so that the sail can spill all its wind, for a moment or two at least. Simply easing out the sheet to feather the canvas then letting go the halyards won't work, because the sail may need help on its way down. Even if it does come down of its own accord, allowing any of it to fall into the raging sea is unthinkable. Furthermore, as you ease the sheet, the boat will start to bear off, so the returns begin to diminish. The alternative is somehow to persuade the boat to come head to wind. In fact, this is not difficult, but the situation will be dynamic. Timing and preparation are vital. You'll only have one clear chance.

First, haul in the mainsheet so the boom is as near amidships as you can get it. This helps the boat to luff and also restricts boom movement during the action that follows. Next, set up the weather topping lift so it's bar taut. This will stabilise the boom completely against the sheet. The main halyards are flaked clear to run and their bitter ends are made fast. This sounds easy, but in practice it really is the hardest part of the operation. If the halyards snag, all will be lost. Since the deck will be swept occasionally by the sea, you may need two or three tries before the halyards are laid out so they'll run free. Needless to say, the sail ties should be rove ready along the boom. If the sail is loose footed, they won't stay there, however, so in this case all hands should stuff their pockets with gaskets.

Now comes the moment. After waiting for a 'smooth' in the sea, the backed staysail which, up until now, has held the boat far enough off the wind to keep the mainsail from luffing, is smartly let draw. The helm is left where it is, lashed down hard, so the boat can do only one thing. She gathers way and swivels into the wind. A good boat, well handled, will luff almost head to wind under this treatment. She won't tack, because she hasn't enough way on, but she won't hang in the wind long either, so you have to be quick. At exactly the right moment, the halyards are let go on the run. By the time the sail hits the deck and all hands have pounced on it, the boat's head will be paying off fast, but that is OK. The sail is down and, hopefully, under control. A boat with a deep forefoot won't fall off too far under reefed staysail in sailing trim (not aback) as long as the helm is lashed down. As she gathers headway, she will try to point up, stall, fall off again, and repeat the cycle; so she can be left to look after herself while you do battle with the main. Because the halyard ends are secure, you can forget about them for the time being as well, to concentrate all your efforts on securing that crazy sail.

In an ideal world, the crew will now rouse out their trysail, but this is invariably a horror job if left until the wind is at storm force. If it can't be managed, or the boat doesn't have one, you are left with either running off before the wind, lying a'hull or heaving to under staysail only.

Running off is not a technique specific to traditional gaff cutters, so it will not be examined here. Lying a'hull is a last-ditch method which I have only been obliged to use in my Colin Archer. This vessel displaced a mere 13 tons. She also had flax canvas sails and in one North Atlantic storm in the 1970s the wind reached such a pitch that carrying canvas in so small a craft was no longer an option. It would have blown away. Our only options were therefore to run under bare poles or to lie a'hull. After many days of foul weather my wife and I – the only crew

Heaving to

Heaving to in the easiest way, this cutter is sailing just off closehauled on the port tack. She is steered through the wind as though tacking, but both headsail sheets are left secured, rather than letting them fly and heaving them in on the new tack. Thus the boat ends up in a close-hauled attitude on the starboard tack with both sails aback. The tiller is lashed to leeward and the boat is now hove to. In this image, the mainsheet has been eased off to encourage the boat to pay off a little. In hard conditions it is left close-hauled, or nearly so.

– were exhausted. We ran as long as we could, but in the end we could no longer find the strength to steer. We snugged the boat down, lashed everything that could possibly move, turned in and left her to it. At this time the waves were certainly 40ft high. The cutter was thrown down on a number of occasions, but she never put her mast in the water and never felt as though she might capsize. In due course, the storm abated to gale force and we were able once more to get under way, having rested as best we could while the boat looked after us. The first time we were obliged to adopt this tactic, we learned the hard way that the helm must be lashed amidships. If it is secured to leeward, the boat may gather way, stall at the top of a wave then fall backwards. That is in fact what happened and the heavy ash tiller, lashed hard against a solid quarter-post, snapped like a carrot.

Modern text books no longer recommend lying a'hull as a method of storm survival. If confronted with such conditions in a modern yacht with a fin-and-spade profile and an essentially flat underbody, I would concur with his viewpoint wholeheartedly. In the Colin Archer, things were different. Not only were we safe, we felt safe too.

Nevertheless, a boat lying a'hull will inevitably spend much of her time beam-on to the seas. This leaves her potentially vulnerable to capsize. Heaving to in a boat that can do it properly avoids this, so it is far better to carry some sort of canvas if it is at all possible. Most pilot cutters have a plumb stem and a deep forefoot, which hold the bow up to the sea. If it's blowing hard enough, such a vessel may well heave to under the reefed staysail with the clew sheeted so as to drive the boat ahead. Experiments with sheet and helm are necessary, though, because all boats are different. With its sweeping forefoot, the Colin Archer type, for example, will not lie to under staysail nearly as well as a Bristol Channel pilot cutter. I discovered this technique in a heavy gale in the Bay of Biscay when I was skipper of the big Le Havre pilot cutter, *Jolie Brise*. In those days her reefing gear was not good and the wind rose too rapidly for us to do anything other than drop the mainsail onto its 38ft boom. Under a staysail sheeted just off close-hauled, with the rudder lashed to steer upwind, she kept gathering just enough way to try to luff up. She never succeeded, but the net effect was to lie 60° or so off the wind. *Hirta* would manage something similar. It wasn't ideal, and if we could have done it, we'd have been far better hove to under main and backed staysail, but it worked on the day and that, in the end, is all that counts.

All boats are different and the only thing one can do is try them, but pilot cutters were conceived by men who knew the sea and had survival high on their priorities list. If we let these boats talk to us rather than trying to force them into doing what we imagine might be right, they will look after us long after we have lost the will to look after them.

Bibliography and Further Reading

TRINITY HOUSE AND GENERAL

A new book on the history of this august establishment under the title *Light upon the Waters* will be published in 2014 and the author is indebted to Captain Richard Woodman, Captain Andy Adams and the Brethren of the House for making their material available to him.

Pilotage Acts 1727, 1754, 1761, 1825, 1854, 1913
An Act for the Amendment of the Law, 5 July 1825
An Act to repeal certain Acts, 11 August 1854
Select committee report on pilotage, 1888
Pilotage Returns 1869/70: The *Spindrift* and the *Fawn*
1910 Department committee on pilotage in the UK
The 1910 Parliamentary report on compulsory pilotage
1911 Departmental committee on pilotage (re Bristol Channel)

Guildhall Library:
Register of sub commissioners, pilot examination, details of vessels, register, returns and minute books of the pilotage committee

The National Archives:
Rail 236/718-16 Letter from North Sea Pilots 1865
MT9 64/M 2046/72 Signal for pilots, 66/M10523/72 Light for pilots, 67/M10893/72 Exemption name marking, 143/M9709/77 Signals Dover Pilot
Rail 1057 Harbour pilots' examination papers
MPR/328/2 Cowes outport letter book
H1544/64 Pilotage at Ilfracombe
H3044/65 Trinity House. By-law to prevent pilots from owning tugs
H4230/65 Pilotage jurisdiction of watermen/compulsory pilotage Thames
H6903/66 Prosecution of 'Bavaria' for not taking pilot
H1840/67 Bridgwater pilotage
H4D1/68 St Ives pilots
H2006/70 Suspension of licence of pilot of *Hippolyte*
Ms 30172 Register of pilots' licences (London) 1808–1929
Ms 30174 Register of pilots' licences (outports) 1808–76 – both groups of pilot's licence records provide pilot's age, residence, qualifications and physical description.

Instructions to Masters of Ships; being a Digest of the Provisions, Penalties, etc of the Pilots Act, together with lists of the Pilots licensed by The Corporation of Trinity House, 1809
Shipping Gazette, 20 January 1880
Illustrated London News 1885

Anon, 'Reply to query on Pilot Boat flags and numbers', *Mariner's Mirror*, 30 (1944)
———, 'History', *The Pilot* (November 2011)
Arrow, Sir Frederick, *The corporation of Trinity House of Deptford Strond: a memoir of its origin, history, and functions* (London: Smith and Ebbs, 1868)
Bowen, Frank C, 'The Corporation of Trinity House', *The Lloyd Mail* (1933)
Folkard, Henry Coleman, *The Sailing Boat* (London: Hunt and Son, 1853)
Greenhill, Basil, and Julian Mannering, (eds), *The Chatham Directory of Inshore Craft: Traditional Working Vessels of the British Isles* (London: Chatham, 1997)
Hignett, Harry, *The History of the United Kingdom Pilots' Association* (London: UKPA, 1984)
———, 'Pilotage History', *The Pilot* (August 2004)
———, 'Pilots and Shipowners', *The Pilot* (March 2012)
Leslie, R C, *Old Sea Wings, Ways and Words* (London: Chapman and Hall 1890)
McKee, Eric, *Working Boats of Britain* (London: Conway Maritime Press/National Maritime Museum, 1983)
Venn, G Barrett, 'Alfred Venn', *The Pilot* (July 2006)

ISLES OF SCILLY

The author is grateful for research work conducted by Sara Stirling.

Cornish Pilot Gig Association

Pilotage returns 76.569/76.575/76.765/76.766/76.5764

Anon, Paragraph on bunkering, *The Scillonian*, 21 (March 1930)
———, 'Loss of ss *Delaware* December 27th 1871. Extracts from *The Cornish Telegraph* 1871', *The Scillonian*, 128 (December 1956)
———, 'End of an Era in the Scillies, Retirement of Senior Pilot', *The Scillonian*, 145 (Spring 1961)
———, 'End of the Albion', *The Scillonian*, 148 (Winter 1961)
———, 'The rescue of two survivors by pilot gig *Albion* from the wreck *Delaware* in 1871', *The Scillonian*, 150 (Summer 1962)
———, 'A Scillonian takes a look at gigs he piloted 30 years ago', *The Scillonian*, 154 (Summer 1963)
———, 'Gig model presented to museum', *The Scillonian*, 174 (Summer 1968)
———, 'Obituary for Mr Jack Hicks', *The Scillonian*, 192 (Winter 1972/73)
Farr, Grahame, 'Shipbuilding in the Isles of Scilly', *The Scillonian*, 55 (September 1938)
———, 'Shipbuilding in Scilly, Part II', *The Scillonian*, 134 (Summer 1958)
———, 'Shipbuilding in Scilly, Part III', *The Scillonian*, 135 (Autumn 1958)
———, 'Shipbuilding in Scilly, Part IV', *The Scillonian*, 136 (Winter 1958)
Gillis, Richard, 'Hazardous exploits of pilot gigs off the Isles of Scilly', *The Scillonian*, 129 (March 1957)
———, 'Pilot Gigs took part in Thrilling Rescues Off the Scillies and Start of the Pilot Gig Race, St Mary's Regatta 1903', *The Scillonian*, 130 (Summer 1957)
———, 'St Agnes Pilot Gig *Daring*'s Last Job that Ended in Disaster', *The Scillonian*, 138 (Summer 1959)
———, 'Details of Scillies Gigs', *The Scillonian*, 140 (Winter 1959)
———, *A Sea Miscellany of Cornwall and the Isles of Scilly* (Harvey Barton, 1968)
———, 'The pilot gigs of Cornwall and the Isles of Scilly', *Mariner's Mirror*, 55 (1969)
———, *The Pilot Gigs of Cornwall and the Isles of Scilly* (Isles of Scilly Museum, 1999)
Harris, Keith, *Azook!: The Story of the Pilot Gigs of Cornwall and the Isles of Scilly* 1666–1993 (Cornwall: Truran, 1994)
Hill, H O, 'The Isles of Scilly Gigs', *Mariner's Mirror*, 42 (1956)
Honiton, E J, 'At Random', *The Scillonian*, 143 (Autumn 1960)
Inglis-Jones, Elisabeth, *Augustus Smith of Scilly* (London: Faber, 1969)
'Islander', 'Weeks I Remember', *The Scillonian*, 50 (June 1937)
Jenkins, A J, *Gigs and Cutters of the Isles of Scilly* (Integrated Packaging Group/Isle of Scilly Gig Racing Committee, 1975)
Jenkins, Alf, *The Scillonian and his Boat* (privately published, 1982)
Jenkins, E R, '*Minnehaha*', *The Scillonian*, 142 (Summer 1960)
Jenkins, Edward R, 'The Story of the Pilot Boats Regatta of 1865', *The Scillonian*, 133 (Spring 1958)
Llewellyn, Sam, *Emperor Smith: The Man Who Built Scilly* (Dovecote Press, 2005)
McFarland, F, 'Regattas of Scilly', *The Scillonian*, 34 (June 1933)

Oliver, A S, *Boats and Boat Building in West Cornwall* (Truro: D Bradford Barton, 1971)
Pender, Clive, *The Friday Night Gig Races on the Isles of Scilly* (leaflet, nd)
Powell, Luke, *Working Sail: A Life in Wooden Boats* (Wimborne Minster, Dorset: Dovecote Press, 2012)
Simper, Robert, *Beach Boats of Britain* (Woodbridge: Boydell & Brewer, 1984)
Tregenna, Lyn, *Cornwall and Isles of Scilly Gig Guide* (privately published, 1991)
Uren, J G, *Scilly and the Scillonians* (Plymouth: Western Morning News, 1907)
Wakefield, V G, 'List of Wrecks in Isles of Scilly, Part III', *The Scillonian*, 103 (September 1950)
Watts, F, 'From Far and Wide', *The Scillonian*, 31 (September 1932)
Whitfield, Rev H J, 'The Changing Population of Scilly 1801–51', *The Scillonian*, 138 (Summer 1959)
Wilkin, Pebbles, 'Pilot Gigs of Cornwall and Scilly', *Classic Boat*, 12 (1989)
Woodcock, Percy, 'Recollections of old Pilot Cutter *Presto* (No 1)', *The Scillonian*, 141 (Spring 1960)

FALMOUTH

The author is indebted to Pilot David Barnicoat of Falmouth; Jim Morrison; National Maritime Museum Cornwall library, especially Roger Barnes; Andy Campbell and Falmouth Packet database at www.falmouth.packet.archives.dial.pipex.com.

Bartlett Library, NMM Cornwall:
Falmouth District Pilot Boat Association registers

Cornwall Record Office:
Dispute between Pilots Dunn and Salt

Falmouth Library:
Cash Book 1919 (1992)
Falmouth Estuary Historic Audit (1992)
Shipping Register Falmouth Custom House 1872

Chart and Compass (journal of British & Foreign Sailors' Society), correspondence re *Gatherer*
Falmouth and Penryn Weekly Times, various
Falmouth Packet, 24 March 1884 & 22 May 1897
Lake's Falmouth Almanack 1887, 1896, 1900, 1902, 1906, 1910, 1911, 1912, 1913, 1914, 1915, 1917, 1918, 1922, 1923
Mercantile Navy List 1889
Shipping World Year Book 1897

Argall, Frank, & Ralph Bird, 'Falmouth pilot cutters 1800–1900', *Mariner's Mirror*, 64 (1978)
Barham, Fisher, *Ships and Shores around Old Cornwall* (Cornwall: Glasney Press, 1982)
Barnicoat, David, *Dodman to Black Head, Falmouth* (Packet Publishing, 1998)
Campbell, Andrew A, *History Notes on the Falmouth Quay Punts*
Carr, Frank G C, *Medley of Mast and Sail*, vol 1 (Brighton: Teredo Books, 1976)
Leather, John, 'The Life and Times of the Southwest Pilot Cutters', *The Boatman* (Dec/Jan 1992/3)
Powell, Luke, *Working Sail: A Life in Wooden Boats* (Wimborne Minster: The Dovecote Press 2012)
Sinclair, W E, *Cruises of the Joan* (London: Edward Arnold, 1934)
Wilson, David, *Falmouth Haven: The Maritime History of a Great West Country Port* (Stroud: Tempus Publishing, 2007)
Woodcock, Percy, 'A Hobble', *The Yachting Monthly and Marine Motor Magazine*, XXXI (May–October 1921)
———, 'Seeking. A day in a Falmouth Quay Punt', *The Yachting Monthly* (1906)

PLYMOUTH

The author is indebted to Martin Langley and Edwina Small for their help.

National Maritime Museum:
Examination taken at Plymouth, Jan–Feb 1710, about abuses by the commissioner including charges of using naval stores for his own purposes and smuggling stores from ships by the pilot vessels
Letter from the Master of Trinity House about Pilots in Plymouth Sound

West Briton, 24 February 1837
Plymouth Port Orders 1858
Shipping World Year Book 1897

Carne, Tony, *Cornwall's Forgotten Corner* (Devon: Lodenek, 1985)
Carne, Tony, & Colyn Thomas, *Images of the Past* (privately published, 1993)
Gill, Crispin, *Plymouth River* (Tiverton: Devon Books, 1997)
Langley, Martin, & Edwina Small, *The Plymouth Pilots* (unpublished)
Leather, John, *Gaff Rig* (London: Adlard Coles, 1970)
Williams, Frank, *The Eddeys of Rame*, www.RameHeritage.co.uk

POOLE

The author is indebted to Elaine Matthews for information on Portland pilots.

Poole Maritime Trust:
Application to Trinity House recommending William Hixon as pilot for Swanage 14.01.1847
Application to Customs House Poole recommending Samuel Hart as additional pilot at Poole 24.04.1848
Poole pilots' reply to complaint by Edward Clark, owner of the Brig *Vivid*, signed by William King, pilot, 17.12.1860
Complaint by Evans Jones, Master of the *Volunteer* of the Poole pilotage deficiencies, etc (nd)
Application to license *Content* as a pilot vessel 24.10.1868 and reply from Custom House 11.12.1869
Laws of Oléron translated from fourteenth-century French

Anon, 'Leaves from an artist's notebook: Poole and its harbours', *The Yachting and Boating Monthly* (May 1908)
Butler, T Harrison, 'Letter', *The Yachting and Boating Monthly* (May 1910)
Perry, Peter, 'The Newfoundland Trade: the decline and demise of the port of Poole 1815–1894', *American Neptune*, 28:4 (Fall 1968)

ISLE OF WIGHT

The author is indebted to John Laing for information about his ancestor, and Art Braunschweiger for his photo of pilot ketch and steamer.

The Portsea Census of 1881

Isle of Wight Record Office:
Information about Arthur Thomas Davis of Sea View and Emma Charlotte Caws

Portsmouth Museums and Records Service:
William Henning Beckett pilot's certificate

Southampton Archive Services:
Information on following vessels, owner and crew – *Pilot, Minnie, Skipjack, Active, Querida, Lively, Deerhound, Solent, Iris, Jessica, Daring* and *Fawn*

Caledonian Mercury (Edinburgh, Scotland, 3 October 1825)
The Journal of the Isle of Wight Family History Society, 33 (May 1994)

Bevis, Tony, 'Trinity House Pilots in the Solent area', *Isle of Wight Family History Society Journal* (2010)
Burdett, David, 'Isle of Wight Pilotage District', www.bembridge.pl/cms.php?pid=359
Burton, Leslie, & Brian Musselwhite, *Crossing the Harbour* (Portsmouth: Milestone Publications, 1987)
Cooke, E W, *Marines de E W Cooke* 1811–1881 (Editions de l'Estran, 1983)
Harding, Di, 'Cowes Pilots 1808', *Isle of Wight Family History Society Journal* (2001)
Leather, John, *Spritsails and Lugsails* (London: Adlard Coles, 1979)
March, Edgar J, *Inshore Craft of Great Britain in the Days of Sail and Oar*, vol II (Newton Abbot: David and Charles 1970)
Radford, John, *Pilot Aboard* (Edinburgh & London: Blackwood, 1966)
Rayner, D A, & Alan Wykes, *The Great Yacht Race* (London: Peter Davies, 1966)
Ruddock, Alwyn A, *Italian Merchants and Shipping in Southampton*, 1270–1600 (Southampton: University College, 1951)

DUNGENESS ON TO LONDON

Dover Museum:
Cinque Port Pilots 1514 to 1988
Dover pilot records for 1891

National Maritime Museum:
Manuscript of Robert Hammond, master of the society of pilots of the Cinque ports, of the southern North Sea in the cutter *Gem* 1841

Adams, Andy, 'The London pilot cutter', www.pilotmag.co.uk/category/history
Freeston, Ewart C, *The Construction of Model Open Boats* (London: Harper Collins, 1975)
Humphreys, Roy S, 'Cinque Ports Pilots', *Bygone Kent*, 3:X
Lane, Anthony, 'The NE Spit Pilot Boats', *Bygone Kent*, 16:VIII
———, 'Trinity House and the Dungeness Pilot Station', *Bygone Kent*, 13:XI

DEAL AND SUFFOLK

The author is indebted to the staff of Deal Maritime Museum and particularly the former curator, Terry Williams.

Guildhall Library:
Ms30204A Dover and Deal expenses 1866–77
Ms30206 Register of vessels from outports

National Maritime Museum:
Trusty 1813–24 Pilots' accounts inwards Oct 1822
Papers relating to loss and salvage of anchors and cables off Deal, with statements of average, Oct–Nov 1822
Commercial Dock receipts 1822–1823

Lowestoft Record Office:
Ms1090/2/2 details of pilots licensed for Lowestoft pilotage early nineteenth century
Ms503/1 Port handbook
Ms841/7/14/2 and Ms841/7/14/1 Pilotage and Beach Companies Southwold

Suffolk Record Office:
LXXXVI: To amend an Act for the amendment of the law respecting pilots and pilotage and also for the better preservation of floating lights, buoys and beacons

Kent History and Library Centre:
Court of Lodemanage and Fellowship of the Cinque Ports Pilots 1496–1855
Commission of Lodemanage 1829
Pilots' examination books 1709–1853
Lists of pilots, 1811–1852
Returns and Pilotage Commission papers 1809–1853
Miscellaneous: journal of a survey of the Cinque Ports Admiralty made by Deal pilots 1841
Epitaph on headstone regarding Tom Edgar, and answer to epitaph written by Daniel Dean, pilot nineteenth century
Deal pilots – Pilot's log book 1840s, List of boats 1821
List of pilots of the Cinque Ports 1834–1852
Account of receipts and disbursements of the surplus rates of pilotage under the Acts of 48 Geo III and 52 Geo III for the better regulation of pilots 1811–1852
Watch House at Pilots Corner 1838–1894
The *Pilote* – salvage 1900
Examination of William Tye of Faversham, sailor, employed to pilot a pink from Rotterdam 1633
Presentment of Robert Hay regarding the stranding of a snow by the pilot Thomas Hammerden, 1766
A remission of fine; and a petition in favour of Deal and Folkestone as pilot stations 1857
Endorsement Paul Bennet pilot 1822
Postcard of Thomas William Burgess swimming alongside his pilot boat during his Channel swim 1911
Payment of £15 15s to pilot 1810
Request for a good pilot 1802
Difficulty over paying for pilot from George Powditch of the schooner *Lucy* 1832
Richard Sackett prevented from serving as pilot due to illness 1819
Detention of a Dover pilot in Holland 1798
Payment to Pilot William Bartlett 1804
Petition opposing Pilot Act
Licences

Le Journal Bordelais, letter regarding English pilots from the captain of *Le Rouennais* (1 January 1849)
The Deal & Walmer Telegram (24 May 1862)
The Ventnor Gazette and Isle of Wight Mercury (October 1887)
Isle of Wight County Press (5 November 1887)

Appleton, G, 'Deal Luggers', *Mariner's Mirror*, 45 (1959)
Bayley, George Bethel, *Seamen of the Downs* (Edinburgh & London: William Blackwood, 1929)
Benham, Hervey, *Once upon a Tide* (London: George G Harrap, 1955)
———, *The Salvagers* (Colchester: Essex County Newspapers, 1980)
Blake, W M, 'The Suffolk Beach Yawl', *Yachting Monthly*, LIV, 414
Bottomley, A F, *A short history of the Borough of Southwold* (Southwold Corporation, 1974)
———, (ed), *The Southwold Diary of James Maggs: 1818–1876* (Woodbridge: Boydell/Suffolk Records Society, 1983)
Bower, Jacqueline, 'A Traditional Community in Decline: Deal Boatmen in the nineteenth century', *Southern History*, 17 (1995)
Carr, Frank G G, *Vanishing Craft* (London: Country Life, 1934)
Cooper, E R, 'The Suffolk and Norfolk Beach Yawls', *Mariner's Mirror*, 13 (1927)
———, *A Suffolk Coast Garland* (London: Heath Cranton, 1928)
Cooper, Ernest R, 'Notes: Beach Yolls', *Mariner's Mirror*, 15
Finnis, Thomas Hornsby, 'Log of a Deal Pilot', *Deal and Kent News* (30 December 1939)
Higgins, David, *The Beachmen* (Lavenham: Terence Dalton, 1987)
Hopkins, R Thurston, *Small Sailing Craft* (London: Philip Allan, 1931)
Leather, John, *The Northseamen* (Lavenham: Terence Dalton, 1971)
Leslie, R C, *A Sea-Painter's Log* (London: Chapman and Hall, 1886)
Malster, Robert, 'Beach companies and their yawls', *Ships Monthly*, 2:4 (1967)
———, *Saved from the Sea* (Lavenham: Terence Dalton, 1974)
Moore, Sir Alan, *Last Days of Mast and Sail* (Oxford: Clarendon Press, 1925)
Oke, P J, 'Deal Galley Punt, Happy-Go-Lucky', *Yachting Monthly*, XXV
Pain, E C, 'The Last of our Luggers and the Men who Sailed Them', *Deal Mercury* (1929)
Pritchard, Stephen, *A History of Deal and its Neighbourhood* (Deal: Edward Hayward, 1864)
Russell, Herbert, 'My Boat', *The Yachting and Boating Monthly*, IV, 19–24 (1907–1908)
Russell, W Clark, *Betwixt the Forelands* (London: Sampson Low, 1889)
Stanton, W H, *The Journal of William Stanton Pilot of Deal* (Portsmouth: W H Barrell, 1929)
Stibbons, Peter, *Crabs and Shannocks: The longshore fishermen of North Norfolk* (Norfolk: Poppyland Publishing, 1983)
Tansley, F J, 'The Lowestoft Beach Yawls', *The Yachting Monthly Magazine*, II (July to December 1898)
Tran, Tri, 'Les Pilotes de Londres au XIXe siècle', *Etudes Anglaises*, 1 (1997)
———, 'Les bateliers de Londres au 19e siècle', *Revue Française de Civilisation Britannique*, IX:2 (1997)
———, 'Les Sociétés de pilotes en Angleterre au XIXe siècle', *Cahiers Victoriens et Edouardiens*, 48 (1998)
———, 'Maritime Pilotage Acts of the 19th Century', *Mariner's Mirror*, 89:1 (2003)

CHANNEL ISLANDS

The author is indebted to the following for their assistance: Priaulx Library; Lionel Frampton; Société Jersiaise; John W Sarre; Major Eddie Parks and the good ship *Vigilo.*

Mackenzie & Co's Almanack 1878
Guernsey Evening Press, article on *Vigilo* (date unknown)
The Star newspaper (February 1904)

Belloc, Hilaire, *On Sailing the Sea* (London: Rupert Hart-Davis, 1951)
Bonnard, Brian, (ed), *Wrecked Around Alderney: The Stories of Retired Alderney Pilot, Jack Quinain* (Alderney: Brian Bonnard, 1993)
Coysh, Victor, and Carel Toms, *Guernsey Through the Lens* (London: Phillimore, 1978)
———, *Guernsey Through the Lens Again* (London: Phillimore, 1982)
———, *Bygone Guernsey* (Chichester: Phillimore, 1989)
Jamieson, A G, *A People of the Sea. The Maritime History of the Channel Islands* (London: Methuen, 1986)
Jean, John, *Stories of Jersey Ships* (Jersey: La Haule Books, 1987)
MacCarthy, Dermod, *Sailing with Mr Belloc* (London: Collins Harvell, 1986)
Renouf, Captain F B, 'At the Turn of the Century', *Société Jersiaise Annual Bulletin* (1966)
Toms, Carel, *Reflections of Guernsey's Past* (Guernsey: Guernsey Press, 1995)

LE HAVRE

The author is indebted to Philippe Valetoux who provided so much of the illustration. Also Dominique Lacassagne.

Le Havre Pilots Association

Auckland Star (1903)

Memoir of Pilot Julien Capard

Besnier, Vincent, *Scenes de la Vie Maritime* (Voiles Gallimard, 1977)
Bonquart, 'Les Pilotes du Havre', *Journal des Voyages*, 406 (11 September 1904)
Briot, Claude & Jacqueline, *Clippers Français* (Chasse-Marée Armen, 1995)
Bryer, Robin, *Jolie Brise. A tall ship's tale* (London: Secker & Warburg, 1982)
Hacks, 'Le metier de pilote aux XIXe siecle', *L'Illustration* (27 August 1892), republished in *L'Hirondelle: Bulletin de liaison de l'association de l'Hirondelle de la Manche*, 37 (November 2008)
Langsdorff, The Princess, *Journal des Voyages et des Aventures de Terre et de Mer* (1904)
Maillart, Ella K, *Gypsy Afloat* (London: Heinemann, 1942)
Marin, P H, and D & S Lucas, *Les quatre vies de Marie-Fernand* 1894–1994 (L'Hirondelle de la Manche)
———, 'Les cent ans de *Marie-Fernand*', *Le Chasse-Marée*, 81 (June 1994)
Marin, Pierre-Henri, *Pilotes, Les Hirondelles de la Manche* (Voiles/Gallimard, 1981)
Martin, E G, *Deep Water Cruising* (Oxford: Oxford University Press, 1928)

Pochulu, Marie-Françoise, *Les Pilotes Maritimes Français – Cent ans de metier* (Edition des Falaises, 2005)

BRISTOL CHANNEL

The author is indebted to the following: Pilot Lewis Alexander's late sons, Norman and Kip; Pilot Bartlett; G Barrett Venn; Peter Stuckey; Malcolm McKeand; John Hart; John Rich; John Robinson; Chris Ellis; Adam Bergius and Ian Denholm; Malcolm Darch; Pilot Buck; Ted Evans; Ron Morgan and Alex Wood for their research on the Gloucester pilots; Clive Roberts for information on John Morgan; Jeremy Smith for information on *Clarice*; Helen Doe for information on Slade's yard; the family of Pilot Peter Evans; the many owners of pilot cutters and relatives of former pilots who have written to me with snippets of information. I thank them all.

Wreck Report for *British Princess*, Board of Trade (1888)
Select committee report on pilotage (1888)
1910 Department committee on pilotage in the UK
The 1910 Parliamentary report on compulsory pilotage
1911 Departmental committee on pilotage (re Bristol Channel)
1906 Barry by-laws
Transcript of a Book compiled by the Scout Leader and the Rover Crew of the 11th Barry Sea Scout Troop concerning the refurbishment of the Pilot Sailing Cutter *Wave* 1926/27

Bristol Record Office:
Bristol Pilotage Fund 1853–1878
List of pilots giving earnings 1877–1890
The Bristol Case 1736
Sailing boat *Pilot*
Pilot boat *Eirene* and crew list 1861–67
Pilot boat *Petrel* and crew list 1898–1910
Pilot boat *Pet* and crew list 1862–1892
Pilot boat *Unexpected* and crew list 1878–1897
Pilot boat *Arrow* and crew list 1879–1894
Certificate and admission of Thomas Berrye 1632
From W Hamilton, John Hyatt to become a pilot 1777
Report on Price Rowland, pilot, 1782
Complaint against pilot by Captain Thomas Richards of *Fanny* 1782
Account of William Gapper, his charges in taking out brig, *Two Friends* 1782
From Captain Shaw re William Gapper, pilot 1782
From Charles Harford re Pilot James Harris 1790
From George Parfitt, pilot, complaint 1816
Pilots' Bonds 1684–1762
Pilots' Petitions 1772–1792
Enquiry into the stranding of the ss *Demerara* with Pilot John Percival 1851
Apprenticeship of James Rowland 1821
Case against a Cardiff Pilot 1858

Gloucester Archives:
Pilot boat *Polly* 1902–1911
Log books of Henry Lewis, Berkeley Canal pilot, 1854–89
Pilot's licences, indentures, etc, of John Brinkworth of Berkeley 1881
Pilot John Hillman
Pilot boat *Alarm* and crew list 1872

Somerset Archive and Record Service:
Minutes of the Bridgwater Pilot Commissioners' meetings 1897–1911
Register of Bridgwater District 1854

Port of Bristol Authority Shiplovers Society and their journal
Alexander, Lewis, '40 Years a Bristol Channel Pilot', *Cardiff Times* (27 January 1934)
Anderson, Winn, *A Rather Special Place* (Llandysul: Gomer, 1993)
Anon, 'Glamorgan Assizes: Witnesses in unseaworthy ship case – Horatio Davies, Cardiff pilot', *Cambrian News*, p8 (6 August 1880)
———, 'Bristol Channel and Swansea Bay regatta. Pilot boat Race', *Cambrian News*, p5 (3 September 1880)
———, 'Norwegian barque *Kong Carl* with Pilot Giles Rowles of Cardiff vanished off Sully Island', *Cambrian News*, p5 (28 January 1881)
———, 'Accounts of shipping damage and losses in snowstorms [Mr Francis, Pilot no 49 mentioned]', *Cambrian News*, p7 (28 January 1881)
———, 'Account of Funeral of Mr Peter Evans', *Cardiff Times* (21 August 1909)
———, 'When Pilotage was a Risky Business', *Cardiff Telegraph* (17 March 1933)
Bemelmans, Ludwig, *On Board Noah's Ark* (London: Collins, 1962)
Birt, Douglas H C, Article, *Trident* (1951)
Campbell-Jones, Susan, *Welsh Sail* (Llandysul: Gomer Press, 1976)
Carr, Frank G G, *A Yachtsman's Log* (London: Lovat Dickson & Thompson, 1935)
Carr, Yvonne, *Shipwrecks around and about Kenfig* (Wales: Kenfig Society, 1994)
Cooper, Derek, 'Ruling those waves again', *South Wales Echo* (26 November 1988)
Cunliffe, Tom, *Topsail and Battleaxe* (Newton Abbot: David and Charles, 1988)
Davies, Horatio, Letter, *Cardiff Times* (7 February 1948)
Elkin, Paul, (ed), *Images of Maritime Bristol* (Derby: Breedon Books, 1995)
Ellis, Chris, *Uncharted Passage* (Isle of Wight: privately published, nd)
Farr, Grahame, 'Bristol Channel Pilotage', *Mariner's Mirror*, 34, 39 (1953)
Farr, Grahame E, *Chepstow Ships* (Chepstow Society, 1954)
Flower, Ellen Barbara, *Under Jane's Wings* (London: Edward Arnold, 1936)
Greenhill, Basil, *The Merchant Sailing Ship* (Praeger, 1970)
Illife, Dave, 'The Return of *Mascotte*', *The Bristol Shiplover*, 20 (1988)
McGrath, Patrick, *Records Relating to the Society of Merchant Venturers of the City of Bristol in the Seventeenth Century*, vol xvii (Bristol: Bristol Record Society Publications, 1925)
———, Letter, *Mariner's Mirror*, 34 (1953)
Morison, Denis, *Frances Ahoy* (privately published by Budbrook & Morison, 2009)
Morrison, Alex, 'Cutters', *Nautical Magazine*, 168 (1952)
Muir, John Reid, *Messing About in Boats* (London: Blackie, 1938)
Port Talbot Historical Society, *Old Port Talbot and District in photographs*, vols 1 & 4 (Port Talbot, 1985)
Robinson, Roger, *The Bristol Channel Pilot Cutters* (unpublished typescript)
Rutherford, Iain W, *At the Tiller* (London: Blackie, 1936)
Smith, Drysdale, *Weekends Afloat* (London: Alston Rivers, 1931)
Stuckey, Peter, 'The Sailing Pilots of the Bristol Channel', *Tideway* (May/June 1969)
———, *Sailing Pilots of the Bristol Channel* (Newton Abbot: David and Charles, 1977)
Tilman, H W, *The Collected Works* (Leicester: Diadem)
Waite, B R, 'Log of Saladin Ocean Race 1926', *The Yachting Monthly*, 247 (November 1926)
———, 'Bristol Channel Pilot Cutters', *Yachting Monthly*, 251 (March 1927) & 338 (June 1934)
Ward-Jackson, C H, *Ships and Shipbuilders of a West Country Seaport* (Truro: Twelveheads Press/National Maritime Museum, 1986)
Waters, Brian, *The Bristol Channel* (London: Dent, 1955)

NORWAY

The author is indebted to the following: Jeppe Jul Nielsen; James Ronald Archer; Arild Marøy Hansen; Malvin Frisnes; the crew and curators of *Frithjof*; Hallvard Bjorgum of Norheimsund and Bergens Sjøfartsmuseum.

Skillings Magazine, 44 (1869)

Ala-Pöllänen, Anne, *The Pilot Boat Sjögren* (Nautica Fennica, 1996)
Archer, James, *Colin Archer, a Memoir* (Gloucester: John Bellows, 1949)
Archer, James Ronald, & Fredrik Lange-Nielsen, *Losskøyta Frithjof* (Larvik, 1996)
Bryhn, B J, Sehyberg, T, and Oestmoen, O T, *Round the World with Ho-Ho* (London: Geoffrey Bles, 1953)
Dumas, Vito, *Alone through the Roaring Forties* (McGraw-Hill, 2003)
Færøvyik, Bernhard and Øystein, *Inshore Craft of Norway* (London: Conway Maritime, 1980)
Gøthesen, Gøthe, *Skagerak Kysten* (Grøndahl, 1977)
———, *Pilot Boats*
Hansen, Arild Marøy, *From a subsidiary source of income to a professional occupation* (Bergen, 2005)
Kemp, Dixon, *Manual of Yacht and Boat Sailing* (London: Horace Cox, 1884)
Kent, Rockwell, *North by East* (New York: Bremer & Warren, 1930)
Leather, John, *Colin Archer and the Seaworthy Double-ender* (London: Stanford Maritime, 1979)
Molaug, Svein, *Var gamle kystkultur I & II* (Oslo, 1935)
Schollert, C, *Lodsliv om Færder* (W C Fabritius, 1884)
Sörensen, Svend, *Colin Archer* (RKE-Verlag, 1989)
Tambs, Erling, *The Cruise of the Teddy* (London: Rupert Hart-Davis, 1950)

SEAMANSHIP

Cunliffe, Tom, *Hand, Reef and Steer: Traditional Sailing Skills for Classic Boats* (London: Adlard Coles, 2005)

Index